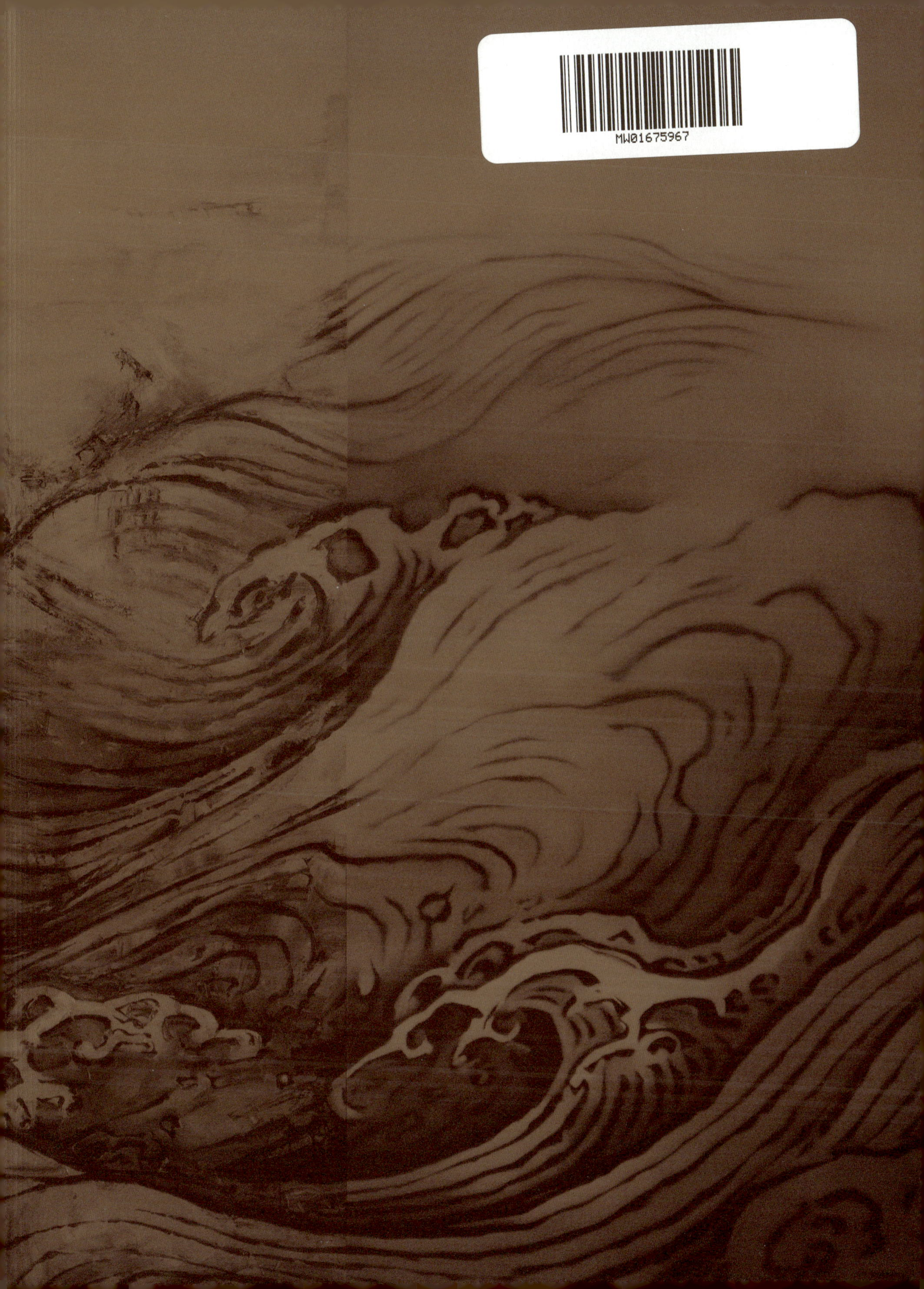

AVATARS AND ANTIHEROES

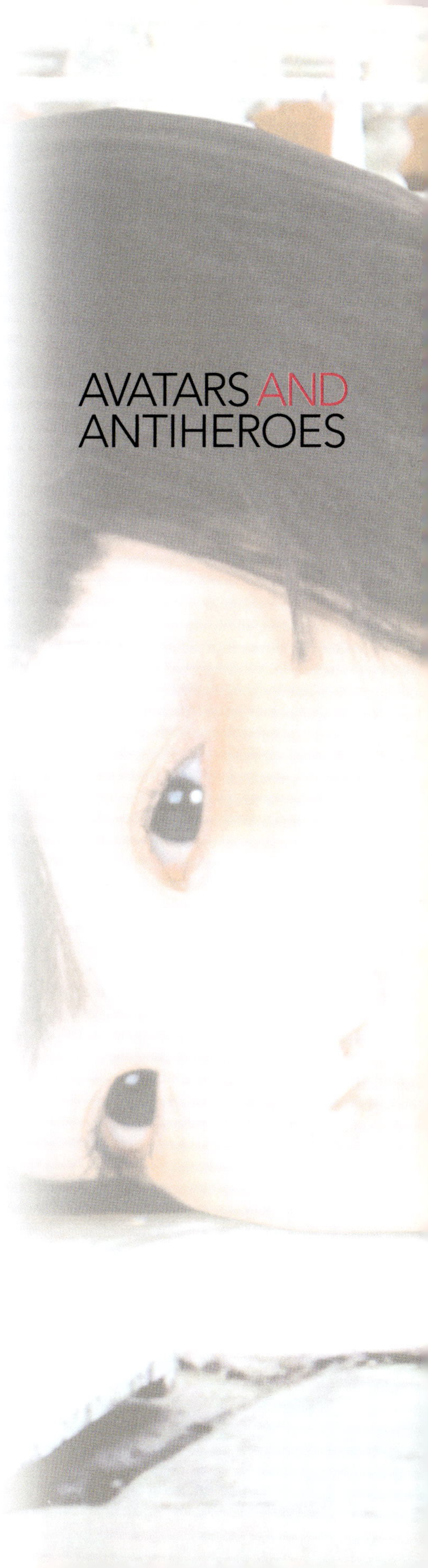

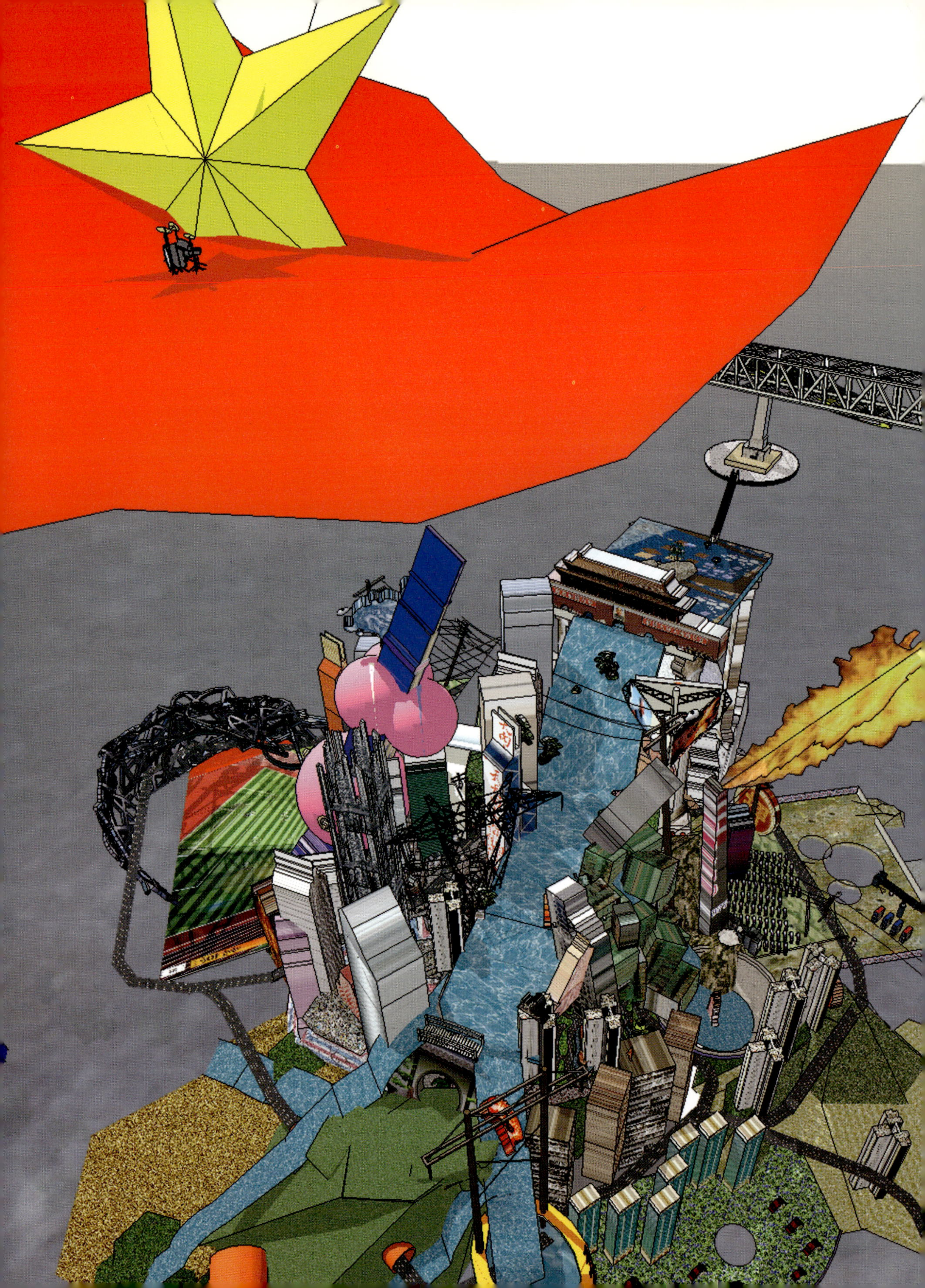

AVATARS AND ANTIHEROES

A GUIDE TO CONTEMPORARY CHINESE ARTISTS

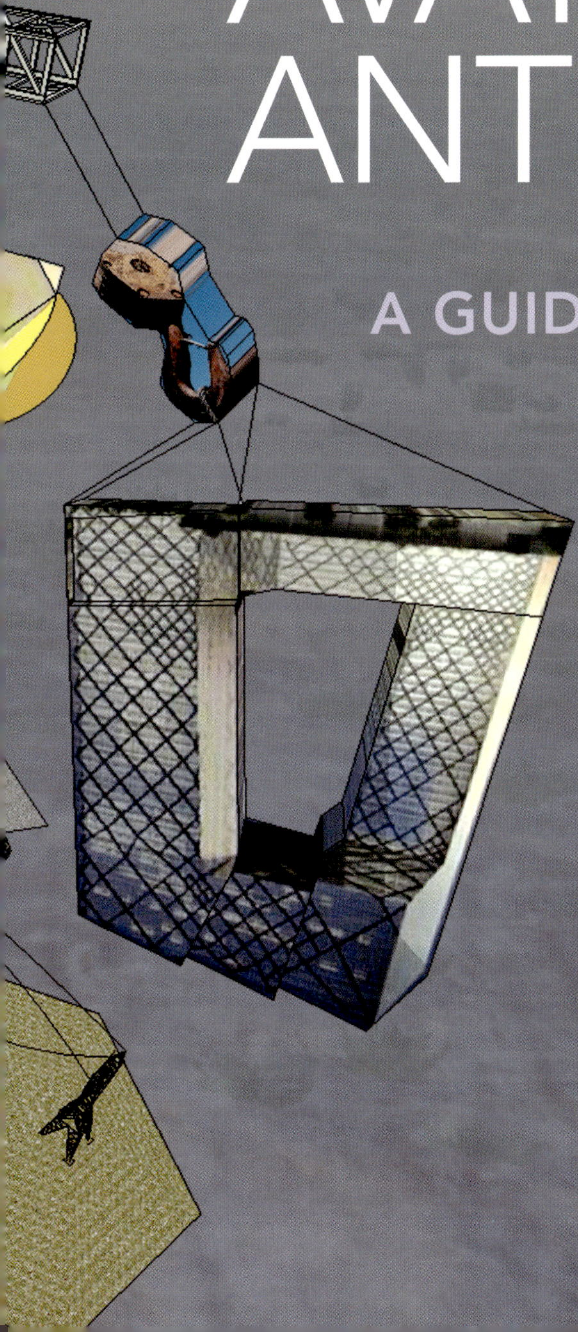

Claudia Albertini

KODANSHA INTERNATIONAL
Tokyo • New York • London

Endpaper illustration *Ma Yuan—The Yellow River Goes Countercurrent* (detail) by He Sen. Courtesy He Sen.

Page 1 illustration *One Day in 2004, No. 6* (detail) by Cui Xiuwen. Courtesy Cui Xiuwen.

Page 2–3 illustration *RMB City* by Cao Fei. Courtesy Vitamin Creative Space.

Distributed in the United States by Kodansha America Inc., and in the United Kingdom and Continental Europe by Kodansha Europe Ltd.

Published by Kodansha International Ltd., 17-14 Otowa 1-chome, Bunkyo-ku, Tokyo 112-8625, and Kodansha America Inc.

First edition, 2008
17 16 15 14 13 12 11 10 09 08   10 9 8 7 6 5 4 3 2 1

Library of Congress Cataloging-in-Publication Data

Albertini, Claudia.
Avatars and antiheroes : a guide to contemporary Chinese artists / Claudia Albertini.
p. cm.
ISBN 978-4-7700-3071-9
1. Art, Chinese--21st century. 2. Artists--China--Biography--History and criticism. I. Title.
N7345.6.A43 2008
709.51'0905--dc22

2007046340

www.kodansha-intl.com

CONTENTS

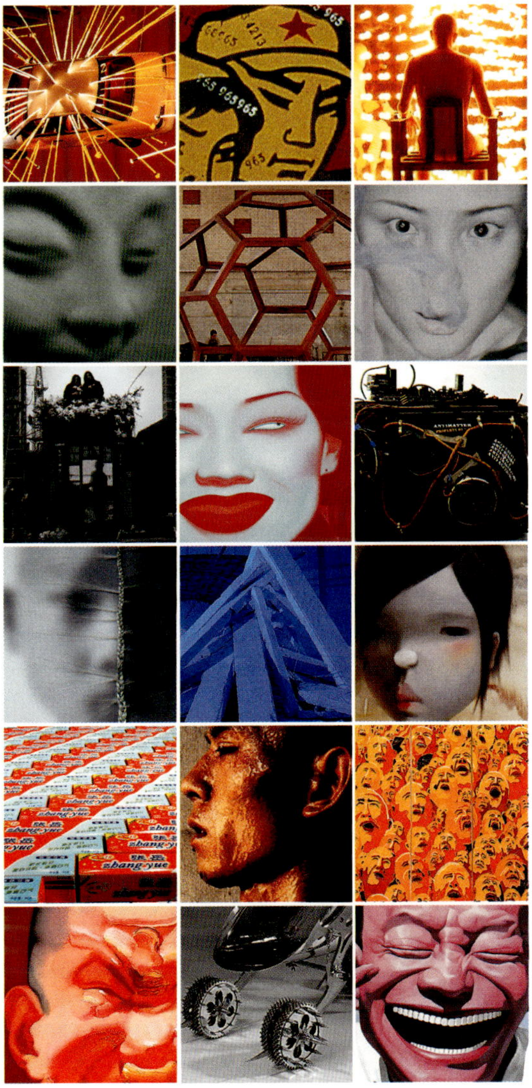

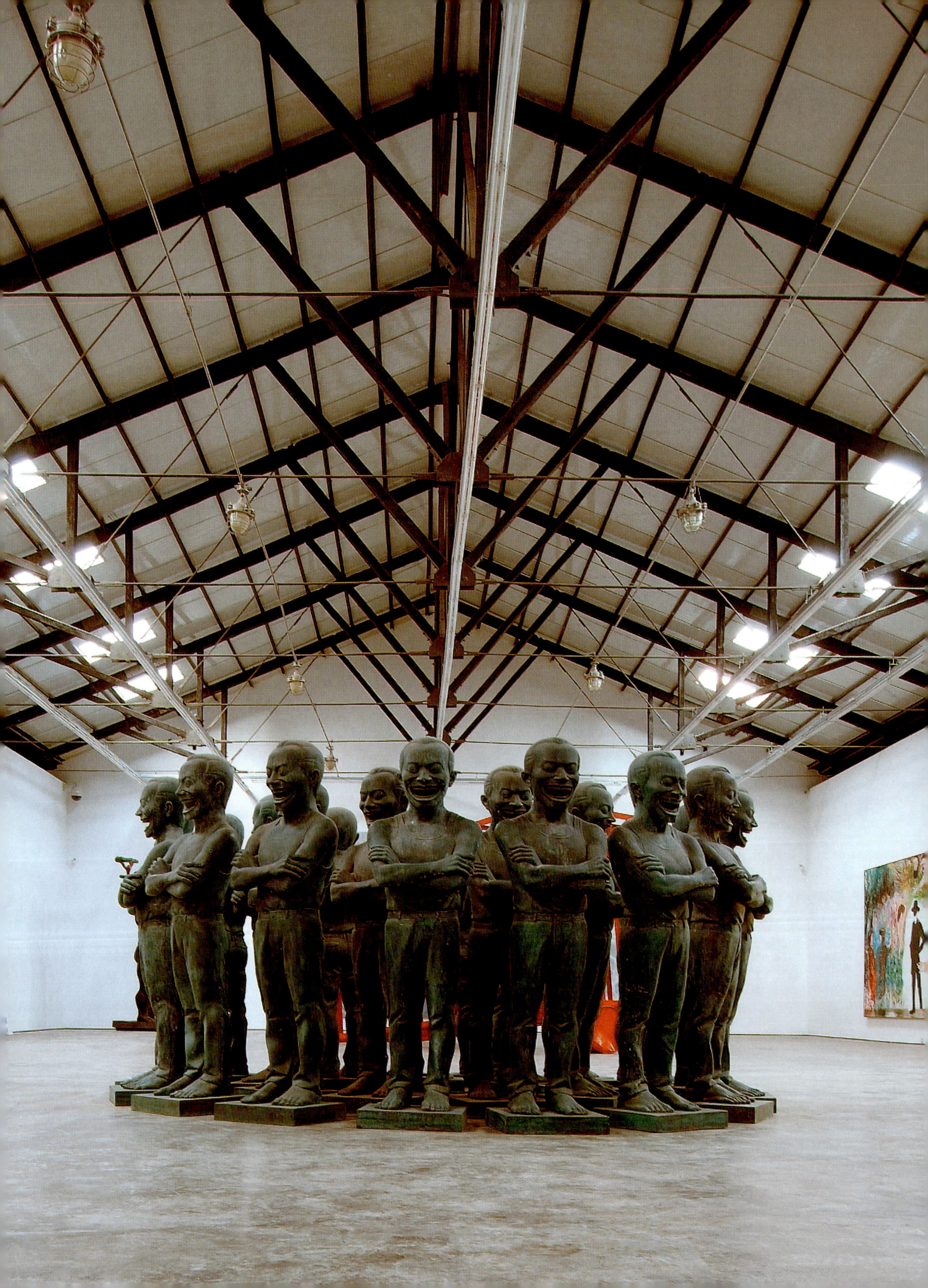

Introduction

September 2007. I was having dinner with a good friend of mine and a Chinese artist in a popular Italian restaurant in Beijing. The three of us were in the middle of quite an intense conversation, when suddenly my friend jumped out with a question: "Why you do art?" she asked the artist. There followed a moment of silence. "You are a smart person," came the artist's reply.

In these years of booming, exploding, sparkling growth, China is a hot topic. Whatever part of the planet we live in, it is hard to avoid brushing shoulders with this immense new world. Articles about China's economic development, its rapid transition from communism to consumerism, and the dizzying changes brought by urbanization, are frequently featured in the international media. Also in the news is China's flourishing new art market, where works of art by contemporary Chinese artists are fetching record-breaking prices at auction houses around the globe. Who are these artists, and why is this boom in Chinese contemporary art taking place at this time of unprecedented economic development in China?

It would be pretentious to attempt to draw up one comprehensive image of this emerging, hitherto unknown character—the contemporary Chinese artist—now entering the international battlefield of contemporary art. It is clear to me, however, that China's fascinating exploding art scene seems already overwhelmingly concerned with the search for identity. In a society that, from Confucius to Mao, has traditionally disregarded individualism for the collective good, contemporary artists are now exploring issues of identity, both individual and national. This book follows the trajectory of Chinese contemporary art from the early eighties to the present. These artists explore China from various perspectives, building bridges between past and present, between East and West. Through their multilayered forms of expression we can identify the connotations of the new globalizing society and its dynamic artistic language. The recent intimidating and radical changes in all aspects of everyday

Yue Minjun's grinning representations of himself as antihero seem to mock the revolutionary heroes of old.

Yue Minjun, *Contemporary Terracotta Warriors*, 2005. Installation view.

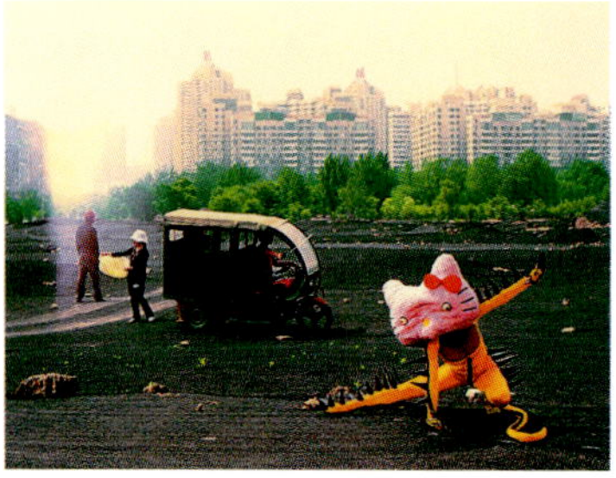

Cao Fei is spearheading China's pop culture generation.

Cao Fei, *Hello! Kitty*, 2006. *UN-Cosplayers* series photography, 35½ x 47 in.

life in China provide a strong creative stimulus for artists, who analyze, investigate, dissect, and rebuild their surroundings, questioning the values and meaning of this still unstable reality. To some, this is an emptied reality that needs to be filled with new principles and ideas; to others, there is no reality if not the one they are trying to create. Artists become thus the indicators of what is happening in society; they question their position and define themselves in relation to the new environment that is taking shape around them.

Hence, *Avatars and Antiheroes* reflects the schizophrenic undercurrents of a nation in continuous fast-forward. From the Cynical Realism and Political Pop movements associated with the post-Tiananmen generation of artists such as Yue Minjun whose grinning representations of himself as antihero seem to mock the revolutionary heroes of old, to the pop-culture generation spearheaded by Cao Fei whose digital avatars live in a world without borders, this book showcases the works of the most important contemporary artists to emerge from China in recent years, artists whose work gives shape to contemporary Chinese identity. Sons and daughters of different revolutions—the Communist revolution, the Cultural Revolution, the more recent economic revolution—these antiheroes, with their often rebellious and cutting-edge attitudes, become the constructors of a new artistic scenario in which the dynamics they create are as much a response to their past as to the present they live in. Experimenting with different media, from painting to sculpture, from photography to installation, from traditional methods to the latest techniques, the forty artists featured in this book reflect a variety of trends on the contemporary scene.

When speaking about contemporary art in China, I use the word "contemporary" to refer to a period that began at the end of the 1970s and continues into the present. After years of intellectual blankness during the Communist regime, the new forms that sprang up at this time were categorized under the common terms of "avant-garde art" or "experimental art." Until the end of the 1970s, strict censorship and rigorous restrictions meant that there was no appreciable contemporary art in China. The slow political and economic liberalization that was the result of the "open door" policy introduced by Deng Xiaoping in 1978, gave artists the opportunity to search for more personal and individual art forms. The quest to explore issues of modernity, nationality, and gender encouraged many artists to step out on the world stage, not to be judged in the context of Western standards, but to have their own unique voices heard. Members of the Star Group, a group of self-taught artists founded in 1979 that included Ai Weiwei, were the first to step out of the official network and bring their art into private spaces. With the desire for freedom of speech and to break away from the rhetoric of power of the previous epoch, the Star Group gained an enthusiastic countrywide following, which culminated in what art critic Gao Minglu termed the '85 New Art Movement, 1985 being a year in which the government appeared to take a much more relaxed approach to censorship of the arts. The '85 New Art Movement saw a flourishing of all artistic fields, from music to poetry, from philosophy to visual art. Conferences and cultural debates were held at academic and unofficial venues. A feeling of general hope spread around the country, thanks to the networking nature of this new art movement, and by 1986 there were artists' colonies in more than twenty-five cities.

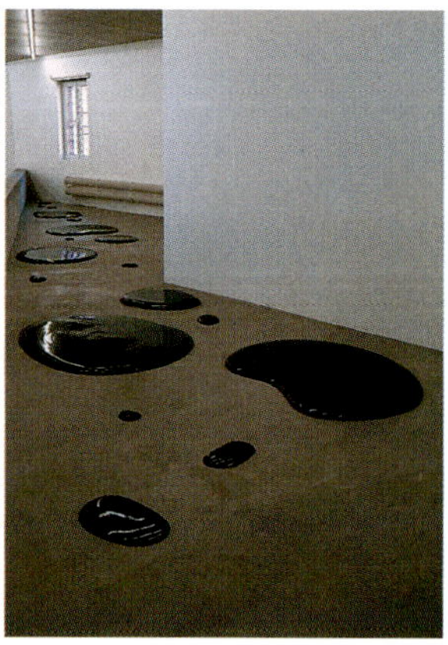

The process of political and economic reform that began in the 1970s gave artists such as Ai Weiwei the chance to step out onto the world stage.

Ai Weiwei, *Oil Spills*, 2006. Porcelain pieces in different sizes.

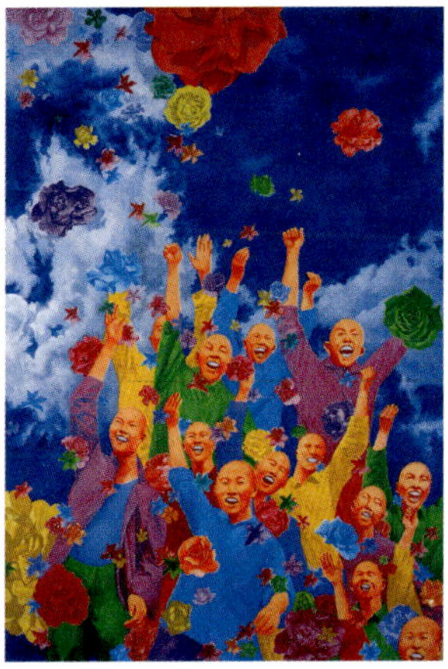

Fang Lijun was one of the initiators of the Cynical Realism movement at the start of the 1990s.

Fang Lijun, *2000.1.30*, 2000. Acrylic on canvas, 141½ x 98½ in.

This nationwide movement, characterized by its collective nature, strengthened antitraditional and antiauthoritarian ideals while spreading new notions about contemporary art throughout the country. Exploring conceptual approaches and promoting communication among art groups, the movement encouraged the diffusion of new art styles and facilitated theoretical discussions about art. All this culminated in the China Avant-Garde exhibition held in 1989 at the National Art Gallery, Beijing. This groundbreaking event, displaying 300 pieces by 186 artists, has become a landmark in the history of contemporary Chinese art, not only for the controversial nature of the works that were exhibited, but also for having shown them in a forum that was one of the official organizations of the Chinese government. It was on that occasion that artist Xiao Lu, as part of a performance piece, opened fire on her work with a gun, an action that caused the authorities to shut down the show. That works of art such as this were shown and performed in an official government space was undoubtedly provocative, and it is widely believed that this event was also related to the social unrest that would ultimately result in the Tiananmen massacre in 1989.

At the start of the 1990s, artists were disillusioned with a system whose professed support for the development of the arts was obviously false. As a consequence, the fracture between official and unofficial art contributed to a widening of the gap between art and society and soon brought an implosion of the previous decade's artistic enthusiasm. Some artists, like Cai Guoqiang—recognized for his choreographed firework displays all around the world—had already left the country to search for their identity as artists overseas, to come back later, or maybe never. In Beijing, artists retreated to a more private dimension and started to gather in artists' colonies located in the outskirts of the city. Beijing's Old Summer Palace, the Yuanmingyuan, became a place where painters would meet, among them Fang Lijun, Yue Minjun, and later Yang Shaobin, initiators of the so-called Cynical Realism movement. Cynical Realism was characterized by a black, ironic mockery, often expressed through portrayals of rows of typical Chinese people, while Wang Guangyi's Political Pop demystified political icons by combining them with commercial symbols. Another artists' colony was Beijing East Village, in the northeast of the city, host to photographers and performers. Ma Liuming's and Zhang Huan's outrageous performances were documented by young photographers such as RongRong and Xing Danwen, both of whom were involved in developing the first experimentation in a field that would come to be defined as "conceptual photography."

If in the 1980s artists believed in idealism and in the value of collective experiments, after Tiananmen they turned toward individual expression. New trends in paintings started to develop all around the country. Within the '85 New Art Movement, the painters of the Northern Group, led by Wang Guangyi, and those from the Southern Group, guided by Zhang Xiaogang, had tried to express on their canvases a combination of Surrealist and Socialist Realist styles, but after Tiananmen artists strove to express their understanding of reality in a more pragmatic way. Wang Xingwei's offbeat scenes from life, and his references to historical photography and Old Master paintings that make his works utterly unique and often difficult to understand, heralded the arrival of a new style of conceptual art.

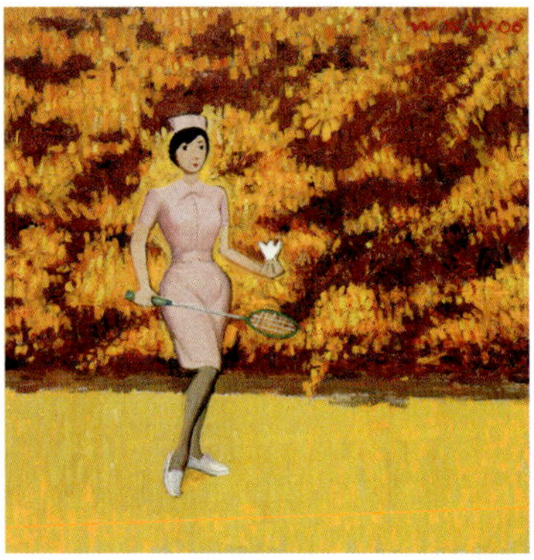

In the 1990s, Wang Xingwei's offbeat scenes from life heralded a new style of conceptual art.

Wang Xingwei, *Untitled (Nurse Playing Badminton)*, 2006. Oil on canvas, 53 x 53 in.

Unlike its Western counterpart, however, Chinese conceptual art did not develop on a basis of an aesthetic autonomy. Chinese artists were committed to the exploration of cultural and social issues rather than only questioning the nature of art. Thus, the first conceptual artists in China adopted what Gao Minglu defined as an "antiart" methodology, which is rather a response to external stimuli from both the social and artistic milieus. Song Dong and Yin Xiuzhen, focusing on the creation of works that were unsellable, materialized the conceptualization of their daily lives and paved the way for what has been labeled "apartment art." These artists created works at home and displayed them only in private spaces to very small audiences. Zhang Peili, soon followed by Yang Zhenzhong, Xu Zhen, and Kan Xuan, pioneered the use of video techniques to conceptualize objects and daily actions. Through the close analysis of everyday objects and their obsession with repeating the same everyday actions, these artists expressed their view of reality with a critical and ironic eye. Yan Lei's exceptional actions took conceptual art into a wider sphere, branching out into broader comments on the state of the arts and art institutions, his discourses questioning the identity of the artist with a bitter irony and a critical distance.

Installation art of the 1990s also reflects an emphasis on the material representation of a concept. Liu Wei, Shi Jinsong, Lin Tianmiao, and Liu Ding, to name a few, are the antiheroes who, with a mixture of the most unthinkable objects, address the relationship between their minds and their surroundings. The appearance of video in China at the end of the 1990s marked a switch in experimental Chinese art from material representation to electronic representation as artists began to experiment with the properties of video in order to present the truth of simple things. At first, a general lack of the advanced technical functions we take for granted today and limited mastery of the camera gave rise to very simple and minimal works. Slowly, more artists started to experiment with new methods. Combining painting, photography, and video, Chen Shaoxiong, for example, expresses an extremely personal narrative realism while observing the unpredictable, constantly changing urban landscape. Wang Jianwei, initially concerned with the mere recording of facts in order to demonstrate the truth, progressed to pieces that were theatrical productions.

Since the 1990s, performance art in China has held a special position among the different forms of artistic expression. Related to the ritualization of the individual body, physical "behavioral" language has in China a subtle symbolism and is therefore a powerful medium for the expression of social critique and moral intuition. He Yunchang and his amazing body discourses, Xu Zhen and Gu Dexin and their use of animals, Ma Liuming and Zhang Huan—they have all chosen a language that to some extent functions as an actual ritualization of the self and of one's own actions.

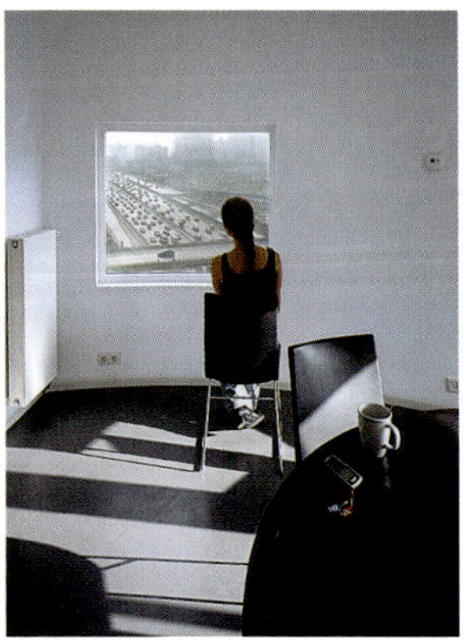

Contemporary artists are exposed to a general sense of nihilism engendered by the passage from the past to the frantic future.

Xing Danwen, *Wall House, image 4*, 2007. Color print, 47½ x 35¼ in.

Where do female artists fit into this historical overview? I think it is interesting to note that the number of female artists in China is blatantly inferior to that of male artists. It is only since the late 1990s that female artists have started to make a sustained impression on the domestic and international scene. The reason can be traced back to the fact that China is a male-dominated country, based on a patriarchal system. After the social unrest of the late 1980s, the period from the 1990s onwards has seen some slight reforms of political and legal systems to recognize women's

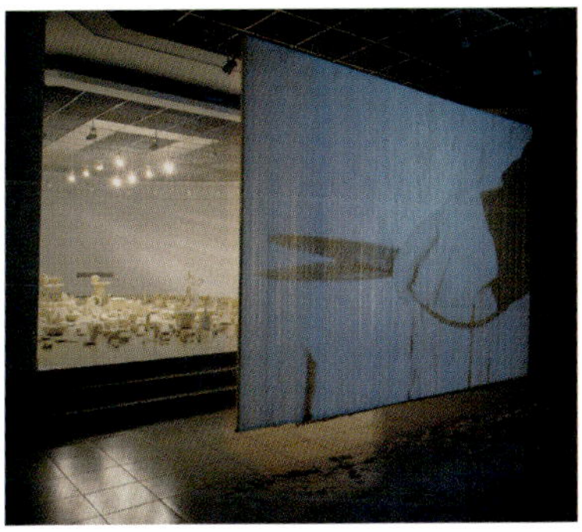

Since the late 1990s, female artists such as Lin Tianmiao have started to make a sustained impression on the international scene.

Lin Tianmiao, *Bound and Unbound*, 1995–1997. Installation.

rights, although the move toward these changes is led by men, a fact that stresses even more that women's status within society is decided by the male establishment. The works of women artists, however, after a period of experimentation, have reached an autonomous degree of maturity, allowing the artists to express their individual ideologies and psychologies, often using their own bodies as a medium. Cui Xiuwen, Chen Lingyang, Lin Tianmiao, Kan Xuan, and Xing Danwen have all made their mark on the international scene, and their works are much in demand both in China and abroad.

Chinese contemporary art, as we have seen, is a phenomenon that cannot be analyzed in isolation from its sociopolitical milieu. This is an era of radical changes, of media saturation, of reevaluation of the personal status under a fastidious symbology dictated by barren social trends, an era in which the privatization of property is taking place at mind-boggling speed. The era has given birth to a new citizen, with a strong individualism. A younger generation of artists is exposed to the general sense of nihilism engendered by the passage from the pre- to the post-, from the past to the frantic future; they experience a general void in which it is hard to define a particular art genre or tendency. This young generation—including Yang Fudong, Liu Ding, Liang Yue, Chen Ke, and Cao Fei, among others—have become the manifestation and incarnation of a society more self-referential. They take distance from the past, from history, to look inside themselves and at their own attitude toward the new momentum taking shape. The result is an indefinable world of dreams, of ecstatic illusions, of pale colors and shadows. They are avatars, the embodiment of the effects of the urbanization, globalization, and commercialization of the times; and in the new virtual reality they seem to be acting as though they are in transition. They don't know where they are going, and they seem to have forgotten their past, but still they look inside themselves in order to narrate a more individual and private story.

And, I wonder, why does an artist do art?

Claudia Albertini
Beijing, 2008

Ai Weiwei

Born 1957, Beijing

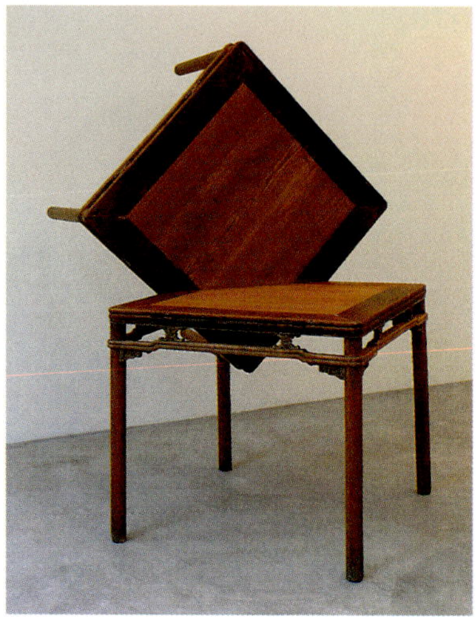

THIS PAGE, TOP: *Tables at Right Angles*, 1998. Tables, late Ming or early Qing dynasty (1368–1911), 69 x 49½ x 68½ in.

THIS PAGE, BOTTOM: *Table with Two Legs*, 2005. Table, Qing dynasty (1644–1911), 73 x 45 x 27½ in.

FACING PAGE: *Fairytale*, 2007. 1001 Chinese visitors, 1001 Qing dynasty wooden chairs. Installation view, Ai Weiwei's studio.

"First, inevitably, the idea, the fantasy, the fairy tale. Then scientific calculation. Ultimately, fulfillment crowns the dream." Ai Weiwei used the famous quote from Russian space theorist Konstantin Tsiolkovsky as the starting point for his work *Fairytale*, a project dealing with the themes of possibility and the imagination that took place at the Documenta 12 art exhibition in Kassel, Germany, in 2007. Ai invited 1001 ordinary Chinese people to come and live their everyday lives in the town of Kassel, home of the Brothers Grimm, as a live installation piece. Encompassing issues of identity and of nation, *Fairytale* drew attention to Ai's social commentaries as a Chinese artist in an international context.

One of the most innovative artists on the contemporary art scene, Ai lived for several years in the northwestern Chinese province of Xinjiang, where his father, poet Ai Qing, had been exiled, accused of "rightism." He then spent twelve years in New York, coming back to Beijing in 1993. In 2003, he founded his atelier FAKE—a name playing on the two Chinese pinyin syllables *fa-ke* whose sounds recall the Anglo-Saxon swearword. With an obvious assertion of inauthenticity, his studio's activities go from architectural practices, including the collaboration with Herzog & de Meuron in the conceptualization of the "bird's nest," as the Olympic Stadium for the Beijing 2008 Olympic Games is known, to artistic productions.

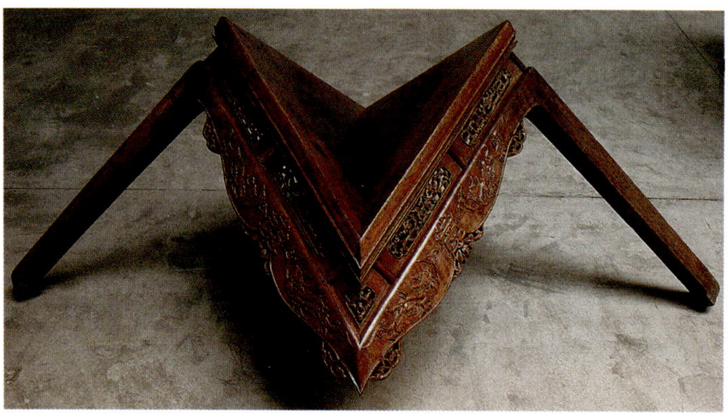

Widely regarded as an agent provocateur, Ai chose art as a means through which to express his disdain for the political pressures of a system condemning society to cultural impoverishment. His work outrages conservative traditionalists, as he questions the role of culture and its historical and ideological nature. *Tables at Right Angles* (1998) and *Table with Two Legs* (2005) were created by remodeling authentic museum quality pieces from ancient Chinese dynasties. His creations for Documenta 12: *Template* (2007) and *Fairytale* (2007) comprise chairs, wooden doors, and windows belonging to destroyed Ming and Qing dynasty houses found in northern China. His work shows an attempt to link cultural and historical sources and to push the boundaries between past and future.

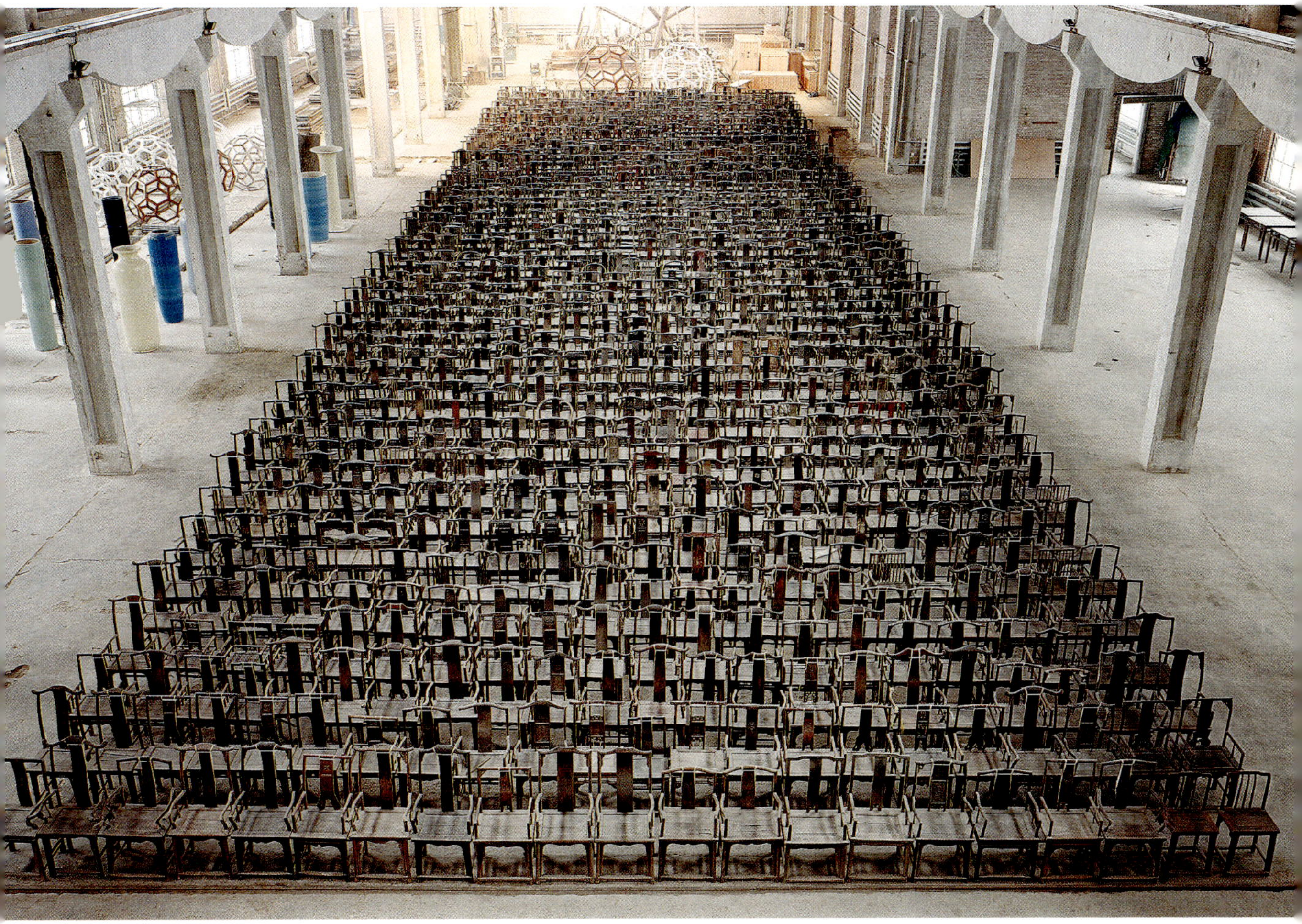

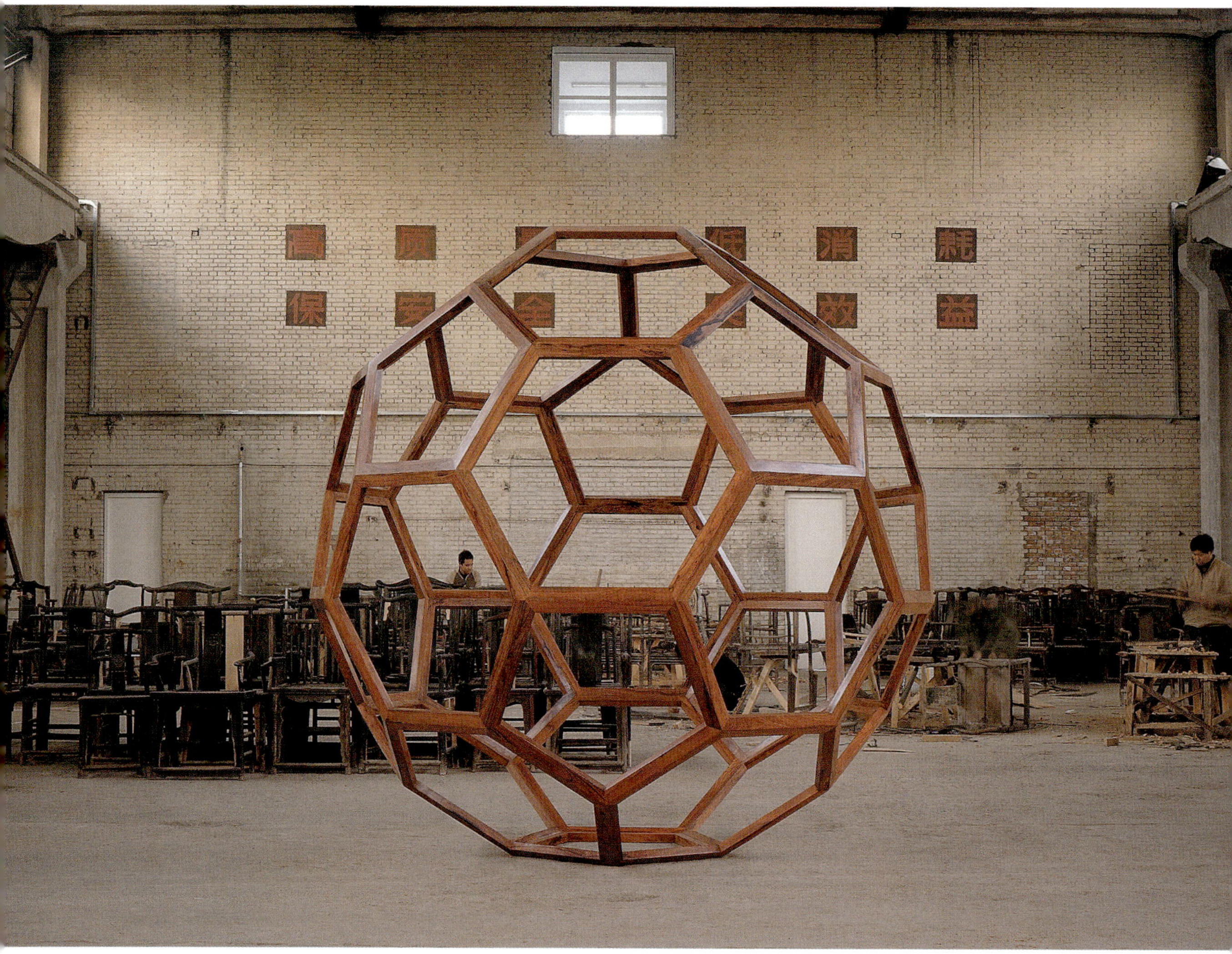

THIS PAGE: *Untitled*, 2006. Huanghuali wood, diameter 109½ in.

FACING PAGE: *Template*, 2007. Wooden doors and windows from destroyed Ming and Qing dynasty houses, wooden base, 23½ x 39 x 28 ft.

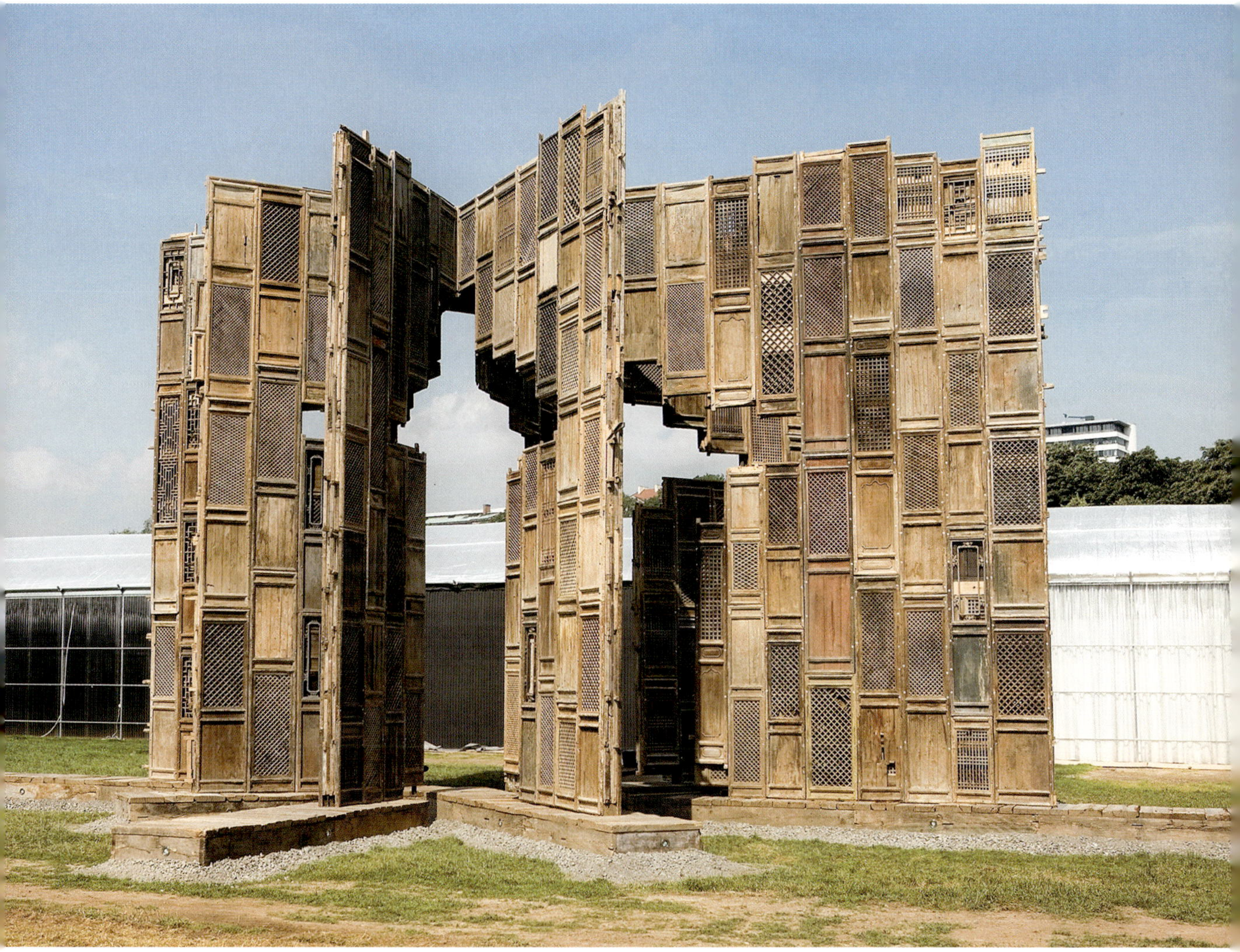

Cai Guoqiang

Born 1957, Quanzhou, Fujian Province

THIS PAGE: *Clear Sky Black Cloud*, daily at noon, Tuesday through Sunday from April 25 to October 29, 2006, approximately 5 to 13 seconds, at The Metropolitan Museum of Art, New York.

FACING PAGE, TOP: *Light Passage-Autumn*, 2007. Gunpowder on paper, 157½ x 236¼ in.

FACING PAGE, BOTTOM: *Head On*, 2006. 99 life-sized replicas of wolves and glass wall. Wolves: papier-mâché, plaster, fiberglass, resin, and painted hide. Dimensions variable.

OVERLEAF: *Inopportune: Stage One*, 2004. Nine cars and sequenced multichannel light tubes. Dimensions variable.

Explosions of supernovas in space, volcanic eruptions on earth: these incredible natural phenomena involve a sudden increase and release of energy while generating a rise in temperature and the release of gases. Master orchestrator of similarly breathtaking feats, Cai Guoqiang is the behind-the-scenes director of the most amazing explosive spectacles.

Trained in stage design, in 1986 Cai moved to Japan, where he started to experiment with the properties of gunpowder in his drawings. After moving to the United States, Cai began to operate on a massive scale, creating evanescent and symbolic patterns using gunpowder that have brought him to international prominence.

One of the four great inventions of ancient China (along with paper, the compass, and printing), gunpowder was already in use during the Song dynasty (960–1279) as a form of entertainment. Cai draws on a wide range of traditions, symbols, and materials, such as Chinese medicine, feng shui, dragons, and cars, to create outstanding compositions of explosions, lights, and sound through his mastery of the black powder. With the aim of attracting the viewer's attention to projects that, paradoxically, he is not sure himself will succeed, Cai plays with the unpredictability of this material, drawing our attention to something that lasts just a few seconds, as in the performance *Clear Sky Black Cloud* (2006).

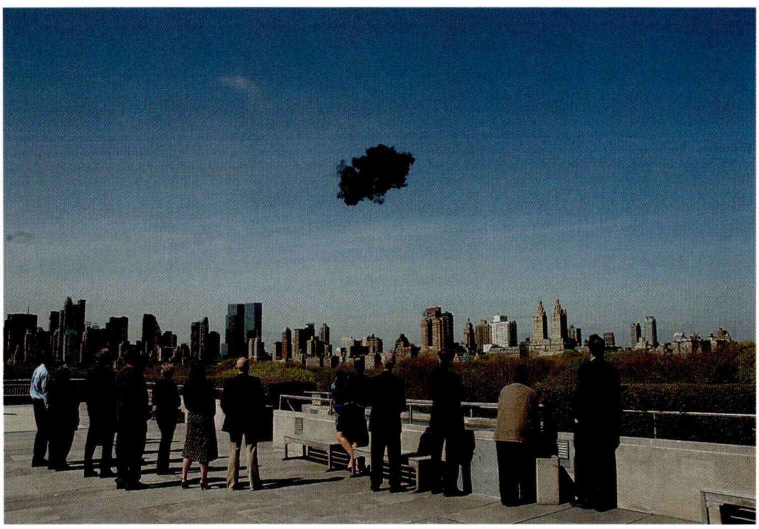

Forcing us to focus on the moment, Cai nudges our senses and builds bridges between East and West, between earth and universe, between past and present. Blending history with politics, he uses his knowledge of metaphysics while showing the ferocity of clashes that exist in our daily lives, as seen in *Head On* (2006). Evoking fictitious and real animals, like dragons and tigers, Cai's installation and performances seem like magic tricks interspersed with interstellar rays, as if the viewer was on the point of being catapulted into space. *Inopportune: Stage One* (2004), with a sequence of nine cars and multichannel light tubes and based on the idea of traditional horizontal scroll paintings, is constructed as though a string of images of a car bombing has been recorded in time sequence by a still camera.

Cai was appointed director of visual and special effects for the opening and closing ceremonies of the Beijing 2008 Olympic Games, and is said to have plans to create an installation on the moon!

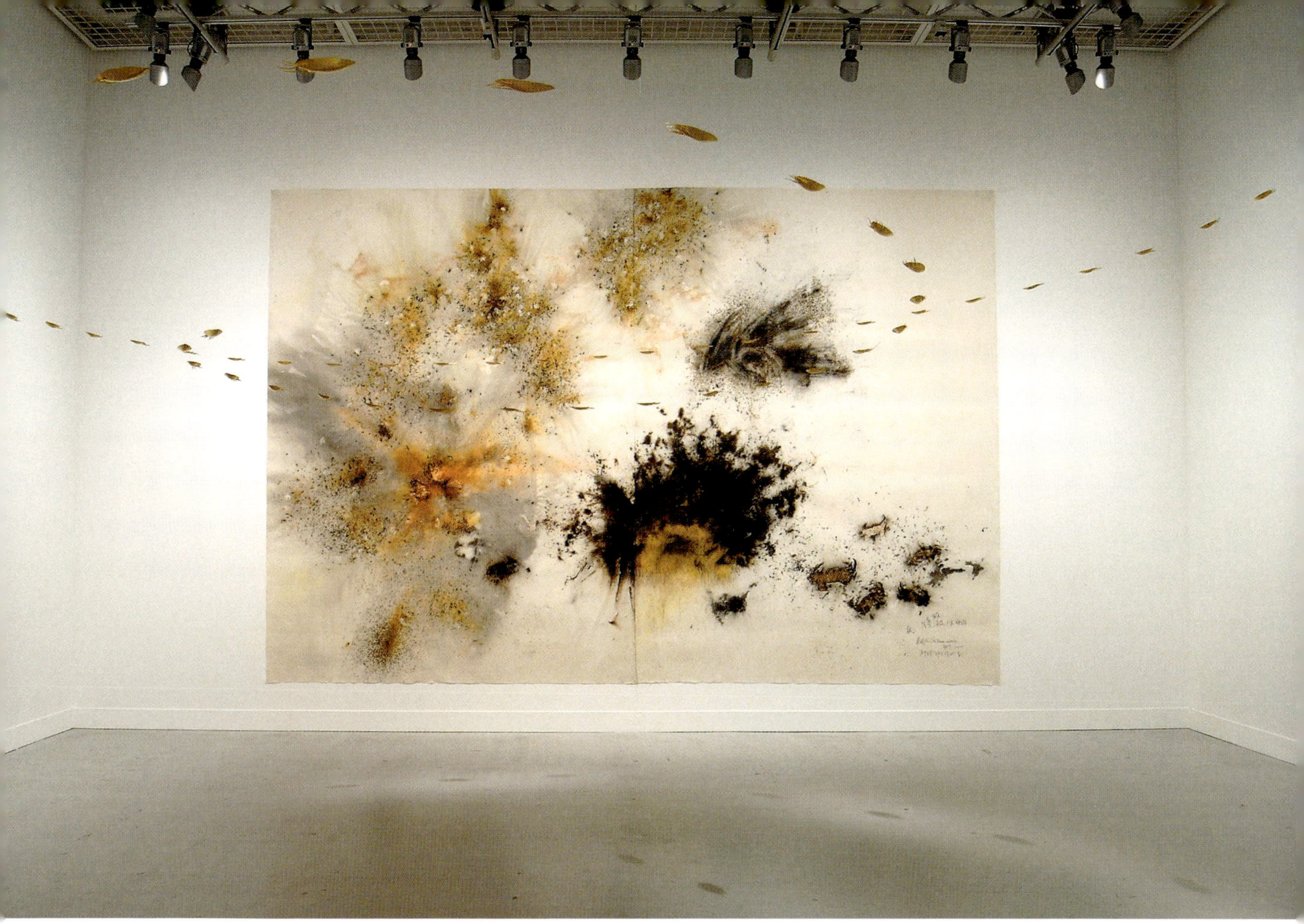

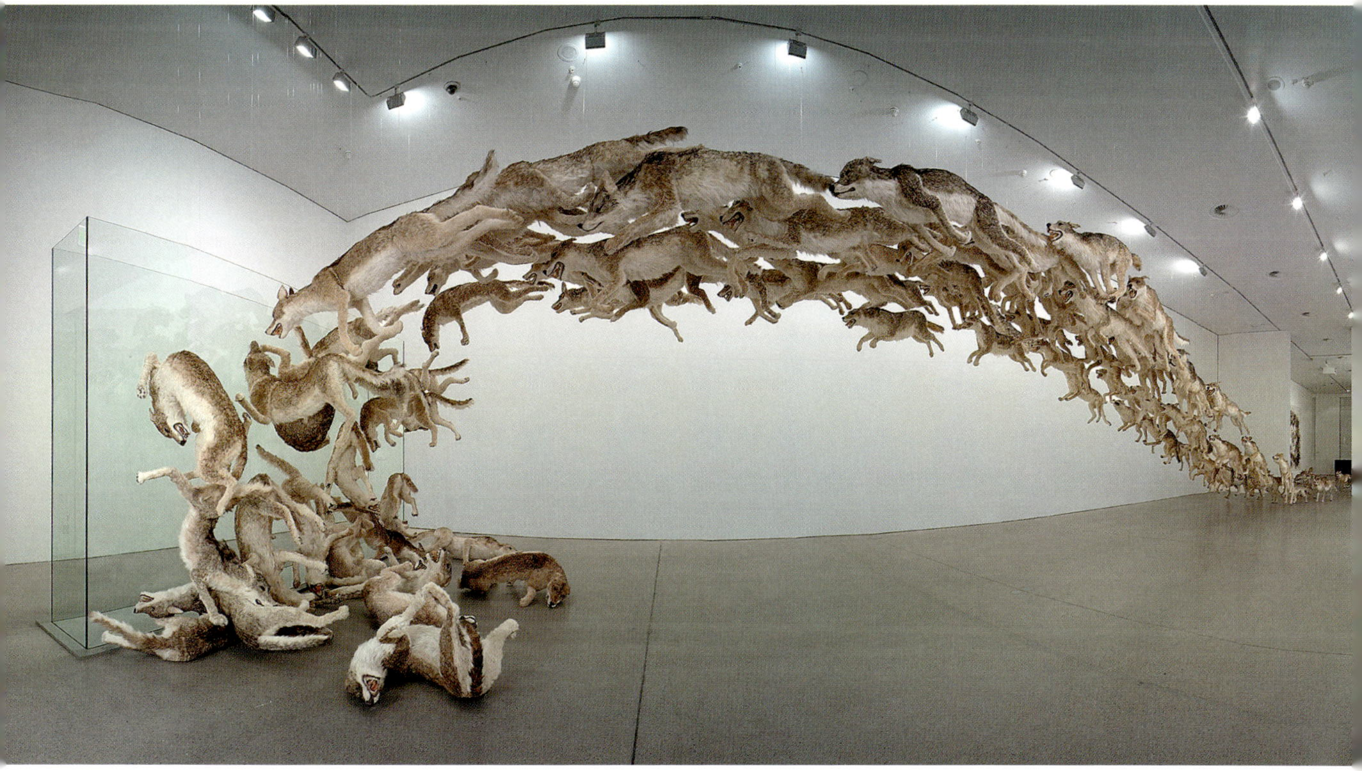

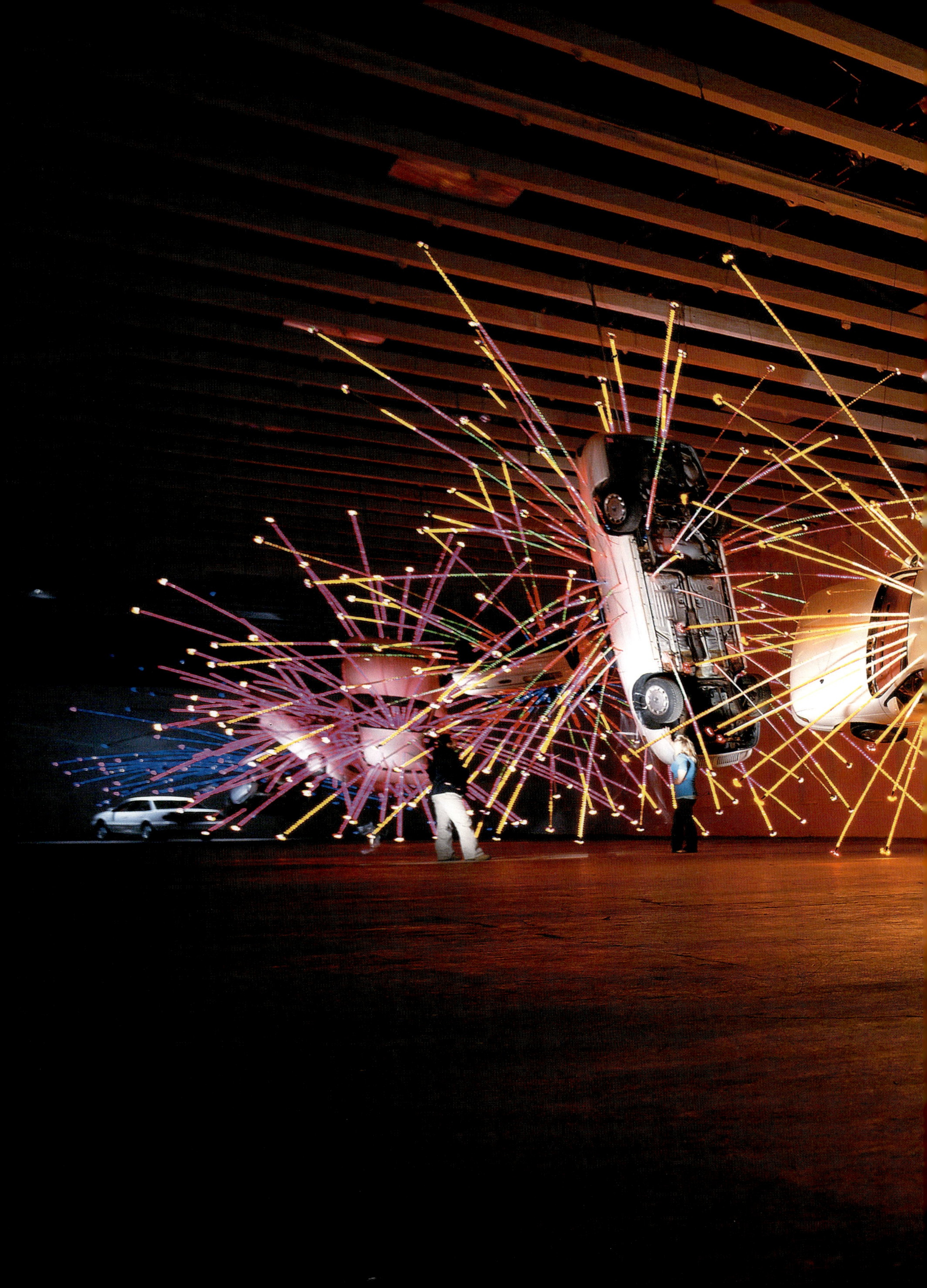

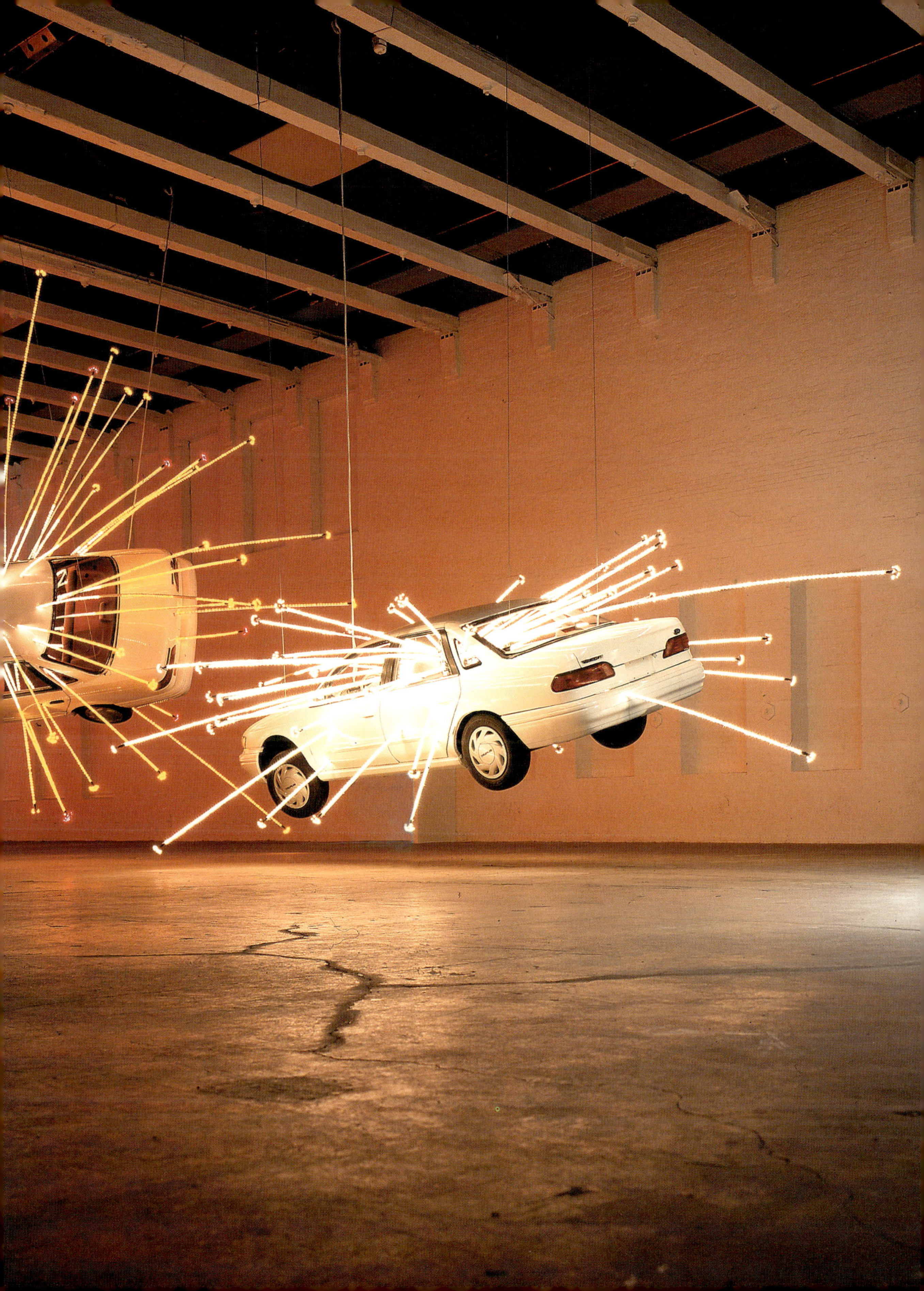

Cao Fei

Born 1978, Guangzhou, Guangdong Province

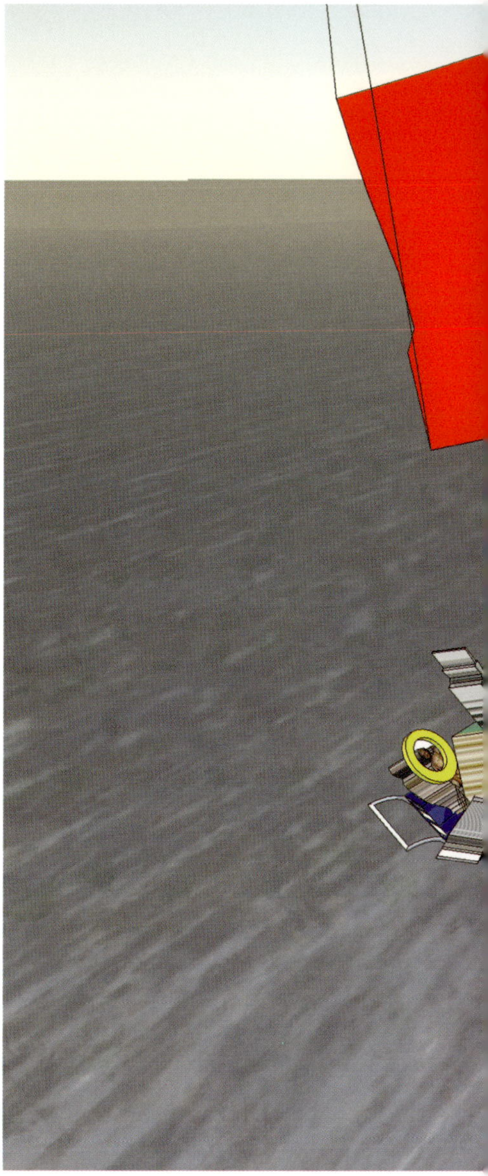

FACING PAGE, TOP: *RMB City*, 2007. Video, 6 mins.

FACING PAGE, BOTTOM: *RMB City* series photography (from the *RMB City* video), 2007. Each 47 x 63 in.

"I construct, and I am constructed in a mutually recursive process that continually engages my fluid, permeable boundaries and my endlessly ramifying networks. I am a spatially extended cyborg" (William J. Mitchell). This is the impressive overture to *I-Mirror*, the documentary film starring and directed by China Tracy, Cao Fei's avatar in the three-dimensional online virtual world Second Life. This project, presented at the 2007 Venice Biennale, explores the boundaries between physical space and cyberspace through the character of China Tracy, digital avatar and founder of the virtual RMB City, who embodies the dreams and the reality of China's younger generation. At the same time, the work is a platform for discussion about the influence the virtual world is exerting on our perception of the real and on our social relationships.

Growing up in the information era, and influenced by Hong Kong and Taiwanese pop culture as well as by the world of new subcultures shaped by Japanese manga, American rap, and Chinese TV drama, Cao is an astute and powerful commentator on the trends of the new millennium. By the age of twenty she had already directed a theater play, and performance remains a central part in all her works. One of the pioneers in the use of digital video in China, Cao explores and documents the new social realities of daily life, focusing on the younger generation, their indifference and sense of alienation, their lack of recognition of the past and inability to project into the future. Her first video, *Imbalance 257* (1999) portrays her friends' lives at art college. The narrative of this piece blurs the boundaries between illusion and reality, rationality and absurdity: "Imbalance is our ongoing experience . . . a disease of adolescence," Cao states. Humorous and ironic, her works narrate dreamlike and bizarre experiences that guide the audience through the realm of this new generation's myths and anxieties.

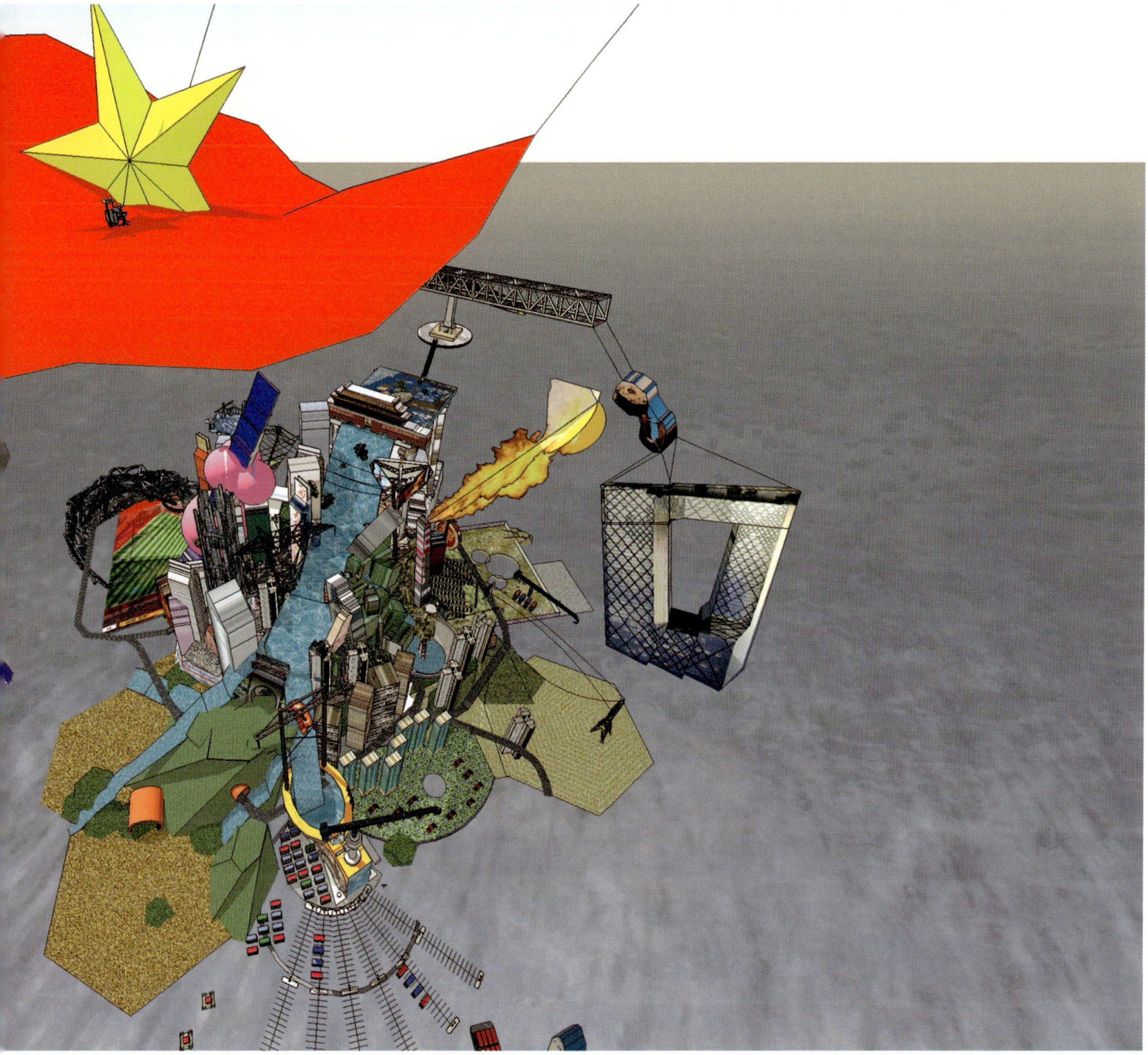

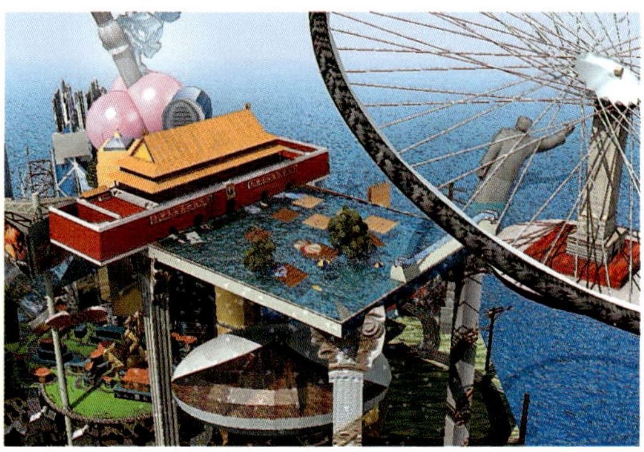

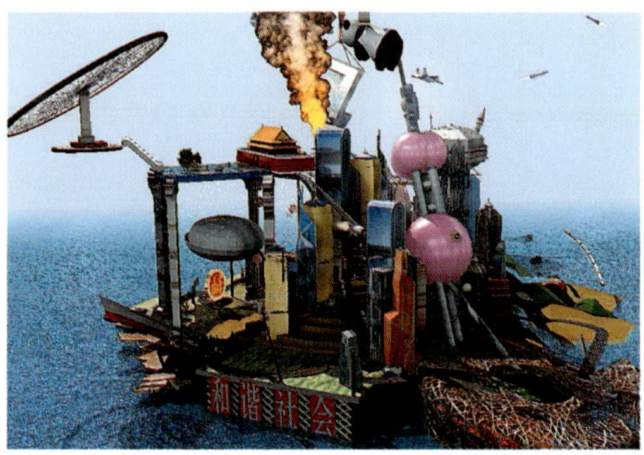
和谐社会

THIS PAGE: *Imbalance 257*, 1999. Stills from video.

FACING PAGE: *Diversionist*, 2004. *Cosplayers* series photography, 29½ x 39½ in.

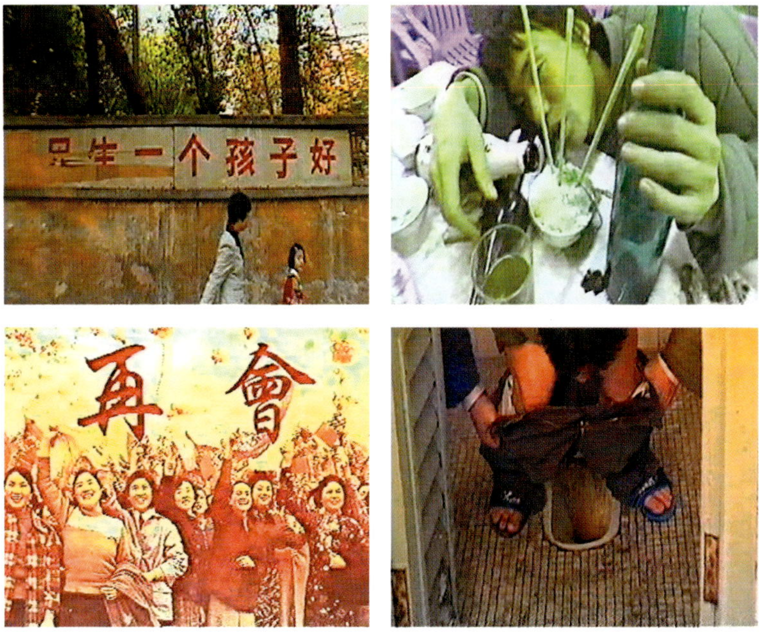

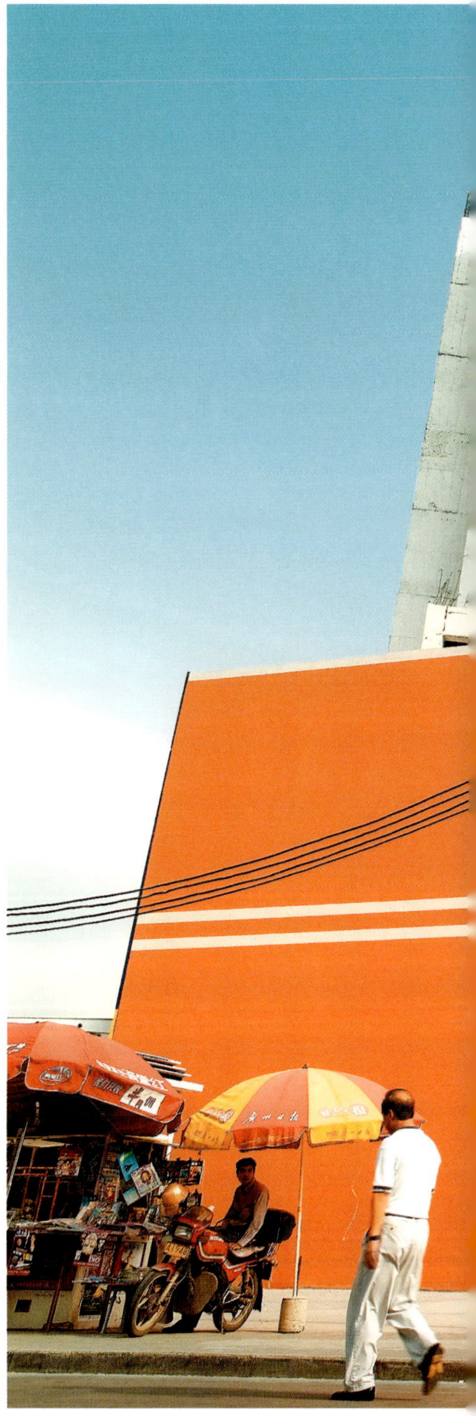

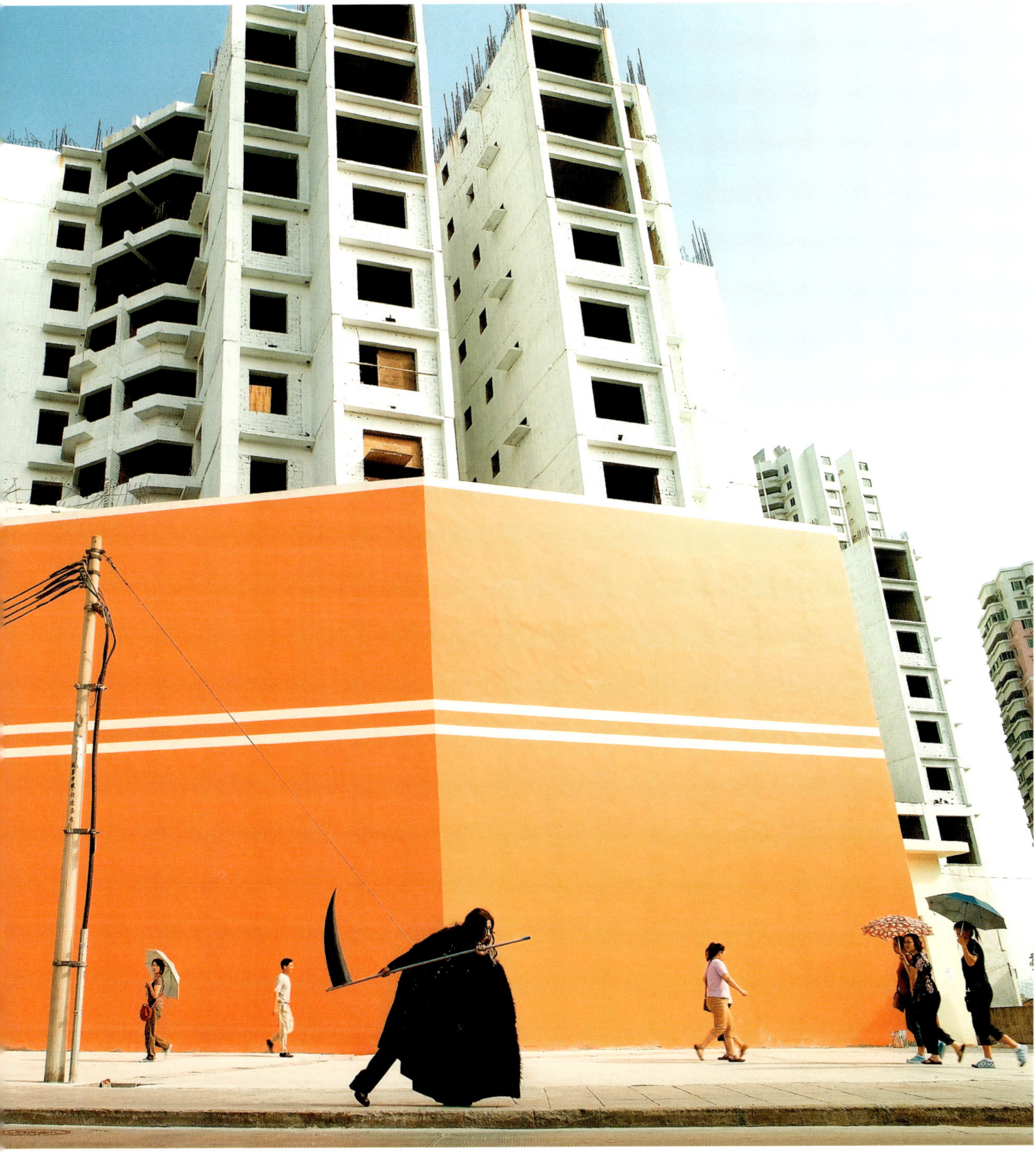

Chen Ke

Born 1978, Tonjiang, Sichuan Province

THIS PAGE: *With You, I Will Never Feel Lonely*, 2007. Installation. Furniture, modeling paste, oil color.

FACING PAGE: *Rainstorm Will Come*, 2006. Oil on canvas, 63 x 63 in.

Educated at the liberal Sichuan Fine Arts Institute, where, due to a lack of existing role models, artists were given ample opportunity to explore their instincts and emotions, Chen Ke was able to analyze a realm she had been exposed to since she was young: "Working in a free environment, it came out naturally. The cartoons and the comic books from my childhood have without doubt influenced me." Stories, stills from a theater performance, fables, and dreams . . . Chen's work is filled with a sense of intimacy that often masks a certain melancholy and solitude.

Chen believes that our "cartoon culture" is a kind of escape or means of fulfilment for the contemporary individual in a society where rapid changes have brought about a general emotional emptiness. "My characters are somewhat sad, isolated, and powerless, and this is exactly how I feel sometimes. My art is as real as my spirit. I look at my canvases as a safe place to deposit my cares. I find release while I am painting. In front of my canvases I can relax and get everything out, as if I was purifying myself."

Chen's style shows influences from Japan, in particular from her favorite artist, Yoshitomo Nara. At the group show Fancy Dream (2006) at the Marella Gallery, Beijing, she presented for the first time an installation of sculptures in fiberglass. "Experimenting with new media makes my work freer, more diverse, and more complete."

The installation *With You, I Will Never Feel Lonely* (2007) is a room, a territory, a space full of memories and dreams. There are old-fashioned wardrobes, desks, chests of drawers, a small bed, a sewing machine, and little items from the artist's past. A miniature painting of a girl—sometimes sad, sometimes hypnotized by her dreams—mysteriously appears on every object in the room. "This is a real space and a mental space at the same time," says Chen.

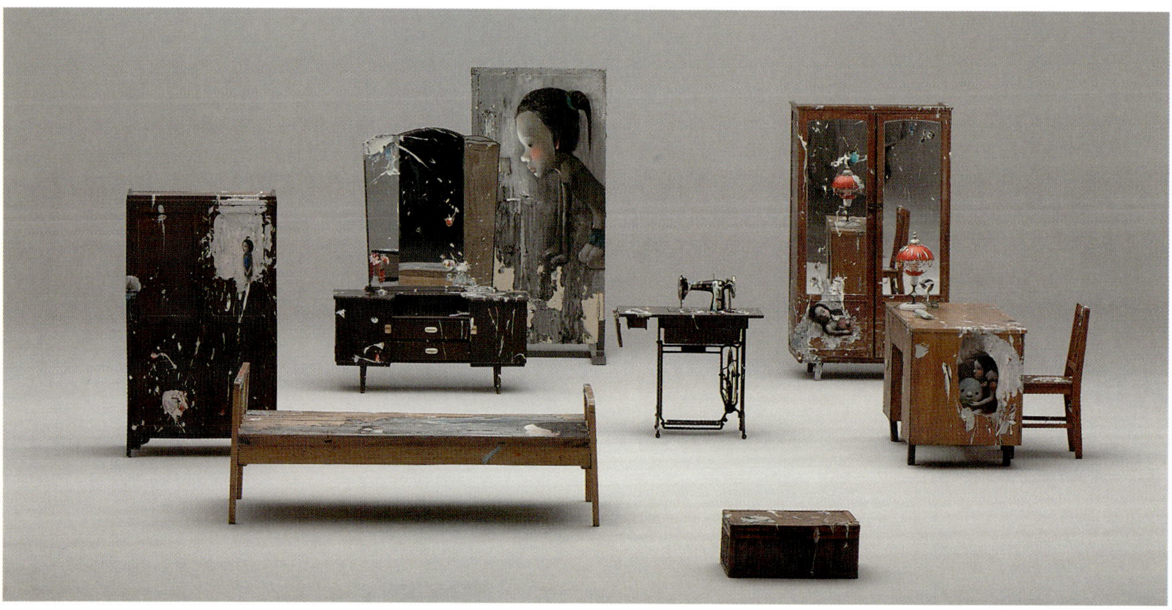

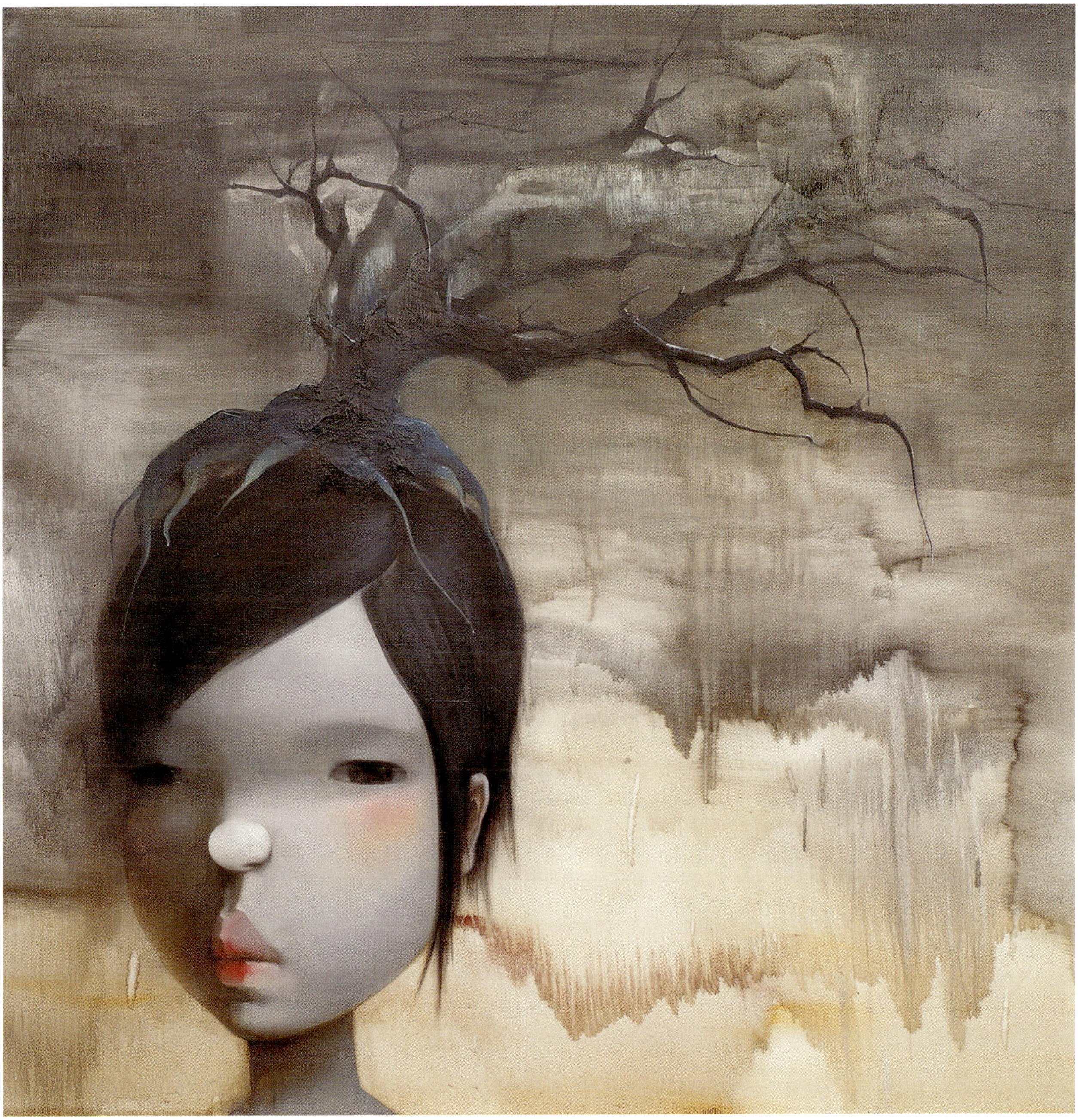

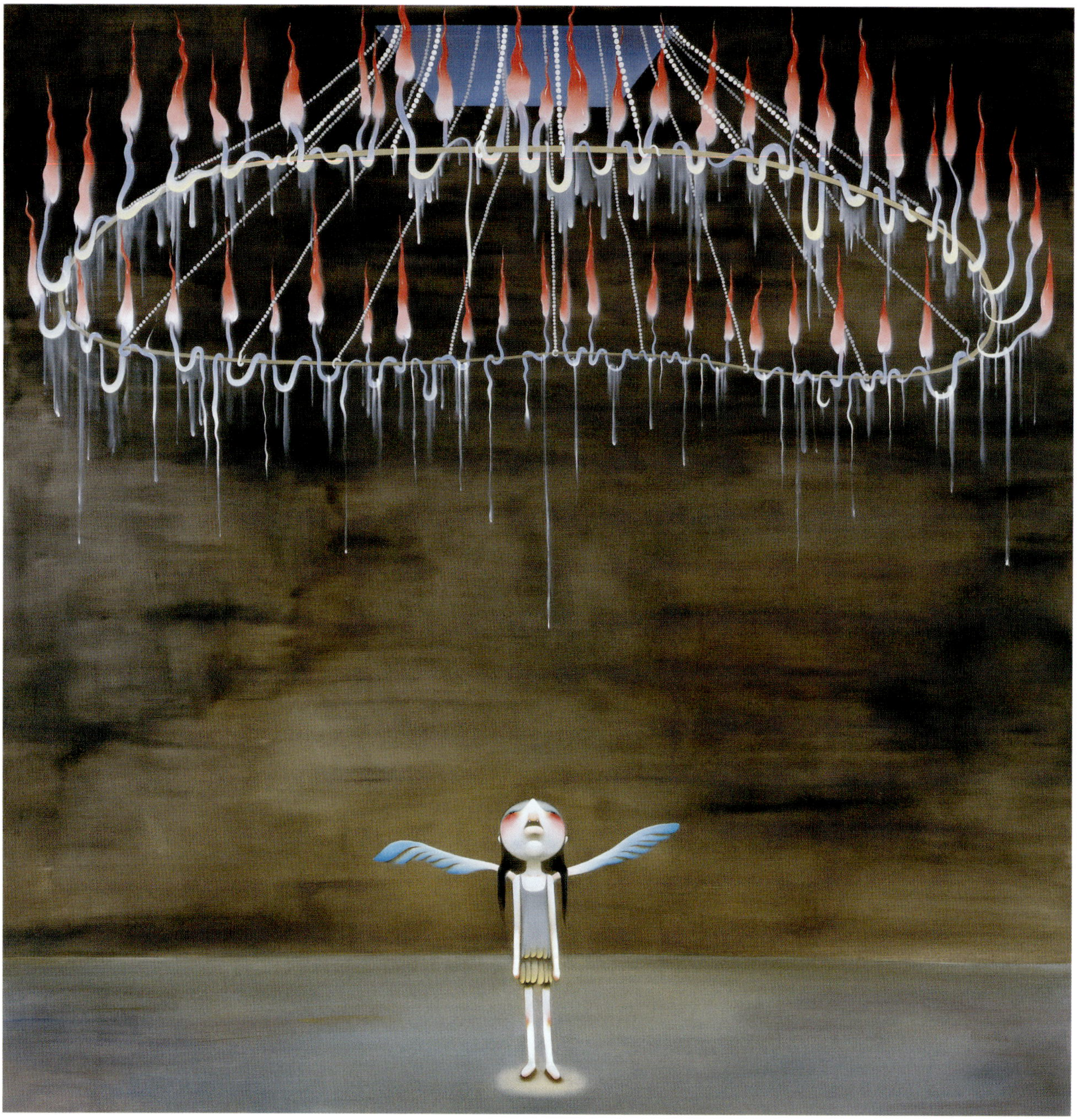

FACING PAGE: *The Higher Life*, 2006. Oil on canvas, 84½ x 84½ in.

THIS PAGE, TOP: *Swordswoman in Night*, 2006. Oil on canvas, 51 x 39 in.

THIS PAGE, BOTTOM: *Watch Fire Between the Banks*, 2006. Oil on canvas, 59 x 118 in.

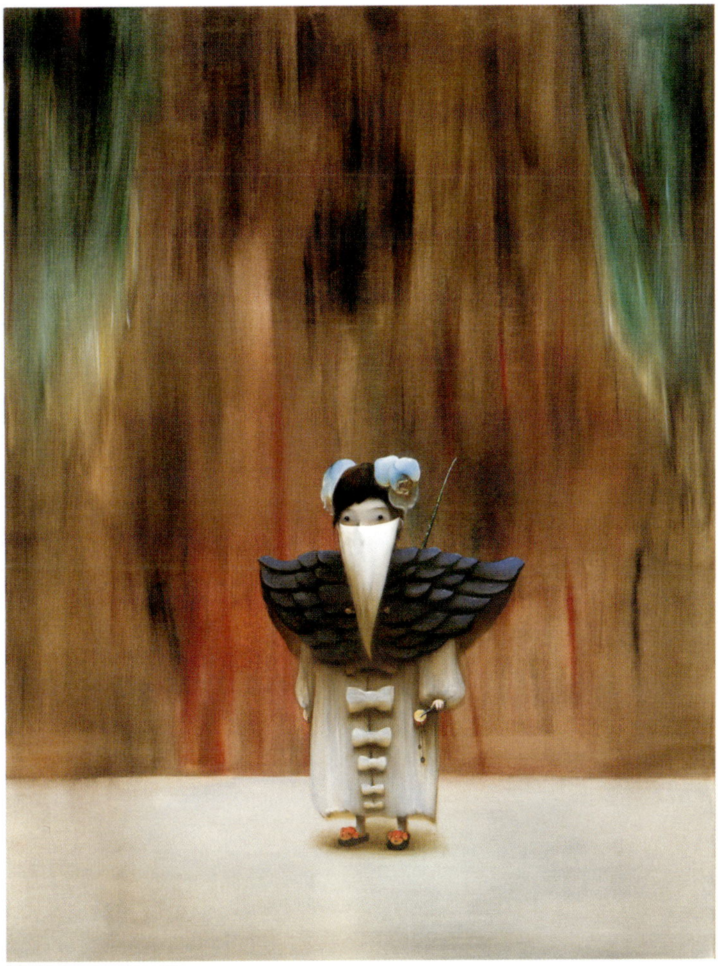

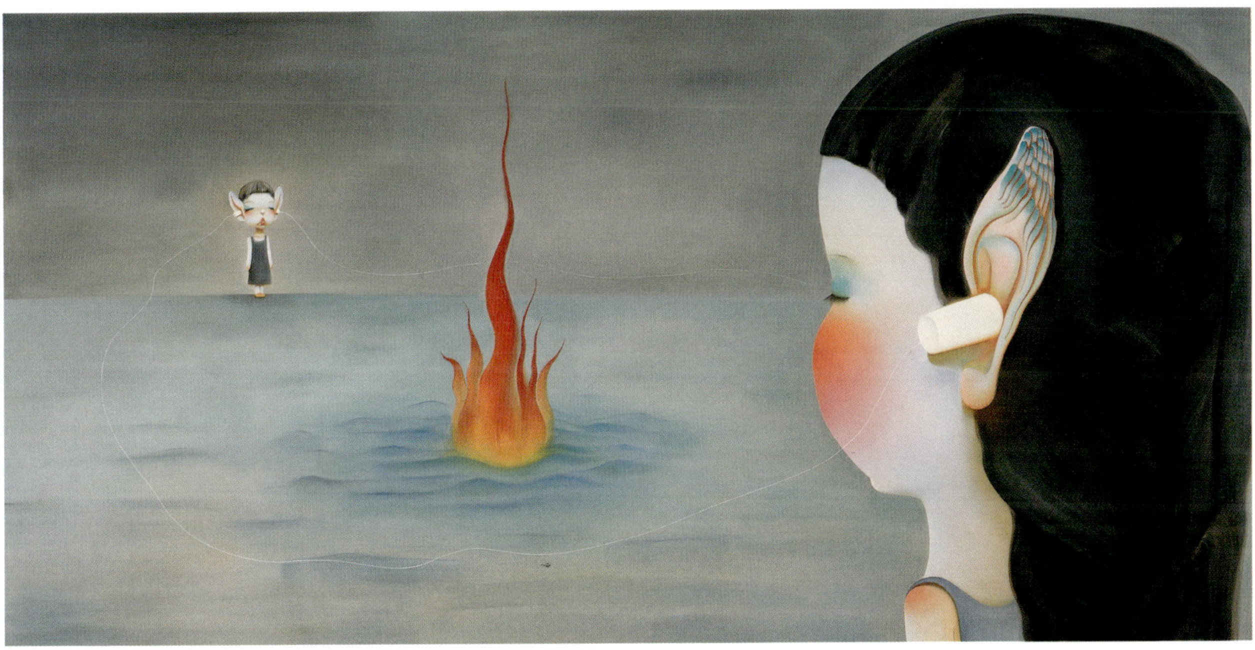

Chen Lingyang

Born 1975, Zhejiang Province

FACING PAGE, TOP: *Menstruation Fairy*, 2002. Video installation, Guangzhou Triennial.

FACING PAGE, BOTTOM: *25:00 No. 1*, 2002. C-print, 47 x 90 in.

OVERLEAF, LEFT: *Twelve Flower Months—The Third Month Peach*, November 1999–December 2000. C-print, 16 x 27½ in.

OVERLEAF, RIGHT: *Twelve Flower Months—The Ninth Month Chrysanthemum*, November 1999–December 2000. C-print, 38 x 41½ in.

A child of the seventies, Chen Lingyang belongs to a generation of women artists who are bravely exploring the sphere of female identity in a period when sex is still something of a taboo subject in China.

Known to be shy, her shyness has not stopped her from standing up and exploring the truth of the female body. Her first work of art caused a scandal: *Scroll* (1999), was six-meter-long strip of toilet paper she used to wipe her vagina during her menstrual period, bearing traces of blood forming marks similar to landscapes. This work, based on the traditional genre of landscapes painted in ink on long pieces of silk and then rolled out to be displayed, has only been exhibited once, at the Fuck Off exhibition in Shanghai in 2001. The traditional silk rolls describe, in their unfolding, the passage of the seasons, and, in *Scroll*, Chen explored femininity through the female body in its passage of time, as marked by its monthly menstruation.

The work *Twelve Flower Months* (November 1999–December 2000) reflects even more sharply the female body in all its carnal truth. In a series of twelve photographs, she presents her vagina during her menstrual period, reflected in a mirror, accompanied by flowers, and framed in a setting recalling traditional Chinese garden design. The flowers are chosen in accordance with Chinese custom, where each month is symbolized by a different bloom. *Twelve Flower Months*, like *Scroll*, draws on ancient tradition to give an honest portrayal of contemporary femininity in a society where so much is hidden from view.

The *25:00* series (2002) portrays a large nude of a female body in a dark cityscape sprinkled with points of light. Chen says: "This female 'giantess' is not actually very brave, that's the reason why she can only freely change her size and make these gestures when the clock strikes 25:00 . . . I often feel that I am weak and helpless, and don't know what to do. I wish that every day there could be a certain time like 25:00, when I could become as large as I like, and do whatever I want."

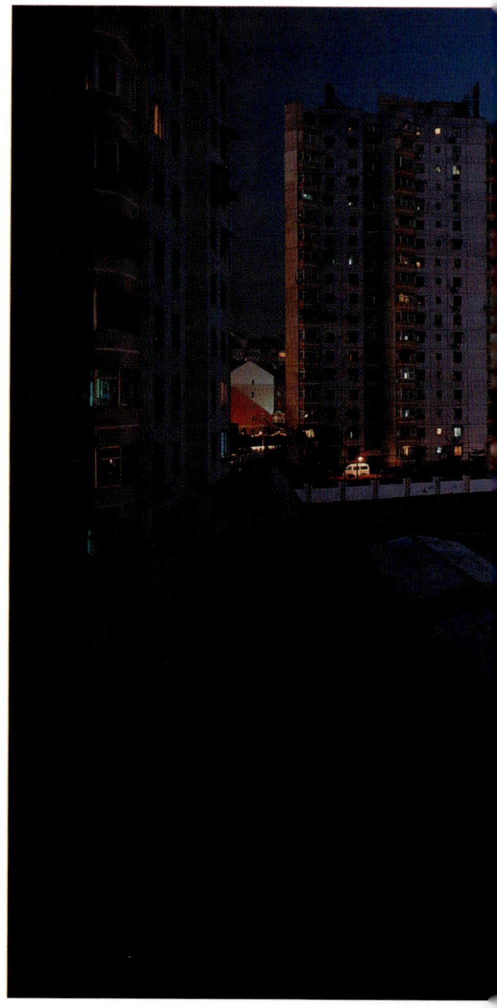

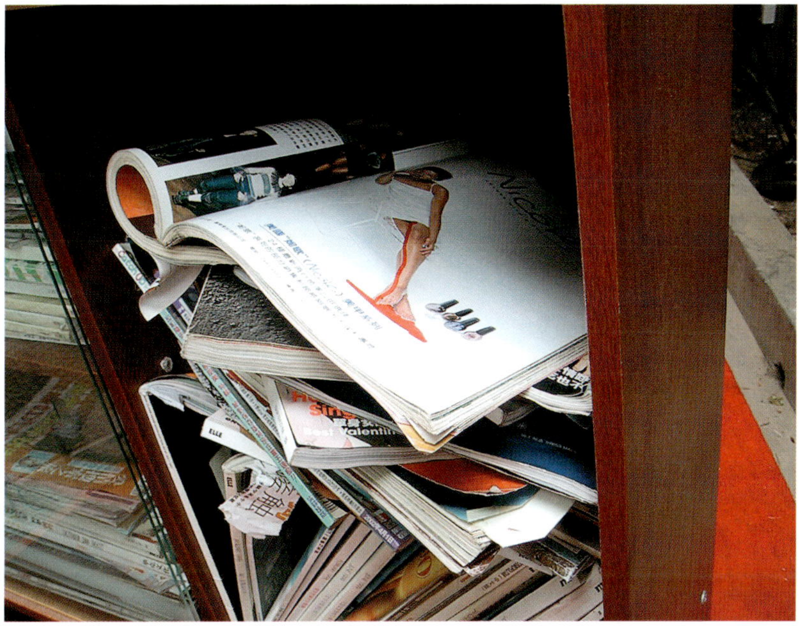

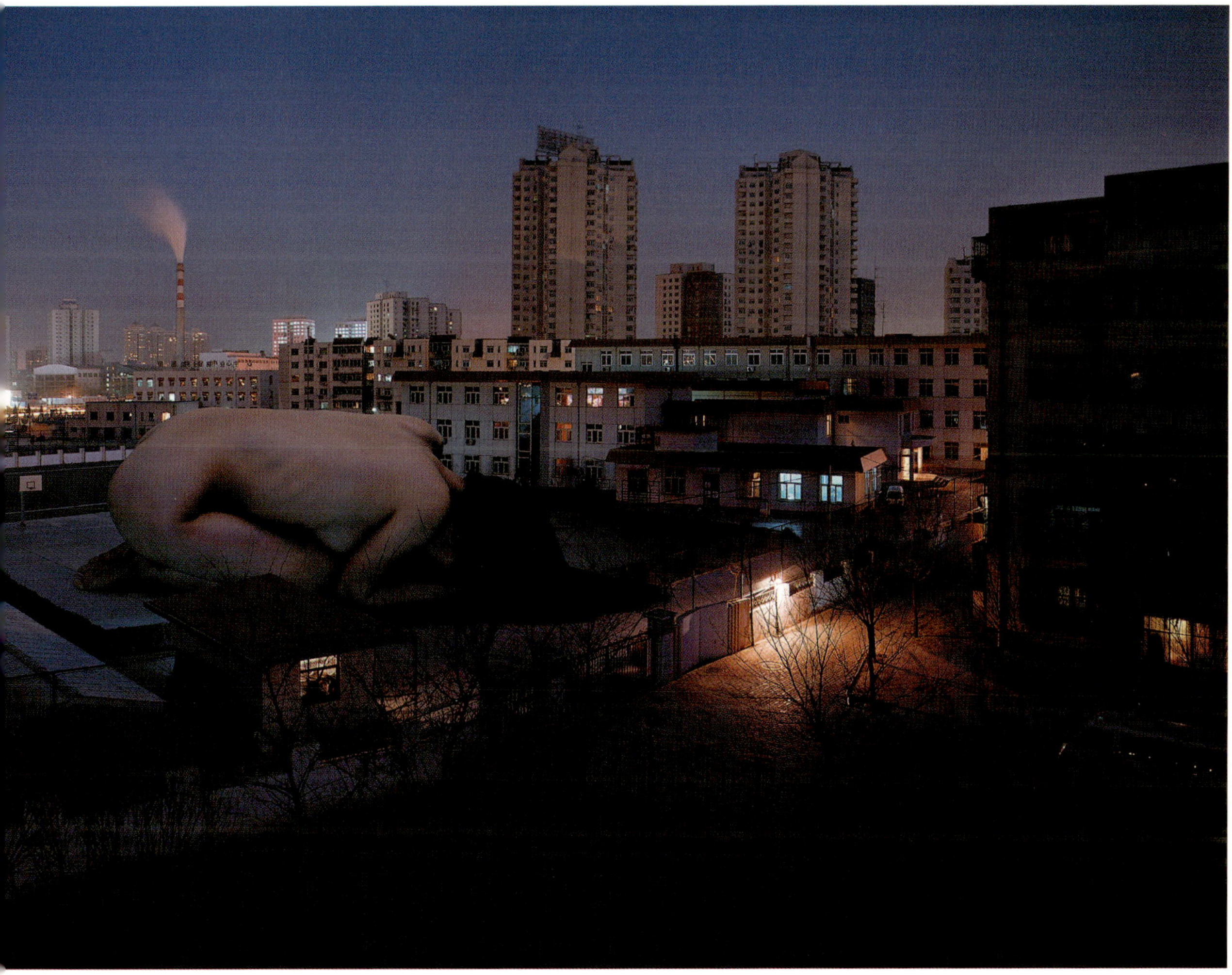

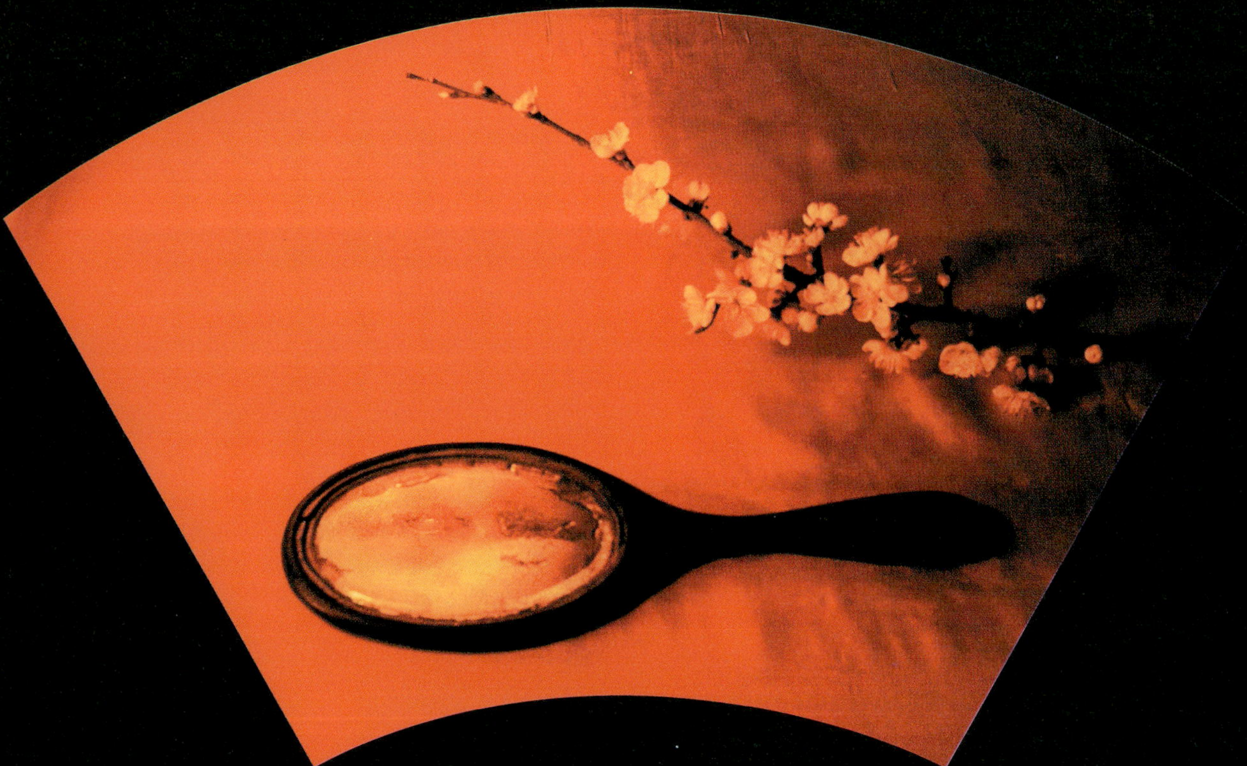

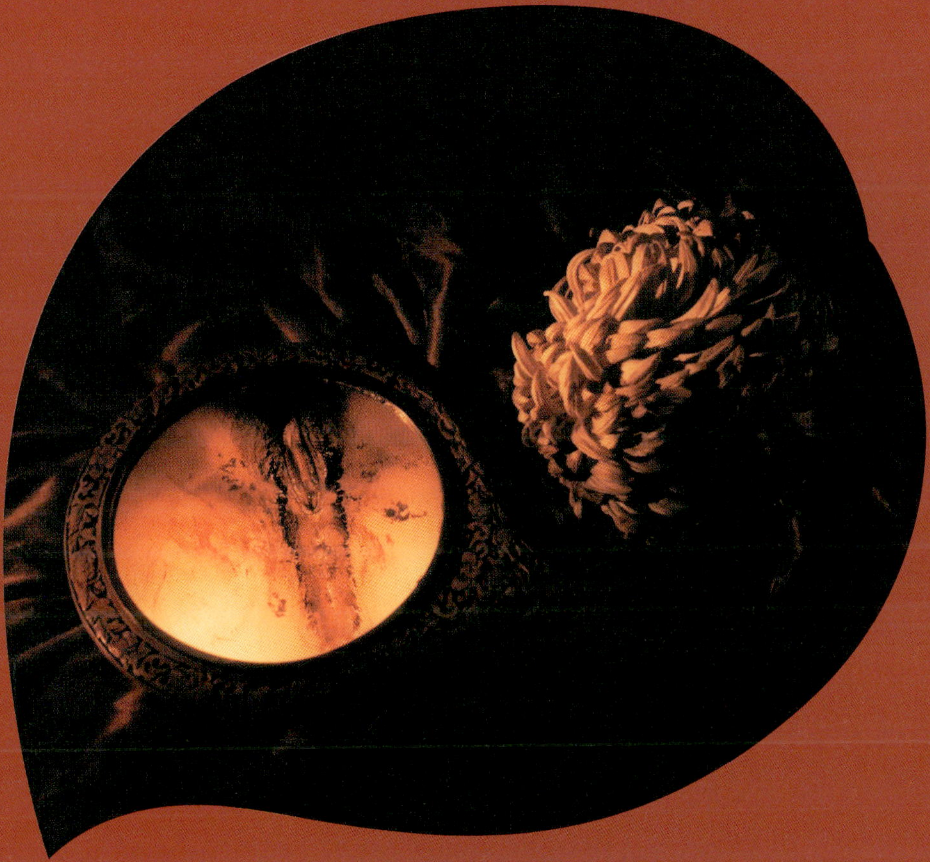

Chen Shaoxiong

Born 1962, Shantou, Guangdong Province

THIS PAGE: *Collective Memory—Tianhe, Guangzhou*, 2006. Chinese ink on canvas, 79 x 118 in.

FACING PAGE: *Ink City*, 2005. Video installation.

Originally trained in engraving, Chen Shaoxiong broke with academic art to found the Big Tail Elephant Group in 1990 with three other artists: Lin Yilin, Liang Juhui, and Xu Tan. Their aim was to critically explore China's rapid economic changes and their effect on urban life. After 1997 when the group broke up, Chen continued to express his fascination with the daily life of the city through video, inks, and photography. "Everything in the city is temporary," he has observed. In the series *Streetscapes* (1997–), the city's dynamics are transformed into a Lilliputian 3-D collage, where miniature figures are photographed and fixed in a series of action-packed scenes, a comment on the transitory nature and artificiality of city life.

In the series *Collective Memory* (2004–) Chen uses monochrome fingerprints to create pixilated images that evoke individual identity and collective consciousness. Fusing new media technology with traditional ink painting in the video pieces *Ink City* (2005) and *Ink Diary* (2006), he creates an extraordinary space in which the reality of the cityscape and our mind's impressions temporarily coexist.

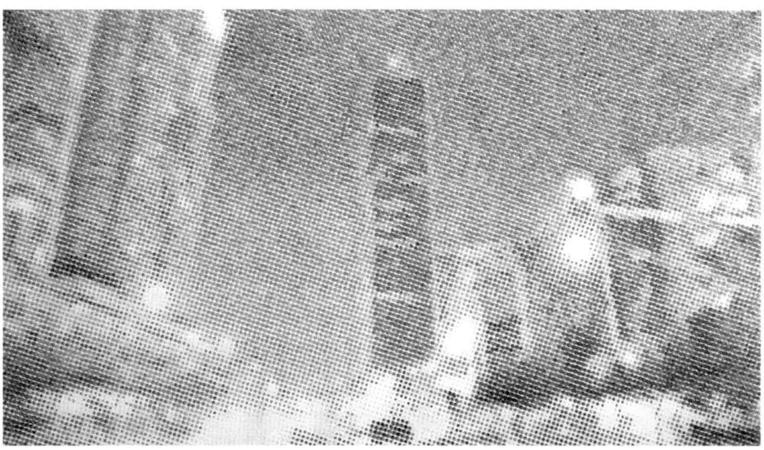

In 2006 Chen collaborated with the Japanese artist Tsuyoshi Ozawa on the project *Summer Holiday*. The artists and their respective families of three spent a twenty-day "summer holiday" in the gallery. Each day the families inhabited a different "unit," and each day they created a new artwork—installation, painting, sculpture, video. Visitors to the exhibition could walk into the units and join in with the activities, with no rules or restrictions. In this experimental piece, the artists explored the themes of personal boundaries and cultural differences using the medium of the family, one of the smallest social cores, where people's interactions and exchanges can be studied in a more genuine and intimate way.

The installation work *Visible and Invisible, Known and Unknown* (2007), comprises the ongoing video series *Ink Things* (2006–) and the paper and canvas works that form the series *Collective Memory*. A model train runs continuously on a looping track parallel to a billboard where the *Ink Things* video is projected; a small camera positioned at the head of the train records the video images and simultaneously projects them onto a screen. Chen invites us to reexamine the way we look at the cityscape as the train passes by the often-ignored images that surround us every day.

In the video *Anti-terrorism Variety* (2002), Chen comes up with a clever idea on how to prevent and fight terrorism, patenting high-rises able to dodge airplanes. Chen's spirit penetrates the bizarre of the everyday, and his witty narrations astonish and amaze.

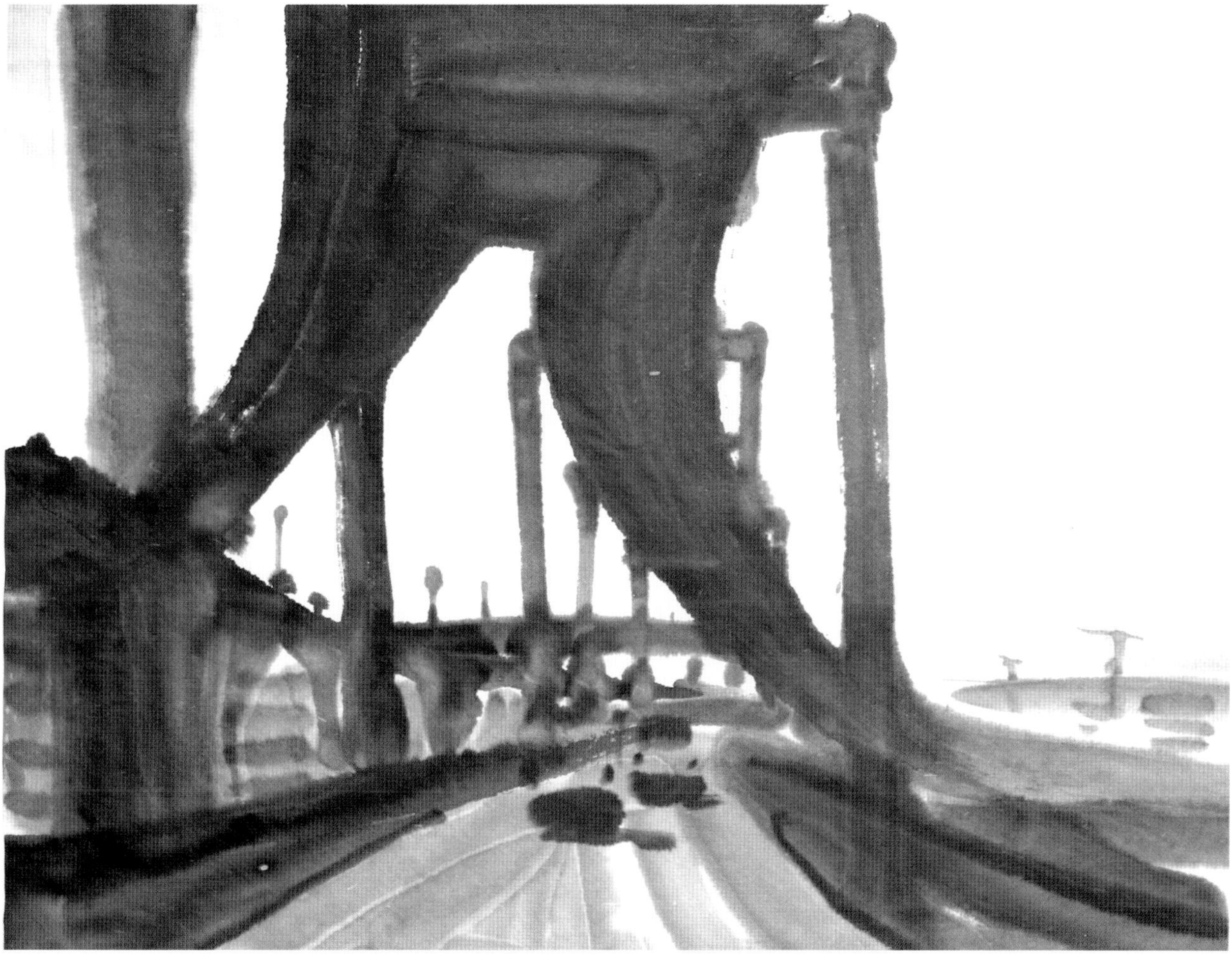

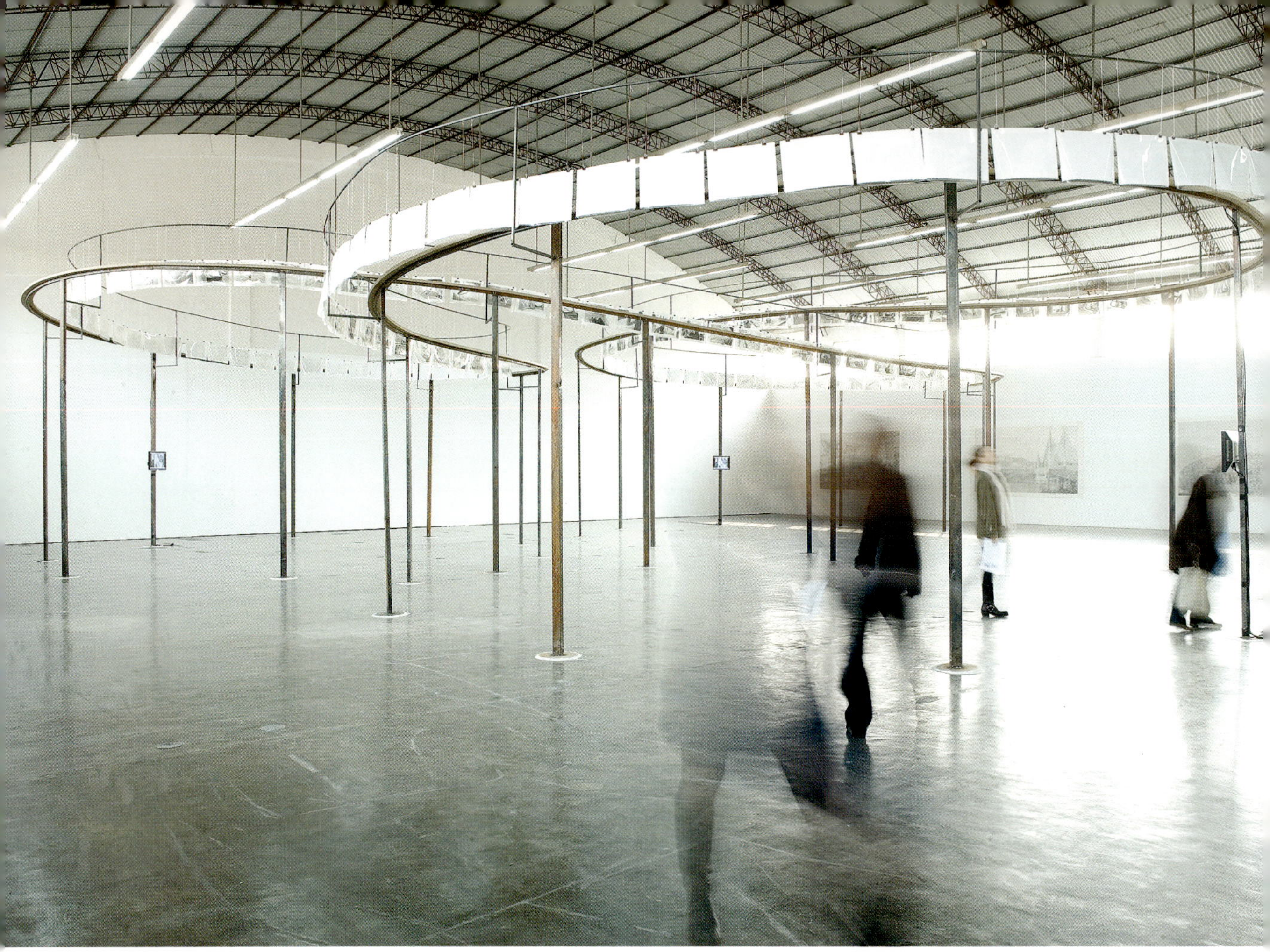

THIS PAGE, TOP: *Visible and Invisible, Known and Unknown*, 2007. Installation view, UniversalStudios-beijing. Rice paper, ink, model train, steel supports, wireless transmitting system.

THIS PAGE, BOTTOM: *Summer Holiday*, 2006. Installation view, UniversalStudios-beijing.

FACING PAGE, TOP: *Anti-terrorism Variety (2)*, 2002. Still from video.

FACING PAGE, BOTTOM: *Streetscape (2)*, 2005. Photo-cut collage, 12 x 12 x 394 in.

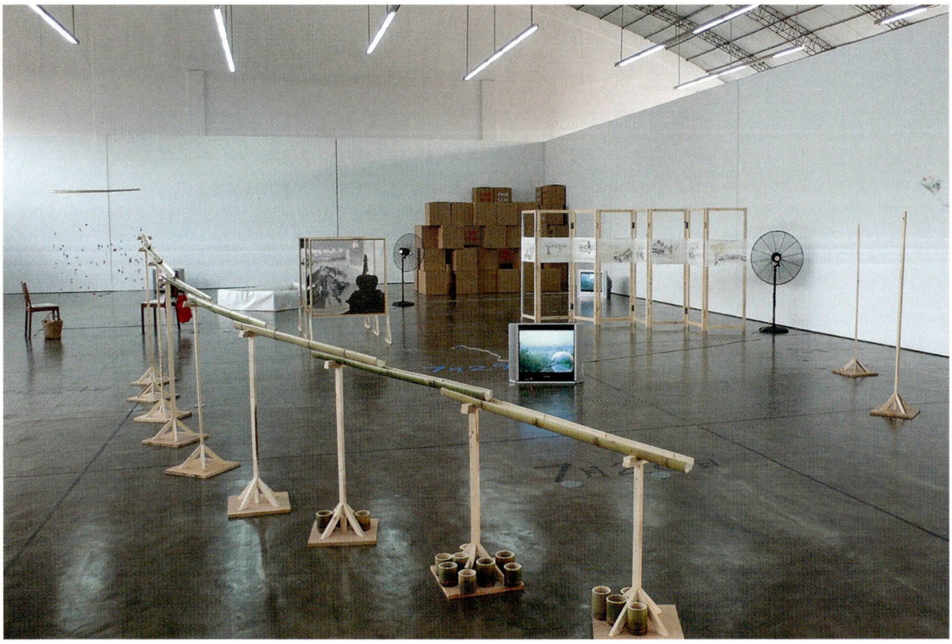

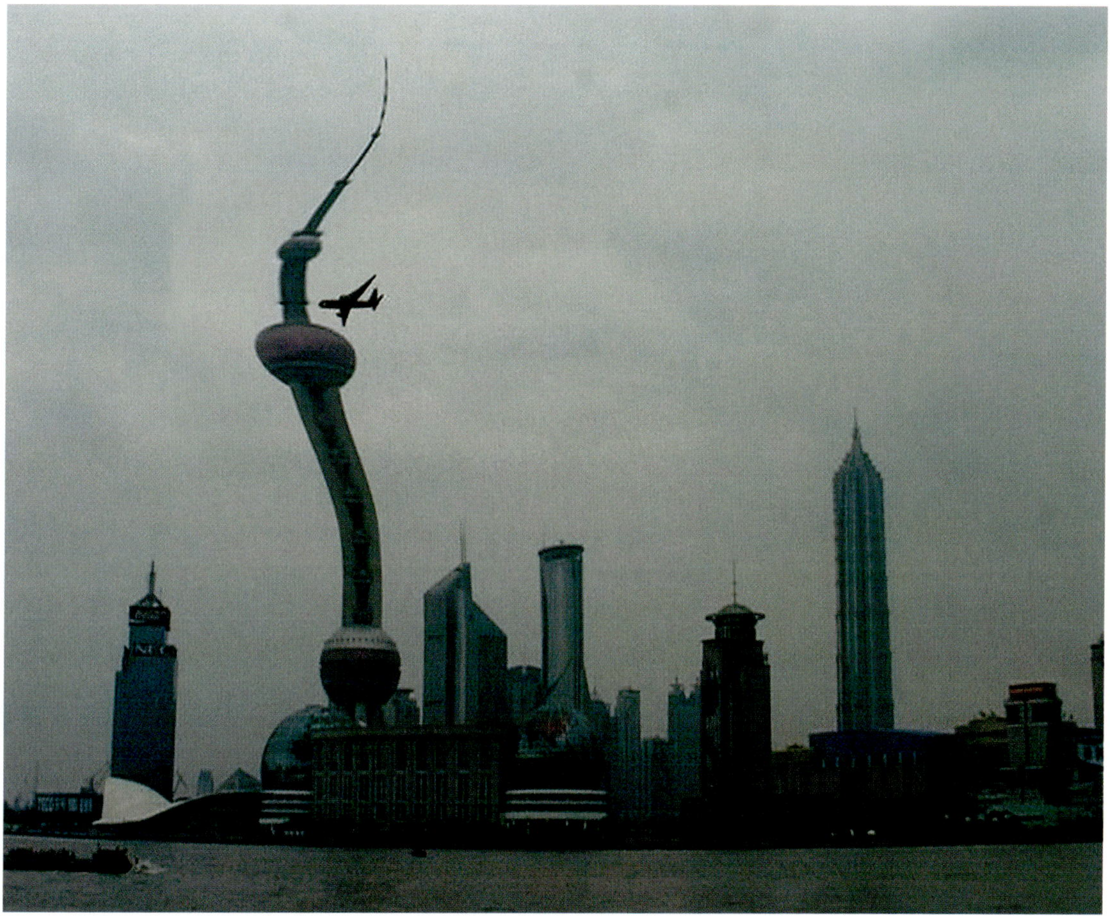

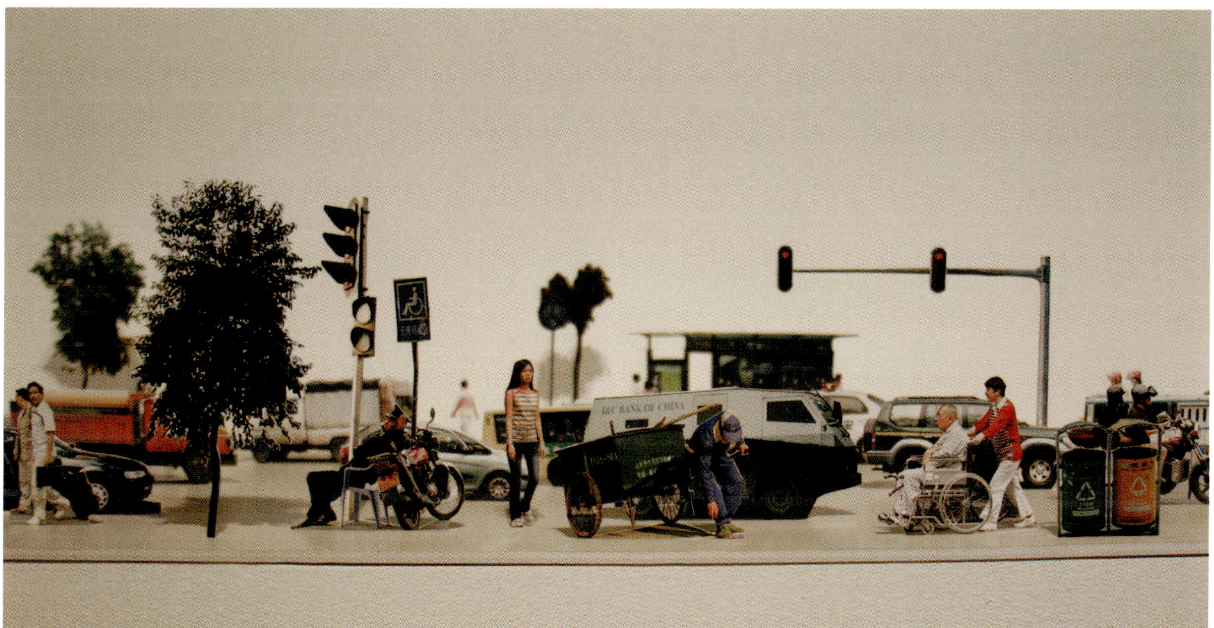
BANK OF CHINA

Cui Xiuwen

Born 1970, Harbin, Heilongjiang Province

THIS PAGE: *Angel No. 1*, 2006. Photograph, dimensions variable.
FACING PAGE: *Lady's*, 2000. Stills from video.

Attractive and self-assured, Cui Xiuwen is highly sensitive to what it means to be a woman in a male-dominated world. She explores and comments on her own awareness of femininity in the new Chinese society, going beyond social morals and superficial appearances. Focusing on the female body and its sexuality, Cui depicts a psychological portrait of womanhood that is often permeated by emotional introspection.

Dealing with provocative and outrageous themes such as the abuse and violence enacted against women in a society where even their status of equality has been gained through a system governed by men, Cui was the subject of magazine articles and TV talk shows as far back as 1998. Her appearances on TV led to her interest in video making and resulted in her most famous work, *Lady's* (2000), in which Cui entered the ladies' toilet of a nightclub in Beijing and, using a hidden camera, filmed the ladies of the title—most of whom happened to be sex workers—touching up their makeup, adjusting their breasts, brushing their teeth, and calling their clients. Highlighting issues of exploitation and isolation, the artist focuses on the female body as constructed by society, plunging into the psychological depths of other women, in this case prostitutes.

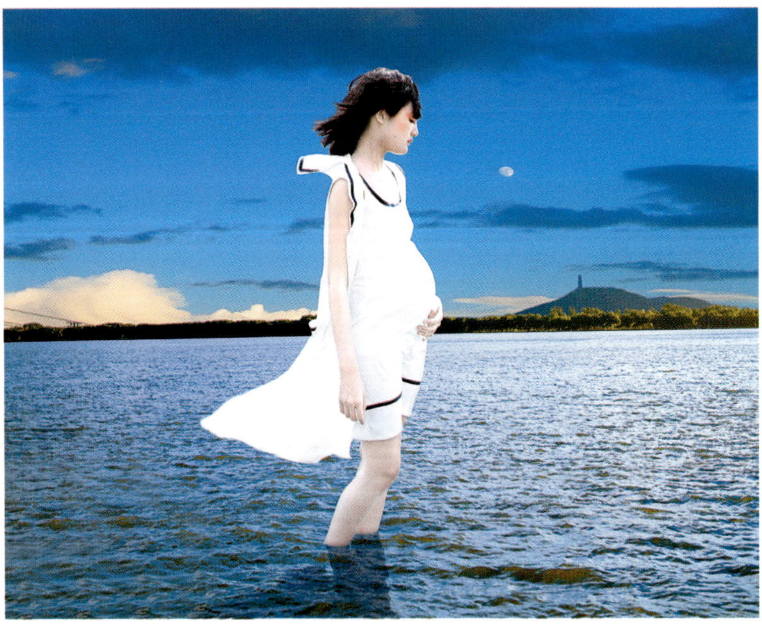

2003 marked a new chapter in the story of Cui's ascent. Working for the first time with a model who was to feature in many of her works, the artist directs her attention to a more philosophical, if not religious, approach to femininity. In the video *Sanjie* (2003), inspired by Leonardo da Vinci's *Last Supper*, the thirteen-year-old model takes her place in front of the camera and assumes the role of each of the apostles in turn, and also of Christ himself. In the video *Drifting Lanterns* (2005), the artist focuses on a single image, rich in spirituality: the oscillating movement of a glowing lantern carried with a chain by the same model. Accompanied by the sound of a Buddhist chant, the girl advances through alleys and courtyards with a ceremonial calmness as the camera follows her path.

In the photographic series *One Day in 2004* (2005), the same young girl becomes a metaphor for oppressed women in an unjust society. In the series *Angel* (2006), the model is slightly older, her body now portrayed in a state of advanced pregnancy. Cui does not make resounding statements; rather, she observes, and offers powerful images that pose thought-provoking questions related to her own reality and the reality of young women living in today's China.

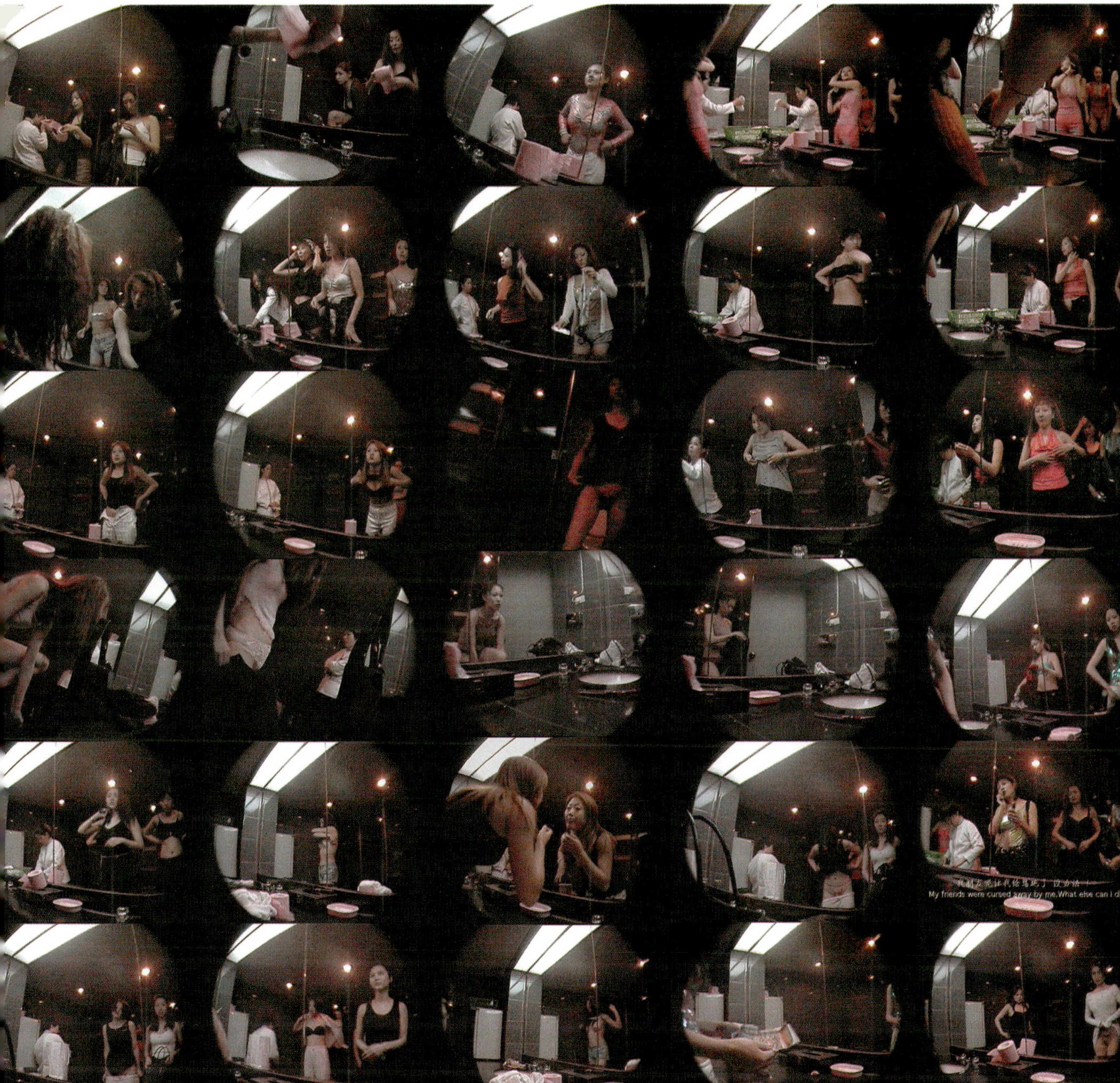
My friends were cursed away by me.What else can I d

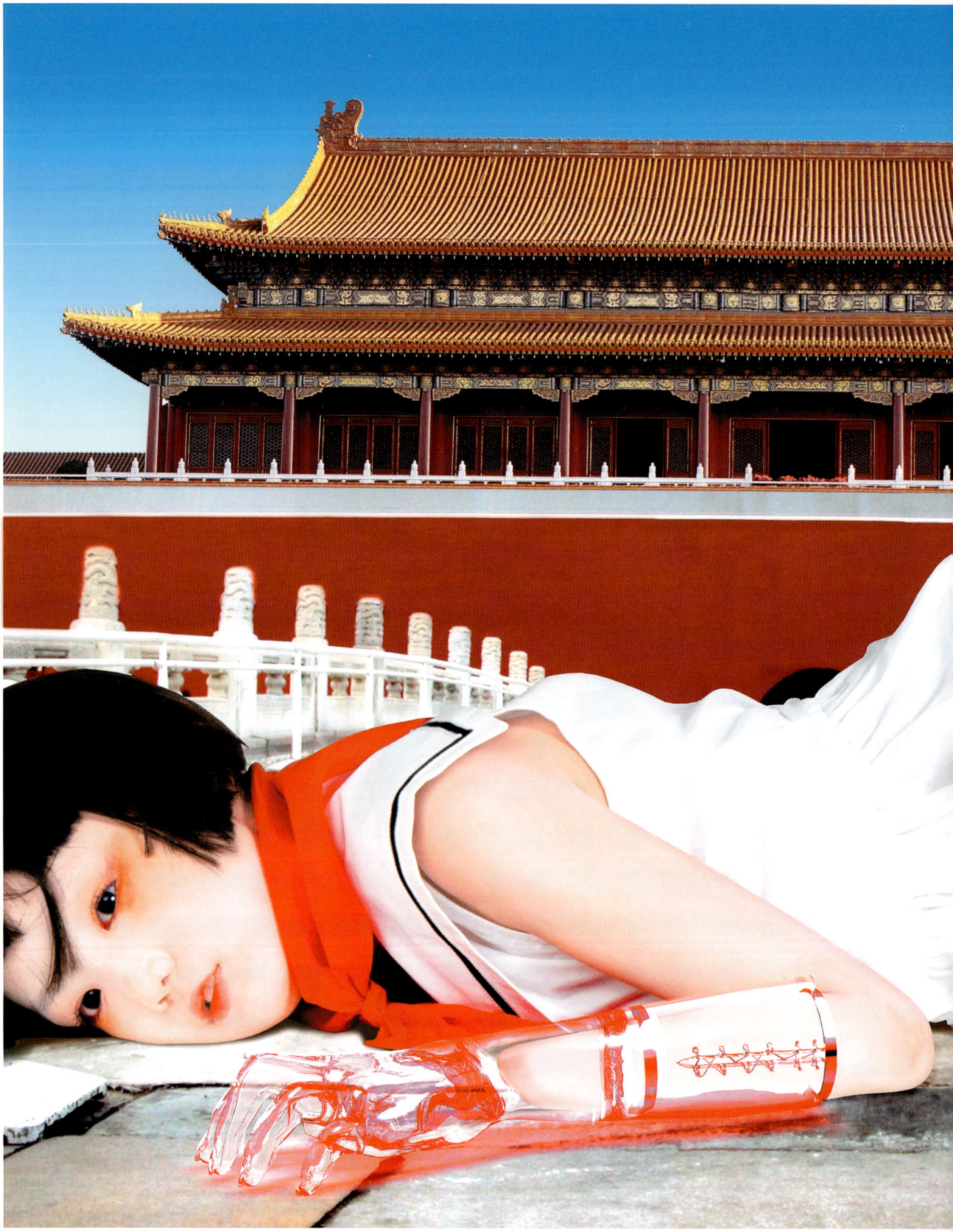

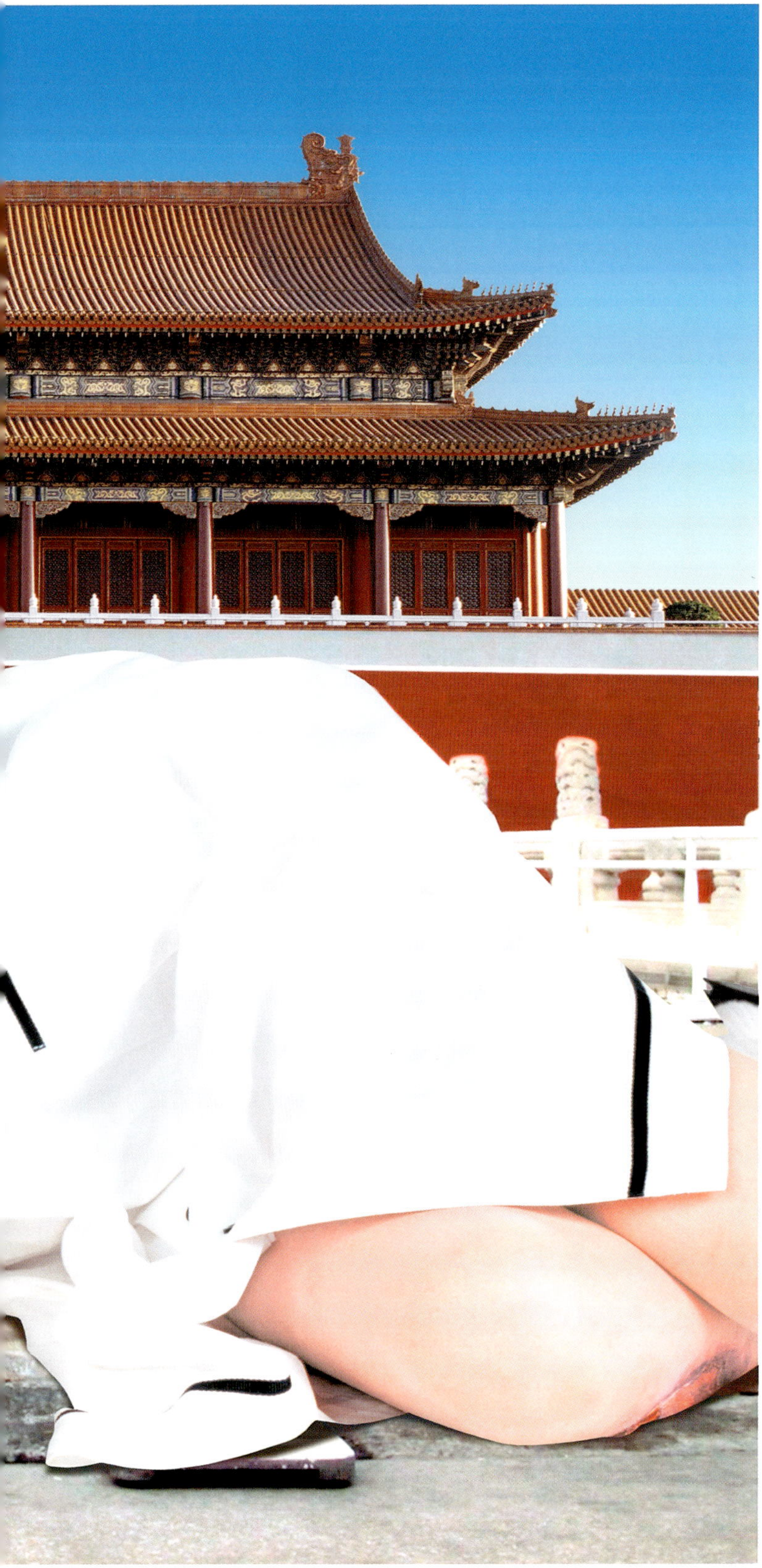

One Day in 2004, No. 6, 2005. Photograph, dimensions variable.

Fang Lijun

Born 1962, Handan, Hebei Province

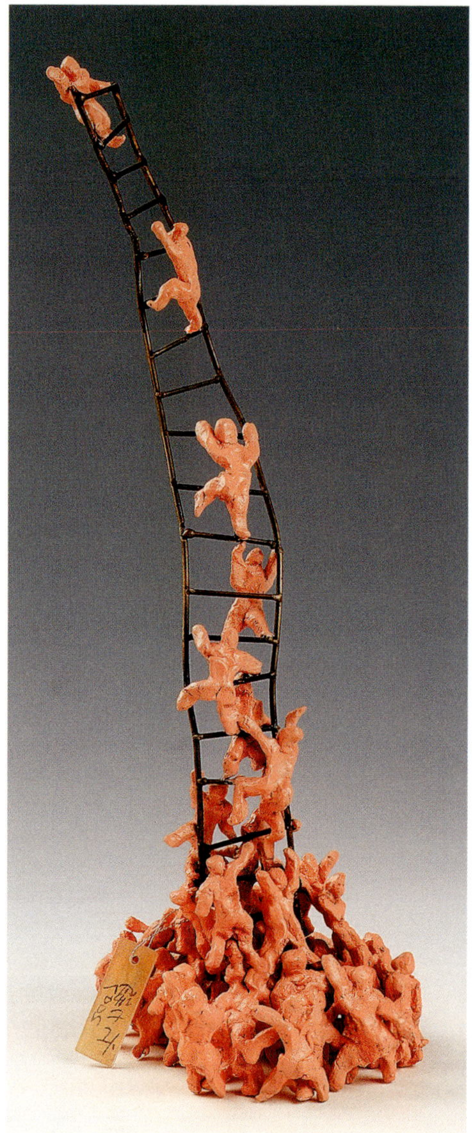

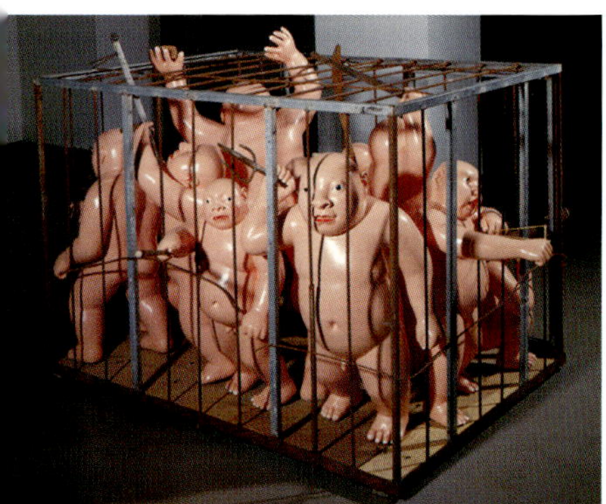

THIS PAGE, TOP: *Untitled*, 2007. Bronze, iron, 17½ x 8 x 6 in.

THIS PAGE, BOTTOM: *2005–06*, 2006. Glass reinforced plastic, steel, iron, stone, 51 x 86½ x 106½ in.

FACING PAGE: *2001–1–10*, 2001. Acrylic on canvas, 141½ x 98½ in.

Dreamlike paintings inhabited by bald-headed figures wandering among the clouds, figures howling, groping, or in yearning poses, heads cast in bronze, swimmers in the water, giant woodblock prints, naked babies, birds, and mosquitoes: Fang Lijun's icons and techniques illustrate Cynical Realist notions of a lost idealism. Indeed, he was one of the initiators of the Cynical Realism movement that developed in the aftermath of the Tiananmen massacre. The movement was an expression of the dissatisfaction of the art world with society and politics of the time, and also a reaction against the hopeless idealism that was typical of the Chinese art scene in the 1980s.

In the first half of the 1990s, feelings of unease, disillusionment, and boredom pervaded Chinese society; Fang was fascinated by this loss of idealism and by the population's general attitude. He became a leading figure at Yuanmingyuan, the artists' village located by the Old Summer Palace in Beijing where, just after the Tiananmen incident, young artists, especially painters, gathered to live and work. The first bald-headed figures started to appear in Fang's paintings at this time, and his trademark character is widely interpreted as symbol of mockery and rebellion.

In all his works, from oil paintings to inks and woodblock prints, Fang skillfully captures the psychological state of his characters, but leaves the viewer with a feeling of ambiguity or ambivalence: among the howling, yearning, rebellious characters are swimmers with flowing movements and relaxed faces, and figures floating in the air surrounded by fantastic clouds and colored flowers, who seem to inhabit a paradisiacal dimension, freed from earthly weight.

Fang does not title his works. In fact, they are distinguished only by a date, which, as art critic Ulrike Munter has noted, suggests that he sees his art as a sort of visual diary, a record of the times.

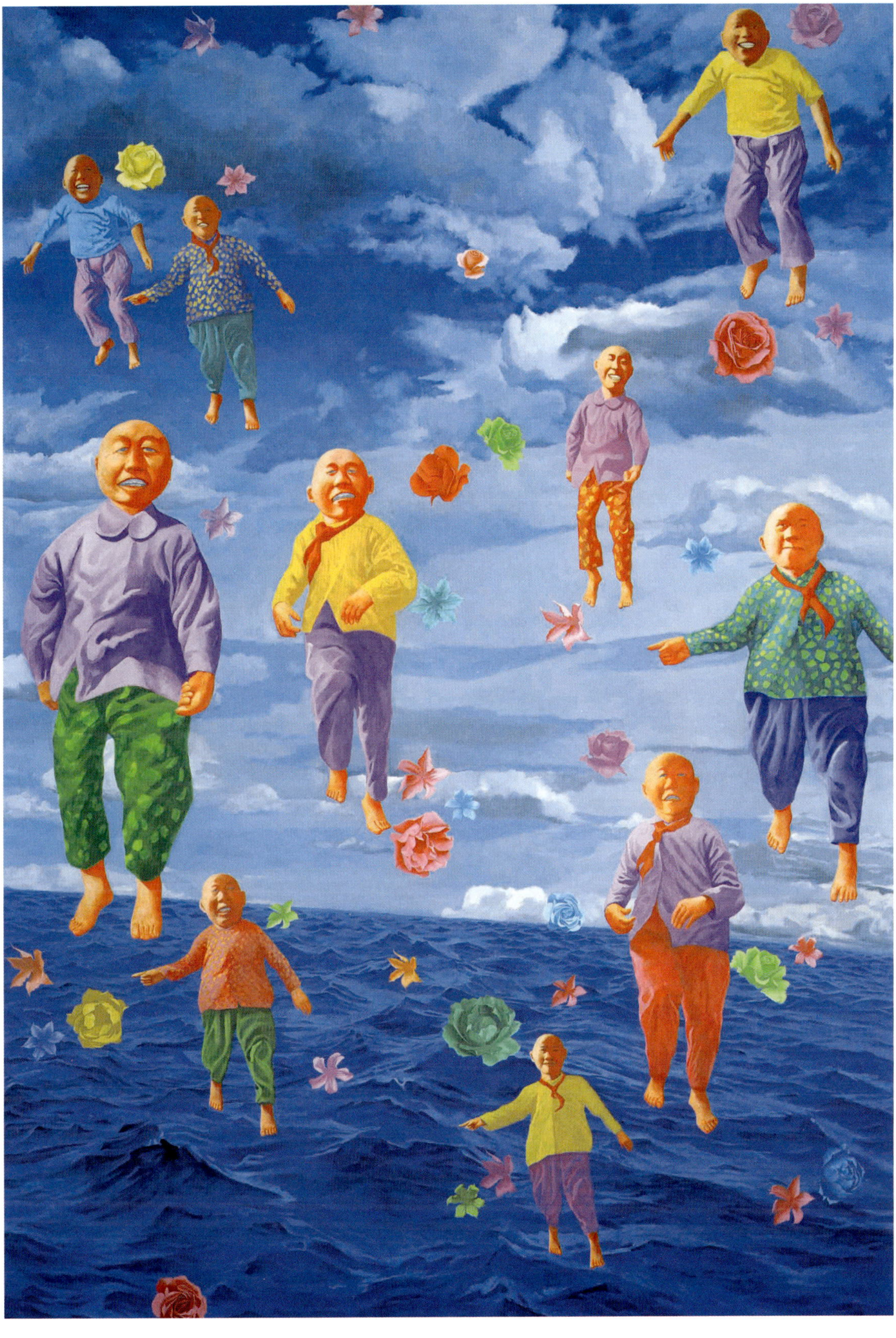

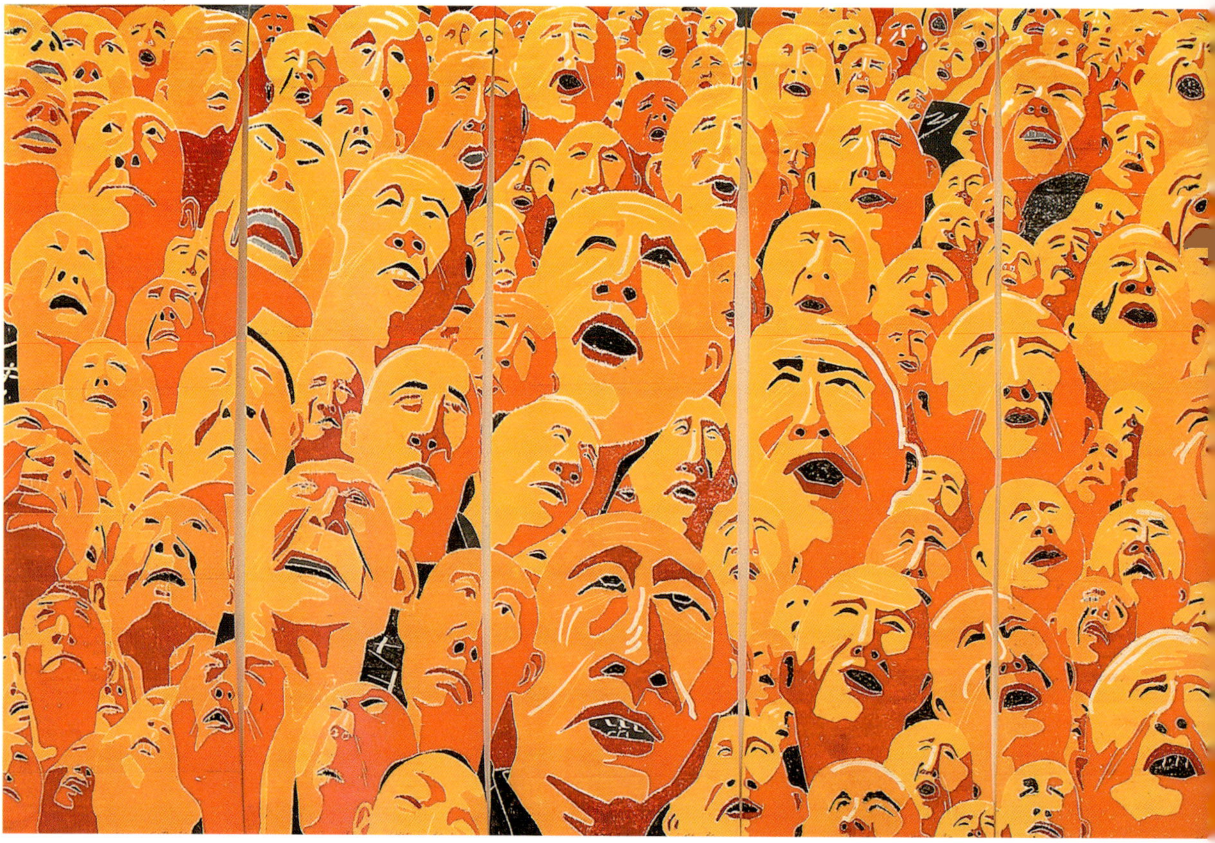

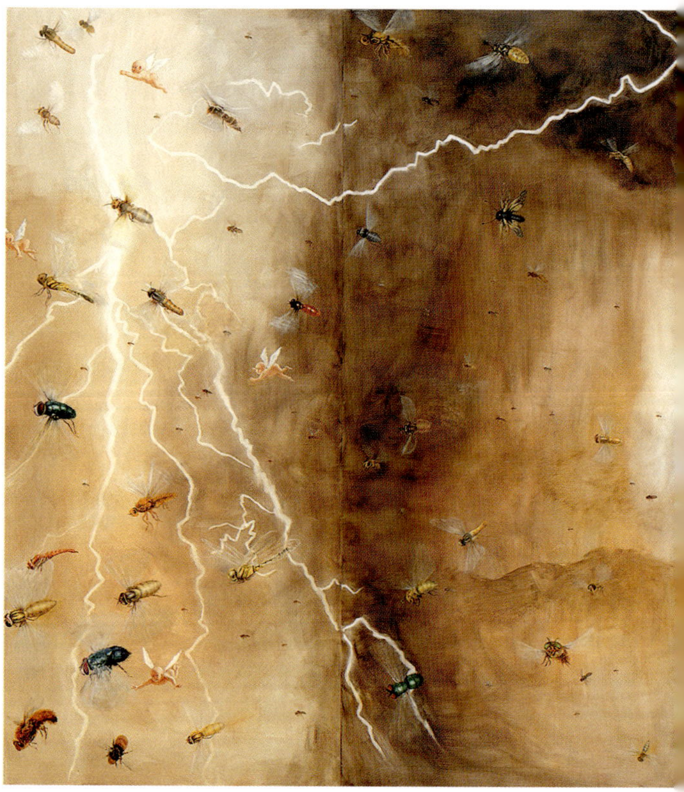

TOP: *2003. 2. 1*, 2003. Woodcut on seven scrolls, 13 x 28 ft.
BOTTOM: *2007–5*, 2007. Oil on canvas, 9 x 32 ft.

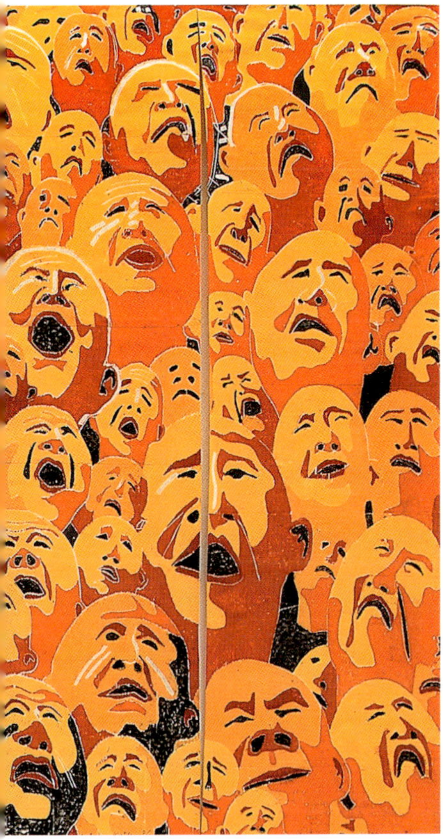

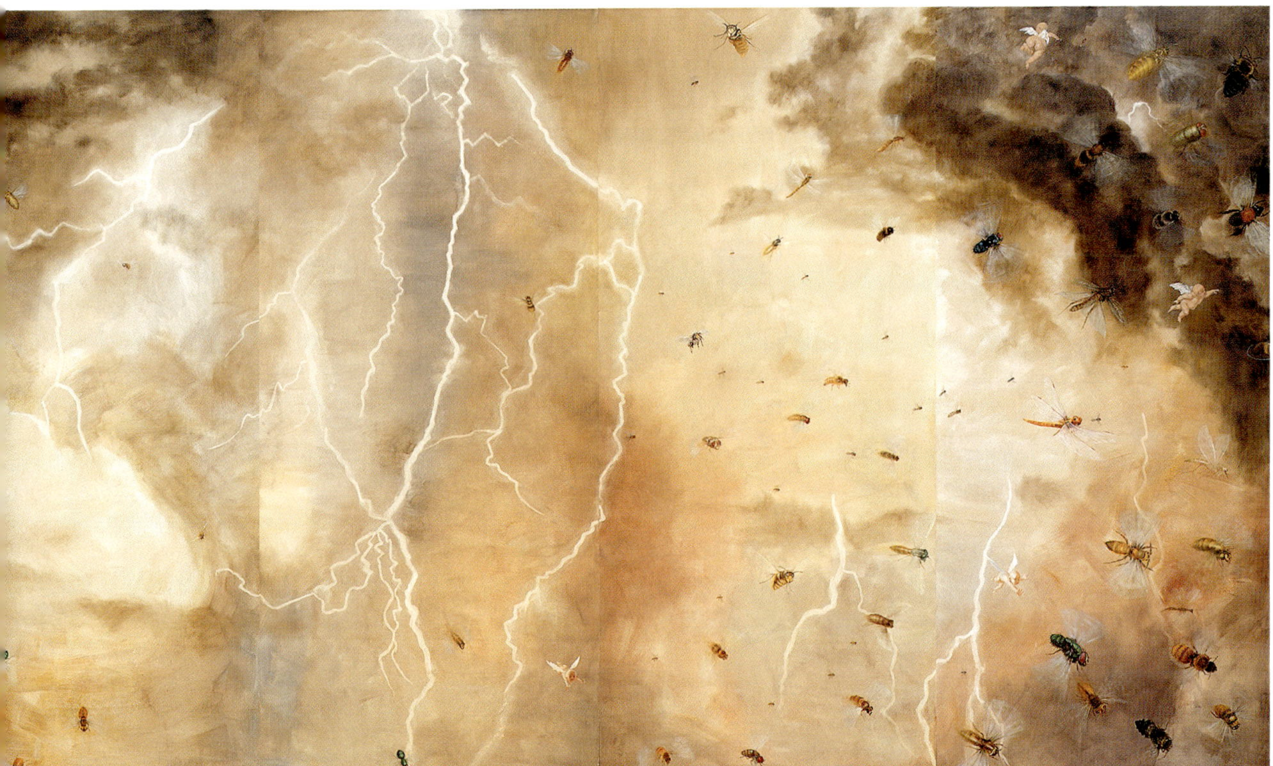

Feng Zhengjie

Born 1968, Sichuan Province

China is red, but it is also green like bamboo, like tea, like jade . . . Red and green, just like the doors of Feng Zhengjie's studio. Bright and shimmering colors, weighty strokes, and winking grimaces are the code to enter Feng's dimension.

Educated at the Sichuan Fine Arts Institute, Feng's early, expressionistic paintings developed into a more personalized and mature technique that came to be known as Gaudy Art. The *Romantic Trip* series (1996) demonstrates this transformation. Considered a turning point in Feng's style, the series has a narrative structure built on real images that are also plastic and fake. Focusing on facial expressions, Feng gives his figures flamboyant colors and affected poses that are kitsch and grotesque, asserting that contemporary consumer culture has become an aesthetic ideology. In the series *Coolness* (2000), he reveals the ever-globalizing characteristics of the body incarnated in "cool" gestures, accessories, and makeup.

With luscious lips, pumped hair, and ostentatious beauty, the women portrayed in the series *China* (2000–) and *Chinese Portrait* (2000–) are fully aware of their dazzling charm. Curator Eleonora Battiston has observed that this display of obsessive hedonism is accompanied by a feeling of emptiness and the absence of ideals and real sentiments, suggested by the vacant eyes of these women who embody not just the superficial, but also the excesses and the alienation brought about by a market-driven culture. The series *Life Like Flower* (2006–2007) moves toward a more personal dimension. "Just as the moon has different phases, waning and waxing, full and eclipse, so do people's lives, they know joys and sorrows, parting and reunion. As flowers bloom and wither, so people's lives have more than one way of being," he explains. Sensitive and profound, Feng is aware of people and their subtle relationships, while thinking that maybe perfection lies in small, simple things . . . like a flower.

RIGHT: *Life Like Flower No. 02*, 2006–2007. Oil on canvas, 118 x 157½ in., 118 x 197 in., 118 x 157½ in.

FACING PAGE, TOP: *Coolness 2000 No. 12*, 2000. Oil on canvas, 75 x 59 in.

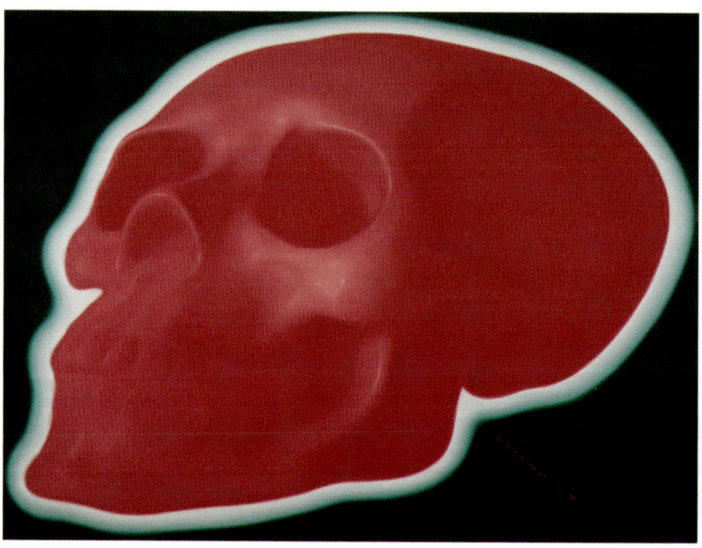

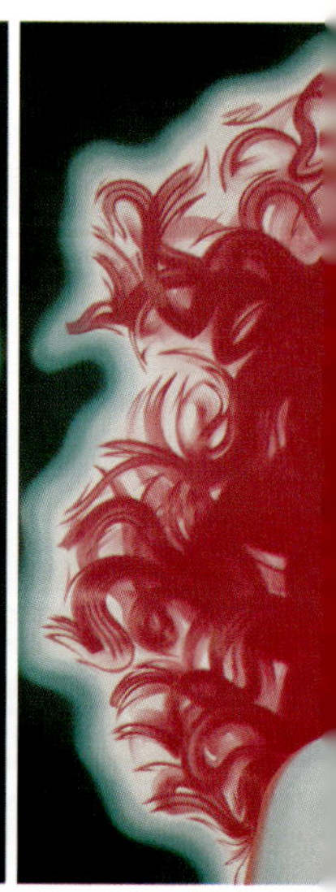

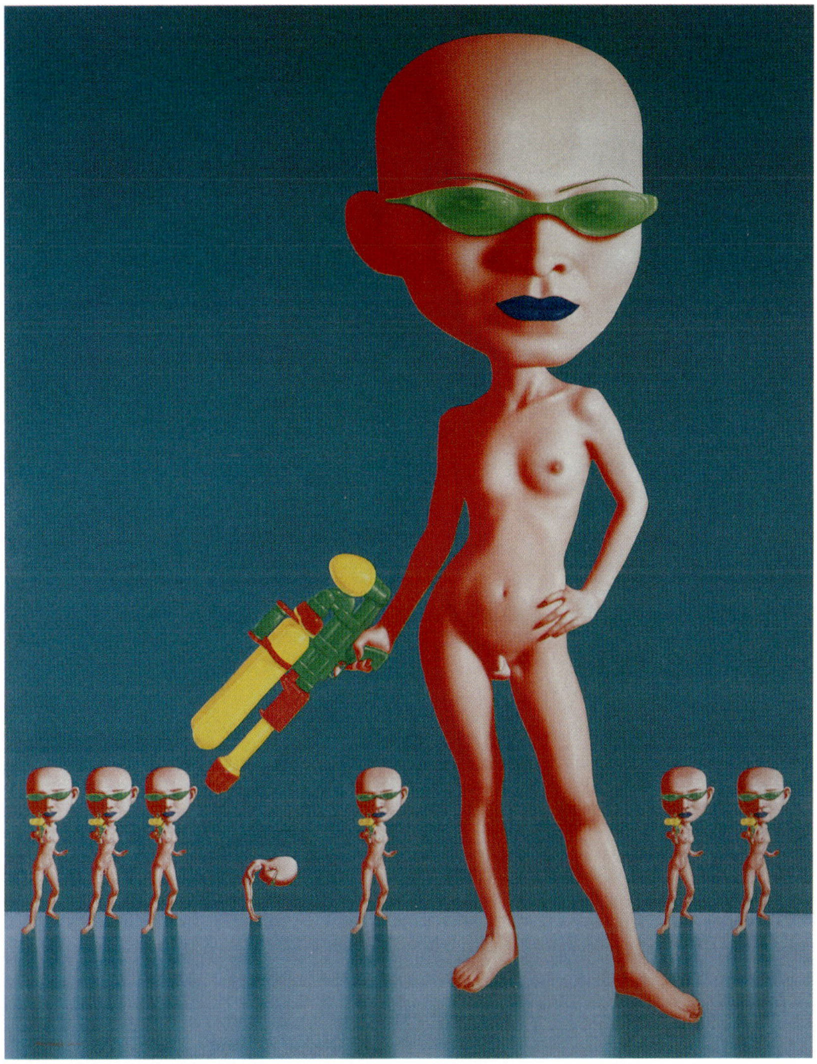

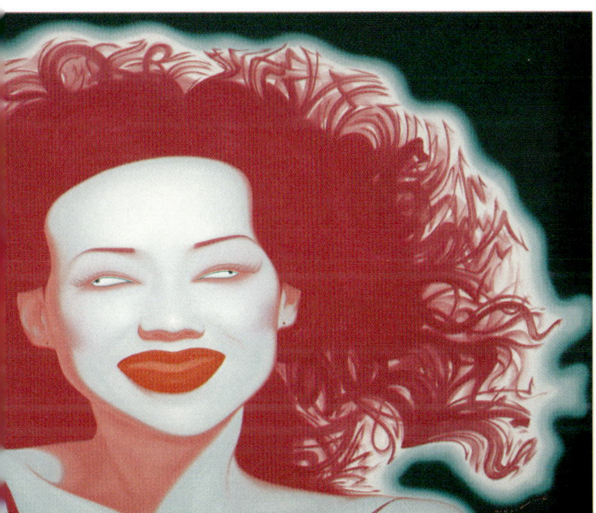

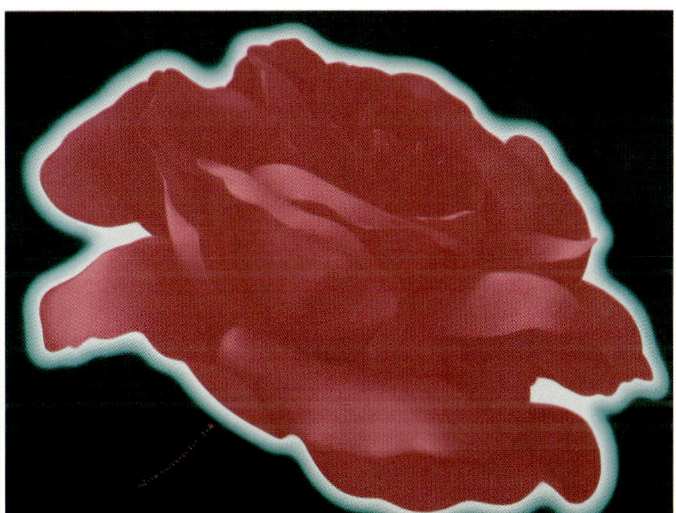

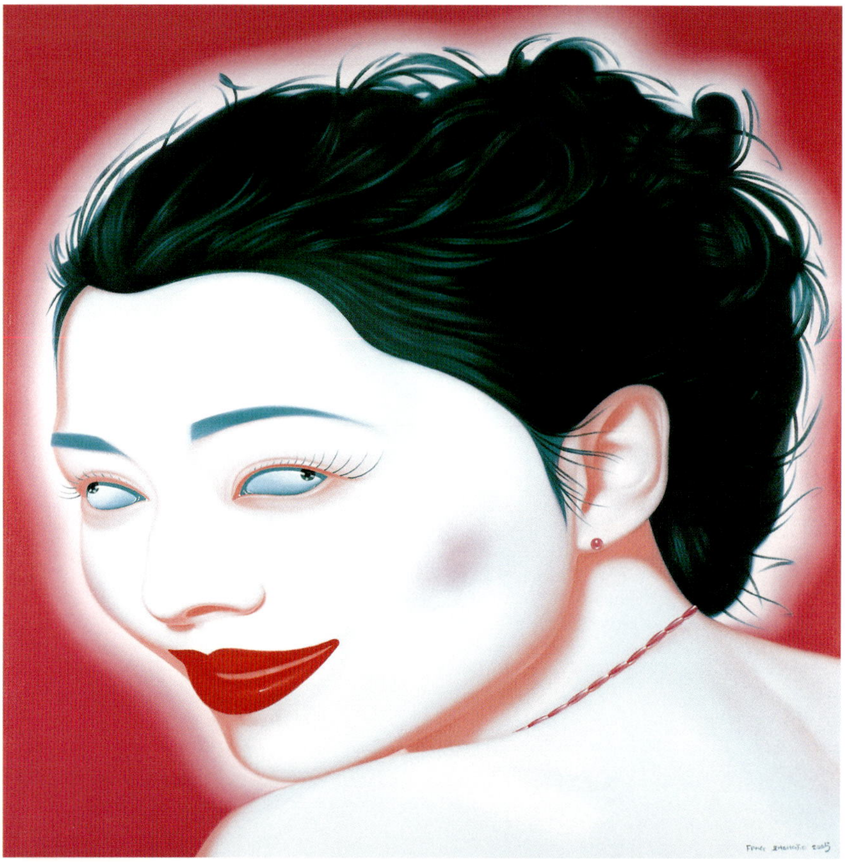

THIS PAGE, TOP: *China 2005 No. 19*, 2005. Oil on canvas, 82½ x 82½ in.

THIS PAGE, BOTTOM: *Chinese Portrait L Series 2007 No. 3*, 2007. 82½ x 118 in.

FACING PAGE: *Romantic Trip No. 21*, 1997. Oil on canvas, 59 x 75 in.

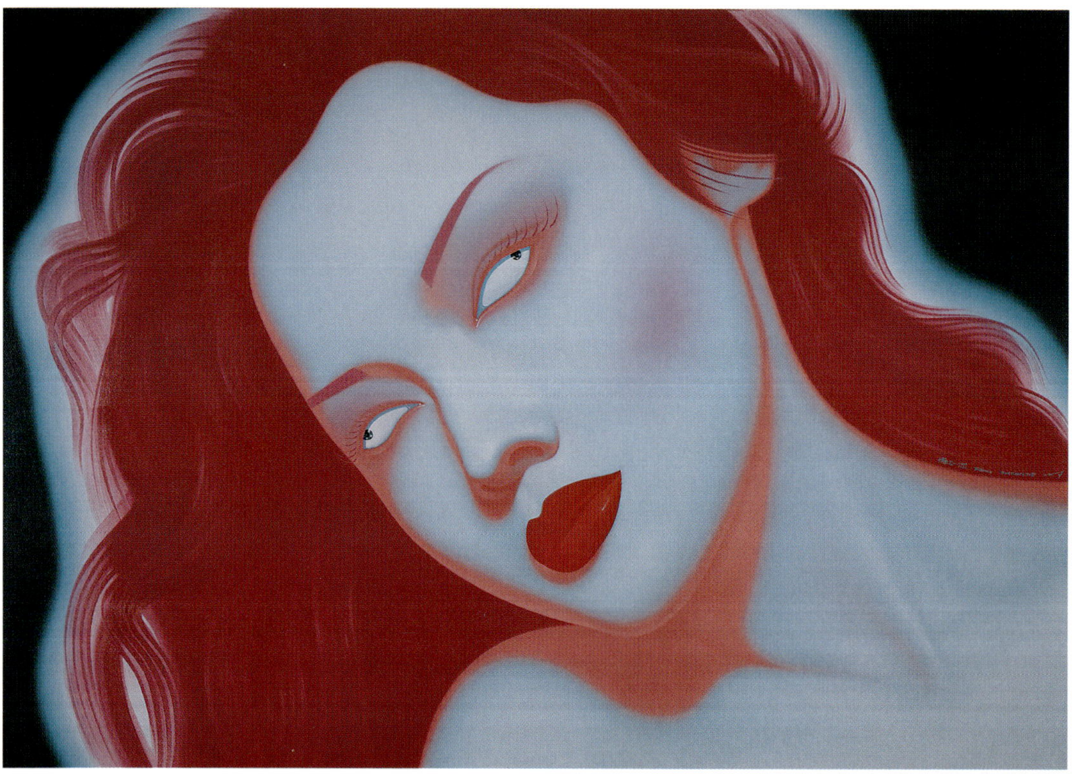

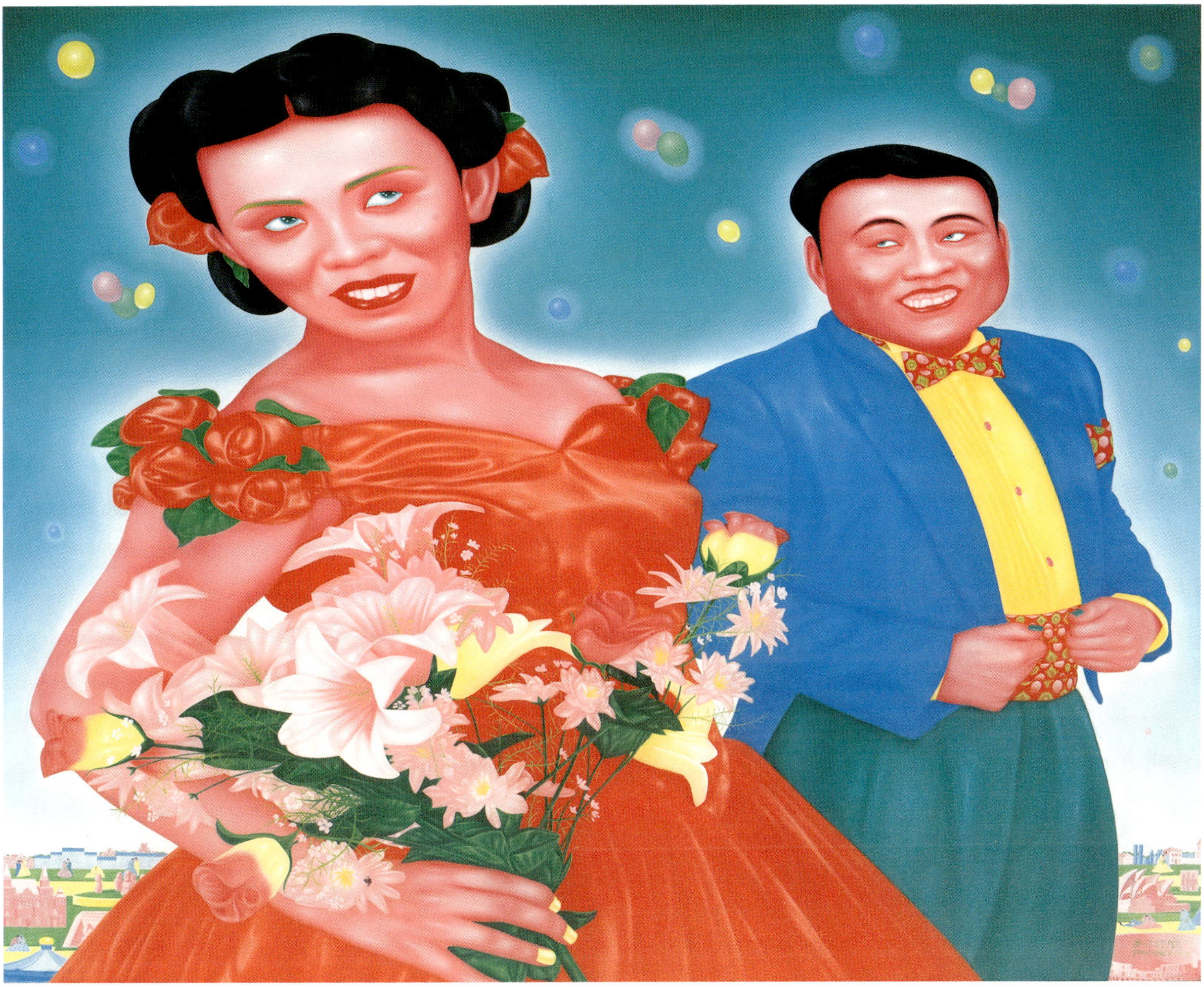

Gu Dexin

Born 1962, Beijing

THIS PAGE: *13.01.2007*, 2007. Installation, Galleria Continua, San Gimignano, Italy. Bananas, steel, marble.

FACING PAGE: *26.08.1996 Meat*, 1996. Photographic record of artist action, dimensions variable.

Gu Dexin comes across as a rather reserved, reticent figure. In fact, his artworks all take the name of their exhibition date so as to let the work speak for itself and allow the viewer's interpretation to be unaffected by any comment from the artist.

Gu's work is an attempt to shake reality and subvert morality, and sometimes embodies a certain level of brutality. His major works are site-specific installations: using plastic and natural materials, such as raw meat, apples, bananas, and even pig brain, he combines the artificial with the organic. Beautiful and hideous, imposing and unpredictable—because of the perishable nature of the materials he chooses, his installations change continuously. The viewer, attracted by their sensorial appeal—often not very pleasant, as some of them carry the odor of putrefaction—is thus faced with an experiment of transformation and alteration; a general allegory for decay that also addresses the physical and psychological aspects of life. His original and bizarre creations deal with people, sex, and violence, and the relationships between human beings and what surrounds them. *29.10.2000* (2000) is a peculiar work: a red chair filled with meat, a red carpet, and a mirror covered in red, positioned as if to symbolize a cycle—the cycle of events in human life. His series of cartoons, *F37* (2003–2006), depicts humans as ridiculous, foolish tools in the hands of a powerful intelligence, and portrays the absurdity of collective taboos, particularly those related to sex.

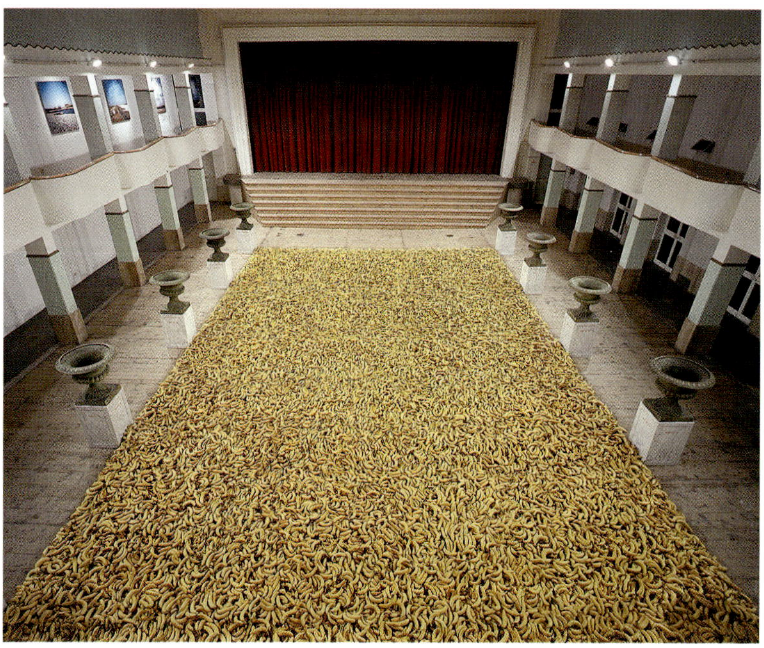

On the occasion of a group exhibition in Spain, Gu's project *13.07.2007* (2007) was based on the idea of connecting the museum building with its surroundings. On the opening day of the exhibition, a transparent tube rising up from a pedestal ran up to the top of the building, where it collected anything that passed in the air. The installation was nothing more than what the tube had captured. *30.03.2007 Lighthouse Funnel* (2007) is a site-specific installation created for the exhibition The Real Thing at the Tate Gallery, Liverpool, in the UK. With a team of workers from a steel factory in Tianjin, Gu recreated the funnel of the last working mobile lighthouse in Liverpool, completely identical to the original in details and size.

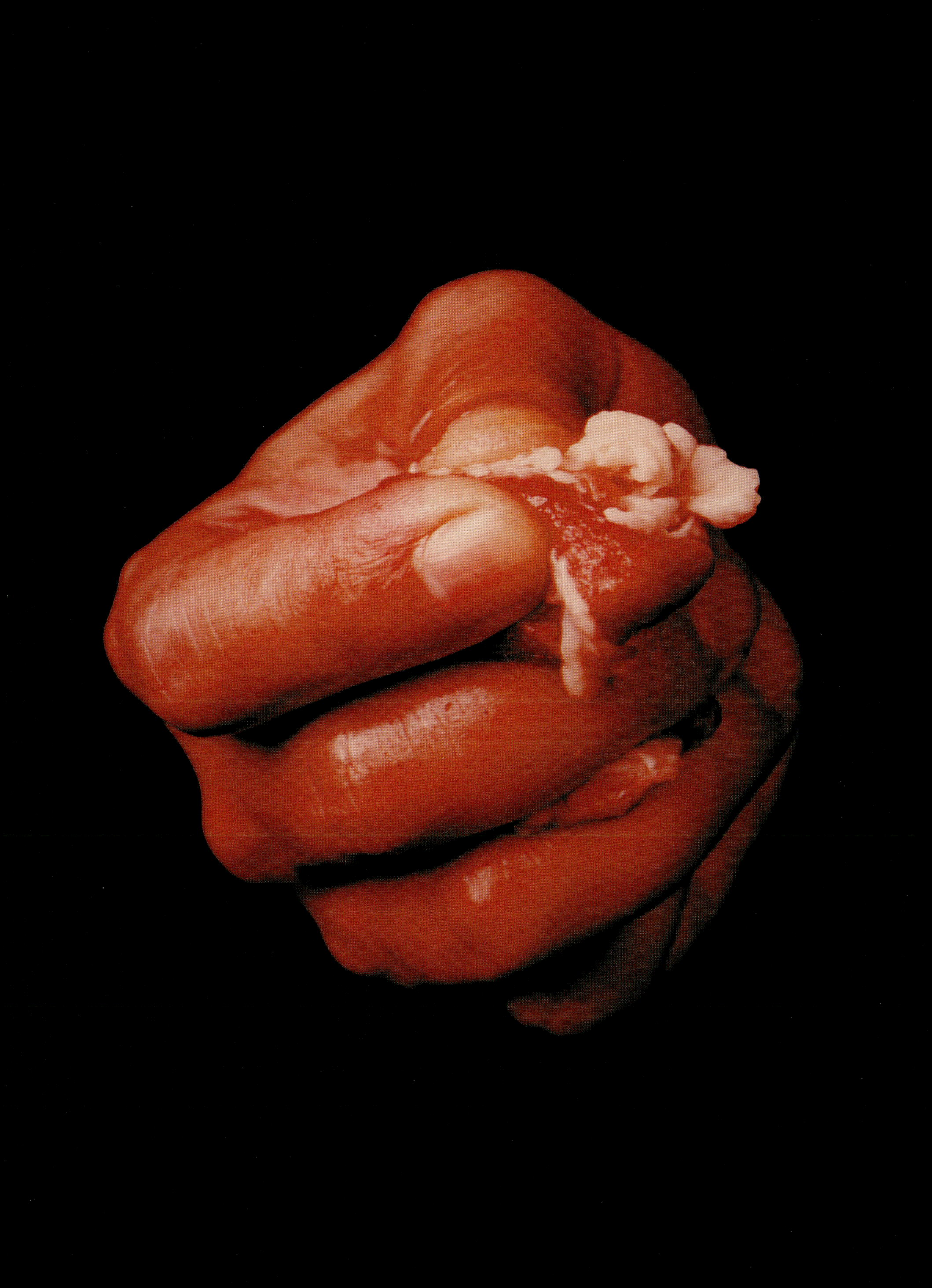

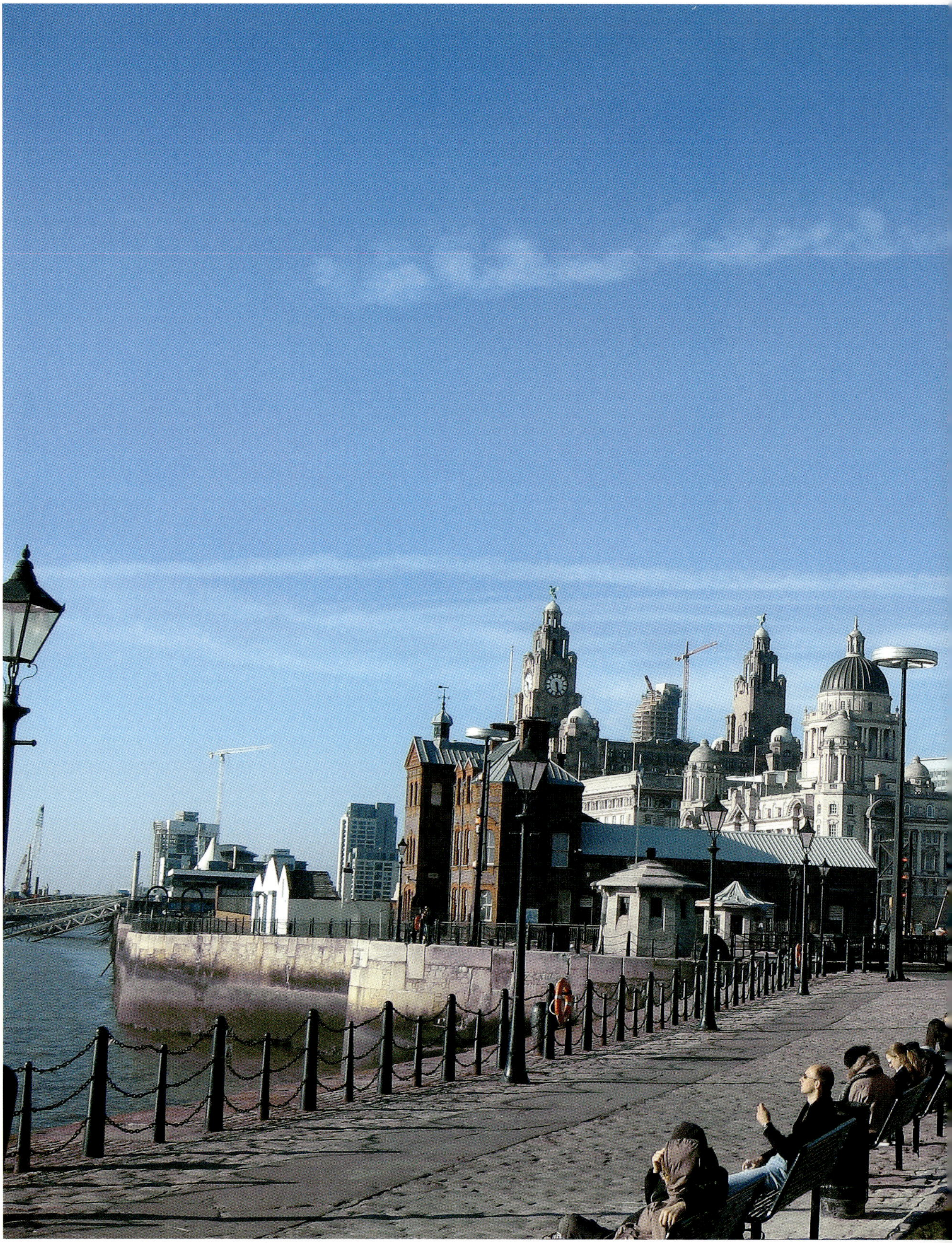

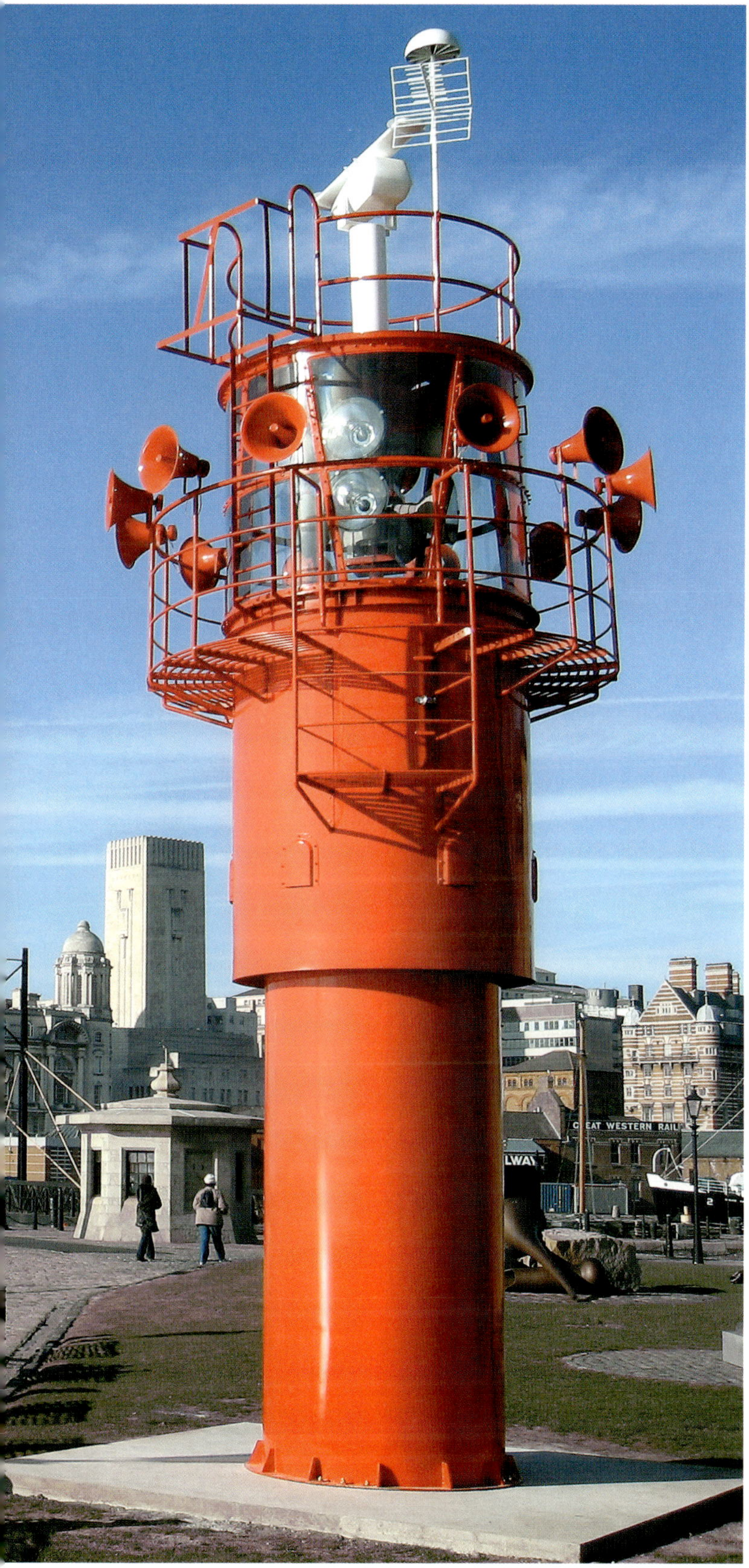

30.03.2007 Lighthouse Funnel, 2007. Installation, Tate Gallery, Liverpool, UK. Grand funnel in steel painted red, sounds from 12 loudspeakers.

He Sen

Born 1968, Kaiyuan, Yunnan Province

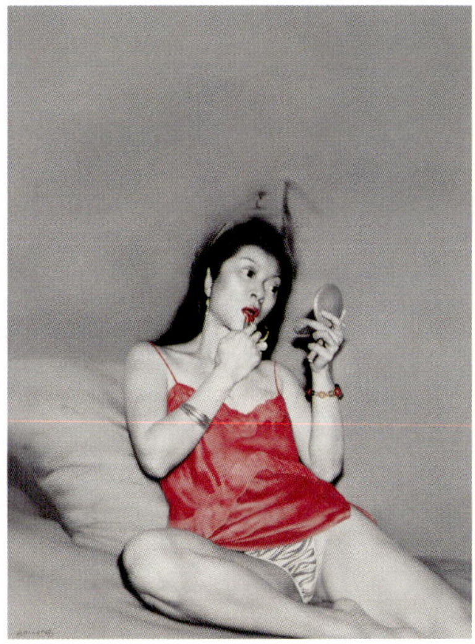

Entering He Sen's studio infuses one with a deep sense of tranquility as if time were somehow suspended there. Music pervades the air; the sound encircles the stunning canvases at the center of the space and traces paths across walls and windows: "Music is more enriching and energetic than paintings," the artist himself admits.

In 1989, after graduating from Sichuan Fine Arts Institute, he started painting still lifes. Rough and repetitive brushstrokes and towering compositions of everyday objects expressed the chaos of his personal life at a stage where everything around him was undergoing change. He concentrated his attention on the social reality of China's modern youth, featuring people, often friends, with cigarettes, trainers, and ghetto blasters. Since then, He has abandoned heavy and complex strokes in favor of smoother surfaces. Stereotyped, glamorous women caught in their daily routines inhabit his canvases. Superficial, artificial, and hollow spirited, some of these women have no eyes. "The women in my paintings have no eyes because I believe that there is a large distance between people, causing them not to see things clearly. They are confused, detached, and turn a blind eye to reality," He explains. His paintings depict the excesses resulting from hyperspeed modernization. Reality appears artificial and skin-deep, just as his women appear beautiful outside but completely lacking in any inner life. In later works, *The Gazing of Luo Yi* (2004) and *Dudu and Makeup* (2005), his sexy and alluring women are depicted with eyes, but the feeling of emptiness remains. His 2006 series of works such as *Ma Yuan—Imaginary Waves Fluctuate* echo the traditional landscape paintings of masters like Ma Yuan, Li Shan, and Xu Wei, but He's deliberately careless canvases become a depiction of a contemporary Chinese society that is superficial and emptied of meaning.

THIS PAGE, TOP: *Dudu and Makeup*, 2005. Oil on canvas, 79 x 59 in.

THIS PAGE, BOTTOM: *Girl with a Toy*, 2000. Oil on canvas, 59 x 75 in.

FACING PAGE: *The Gazing of Luo Yi*, 2004. Oil on canvas, 79 x 59 in.

OVERLEAF: *Ma Yuan—Imaginary Waves Fluctuate*, 2006. Oil on canvas, 118 x 197 in.

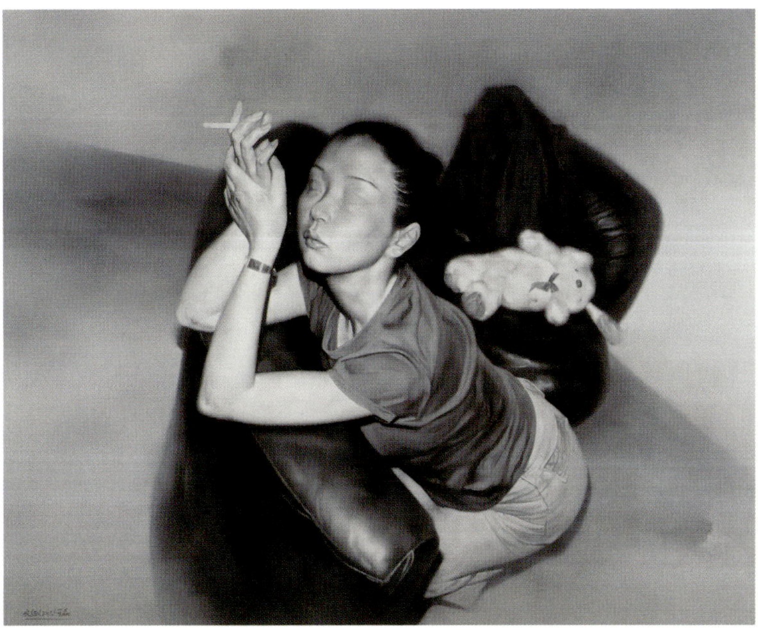

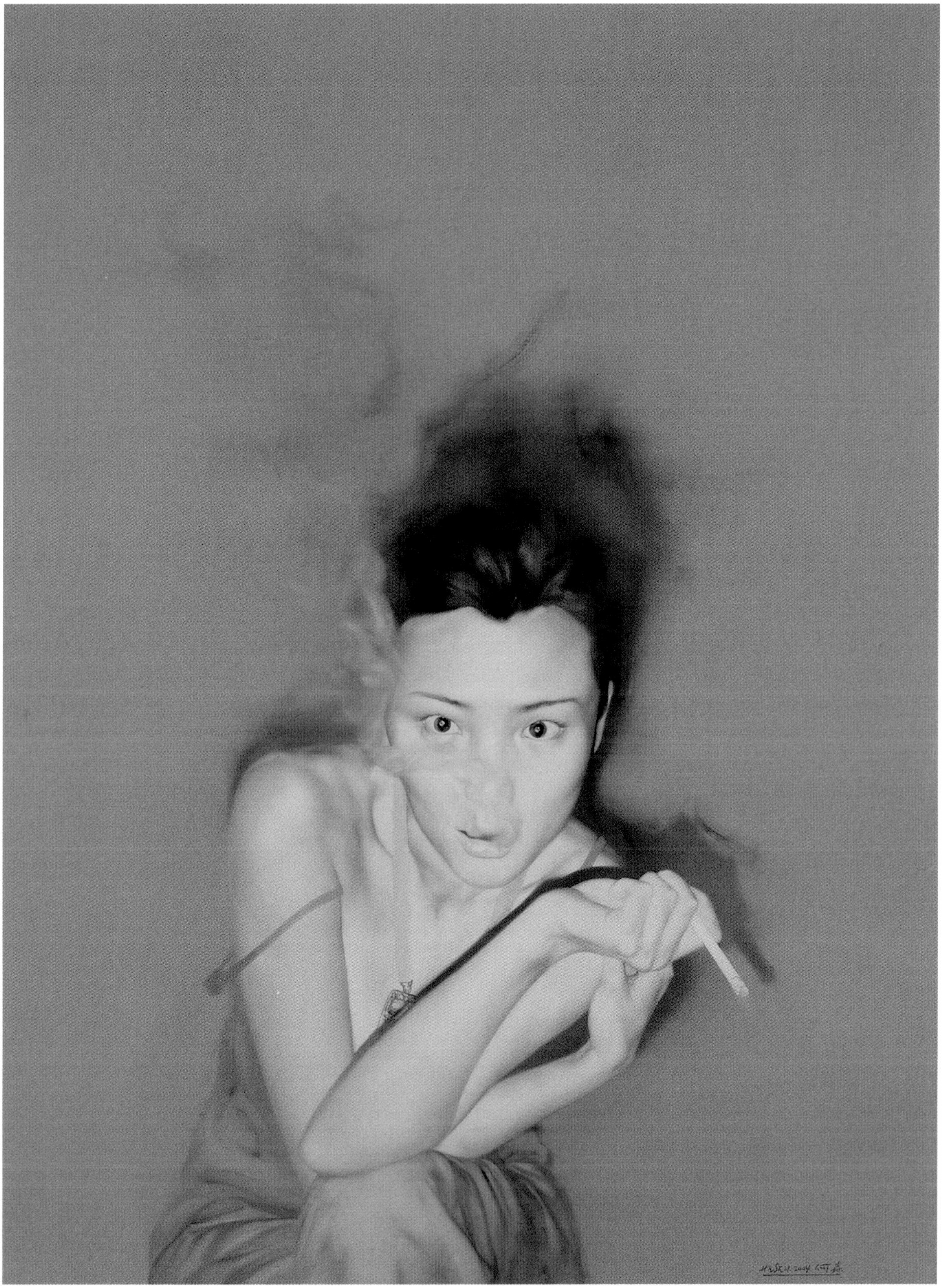

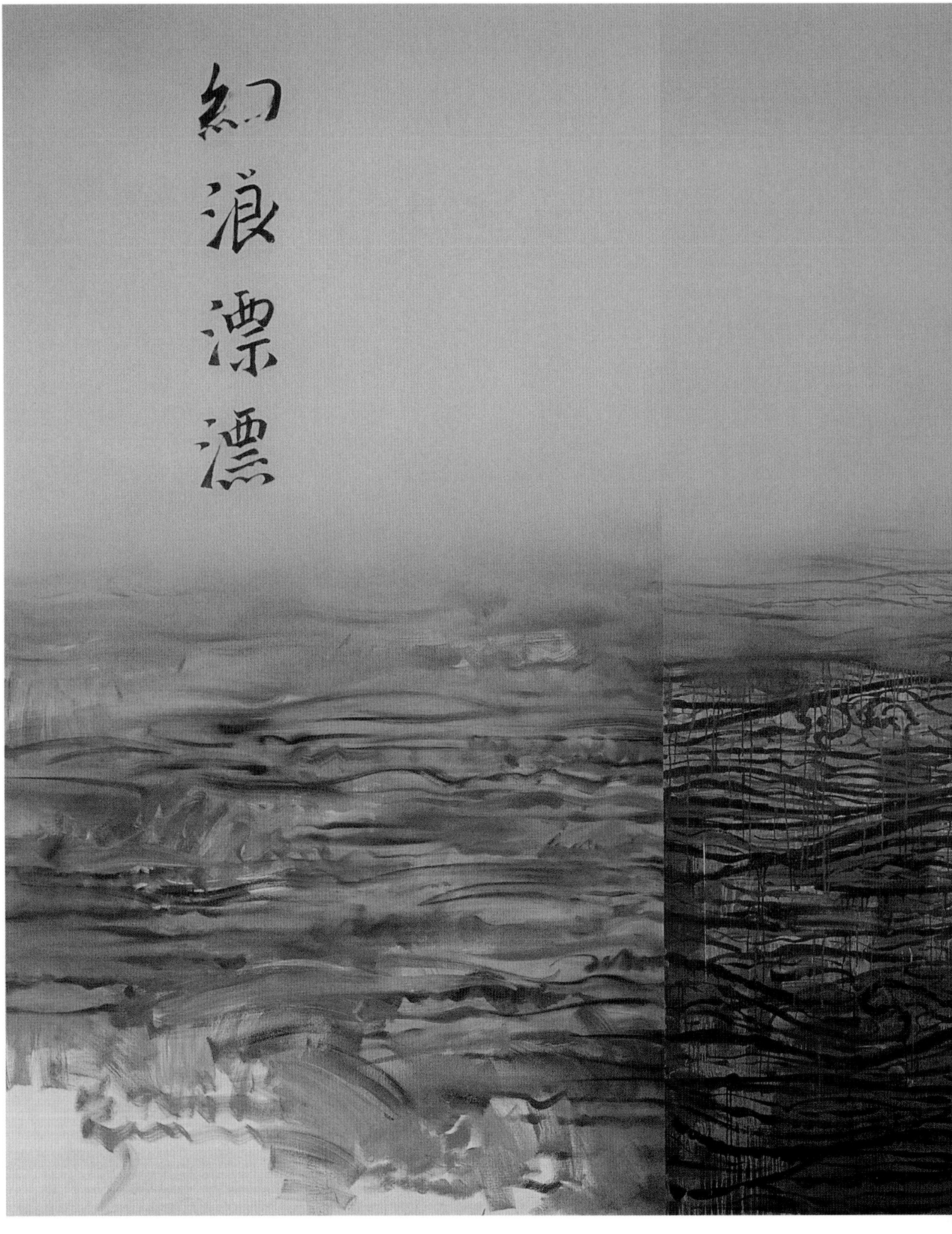
幻浪漂漂

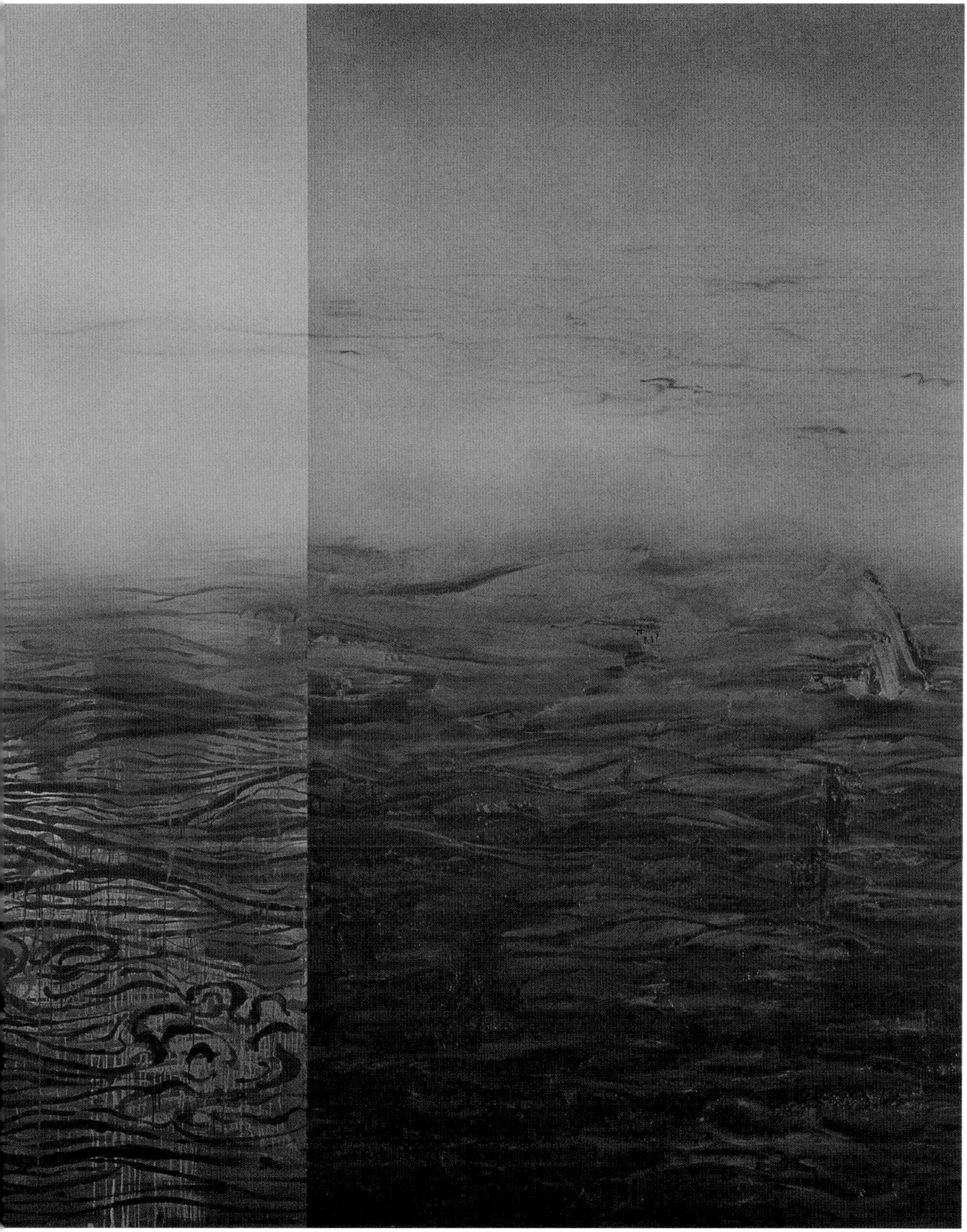

He Yunchang

Born 1967, Kunming, Yunnan Province

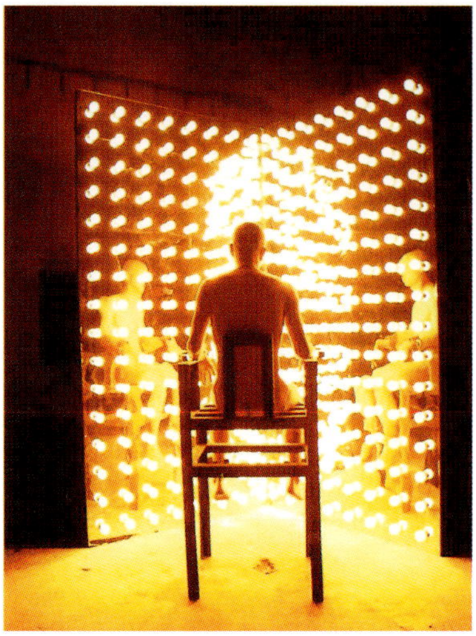

THIS PAGE, TOP: *A Test of Sight*, 2003. Performance.

THIS PAGE, BOTTOM: *Dragon Fish*, 2006. Performance at Newcastle Central Square Building, Great Britain.

FACING PAGE, TOP: *Touring around Great Britain with a Rock*, 2006–2007. Performance. Starting from Rock in Northumberland, He Yunchang walked to the nearby coast at Boulmer, where he selected a rock and carried it around Great Britain, a journey of 3,500 miles over 101 days.

FACING PAGE, BOTTOM: *Casting*, 2004. He Yunchang was cast into a cement block and stayed inside for 24 hours with a mobile phone. Performance at BTAP, Tokyo Gallery, Beijing.

He Yunchang is a performance artist who places incomparable physical demands upon himself: wrestling with one hundred people for sixty-six minutes incessantly in his performance piece *Wrestling: One and One Hundred* (2001), or circumnavigating Great Britain on foot carrying a rock he would return to the place he took it from, in *Touring around Great Britain with a Rock* (2006–2007).

"What will be the result of my artworks?" he says, "I don't know! Look at my hand, after I've cast it in cement for twenty four hours I can't use it properly anymore. I use my body to express what I think, and I believe this is a very intimate and profound way of doing it. Performance art is changing these days; it's becoming a way of acting, and artworks are just products to be sold. From my point of view, performance art is not acting; it's a way of being. Works of art are not products; I do not trust products! A product doesn't last forever, it is consumed. A good artwork will remain!"

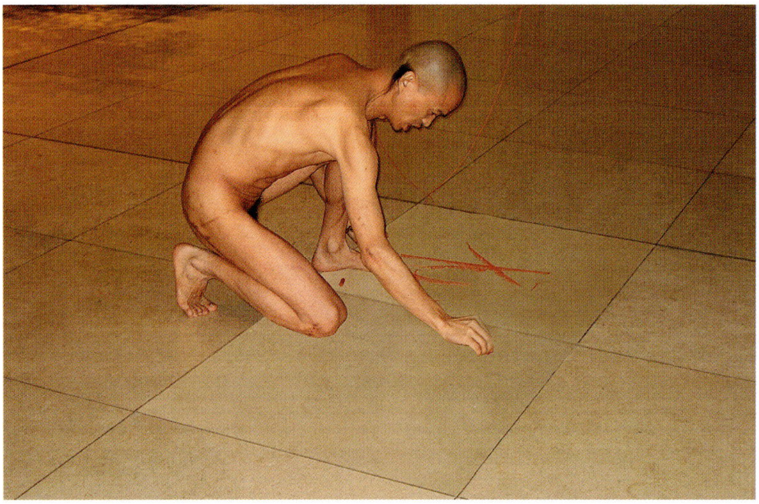

Carrying members of the audience on his back, shoulders, or in his arms in *Catching a Dragon In Mid-Air* (2002), staring at ten thousand watts of light for an hour "to make my eyesight worse," in *A Test of Sight* (2003), or, in *Dragon Fish* (2006), running continuously in a circle around the word "Dragon Fish" written on the floor, for twenty-four hours, with his naked body tied to a cord attached at one end to a piercing around his collarbone and at the other to the roof of the atrium in which the performance took place, He combines the challenge of performance with the desire to spread a message. *Dragon Fish*, for example, draws our attention to the physical and mental violence suffered by North Koreans when caught trying to escape over the border to China. "Art is a way of changing society, to better understand people's lives and relationships. Through my works I say something really deep and personal. My works are a 'moment' I cannot repeat. While I'm performing I often feel I won't be able to complete my work—I am scared. After I've finished, I am happy. I am a simple person," he smiles.

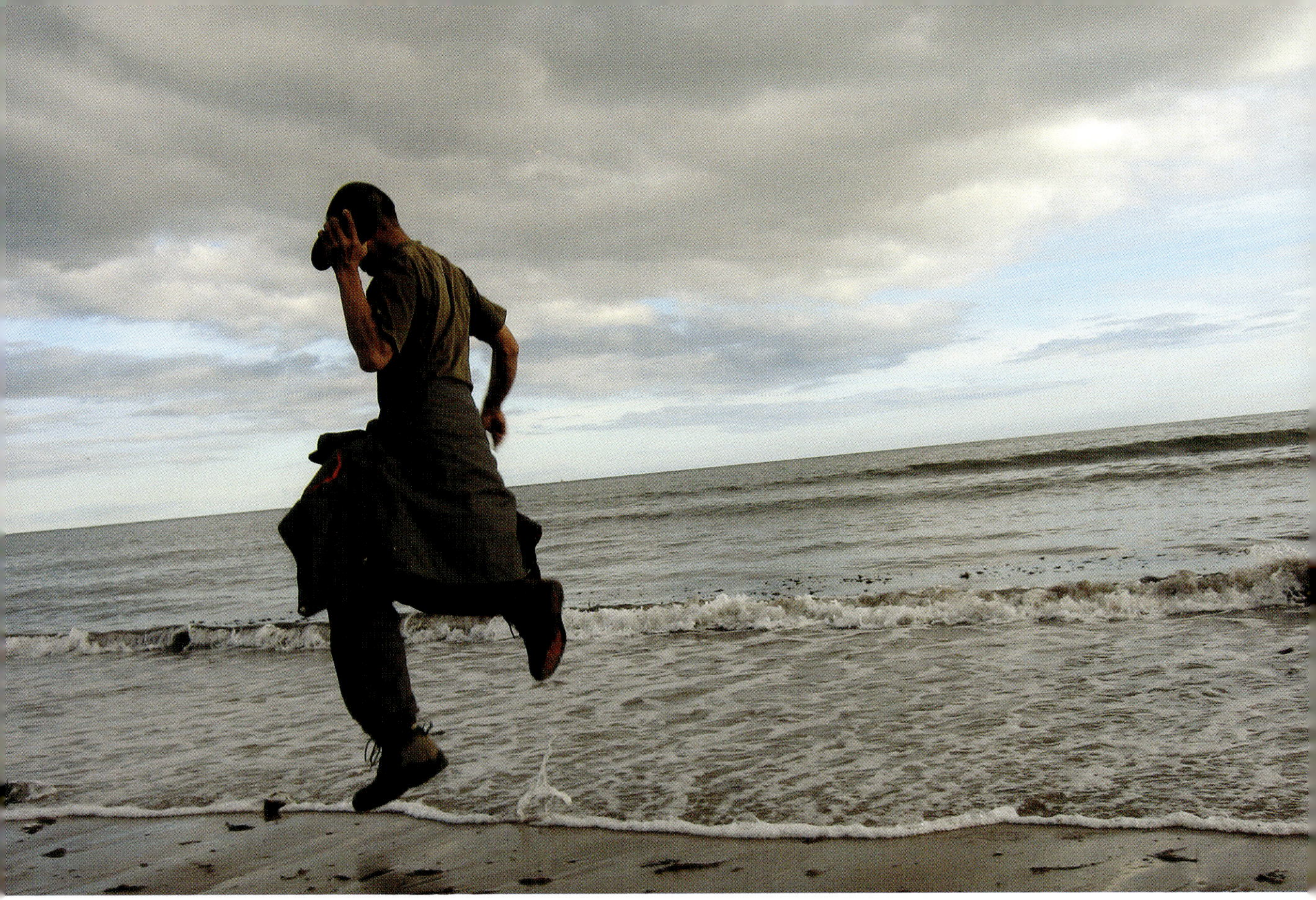

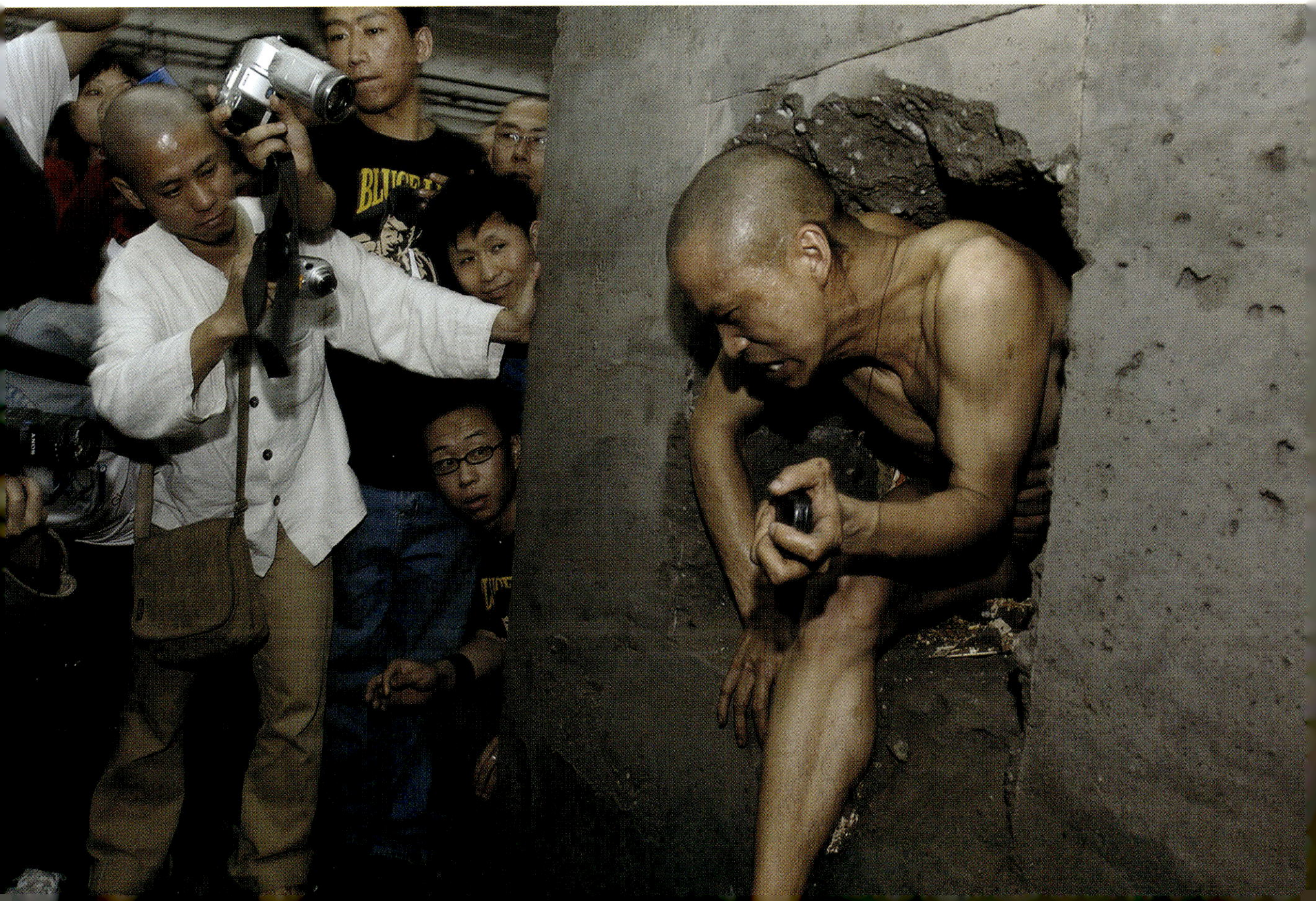

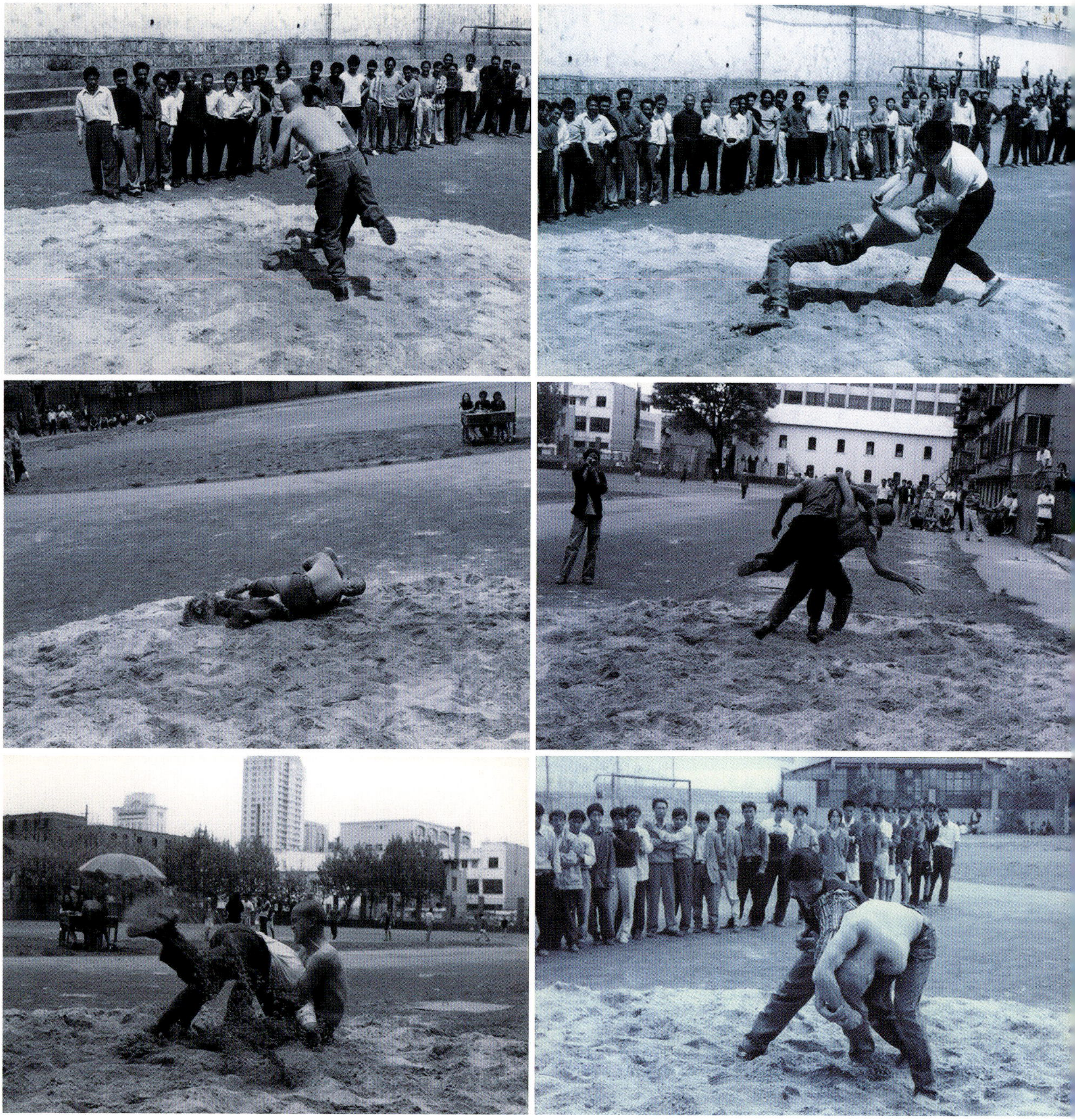

Wrestling: One and One Hundred, 24 March, 2001. Performance at Kunming, Yunnan Province, China. He Yunchang wrestled with one hundred people, one after the other, for 66 minutes. He won 18 of the matches.

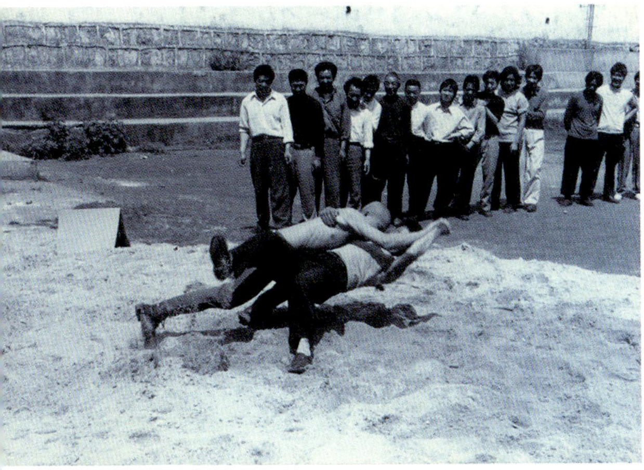
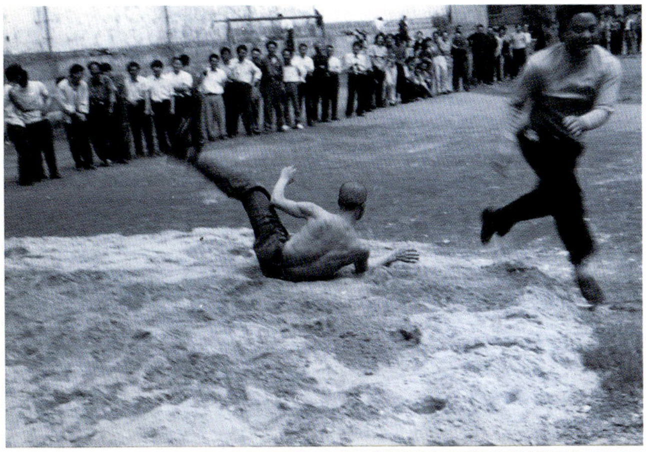
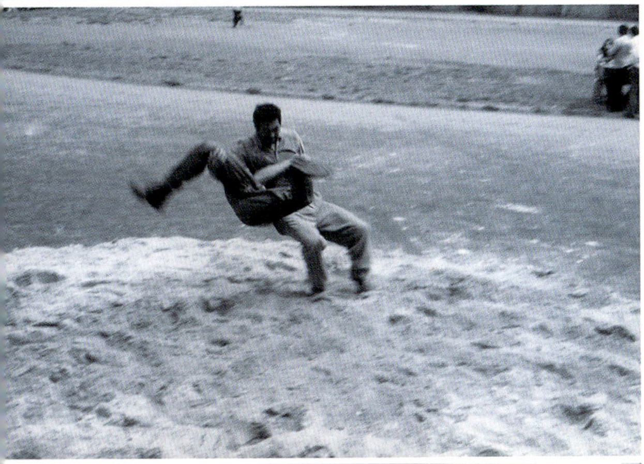
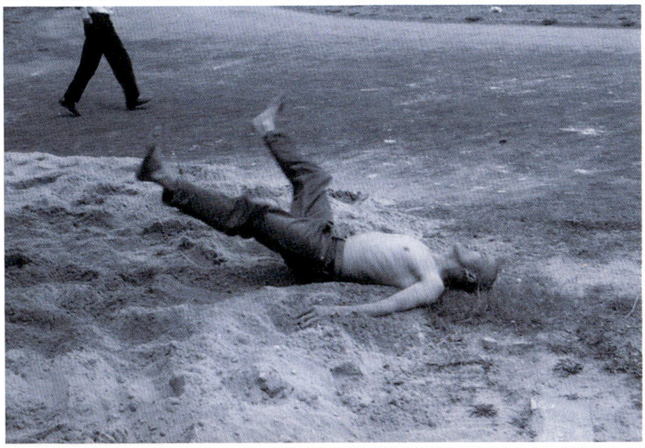
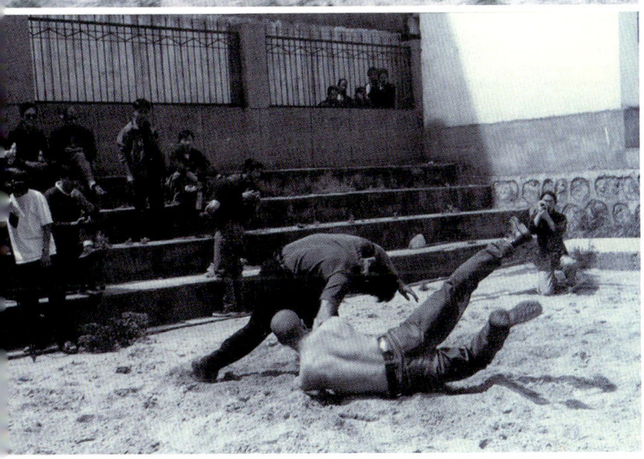
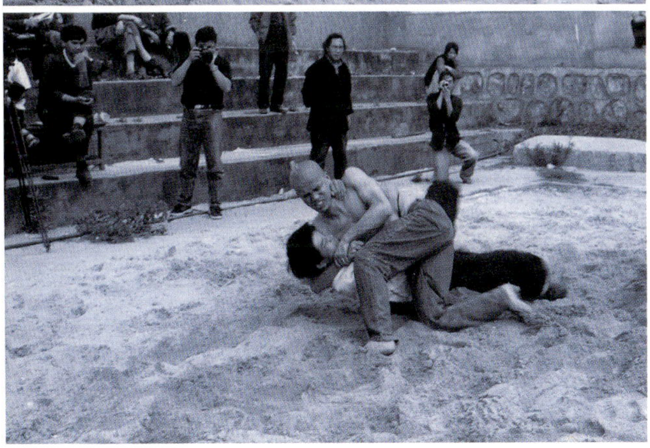

Jiang Zhi

Born 1971, Yuanjiang, Hunan Province.

One of China's most important video artists, winner of the Chinese Contemporary Art Award from the Chinese Contemporary Art Association in 2001, Jiang Zhi reflects on various aspects of modern China's turbulent society, from the estrangement of individual existence to the hectic pace of our social lives.

In an early video, *Fly, Fly* (1997), he films a hand mimicking the flapping wings of a bird in a cramped city apartment. Confined in a small room, one feels subjugated to the self and to everything around; at the same time, one experiences tranquility, fantasies, boredom, and passion—all ways of transcending reality and escaping, just like flying. "Can we shake off heaviness for lightness?" asks the artist. "In which direction we shall choose to fly?" In Jiang's work, reality often mingles with dreams. In *Things Would Turn Simpler Once They Happened* (2006), people whose lives seem to be directed by external forces are waiting to be rescued from the humdrum repetition of the everyday. "In this age of changes, people expect something to happen, something that throws light on them like a spotlight. Everything then will become simpler," Jiang says.

Things Would Turn Nails Once They Happened (2007) shows the stunning image of an old house surrounded by new development, a symbol of the atrocious consequences of destruction and reconstruction. *Dingzi hu* in Chinese means "nail house," and is popular parlance for those households determined to resist displacement directives. This work captures a real house, whose owners are trying to resist the momentum of modernization. The video installation *Onward! Onward! Onward!* (2006) depicts Chinese leaders Mao Zedong, Deng Xiaoping, and Jiang Zemin, running, one after the other. Their action of endless moving depicts faith in progress, summed up in the popular slogan, "As long as we are running we are always advancing," while emphasizing that the concept of fate is deeply rooted in this society. The installation *I Am Your Poetry* (2006–2007) marks a new stage in the artist's development: comparing the works that make up this series to the verses of a poem, Jiang explores the theme of skin—a layer, a container in which our essence lies, which mutates with the passing of time. Skin represents something passing, changing, and fading away.

THIS PAGE: *I Am Your Poetry No. 4*, 2007. Installation. Silicon gel, red woolen thread, light, tree, grass, plaster, rocks, and sand.

FACING PAGE: *Onward! Onward! Onward!*, 2006. Video installation.

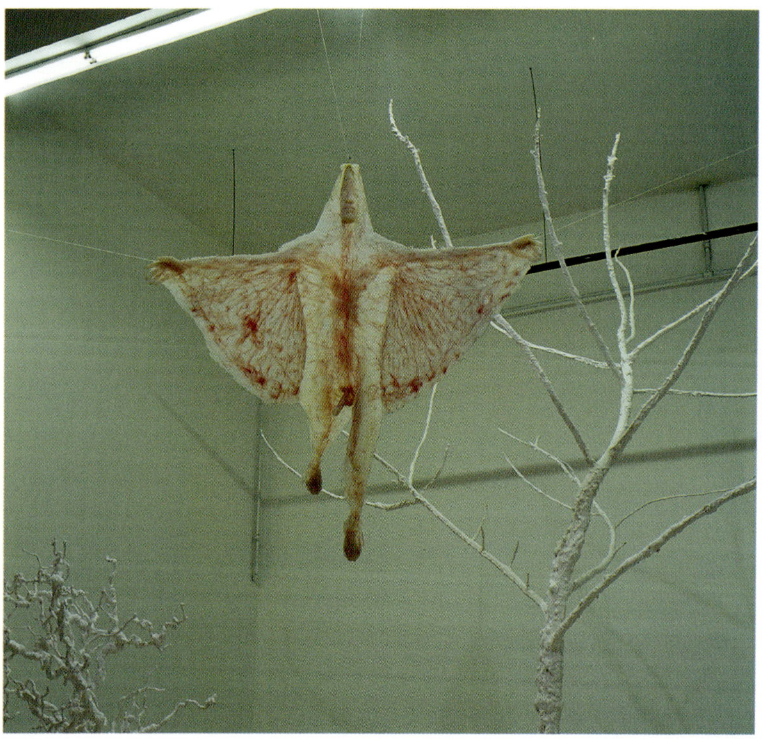

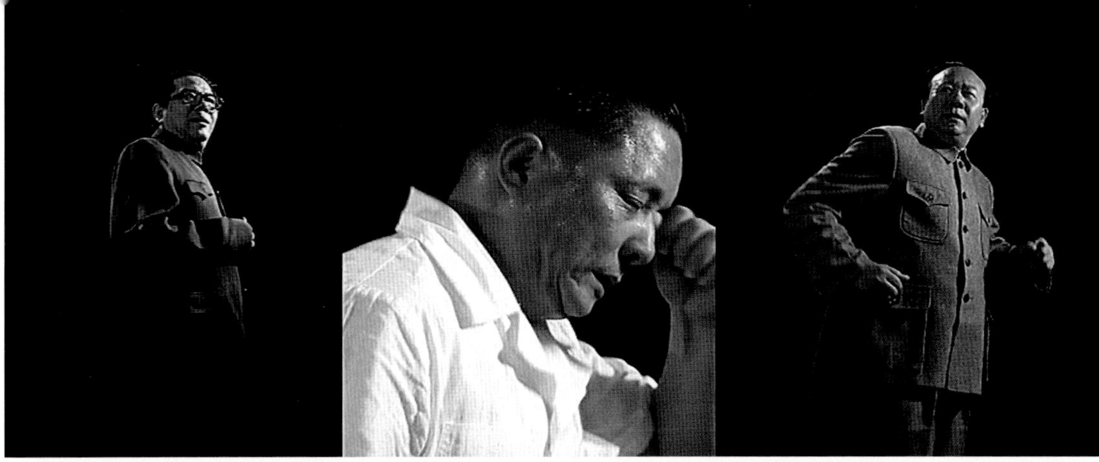
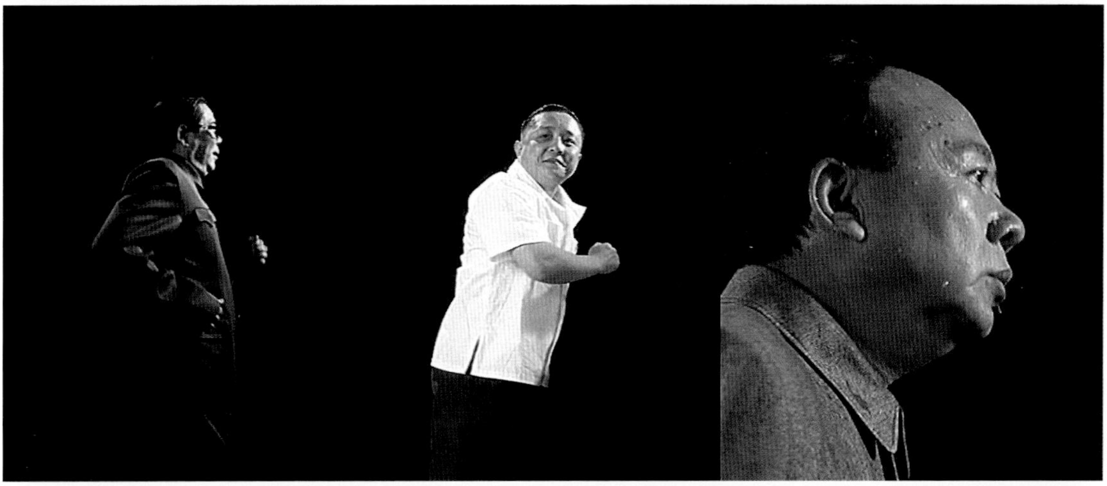
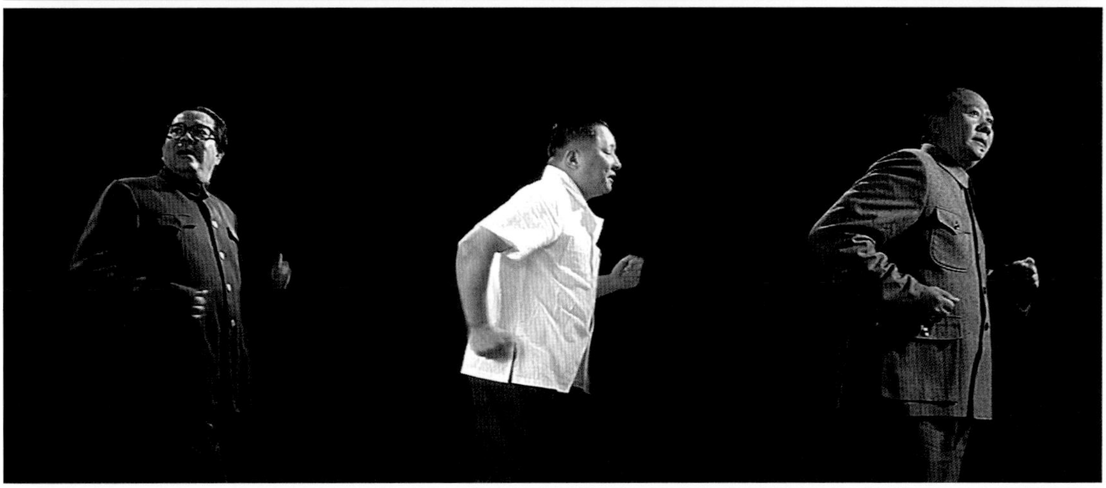
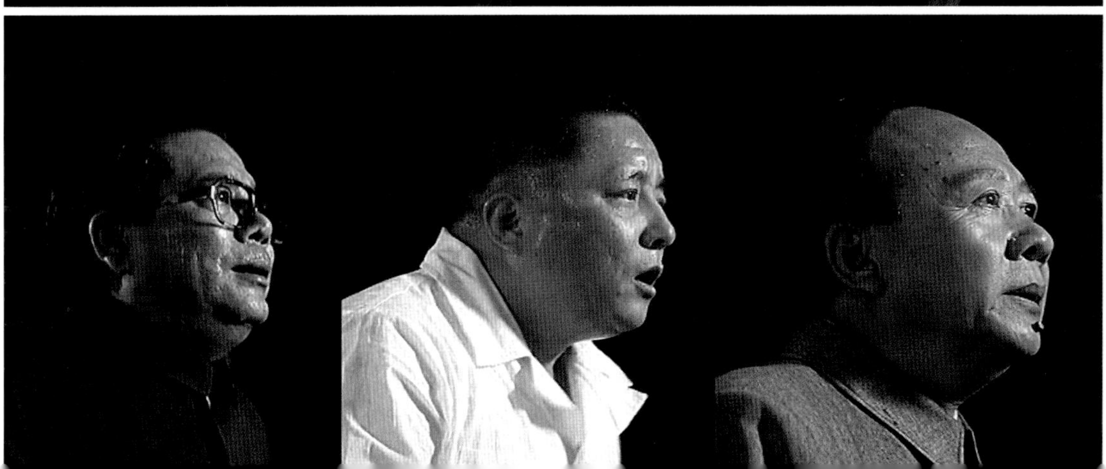

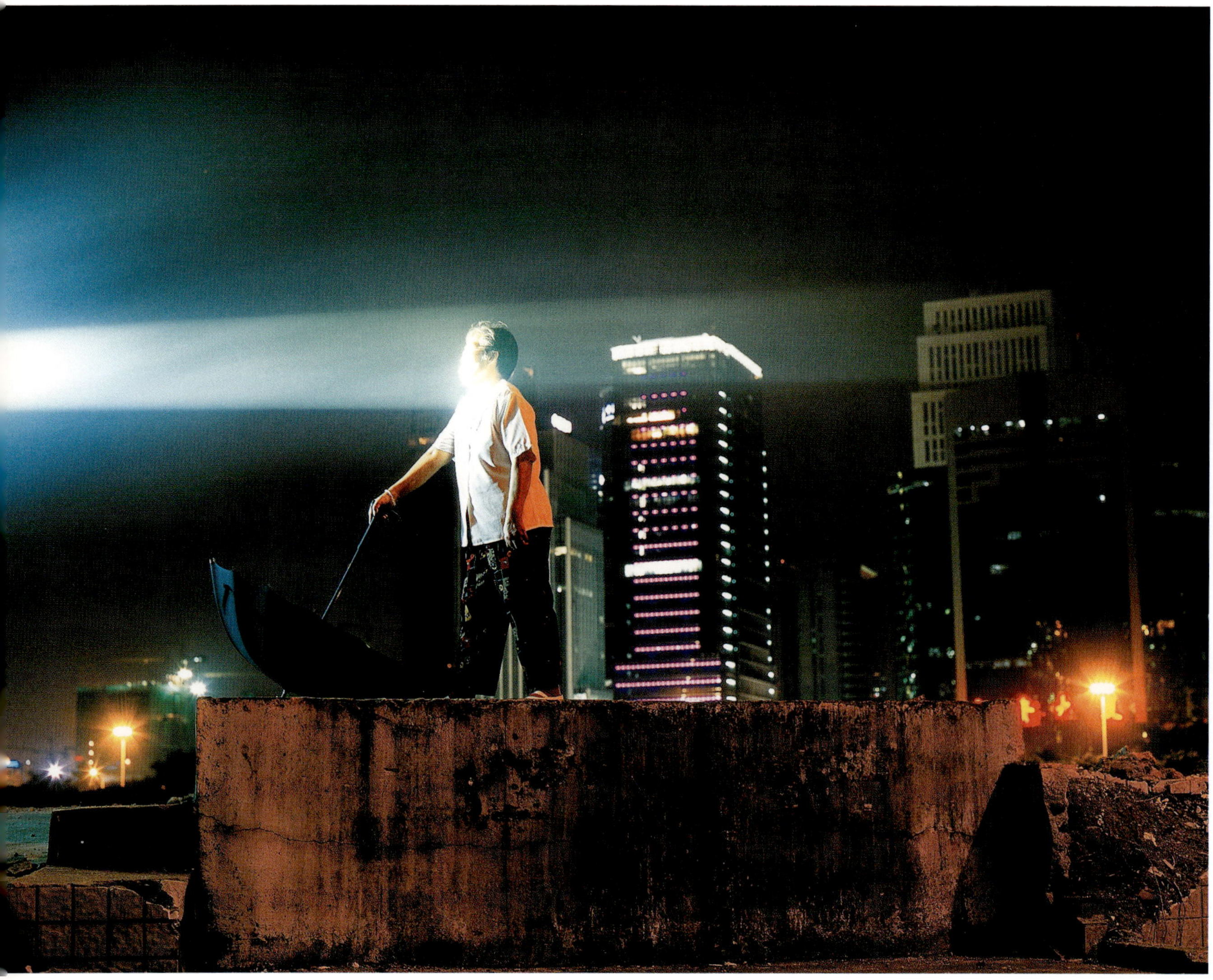

THIS PAGE: *Things Would Turn Simpler Once They Happened No. 1*, 2006. C-print, 59 x 78½ in.

FACING PAGE: *Things Would Turn Nails Once They Happened*, 2007. C-print, 59 x 78½ in.

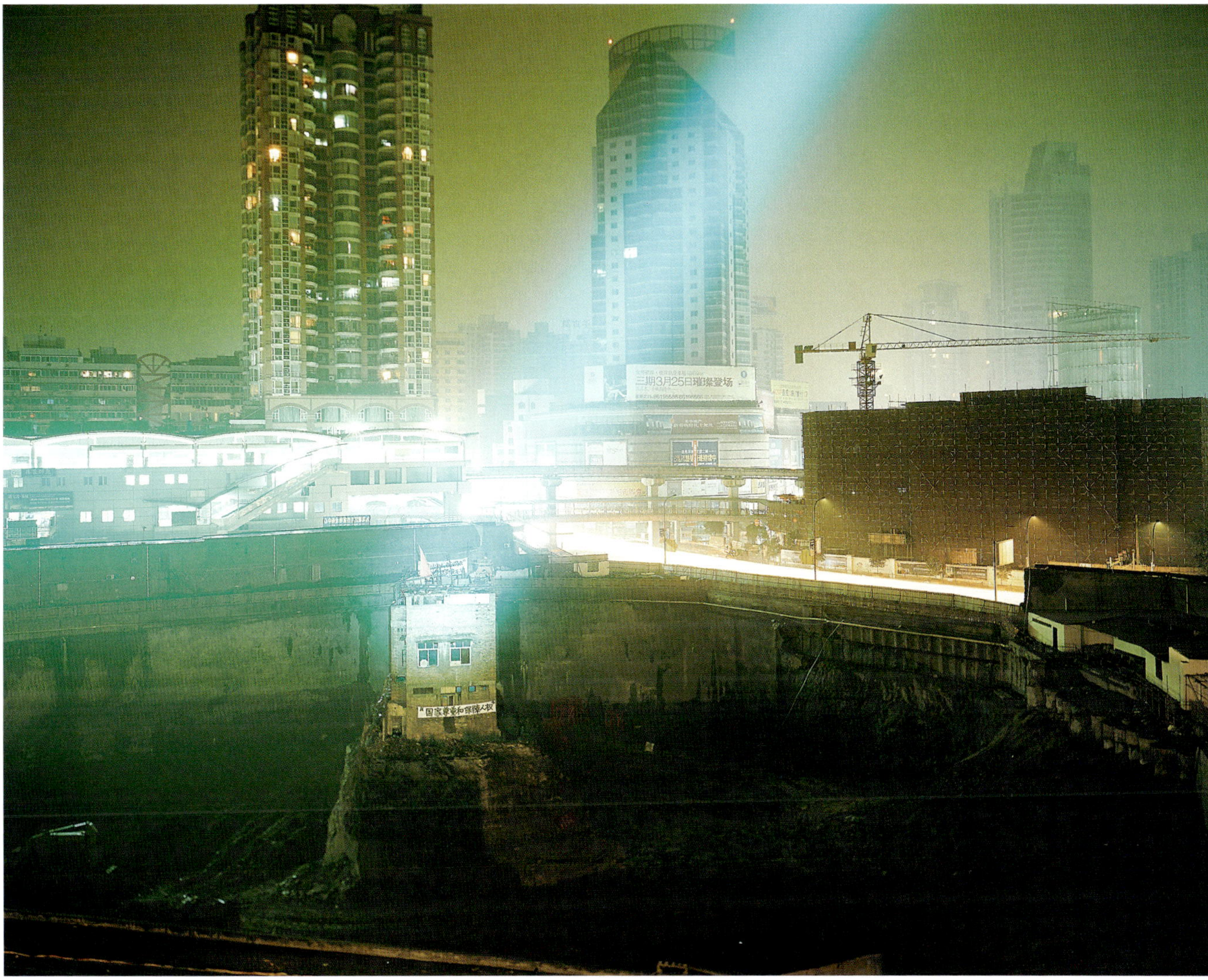
三期3月25日璀璨登场
“国家尊重和保障人权”

Kan Xuan

Born 1972, Xuancheng, Anhui Province

THIS PAGE: *OBJECT: Egg Is Grey*, 2006. Still from video, 37½ x 47 in.

FACING PAGE: *OBJECT: Sugar Is White*, 2006. Still from video, 34½ x 47 in.

Kan Xuan appeared on the Chinese art scene in 1999 with a series of short four- to five-minute films all based around a close-up shot with the camera held motionless. Although she trained as a painter, Kan had been making her living working for a multinational advertising and production company before becoming an artist. Her interest in installations led her to learn the tricks of video art and editing on her own.

In her early works it is possible to read a search for identity, a reference to her own status as an artist in China, and deep analyses of how reality is perceived in a country where the truth is often disconcertingly hidden. Along with other young female artists, Kan's first works can also be interpreted from the point of view of an artist questioning female identity in society. Her expression is delicate, yet intense, and her unique style is defined by fleeting images and highly spiritual language. In later works, Kan seems to be preoccupied with more personal experiences. In the video *Endless* (2000), she filmed herself completely naked, going up and down the staircases and corridors of a monastery in subzero temperatures. In this film, Kan expresses the emptiness of life and something of the status of artists in China, and goes further to physically experience this with her own body. In order to exorcize her own fears by facing them, she often puts herself in difficult positions; in the video work *Kan Xuan! Kan Xuan!* (1999), we see her fervently wandering through subway corridors as though in search of someone, but all the time calling out her own name, while in *Looking, Looking, Looking For . . .* (2001), she allows spiders to crawl over her body. Playing with the senses, Kan highlights with a deep irony, and often with dramatic scenery as a backdrop, the trivial elements, sensations, and feelings we experience every day, but that often we barely notice, as seen for example in her attentive treatment of an egg and sugar cubes in the video work *Object* (2006).

At the 2007 Venice Biennale, Kan presented her most significant videos, among which was *Or Everything* (2005). This extremely poetic piece, inspired by Zen spirituality and composed of a combination of ten different Buddha images, attempts to achieve a kind of enlightenment in the viewer by leading him or her into a mysterious world that goes from the most ordinary to oblivion.

"My videos are slow, quiet, beautiful, and somewhat sad," says Kan about her work. "When you feel happy, there is movement in your mind. Emotions are small intervals of time that have a beginning and an end."

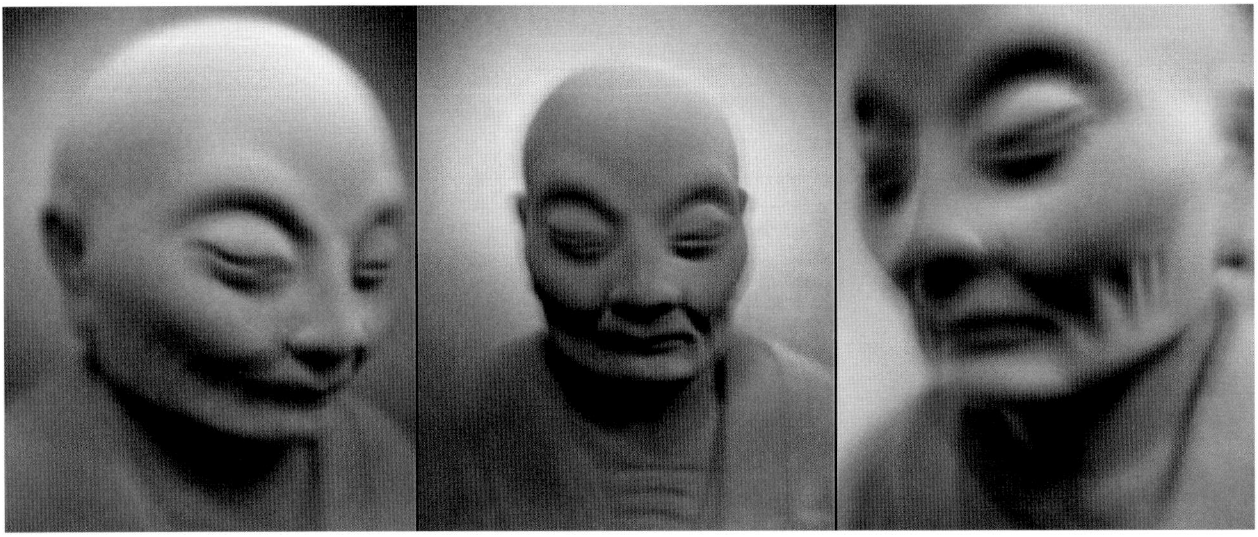

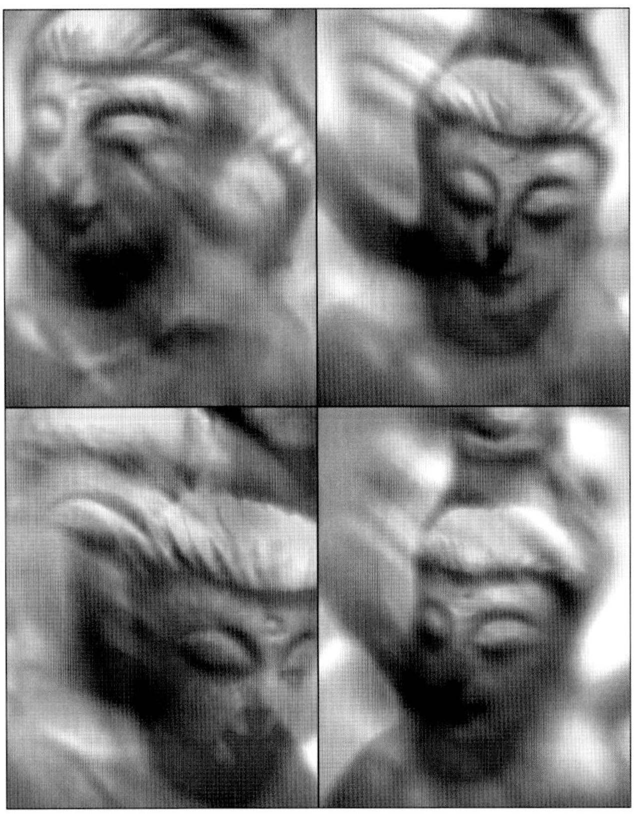

THIS PAGE, TOP: *A Monk*, 2005–2006. Video installation, loop.

THIS PAGE, BOTTOM, AND FACING PAGE: *Or Everything*, 2005. Video project with 10 combined Buddha images. Video installation, loop.

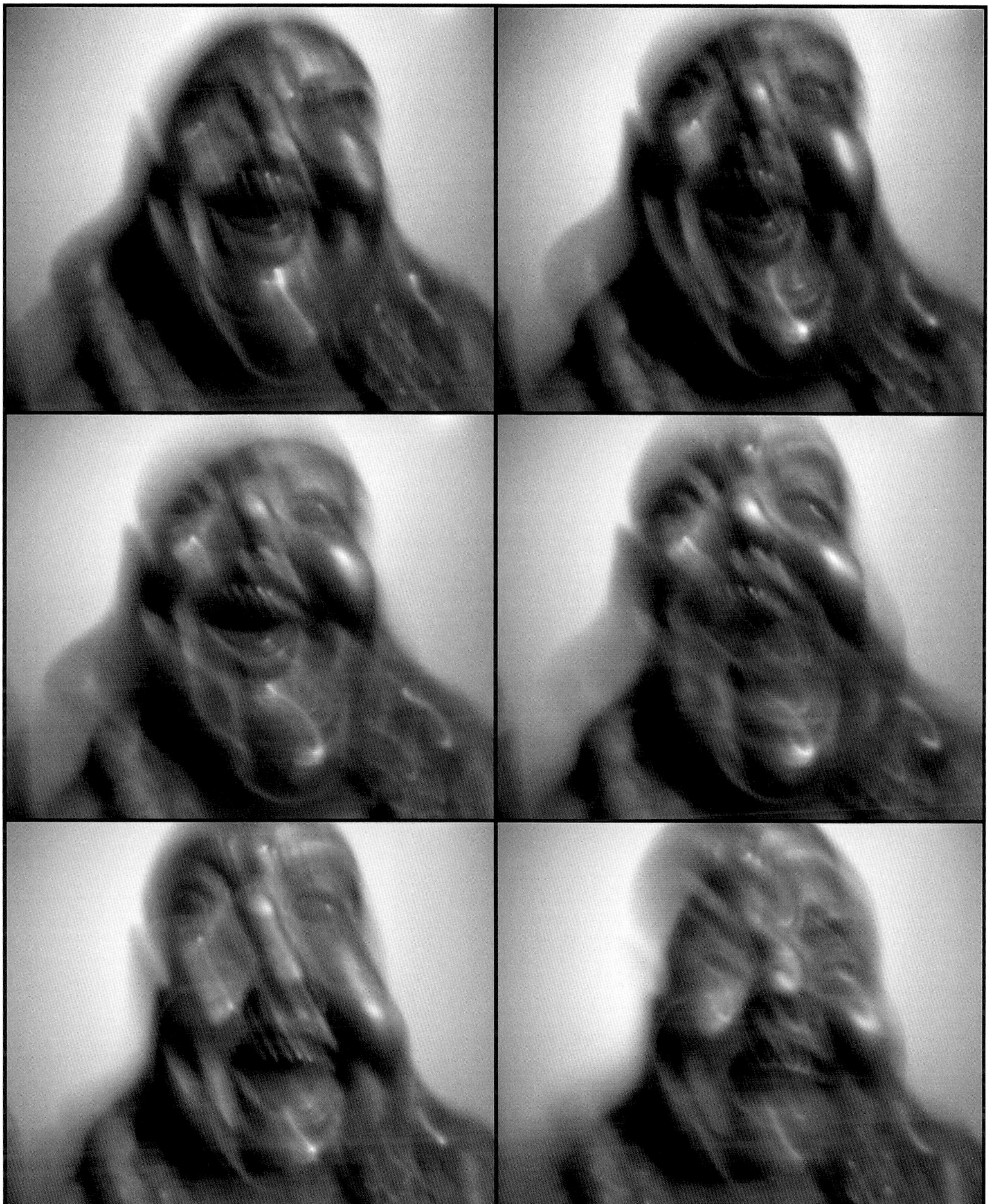

Liang Yue

Born 1979, Shanghai

A clarinet player as well as a visual artist, Liang Yue is a spokesperson for the younger generation in Shanghai. Experiencing a world in which people are constantly faced with chaos, which they either confront or embrace, she fuses opposite sentiments in an understated and elegant manner. Isolation, alienation, and impermanence are the themes running through her photography and videos. Her seemingly straightforward representations of everyday landscapes and situations stealthily draws us into a deeper awareness of the physical and social architecture of Shanghai.

Her photographs are characterized by a fascinating dichotomy between the public and private sphere, between feelings of familiarity and of strangeness. In the series *Several Dusks* (2002–2003), Liang chooses the light of dusk to record an impalpable moment between day and night. She creates a moment in suspension as if she wants to stress the paradoxical sense of isolation young people experience in contemporary society. Signaling "I love you" with a torch in the half-light in *Morse Code* (2003) or following the scent of an unknown Lily—maybe a girl, maybe just the random solitary soul of a flower—through a crowd in *Lily's Afternoon* (2002–), Liang draws the viewer along a dreamlike track interspersed with memories. Through the recording of movements, Liang attempts to portray her own and her subjects' states of mind and attitudes toward life, and the general sense of emptiness felt by young people in particular.

Characterized by dialogue-free narratives, Liang's videos have melancholic soundtracks, often clarinet melodies, eliciting from the audience an intimate and personal response to Shanghai's rapidly changing environment. Liang's camera lens zooms in and out as she looks for another world she knows is out there but finds hard to capture. Fascinated by small things, by elusive, subtle details, Liang's works are like an illusion. The video piece *Stop Dazing*, completed in 2004, swings from a very introspective, profound, and private angle to a humorous record of events related to daily life and the environment.

"Many people see my work as melancholy and sad," says Liang. "In everyone's life there are sad or difficult moments. But the cruelest thing is that no one will ever be able to fully understand or experience what another person feels. Hence solitude is the ultimate necessity when you come to face the coldest, hardest things. But this sadness is just one part of me—I am also a very entertaining and funny person, and I love being with people!"

THIS PAGE AND OVERLEAF: *Morse Code—Several Dusks* series, 2003. C-print.

FACING PAGE: *Stop Dazing*, 2004. Stills from video.

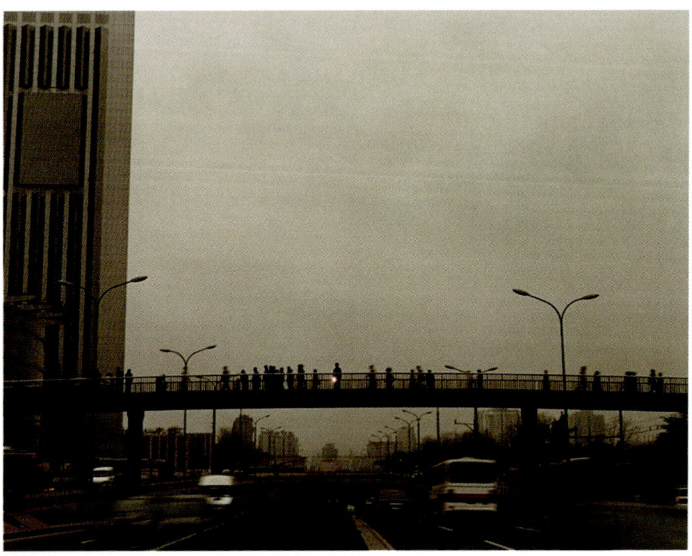

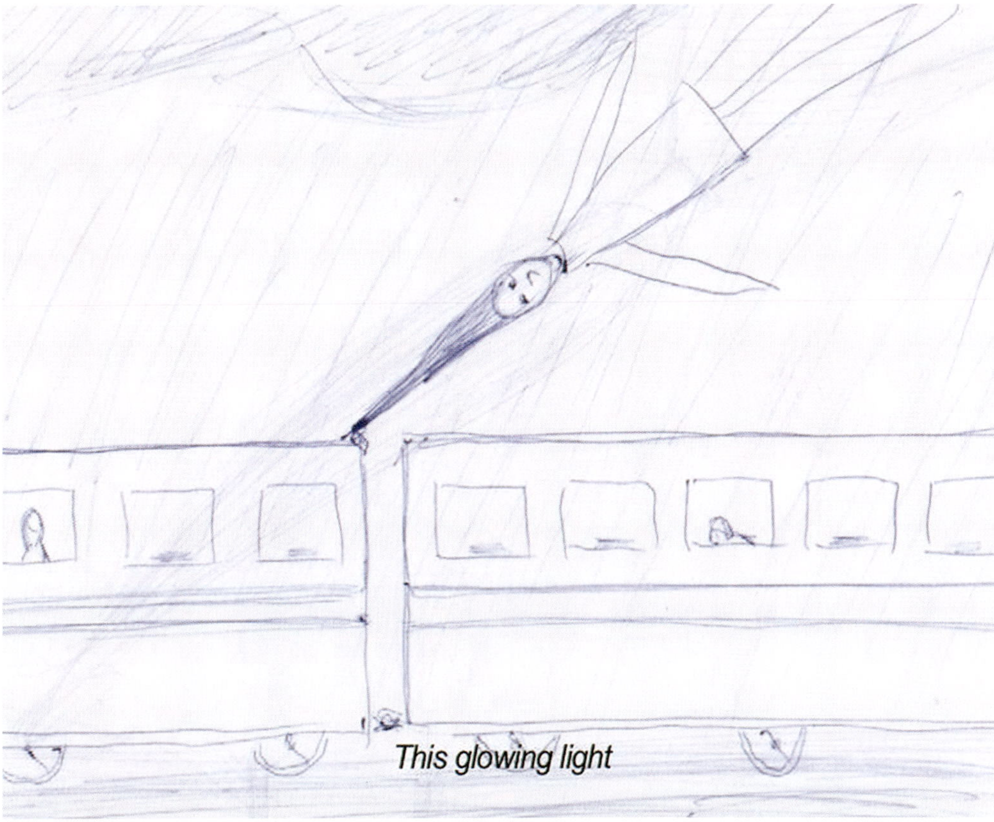
This glowing light

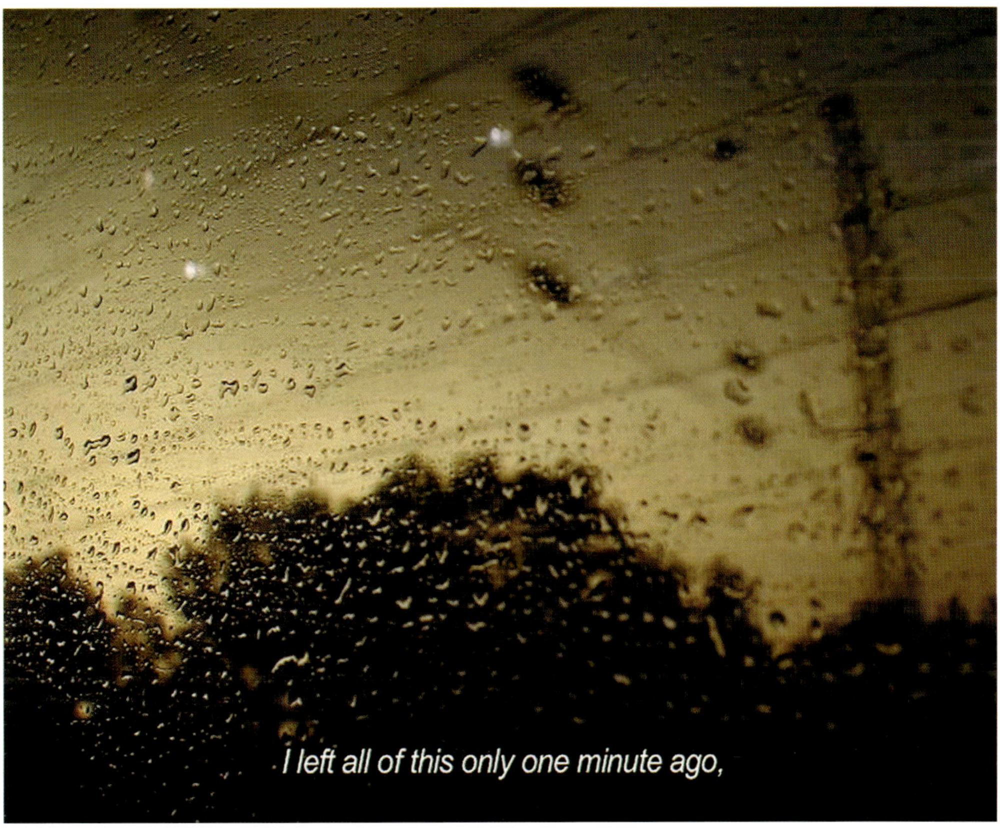
I left all of this only one minute ago,

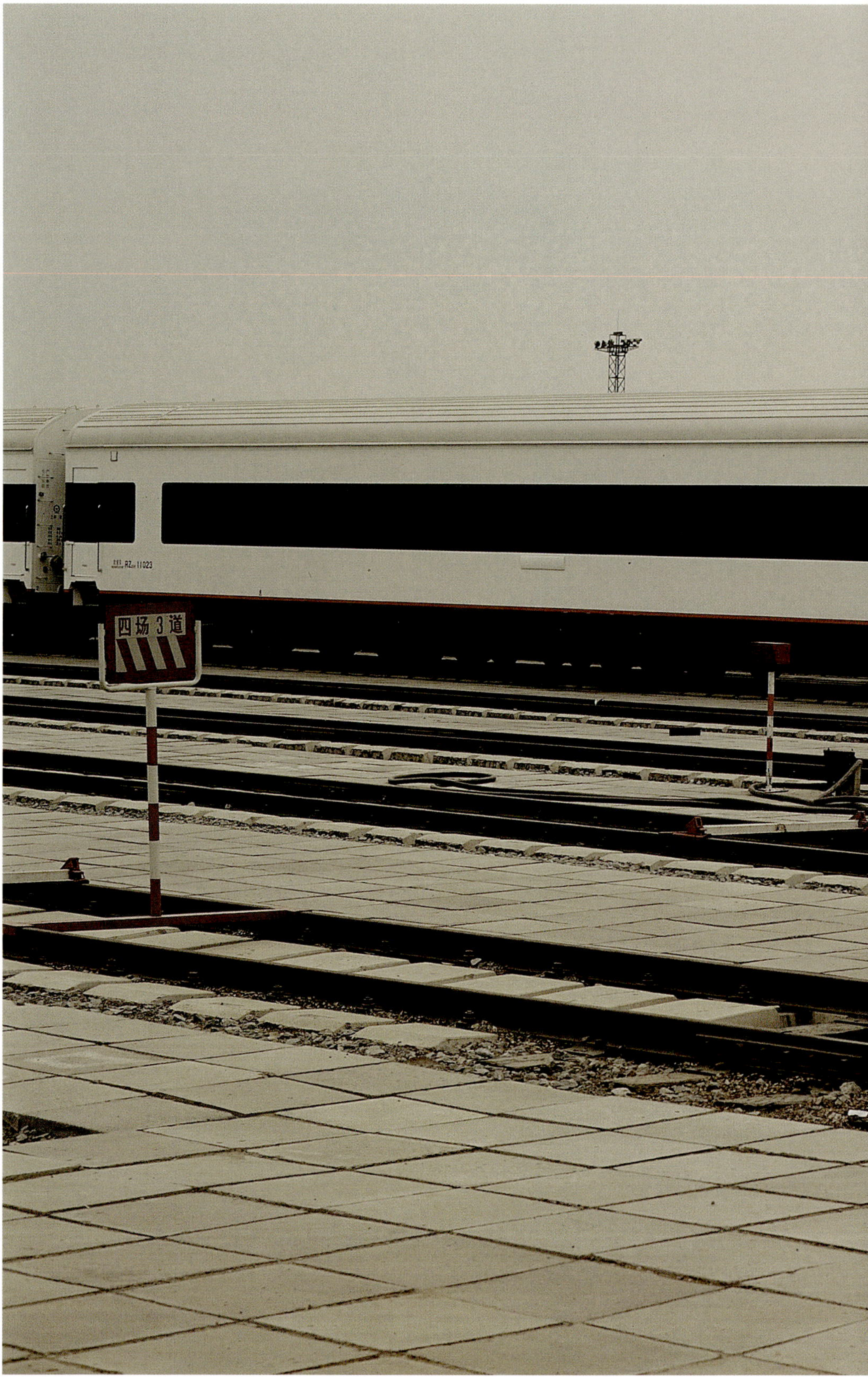
四场 3 道

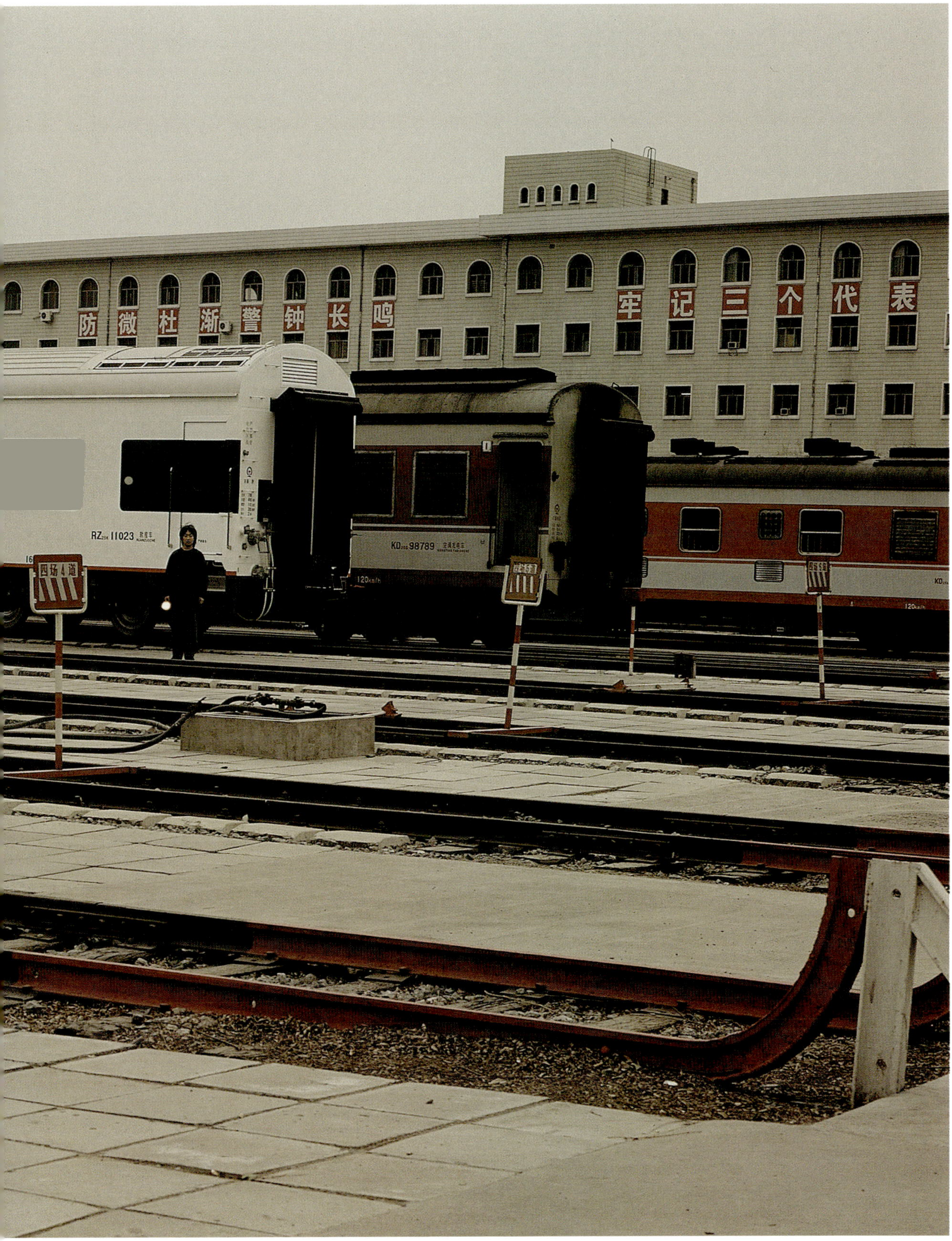
防微杜渐警钟长鸣
牢记三个代表
四场4道
RZ 11023
KD 98789
120km/h

Lin Tianmiao

Born 1961, Taiyuan, Shanxi Province

Gifted with innate tactile power, Lin Tianmiao explores issues of female identity through amazingly intricate installations featuring old-fashioned and everyday objects wrapped in cotton thread.

Works such as *Bound and Unbound* (1995–1997) and *The Proliferation of Thread-Winding* (1995–1997) took a long time to complete, and required the help of various family members and friends. Lin's creations echo the repetitive, redundant duties of female labor. The intense process of wrapping and encasing objects has a dual meaning, hinting at preservation while also making objects futile.

In the installations *Focus* (2001), *High* (2000–2003), and *Hand Signals* (2005) Lin uses digital technology to alter the human body into a ghostly white form, as though to mystify our perceptions of sex and status. The "threads" theme that runs through her work could be seen as a metaphor for all the small habits that characterize a particular culture or even the intricacy of human relationships. The female image she uses in *Initiator*, an almost perfect beautiful woman, symbolizes "the moment in life in which one can be seduced and captured by things of the external world," stated Lin in an interview with Chinese curator Pi Li.

The Proliferation of Thread-Winding, in which hundreds of threads tied to a myriad of needles radiate across a bed and onto the floor, deals with the theme of the violation of privacy (the bed)—"a woman thing"—and the complexity of the world's affairs (the needles). A video on the pillow shows Lin involved in the repetitive work of winding balls of thread, which, as curator Karen Smith has pointed out, seems to emphasize the artist's endurance and her desire to escape strong emotional ties.

THIS PAGE: *Bound and Unbound*, 1995–1997. Installation. White cotton thread, video projection, household objects.

FACING PAGE: *The Proliferation of Thread-Winding*, 1995–1997. Installation. White cotton thread; 20,000 needles 5–6 inches long; TV screen; video; bed; rice paper.

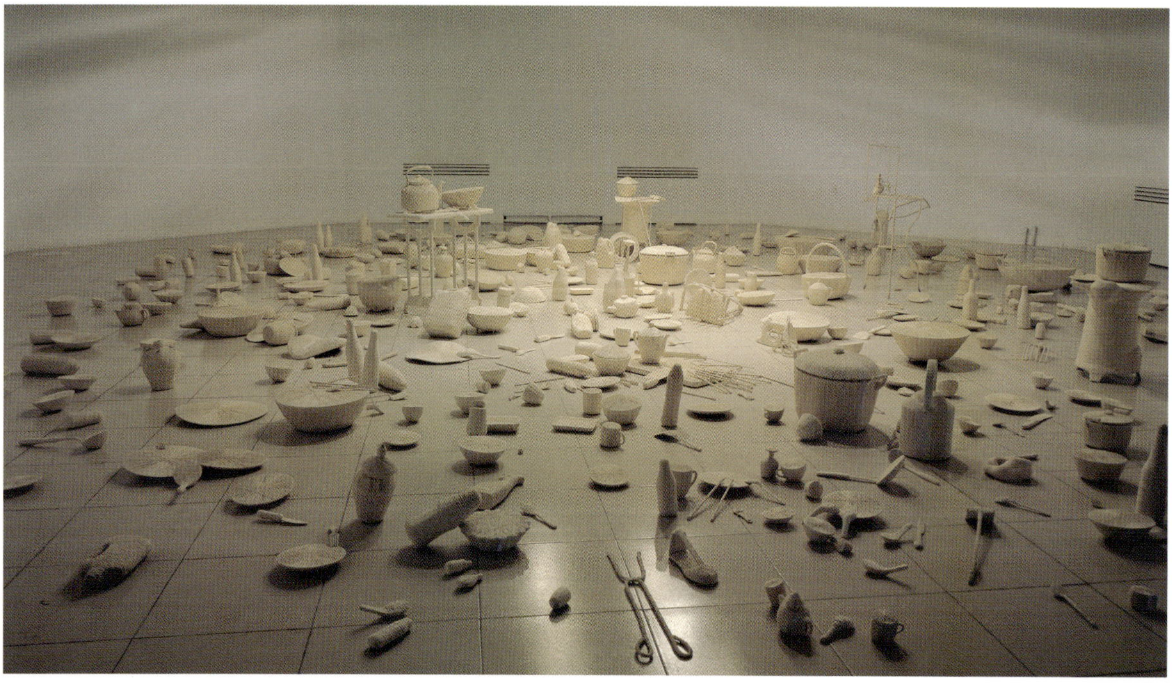

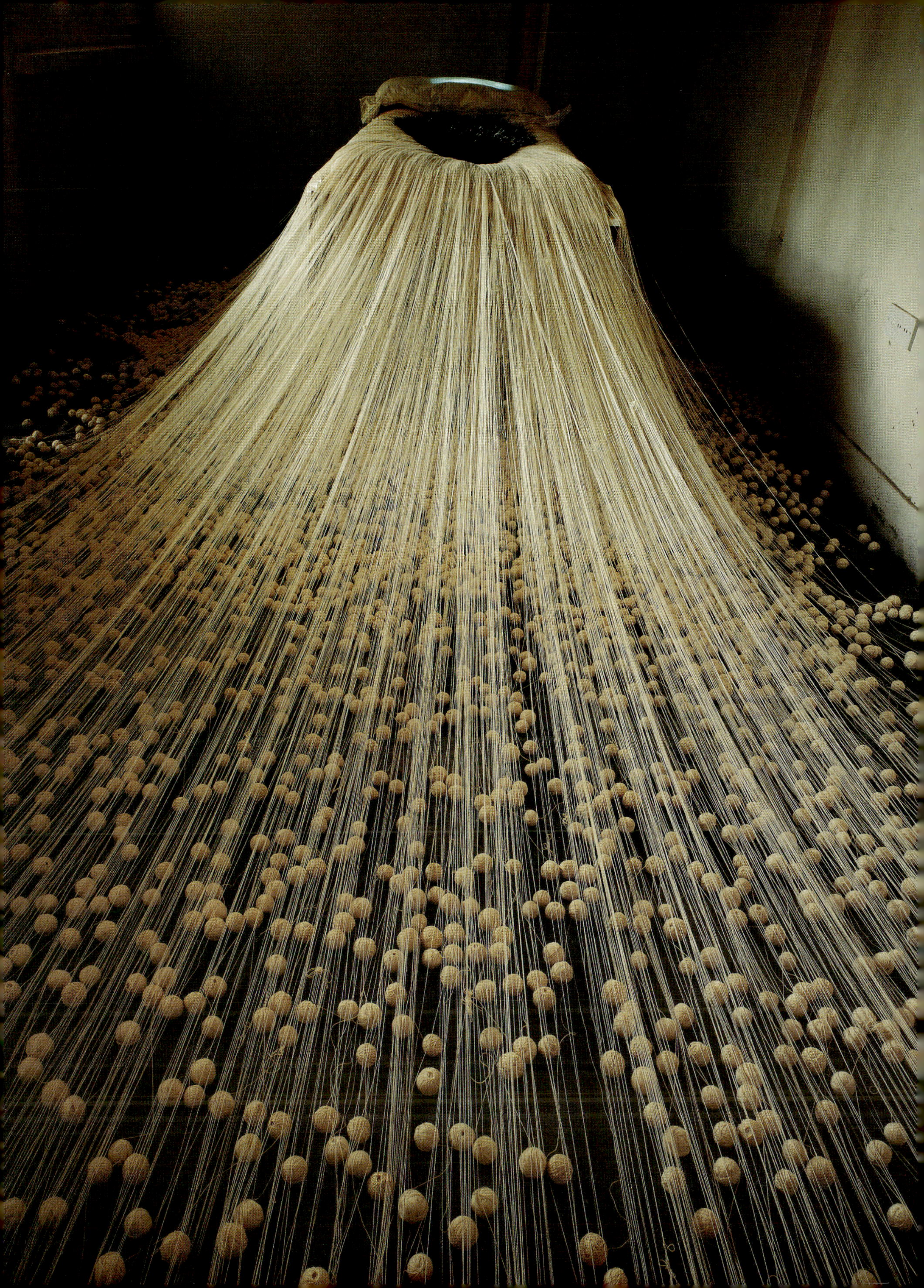

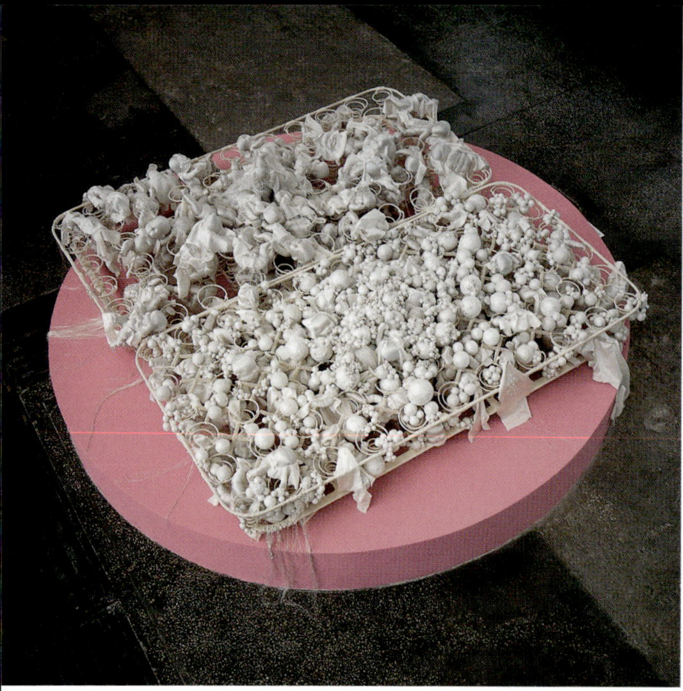

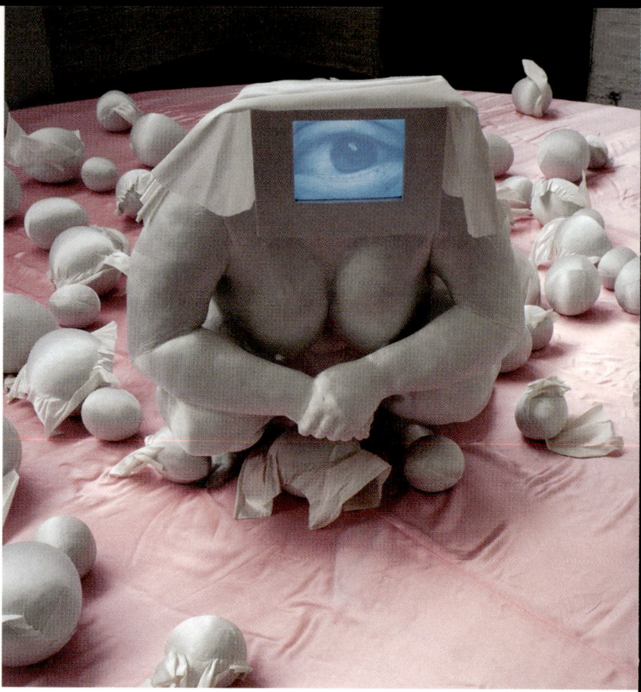

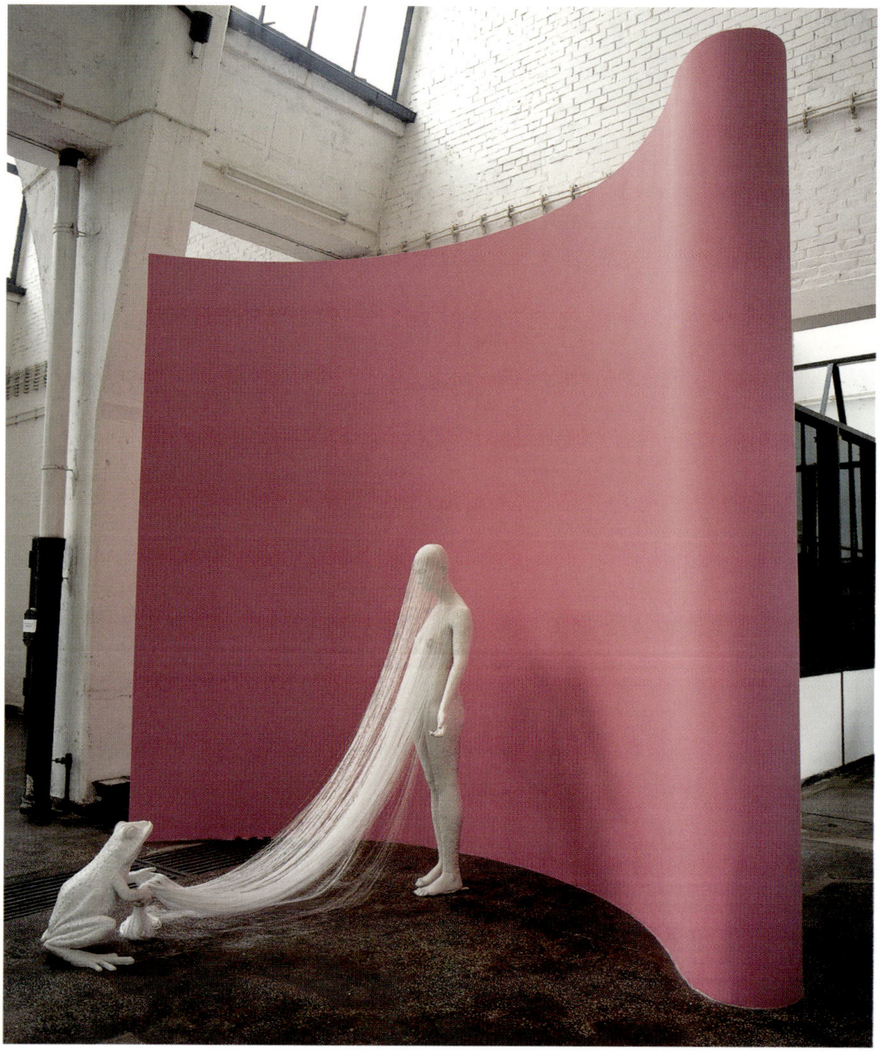

THIS PAGE: *Slumbering* (top left), *Procreating* (top right), *Initiator* (bottom), 2004. Installation. Mixed media, fiberglass, silk, mixed techniques. Dimensions variable.

FACING PAGE: *Focus*, 2001. Installation. Digital photograph, thread, hair, 83½ x 64 in. (Size with frame.)

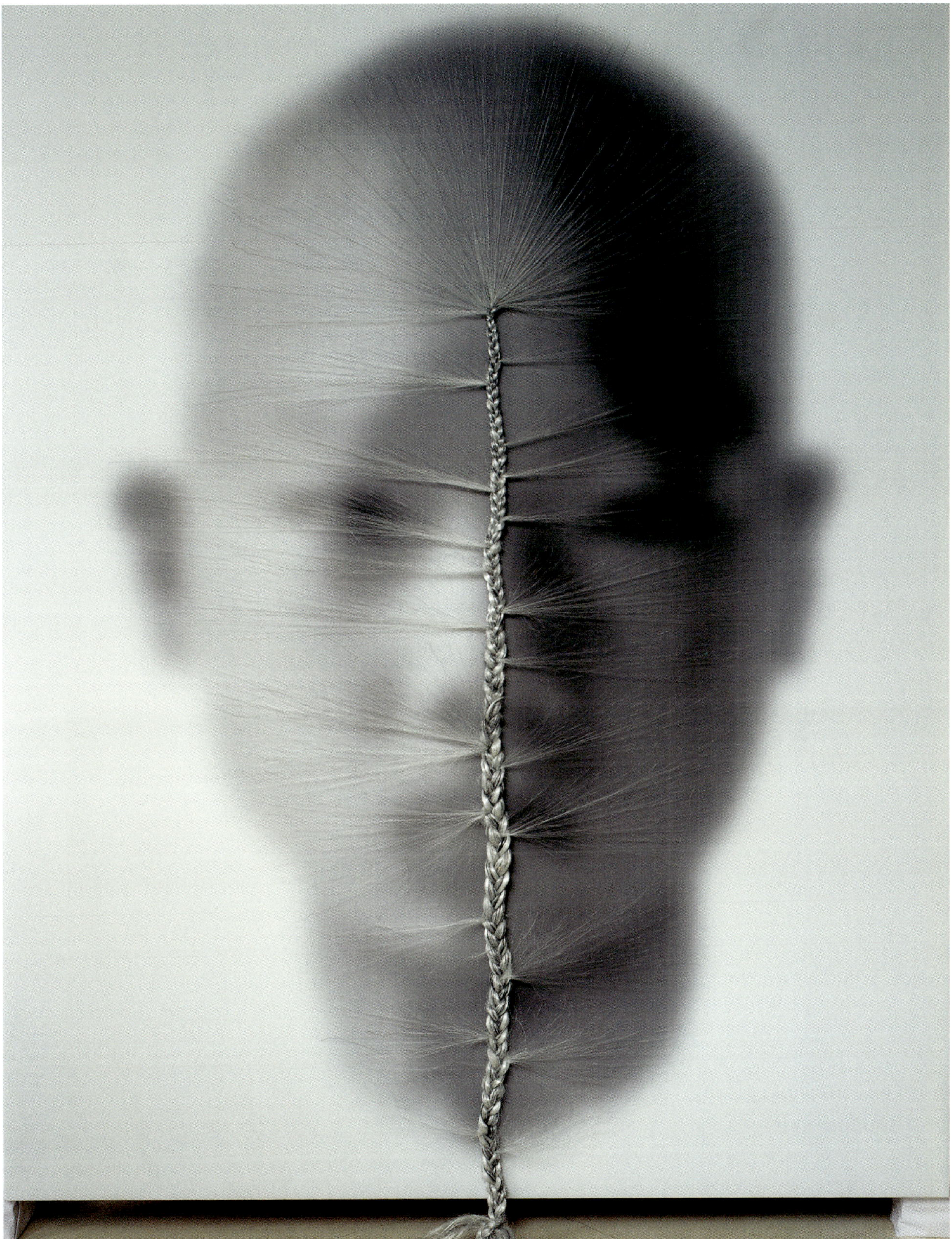

Liu Ding

Born 1976, Changzhou, Jiangsu Province

THIS PAGE: *Power*, 2006–2007. Porcelain, aluminum, acrylic, spotlights, height 43 in., diameter 59 in.

FACING PAGE, TOP: *Products*, 2005. Performance view at the 2nd Guangzhou Triennal, Guangzhou Museum.

FACING PAGE, BOTTOM: *Products*, 2005–2006. An installation of the 40 paintings from the performance at the Guangdong Museum of Art. 40 paintings in gilded frames, each 27 x 39 in., traditional living room furniture.

OVERLEAF: *Tiger*, 2007. Concrete, fluorescent lights, artificial tiger skin, mirrors. Dimensions variable.

Liu Ding's bold and playful works are characterized by a luminous quality and sophisticated concepts. Installations remain his mainstream productions, although he often expresses himself through paintings, photography, and stage design, and has taken part in exhibitions and projects around the world. His themes include social boundaries, the position of the individual in China today, and the damage we inflict on the environment in the name of progress. Liu gives shape to his biting social commentary through bright colors, minimalist sculptural objects, glazed capsules, shiny porcelain, skulls, and jewels. The installation *Tiger* (2007), inspired by a story by Jorge Luis Borges, is a comment on the thirst for power we feel as human beings. Symbol of energy and supremacy, the tiger is also a metaphor for the dynamism of contemporary society. *Power* (2006–2007), is a pyramid of gilded skulls through which the artist reinterprets the concept "all life is vanity."

Products (2005–2006) is part of Liu's *Sample from the Transitions* project that analyzes social and political phenomena that affect contemporary society on a microcosmic level. In Dafencun, southern China, there is a thriving industry based on the mass production of classic oil paintings for export to the West, and in *Products*, Liu invites the "masters" who reproduce these paintings to carry out their work inside an art museum as a performance, thus exploring the contradictory dualism of these masters as creators and manufacturers in a space that becomes both an exhibiting and a production milieu.

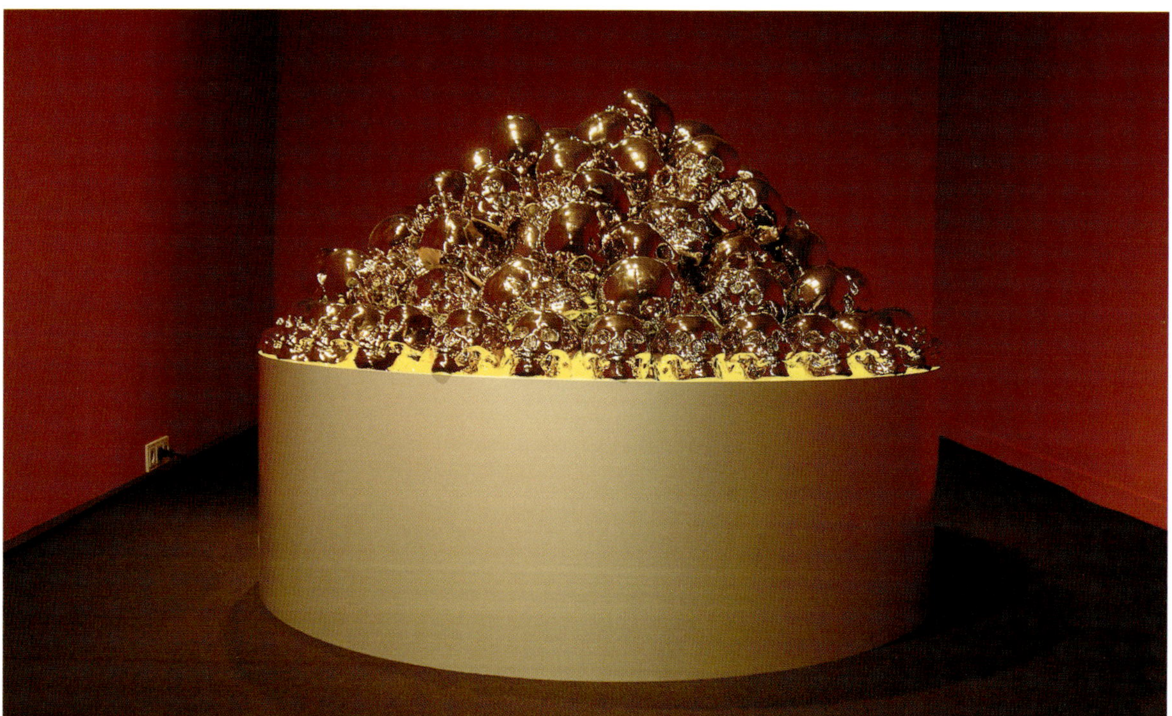

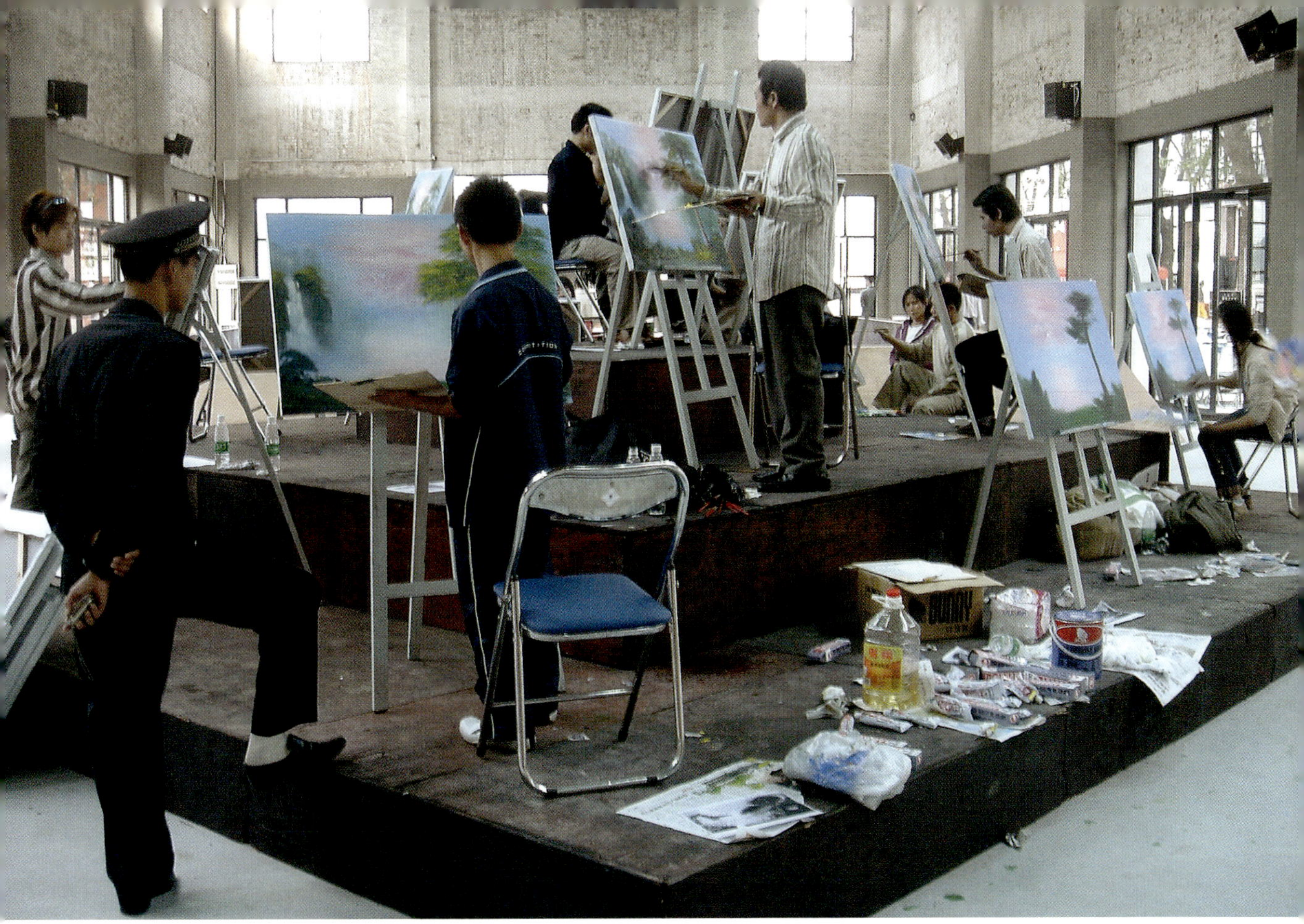

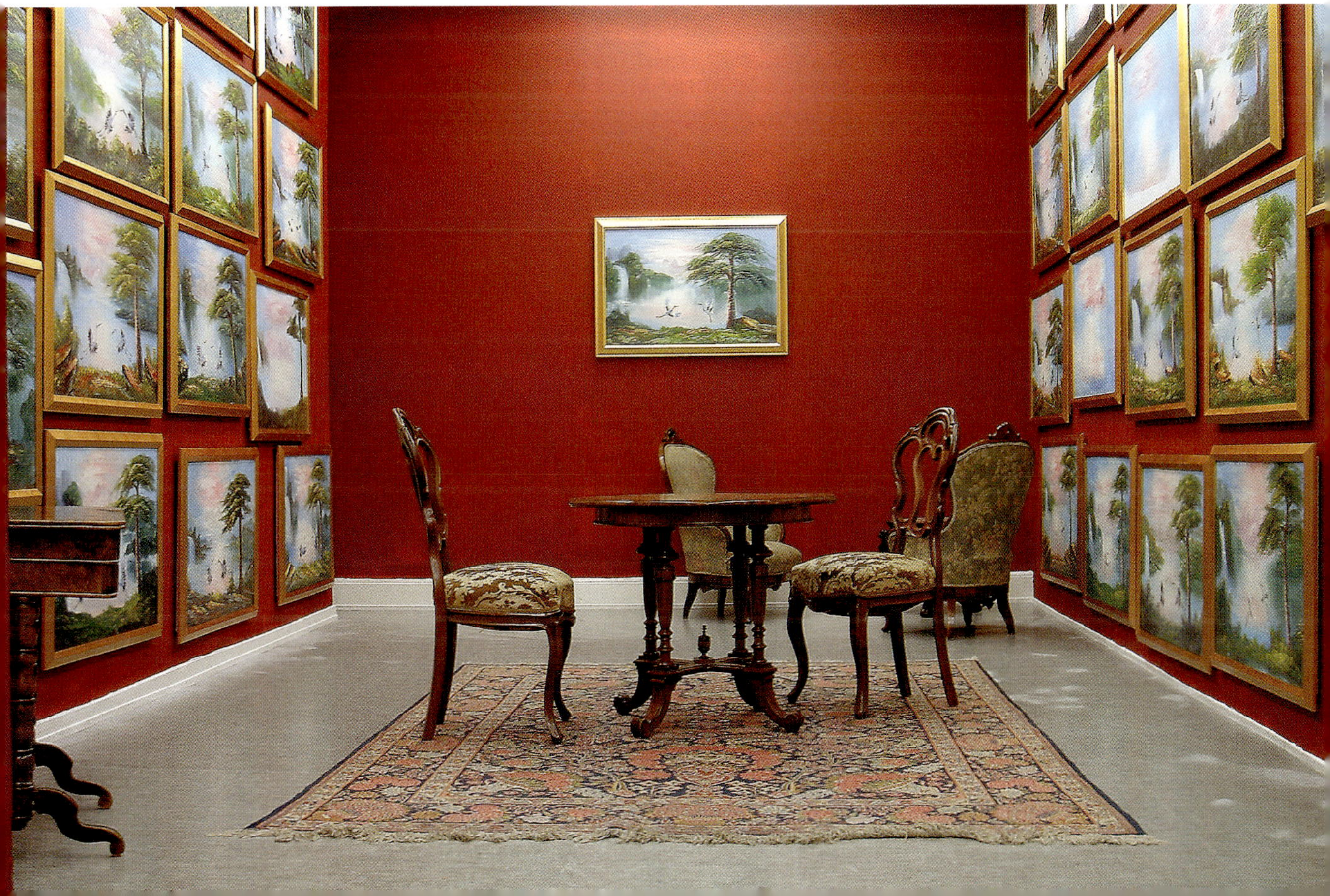

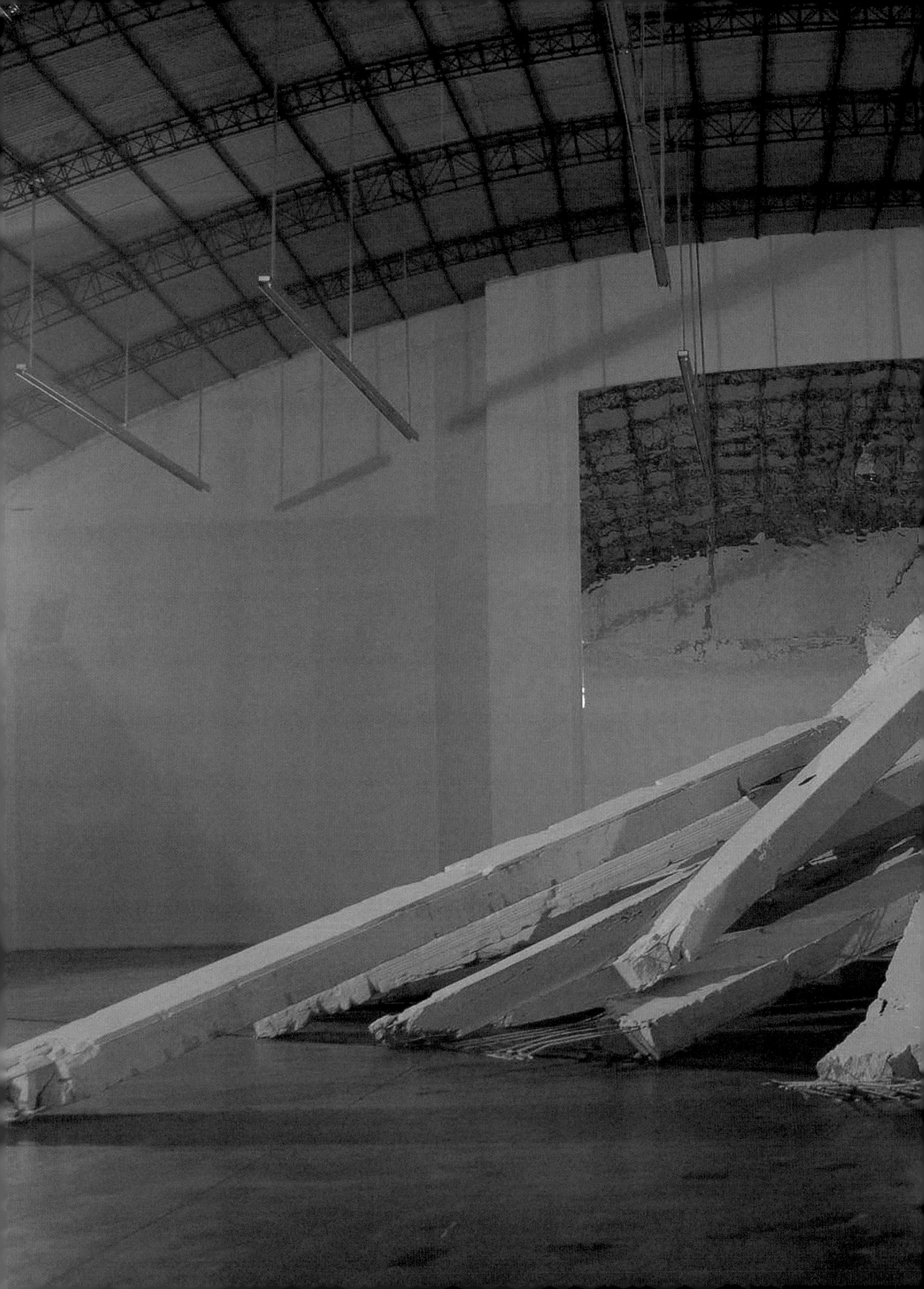

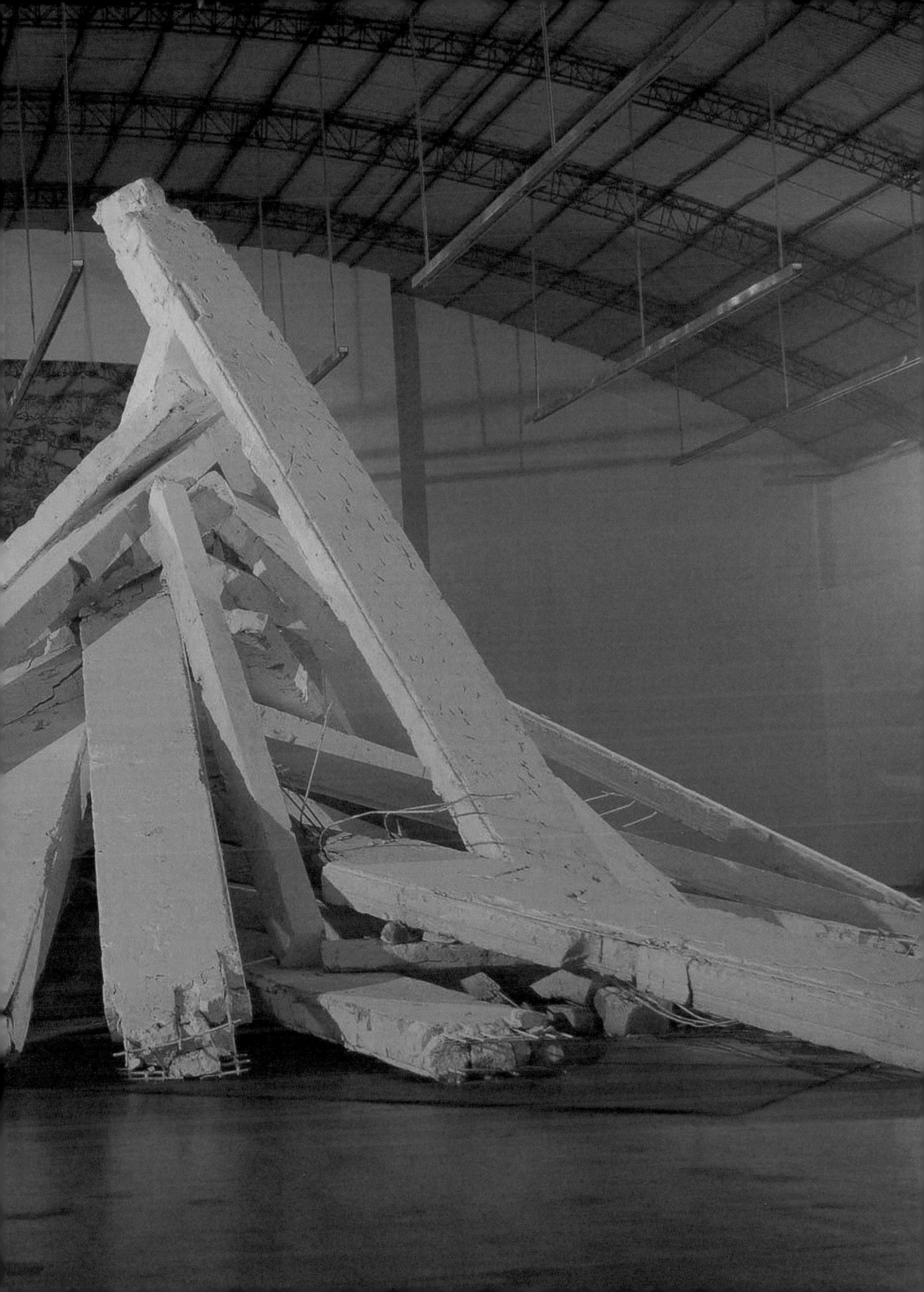

Liu Wei

Born 1972, Beijing

"It all depends on the single individual, on personality. I believe in people's willpower." For Lui Wei, self-knowledge and the confidence to freely express one's personal ideas and concerns while maintaining an awareness of the context of the wider culture is the key to creating good art.

Using everyday objects and materials, Liu has created a wide range of explicit installations and artworks. In his exhibitions, every single object is perfectly linked to the other, and thus what emerges is the perception of completeness resulting from his straightforward mental organization. The show Outcast (2007), for example, was a comprehensive discourse expressed through various media including paintings, light boxes, and the 150-square-meter installation, *Untitled*, made out of hundreds of fragments of broken doors and windows that had been discarded as waste in the process of urbanization. A satirical commentary on the cultural decay, corruption, and aggression that pervade society, Liu invites us to reexamine the nature of what we are surrounded by and the power we invest in it.

On some of his works appears the label "Property of Liu Wei," which could be mistaken for the artist's egocentricity, but this is not the case. By drawing our attention to the idea of property, Liu forces us to consider the complex nature of social changes taking place in China, the nature and production of power, the surging force of materialism, the widening gap between rich and poor, and the unbelievable speed of the redevelopment of the country. Through works such as *Porcelain III* (2006), a space satellite made out of everyday porcelain objects such as cups and plates, through the ragged and warped exteriors of world famous buildings in installations such as *Love It, Bite It* (2006), Liu gives a vivid portrayal of the disposable nature of contemporary reality, a reality that engenders social alienation and emptiness.

THIS PAGE: *Love It, Bite It*, 2006. Installation made of biting rubber (for dogs), dimensions variable.

FACING PAGE: *Outcast No. 2*, 2007. Oil on canvas, 283½ x 181 in.

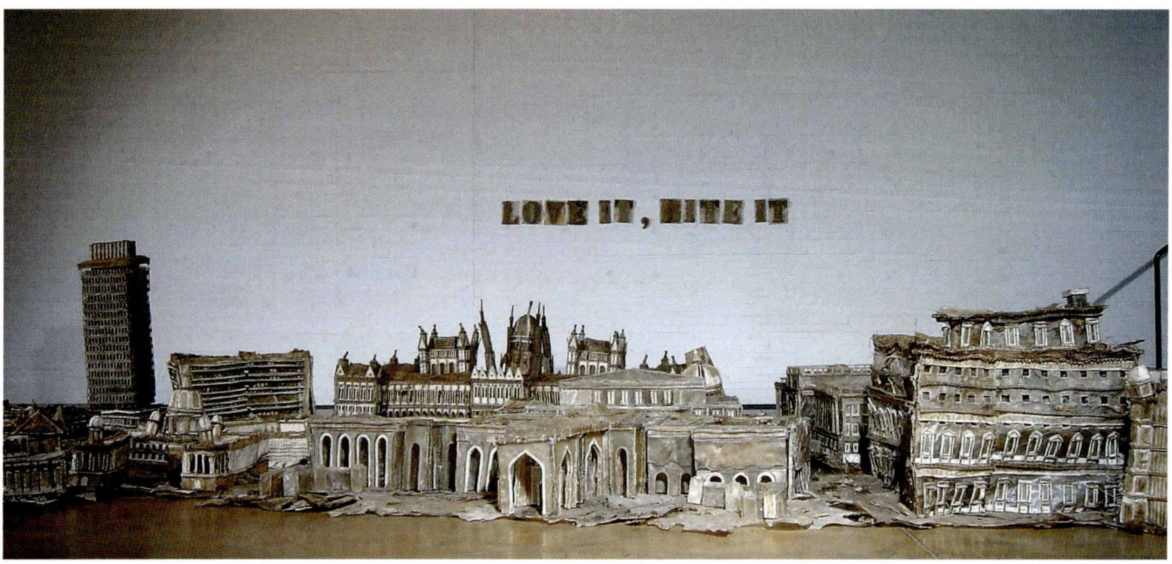

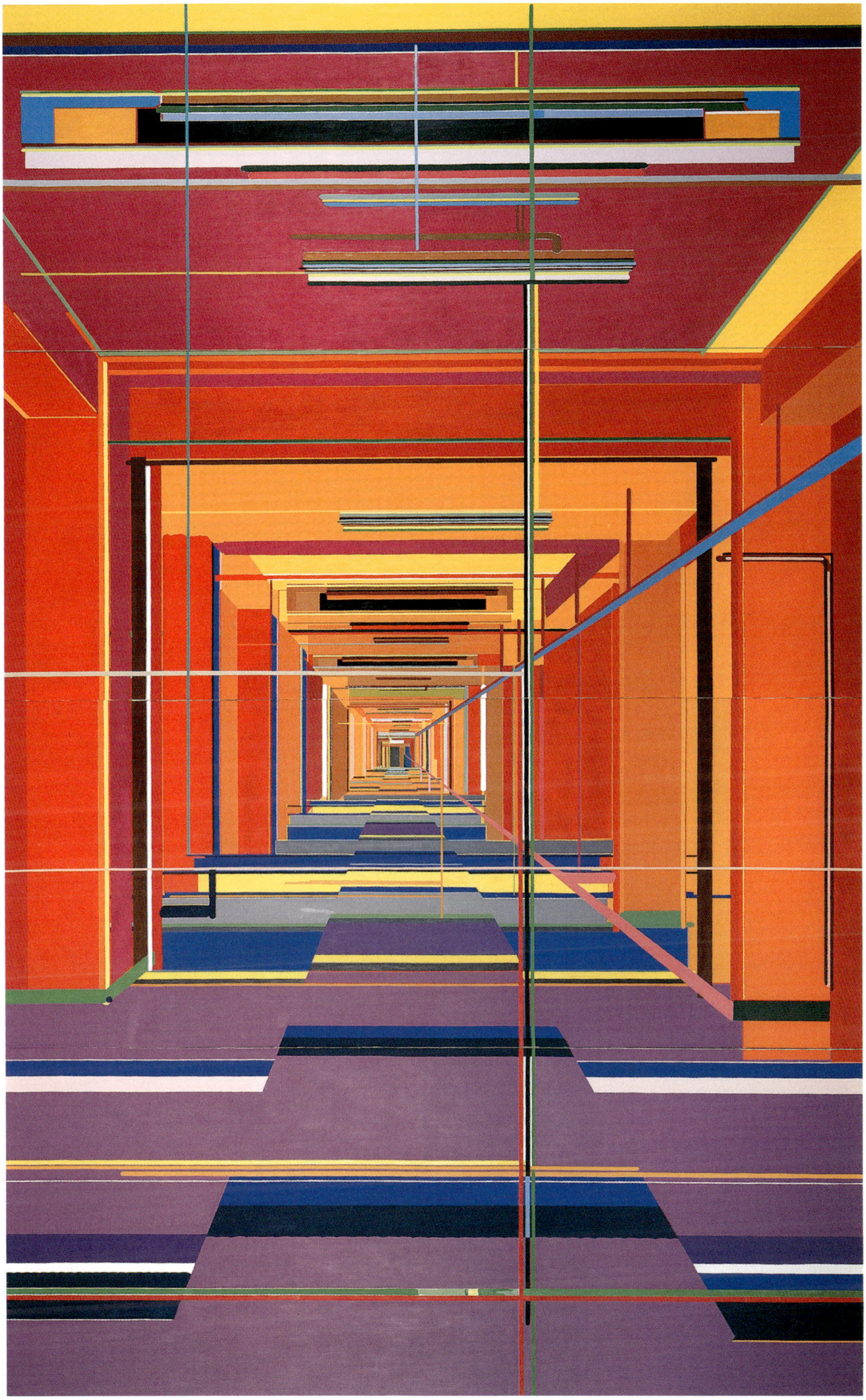

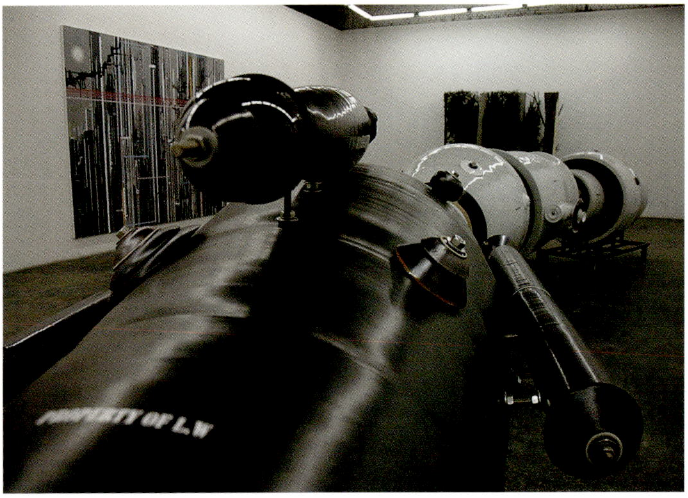

THIS PAGE, TOP: *Porcelain III*, 2006. Porcelain, 108 x 374 in.

THIS PAGE, BOTTOM: *A Life Style*, 2007. Colton steel, 118 x 354 x 98½ in.

FACING PAGE, TOP: *Outcast—Untitled*, 2007. Old windows, steel supports, earth, tables, chairs, lights, fans, trash, pine trees, 15 x 56 x 39 ft.

FACING PAGE, BOTTOM: *Anti TV Set*, 2006. TV, 21 x 27½ x 20½ in.

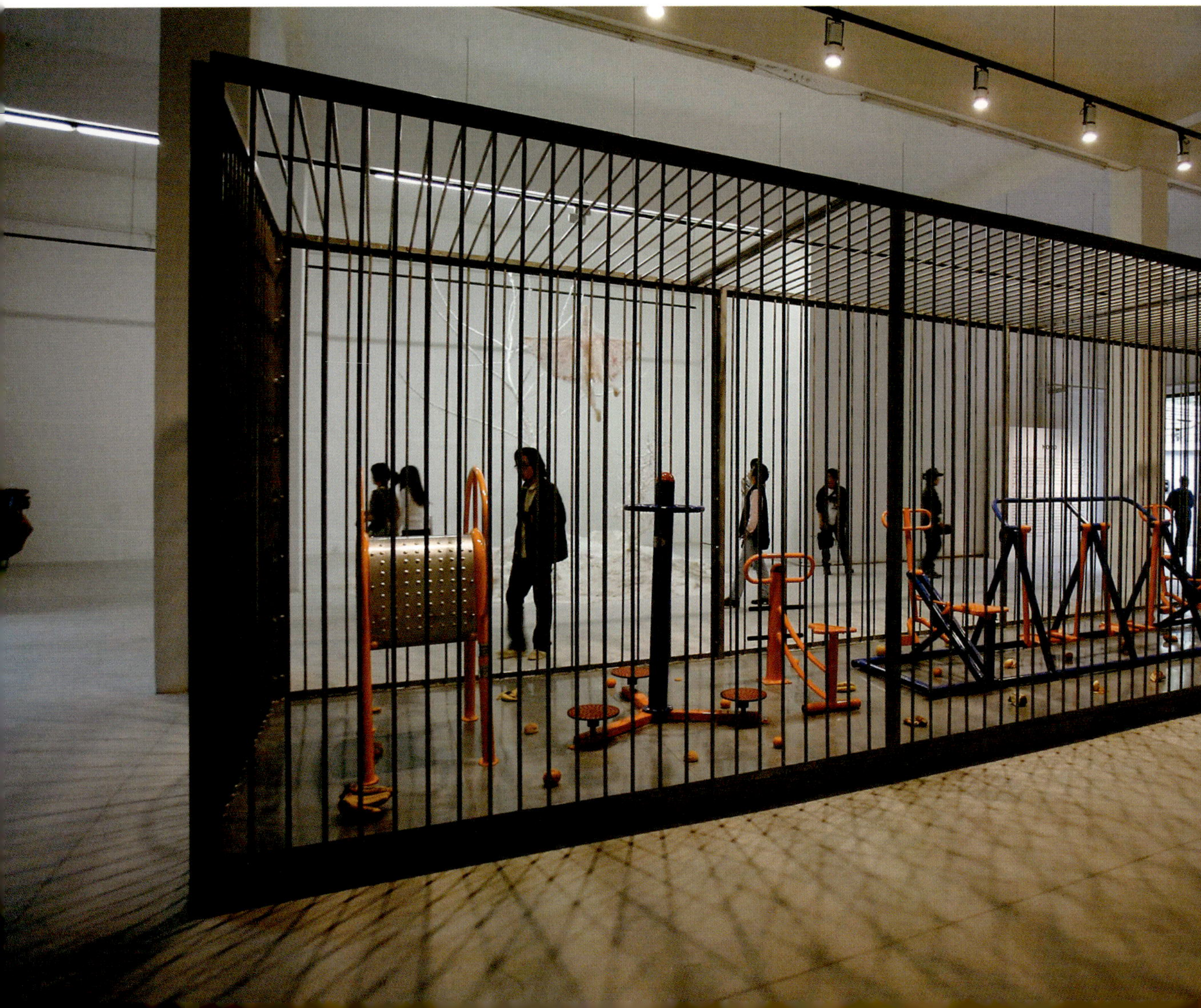

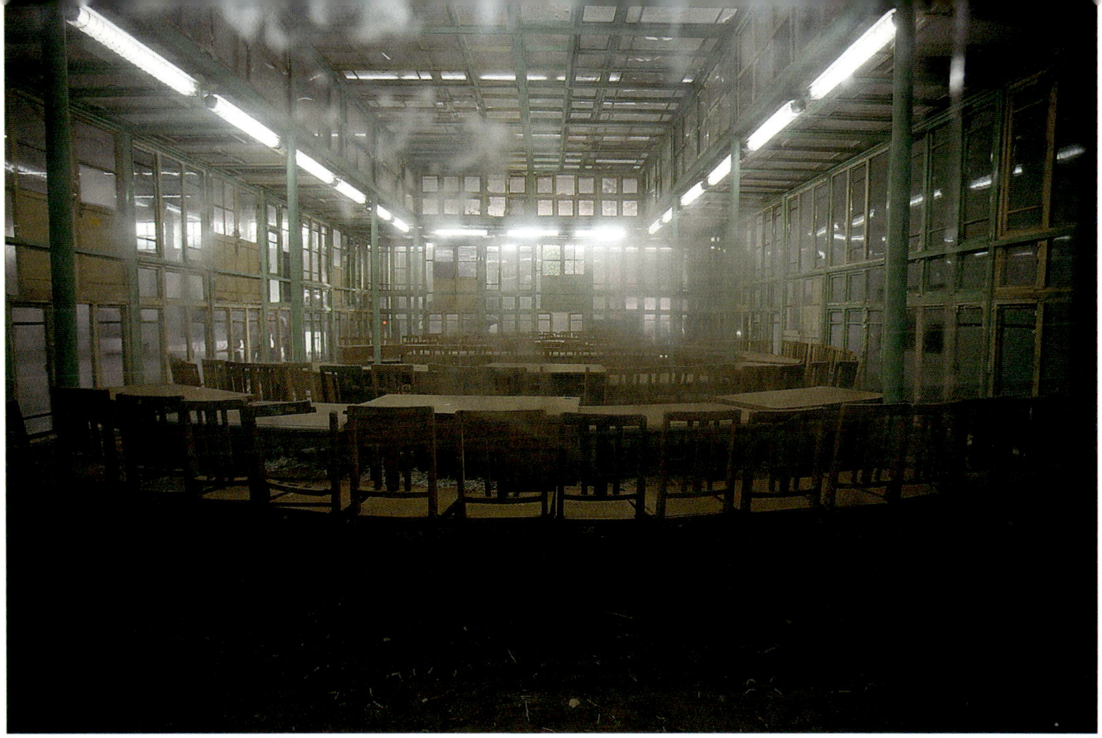

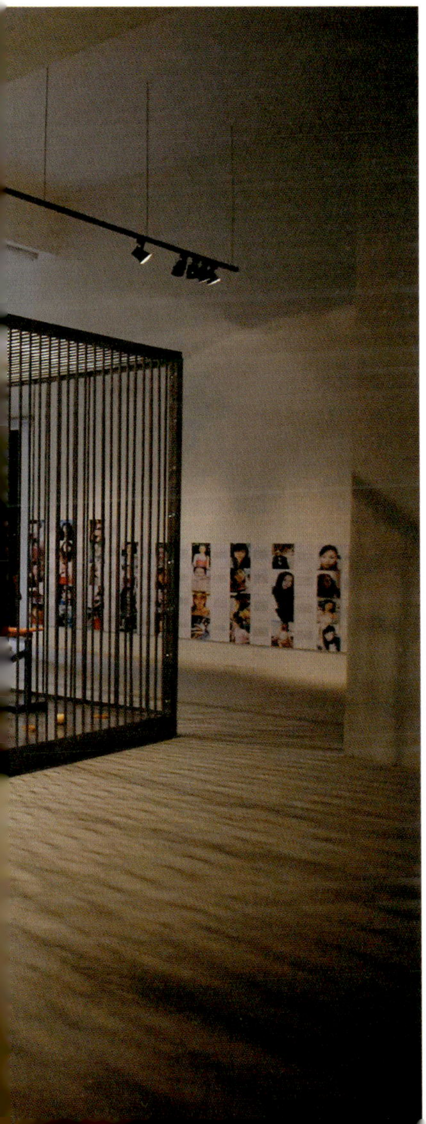

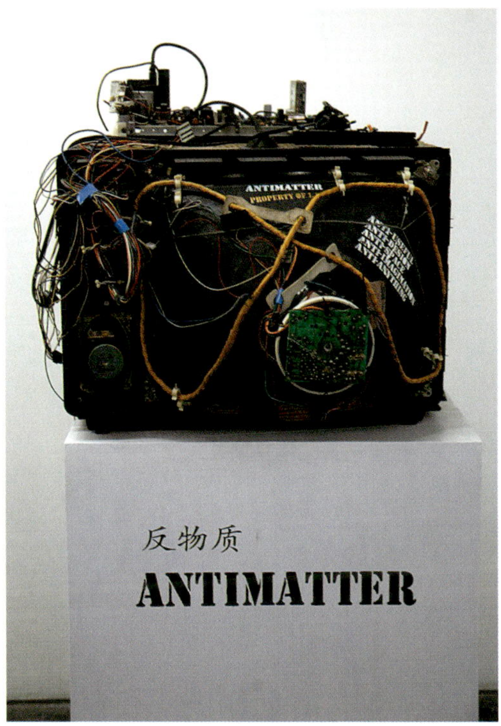
反物质
ANTIMATTER

Ma Liuming

Born 1969, Huangshi, Hubei Province

THIS PAGE: *Painting No. 20*, 2006. Oil on canvas, 79 x 59 in.

FACING PAGE, TOP: *Painting No. 19*, 2005–2006. Oil on canvas. 79 x 59 in.

FACING PAGE, BOTTOM: *Painting No. 18*, 2006. Oil on canvas, three panels, each 79 x 59 in.

OVERLEAF: *Fen-Ma Liuming Walks on the Great Wall*, 1998. Performance, Beijing.

Known for his mutations into his feminine alter ego Fen-Ma Liuming, for performances where he marches barefoot on the Great Wall or falls asleep naked in front of the audience, and for the distorted self-images that inhabit the center of his canvases, Ma Liuming is a multitalented artist whose narrative represents and transgresses the human form.

The images he offers are a subtle and profound analysis of the state of the human race; his vigor lies in the ability he has to abstract and transcend reality to reach an elevation from which he challenges us to question our existence. Working from opposite poles: feminine and masculine, negative and positive—or yin and yang as expressed in Chinese philosophy—the character of Fen-Ma Liuming is separated from reality: Fen is a female name but also has the same pronunciation as the Chinese character meaning "separation." The artist likewise separates himself from the world and from the demands of aggressive contemporary society, an isolation that allows him to rediscover an interior harmony.

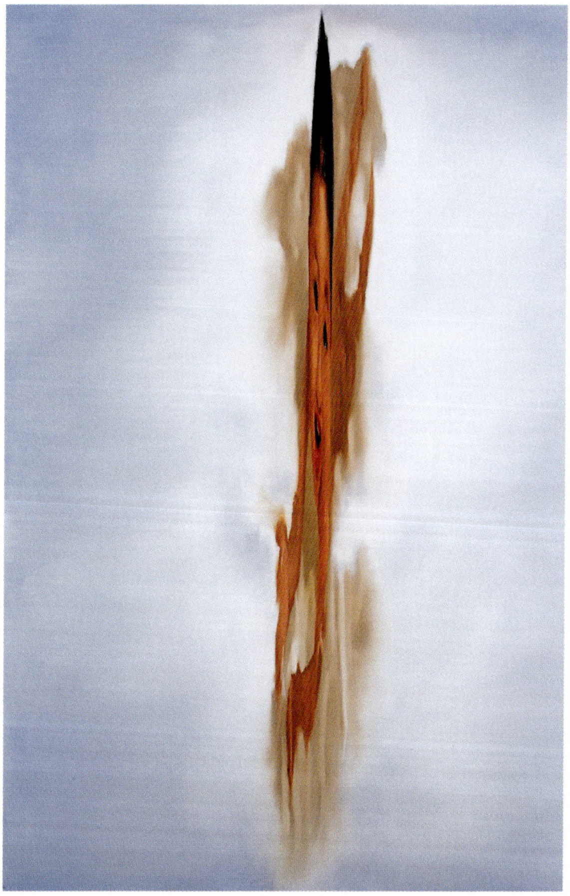

The Fen-Ma Liuming portrayed in the artist's performances is transported onto his canvases where the black and white body with colored face mutates into a baby's body combined with Ma Liuming's own face: another unreal existence. In his 2005–2006 untitled series of paintings, the representation of the self is a stretched-out central slice against a background of black infinity: a "biomorphic" presence on the inanimate fabric of the canvas. In his work it is possible to read a direct link to Chinese metaphysics, where the concept of permanence is expressed through a fluid narration. Ma's attempt to detach from contingency and materiality in order to reach the essential is evident in the structure of his evolving iconography. The mutations continue and his face appears now split into two halves, his forehead and eyes on the bottom of the canvas, his mouth and chin at the top. Ma constantly reproduces his own persona as a way of projecting universal analyses of the self. A further development in the artist's work has coincided with the birth of his son with whose images he alternates his own in a new metaphoric representation of continuity.

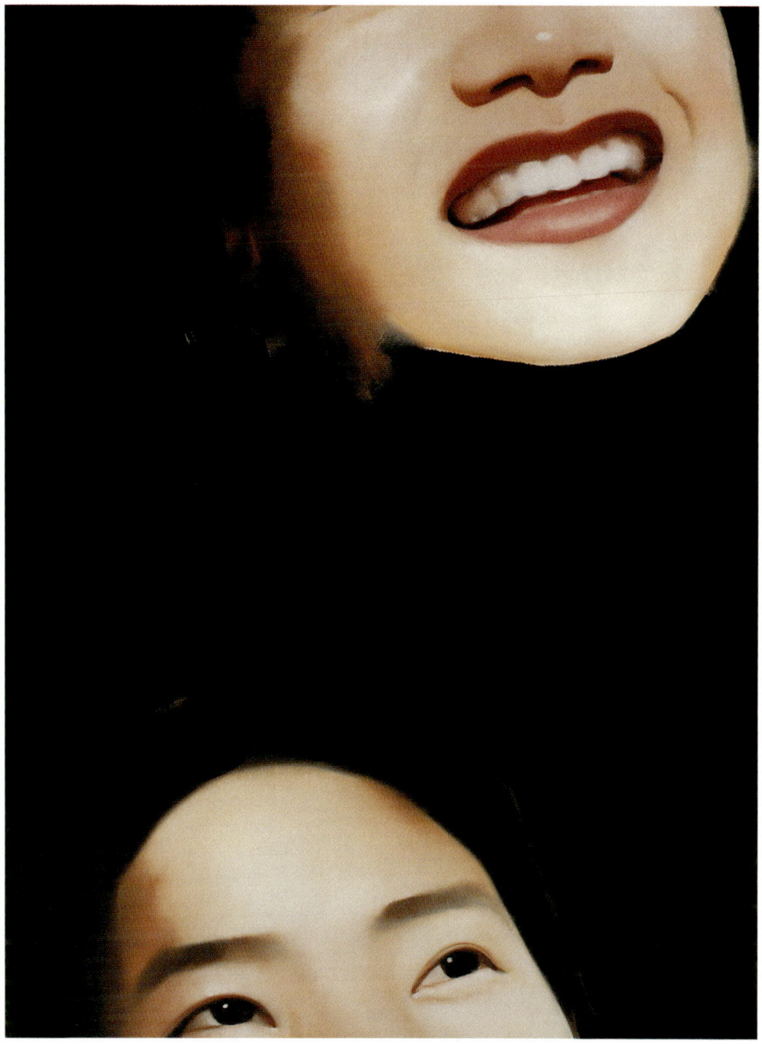

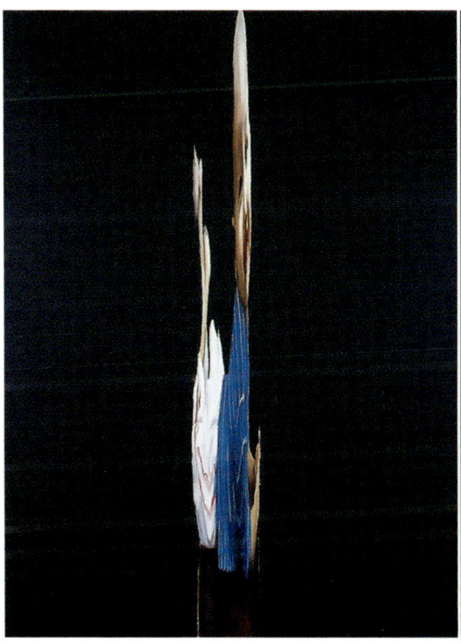

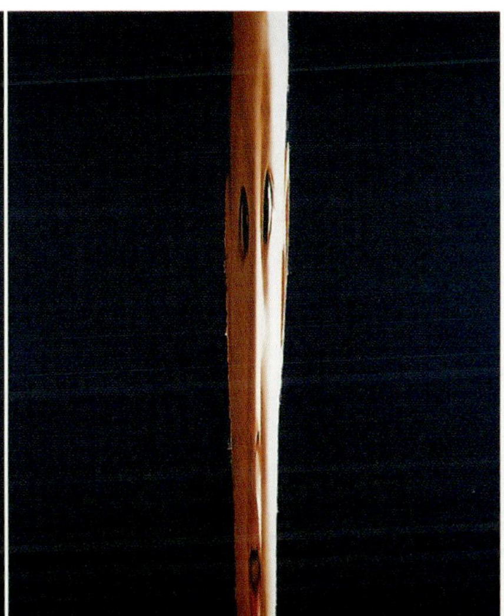

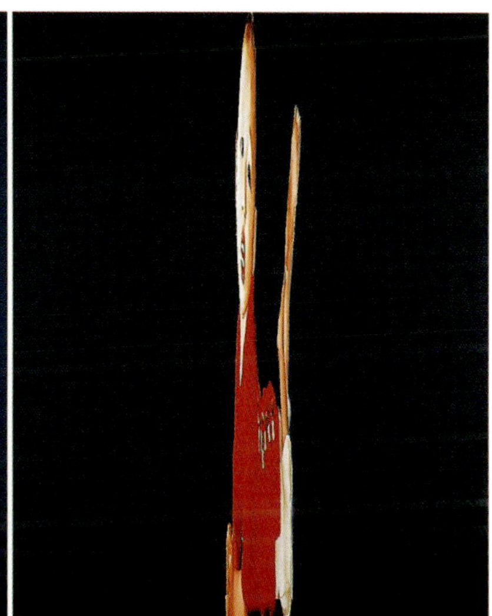

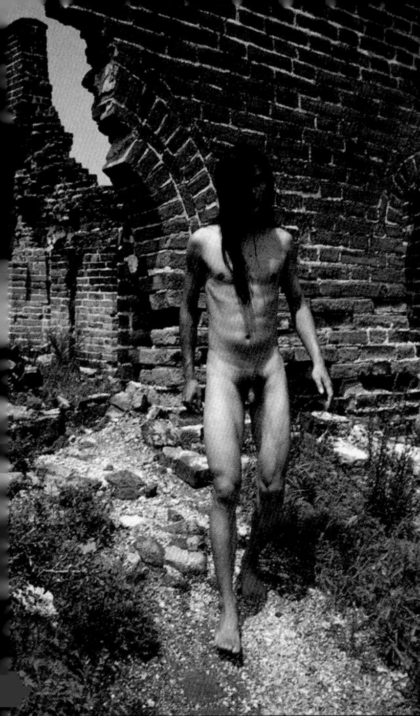
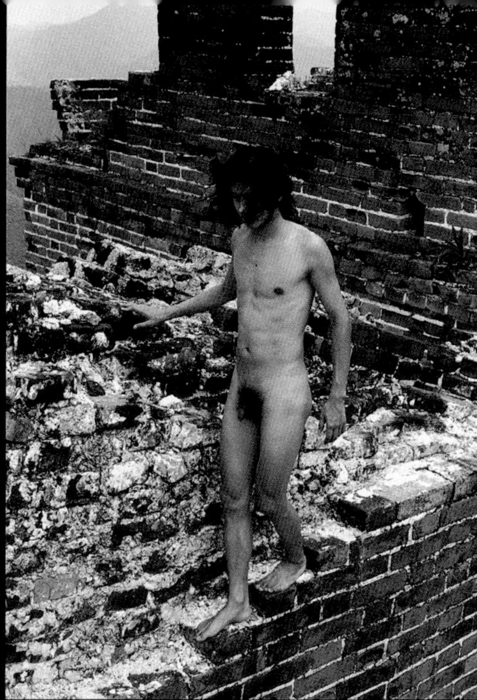
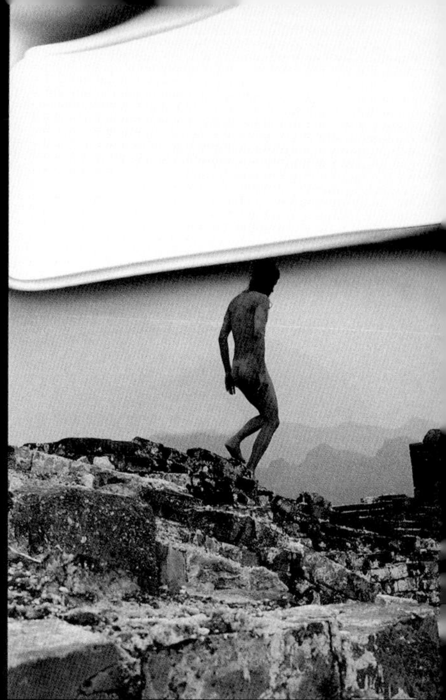
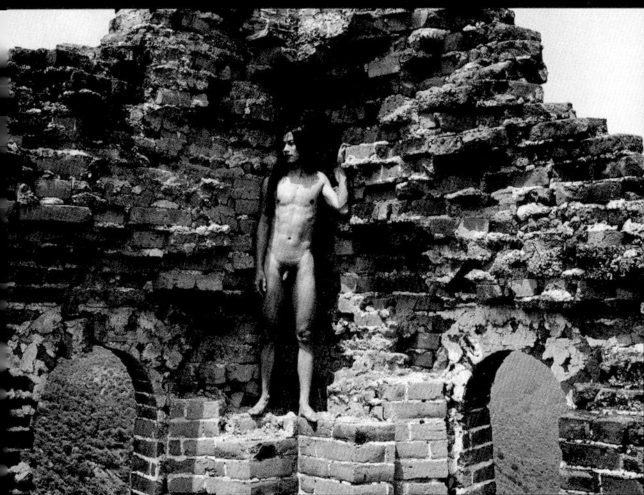
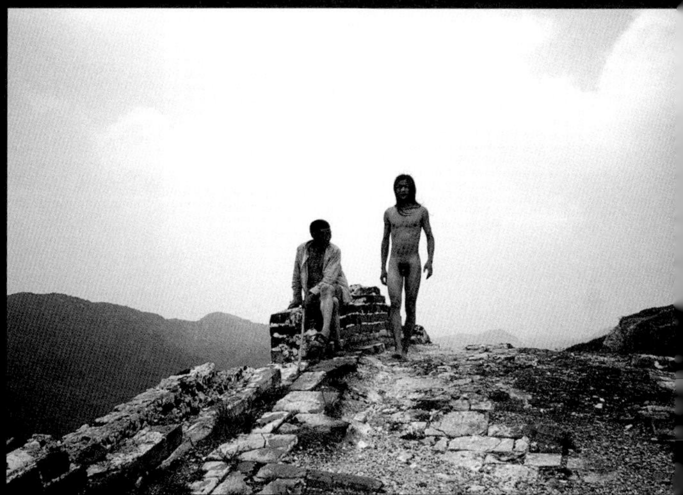
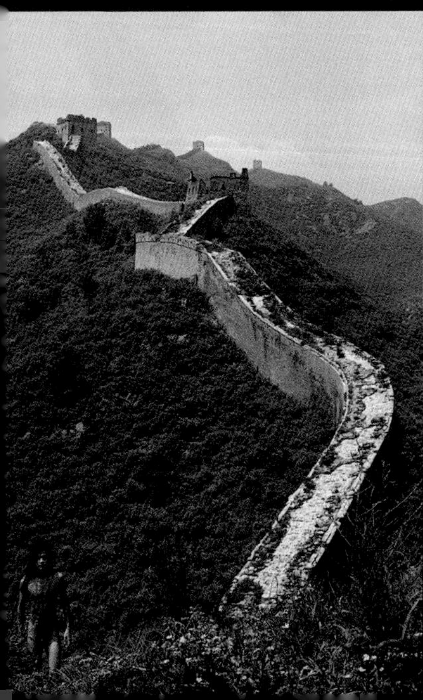
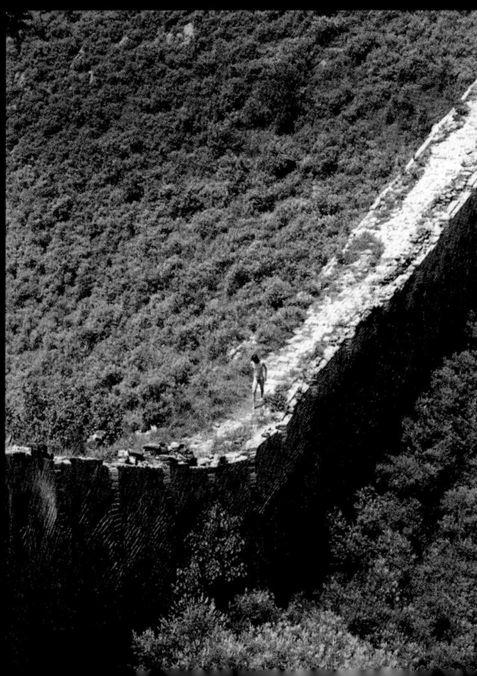
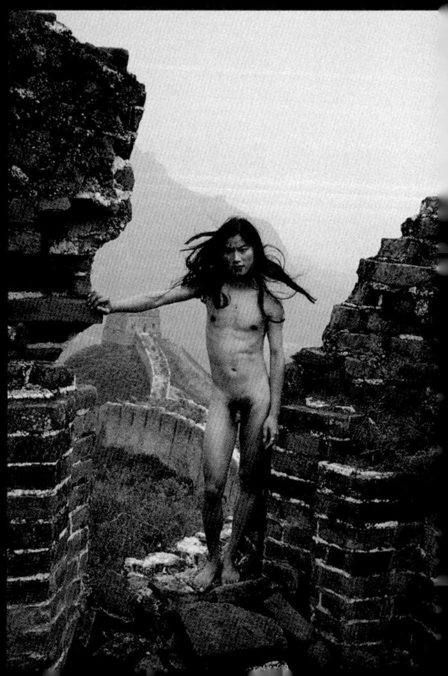

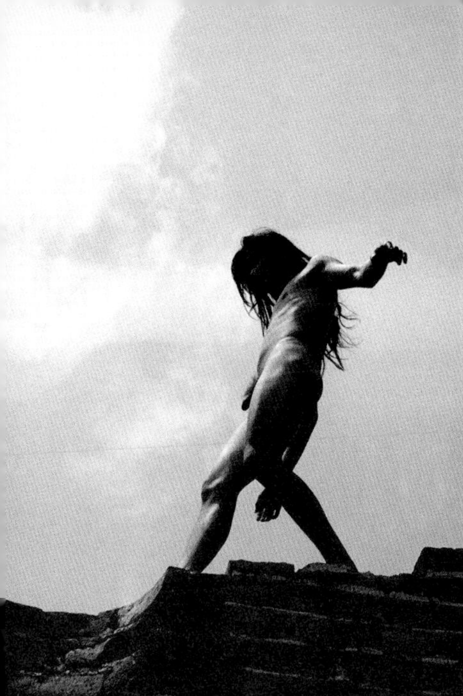
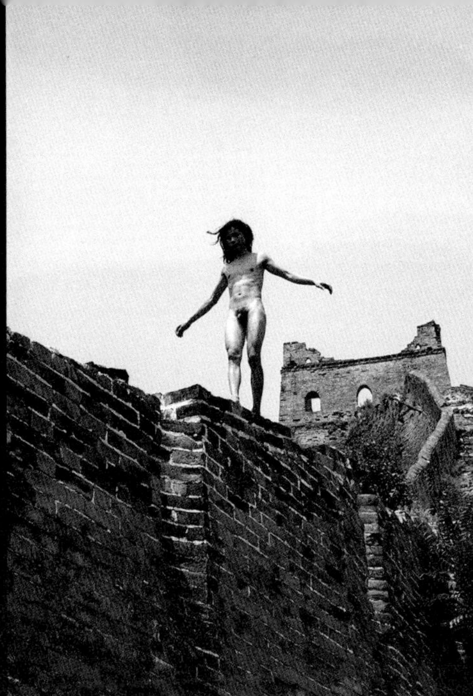
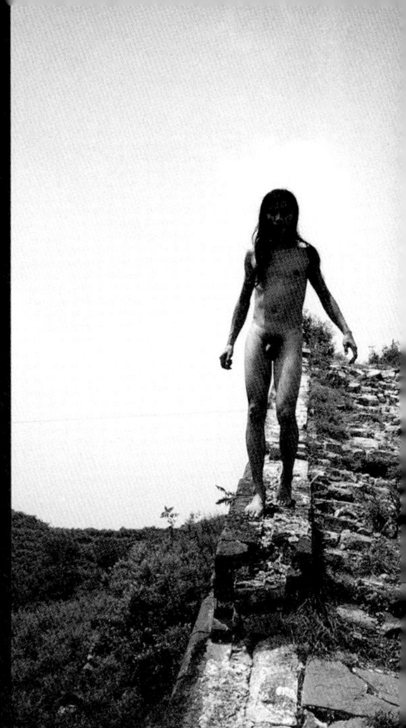
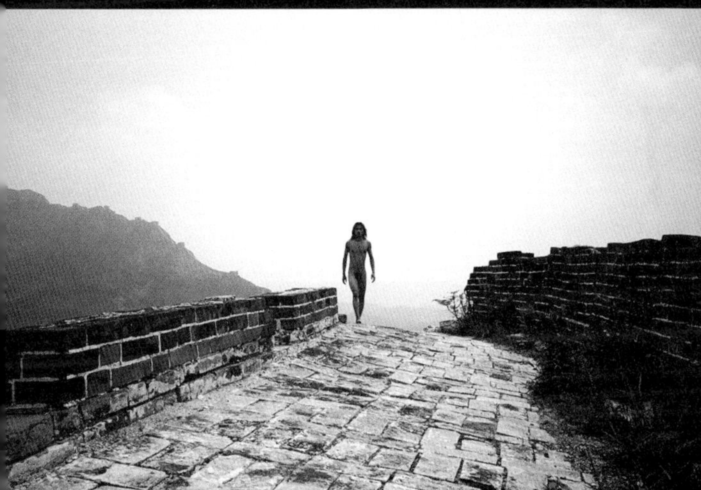
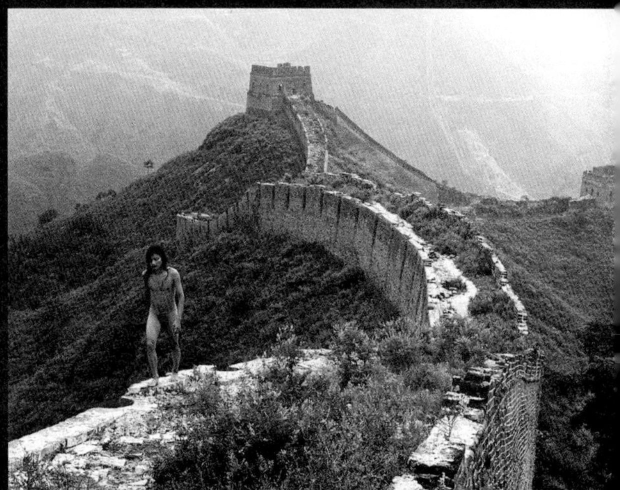
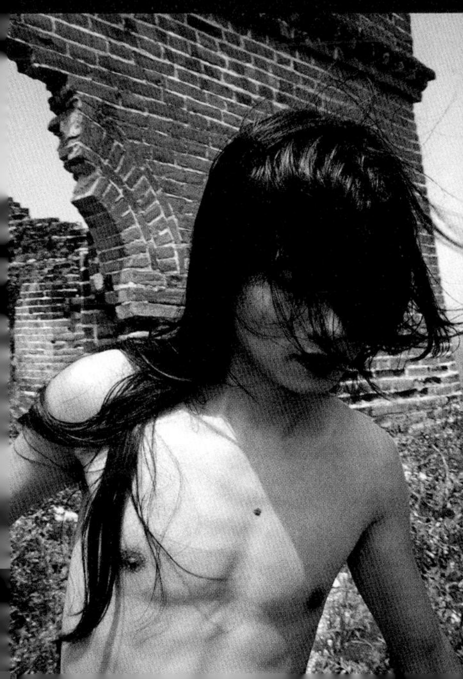
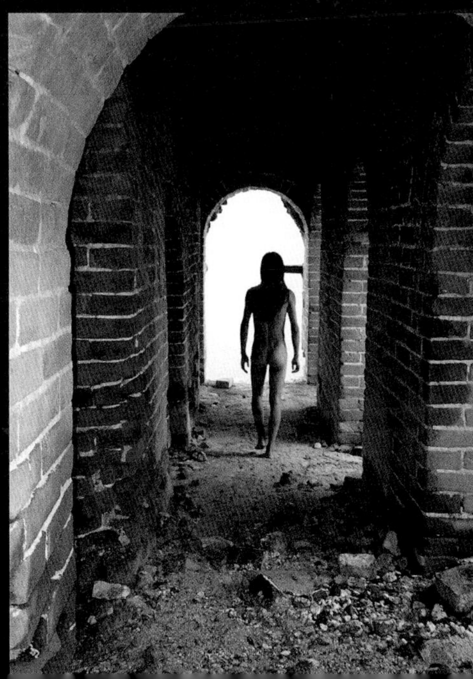
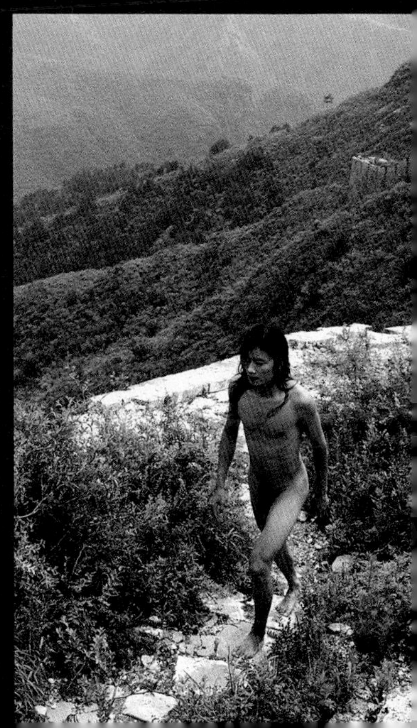

RongRong & Inri

RongRong born 1968, Zhangzhou, Fujian Province
Inri born 1973, Yokosuka, Kanagawa Prefecture, Japan

THIS PAGE, LEFT: RongRong, *No. 20, East Village, Beijing* series, 1994. Gelatin silver print, dimensions variable.

THIS PAGE, RIGHT: Inri, *1999 Tokyo*, 1999. Gelatin silver print, dimensions variable.

FACING PAGE: *In Fujisan, Japan* series, 2001. Gelatin silver print, dimensions variable. Top, from left to right, *No. 7, No. 8, No. 14.* Bottom, *No. 1.*

Yuan fen. There is no English translation for this word, nor a way of describing what the Chinese characters for these words mean in a polished manner—perhaps "fate" is the closest we can get in English. The art of RongRong and Inri, however, can maybe help us understand. The moment you see their work, something almost ecstatic penetrates the skin and enters the heart.

RongRong and Inri met in 1999. They couldn't speak the same language, but they were fascinated with each other's images. Perhaps *yuan fen*—fate—made that happen. When they met, RongRong was already a fundamental figure in contemporary Chinese photography as a member of the experimental art community Beijing East Village, the eye documenting the audacious performances of Zhang Huan, Ma Liuming, and others. Inri, at that time, was a photographer in Tokyo. Her images, focusing on the human form, explored the theme of reason, and how reason gives us as much instability as power, for we cannot control the universe we live in. When the two artists met, their interests moved from a personal introspection to an opening up to the world in order to discover their relationship with the landscape around and to create their own space in it. In the way ancient artists might accompany a painting of a landscape with a poem, RongRong and Inri use their own bodies to add a note of lyricism to the landscapes they discover. Their art is a penetration of nature and a perfect symbiosis, as can be seen in the series *In Fujisan, Japan* (2001).

RongRong and Inri are not performers; there is no audience to watch them. They document their experiences through photographs. Perennially spontaneous, their actions are controlled only by three fundamental conditions: *tianshi* (the moment), *dishou* (the place), and *renhe* (harmony). Sharing a perfect chemistry, simple, sensitive, full of calmness and lyricism, RongRong and Inri hypnotize the viewer.

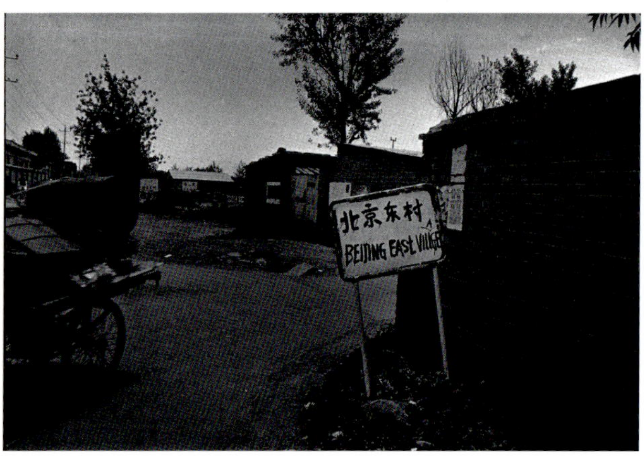

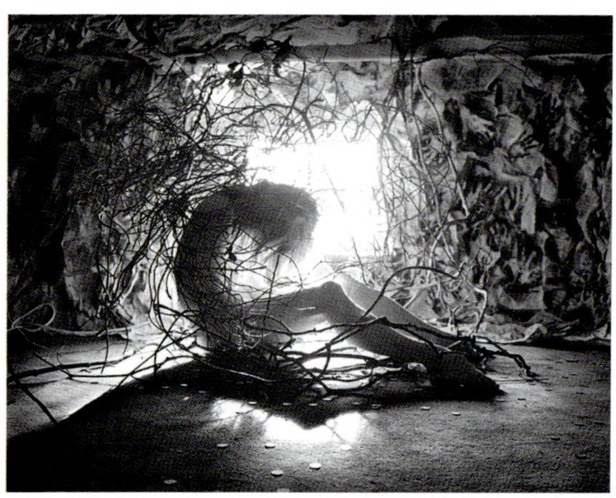

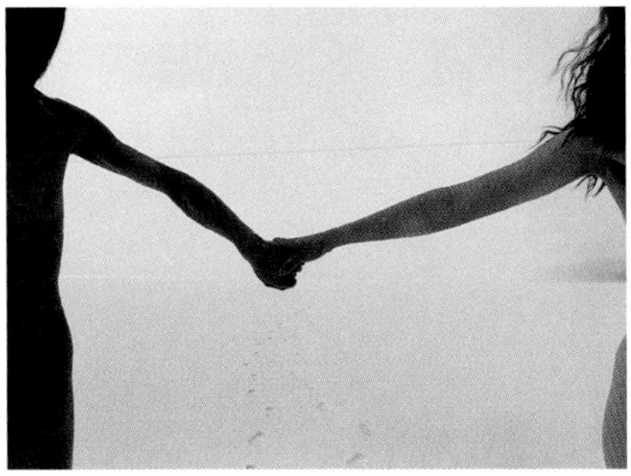
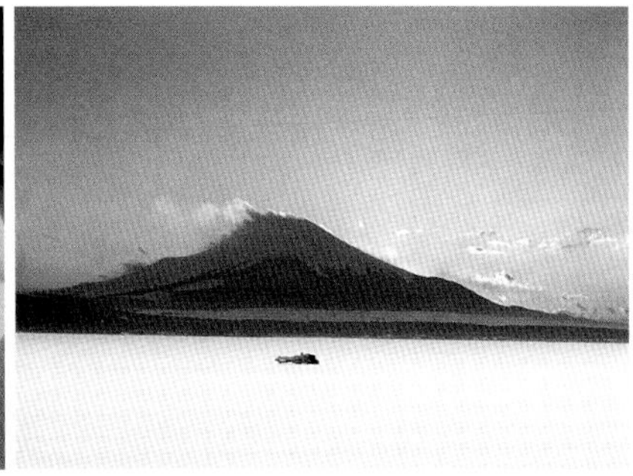
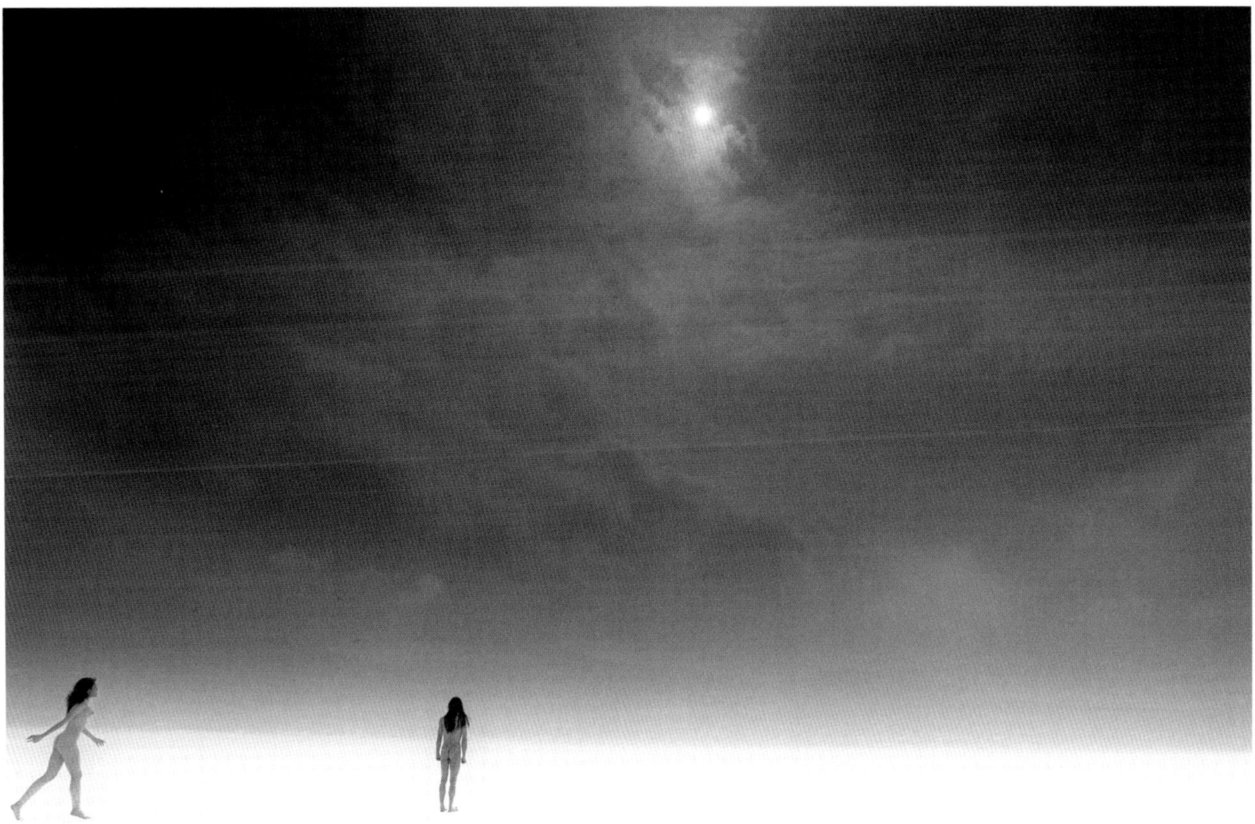

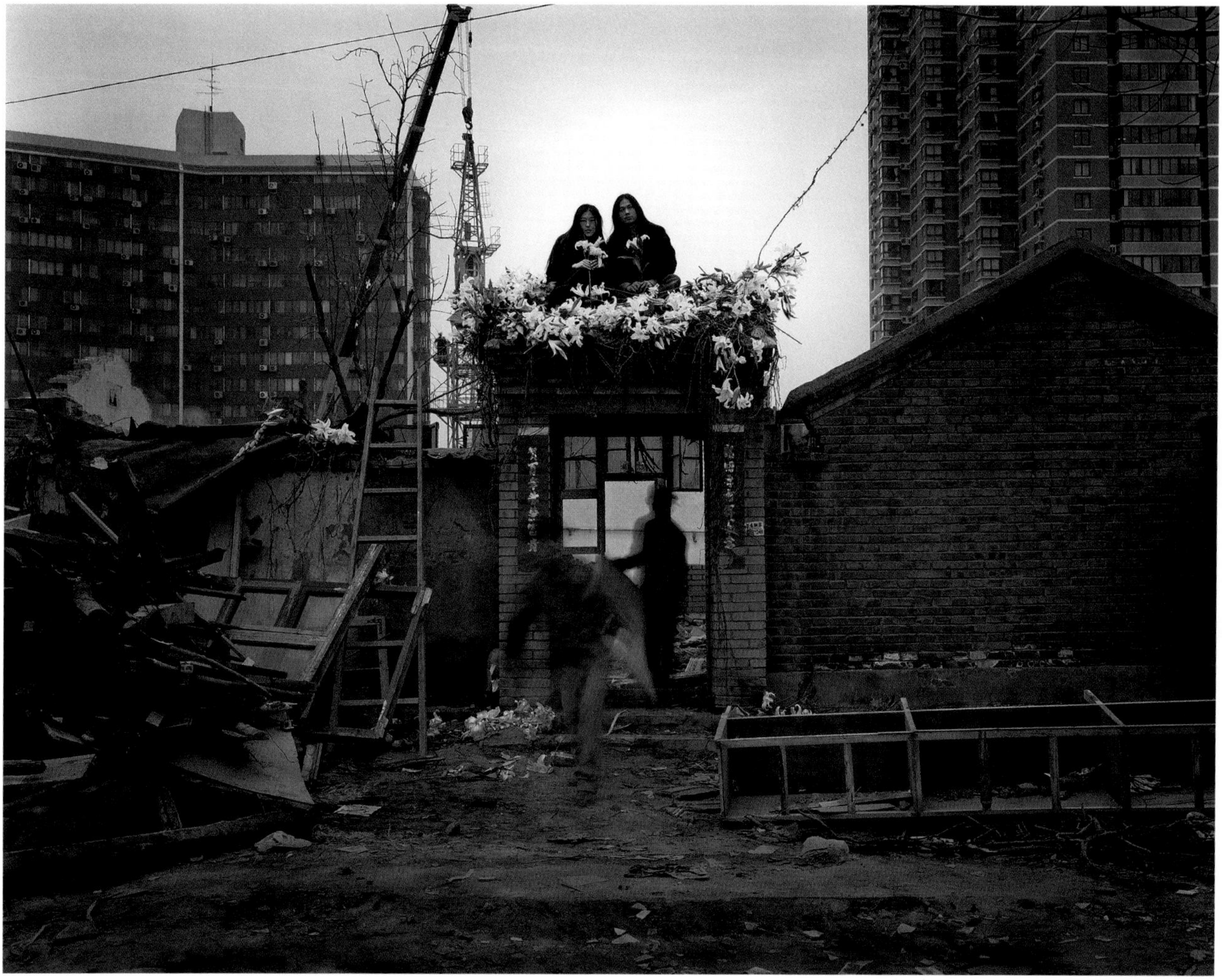

THIS PAGE AND FACING PAGE: *In Liulitun, Beijing* series, 2003. Gelatin silver print, 43 x 59 in. This page, *No. 1*, facing page *No. 2*.

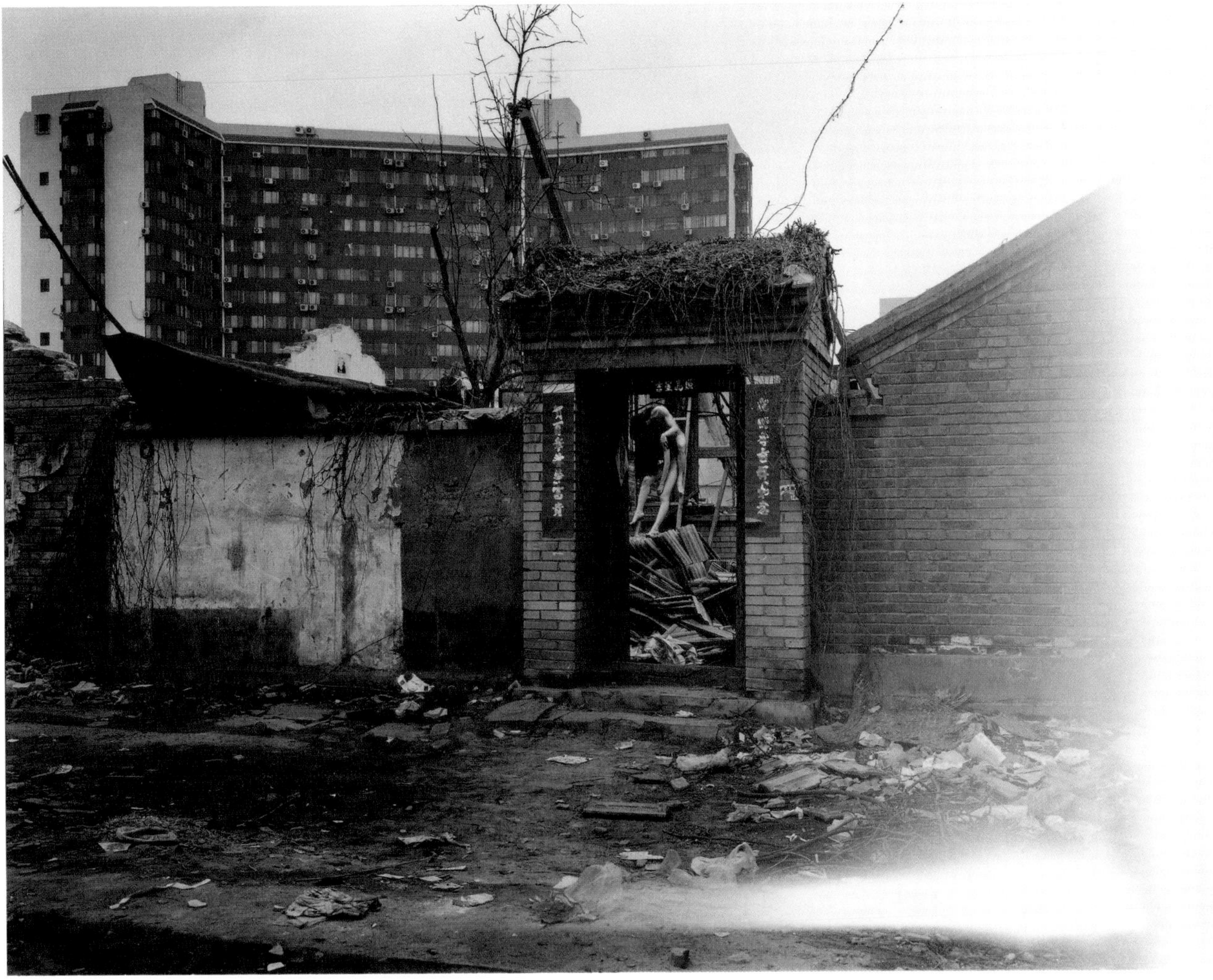

Shi Jinsong

Born 1969, Danyang, Hubei Province

THIS PAGE: *Secret Book of Cool Weapons*, 2002. Various razor-sharp shapes in steel.

FACING PAGE: *Na Zha's Baby Stroller*, 2007. Steel, 39 x 39 x 27½ in.

Shi Jinsong is a great observer of forms and a skillful craftsman when it comes to reproducing them. Mastering different sculptural techniques, he plays with various materials—from branches and leaves to sugar and steel, reproducing shapes and forms that are very common to us. His aim is often to stress the ephemeral nature of these everyday objects, and his choice of materials is always particular to this task. In *Sweet Life* (2001), a series of objects cast in caramel are lined up on a shelf to melt during the course of the exhibition. In the 2007 series *Black and White Bikes* and the installation *Chanting Willow Tree*, he shows a move toward natural materials to express his perception of the impermanency of things.

Shi's work is also a reflection on the exertion of control in contemporary society, on the relationships between state and institutions and the individual. In his work, everyday objects become not just material possessions but also deadly weapons; the series *Secret Book of Cool Weapons* (2002) is a collection of weapons that resemble familiar corporate logos, showing how material possessions can become powerful and harmful tools that define our lives. The theme is repeated in the *Office Equipment* series (2004): razor-sharp sculptures become the visual metaphor through which office workers are depicted as victims of an authoritarian power.

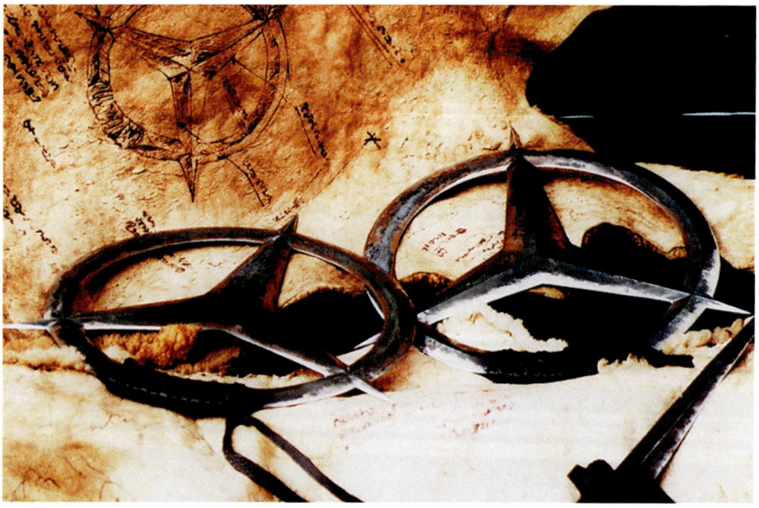

Shi's pieces show influences from Zen Buddhism, Taoism, and Chinese mythology. In the series *Baby Boutique* (2005), Shi presents consumer products for babies—a life-size stroller, cradle, and walker are assembled in stainless steel in an aggressive language of points and bladelike sharp curves. Here, Shi is initiating a dialogue between mythic Chinese culture and forms of modern consumerism: Na Zha is a deity of Chinese folklore, a child warrior celebrated for his supernatural powers, bravery, and strategy on the battlefield. Shi believes that Na Zha is "created from the desires of adults, combining Chinese and Western legends, and based on the value structures of the adult world." The works in this series generate contradictory feelings in the viewer, who is perversely attracted by the beauty of the dangerous blades and spikes.

Shi is also concerned with forms of representation, and is obsessed with the illusion of precision dictated by the design process and the blueprint, both of which draw on the accuracy of mathematical calculation. He believes that these blueprints reflect our psychological reality, and all the objects he creates are accompanied by intricate plans and drawings.

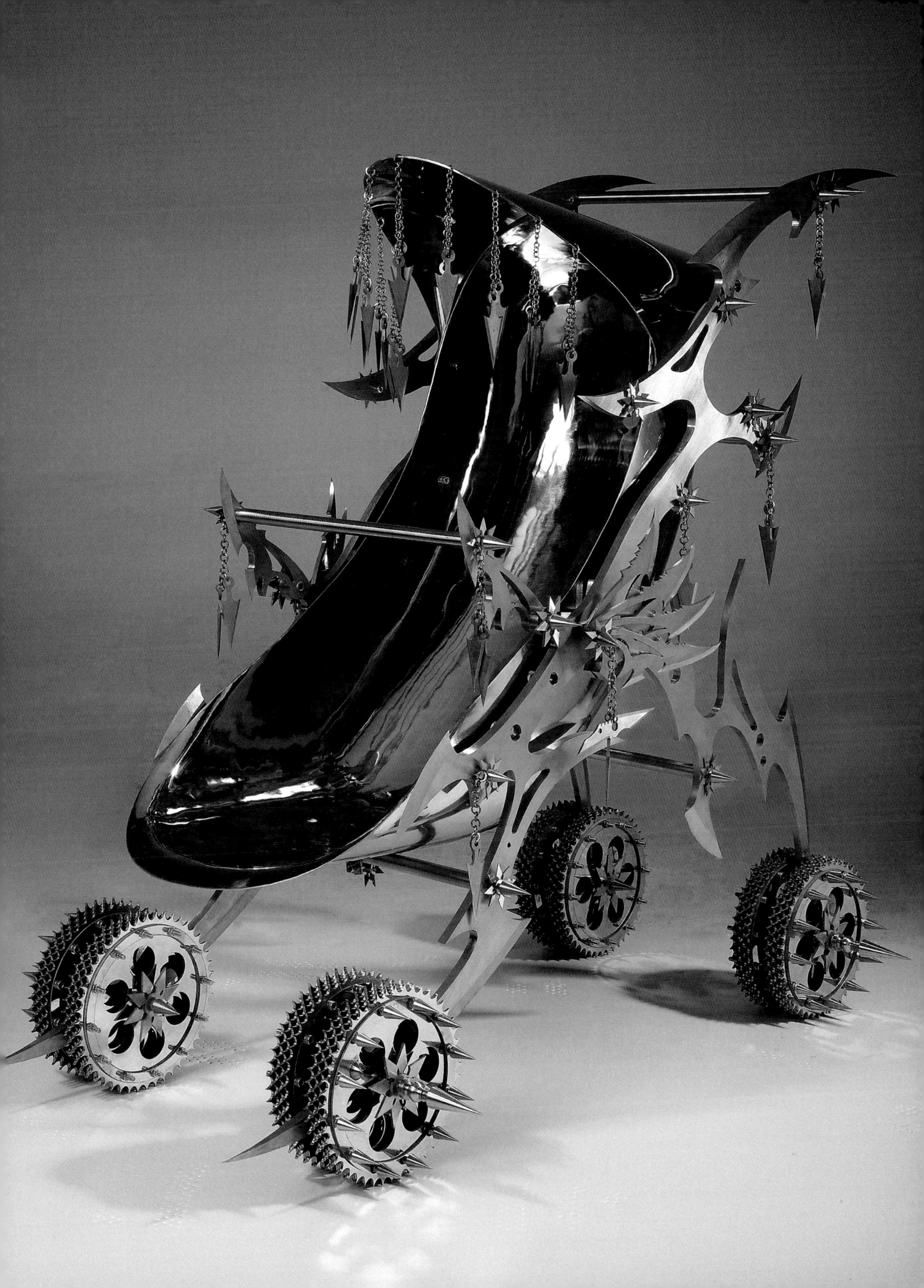

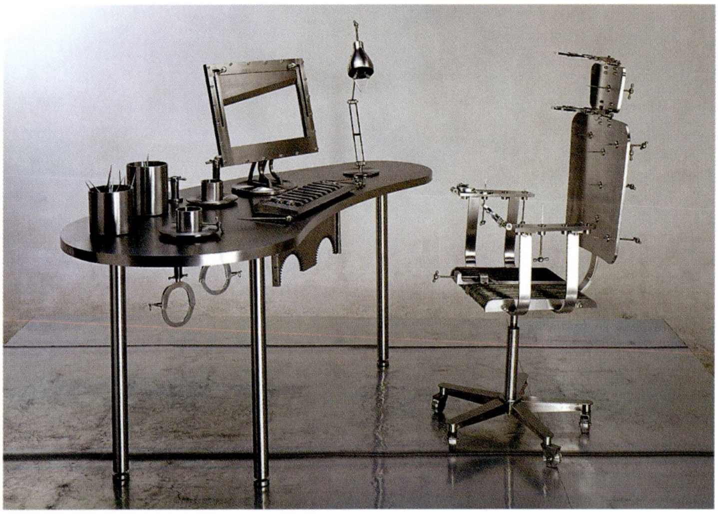

THIS PAGE, TOP: *Torture Instrument No. 1*, 2004. Steel. Variable dimensions.

THIS PAGE, BOTTOM: *Chanting Willow Tree*, 2007. Wood and steel screws, 134 x 94½ x 102 in.; 110 x 86½ x 98½ in.; 126 x 79 x 94½ in.

FACING PAGE: *White Bike*, 2007. Wood, plastic leaves, needles and threads, motorbike, 92½ x 43 x 68 in.

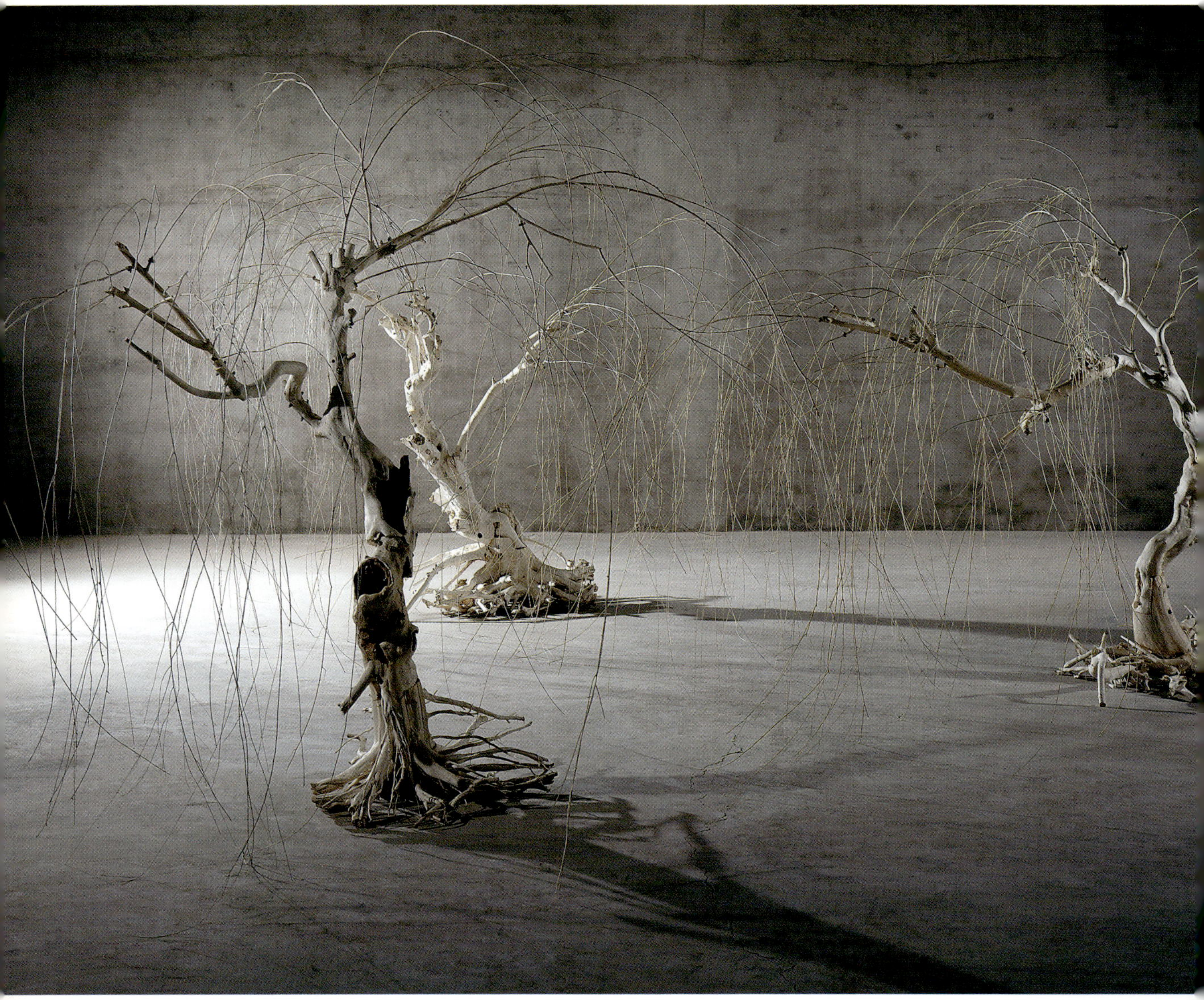

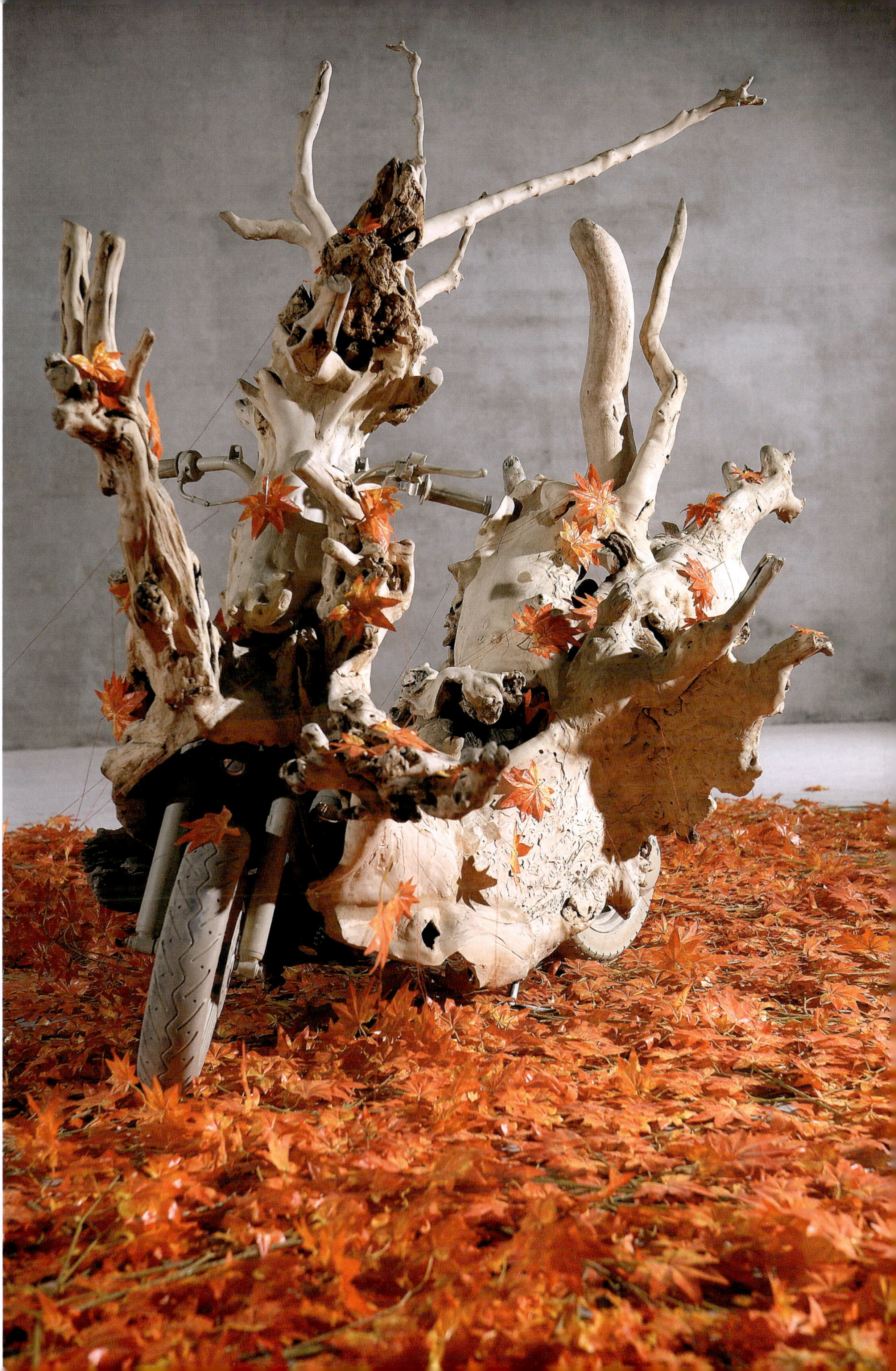

Song Dong

Born 1966, Beijing

THIS PAGE: *Touching My Father*, 1997–2000. Stills from video of performance.

FACING PAGE: *Breathing*, 1996. Photographs of performance, each 47 x 71 in.

Dealing with issues of identity and ephemerality, Song Dong is famous for his video and performance pieces. Song believes, in fact, that the recording of a process is more important than the performance itself because the recording is what will remain forever. In the video *Touching My Father* (1997), the artist projects an image of his hand onto an image of his father as if he is caressing his father's body, while in *Father and Son* (1998), his own image is superimposed onto his father, raising questions of identity. In the celebrated performances *Broken Mirrors* (1999) and *Burned Mirror* (2001), Song records the idea of destruction, of fragmentation, showing how an image viewed through a mirror is perceived as artificial, but when the mirror breaks, the image has a more powerful reality.

In an ongoing project *Writing Diary with Water* (1995–) Song uses a brush and water to write daily diary entries on a particular block of stone, fully aware of the fact that no one will ever read his writing and his thoughts will remain secret. Playing with the dichotomy of absence and presence, the water diary has become a fundamental part of the artist's life and art.

Often using references to traditional Chinese idioms to title his works—for example, *Wangyan yuchuan* (Longing), *Leng kaishui* (Cold Boiled Water), *Haqi* (Breathing)—Song shows his sensitivity to hidden forms: these titles are nearly impossible to translate idiomatically into other languages because they are so peculiar that they can only be fully understood in their original form. Song becomes the secret producer whose work is like a "blind spot" in contemporary art, in the words of curator Leng Lin. In the performance *Breathing* (1996), Song, in a sort of feat of self-endurance, lies on the sidewalk in two different locations in Beijing and breathes onto the ground for forty minutes. Experiencing the relationship between man and environment in an almost ritualistic way, he obtains two different results in two different locations. In Tiananmen Square a thin layer of ice is formed beneath his mouth that melts as soon as he leaves; at Lake Houhai nothing changes at all.

Waste Not (2005) was a project carried out by Song with his mother, addressing the emotional ties of family relationships. By transporting their old house and all its contents to the exhibition space, they revived their attachment to the past and to deeply rooted family traditions. The title *Waste Not* refers to a time, not long ago, when shortages of goods meant never throwing anything away.

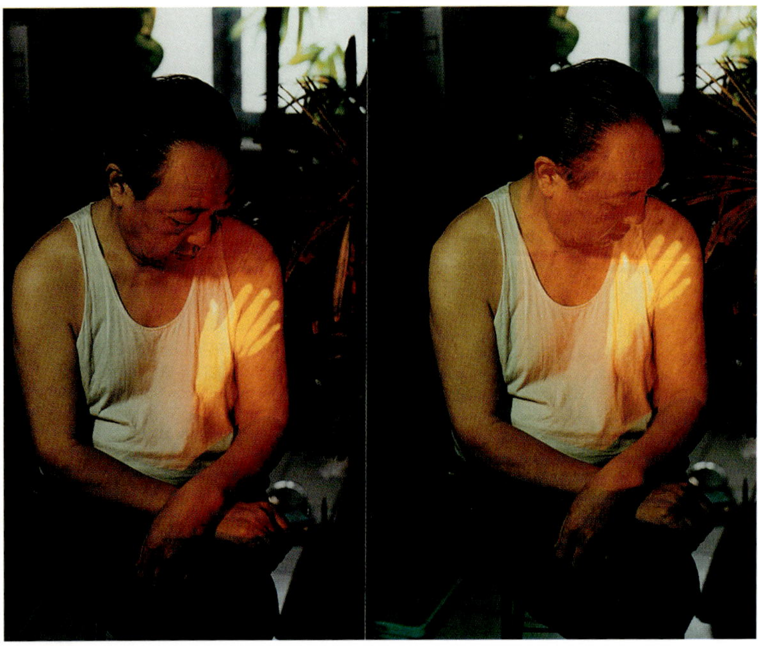

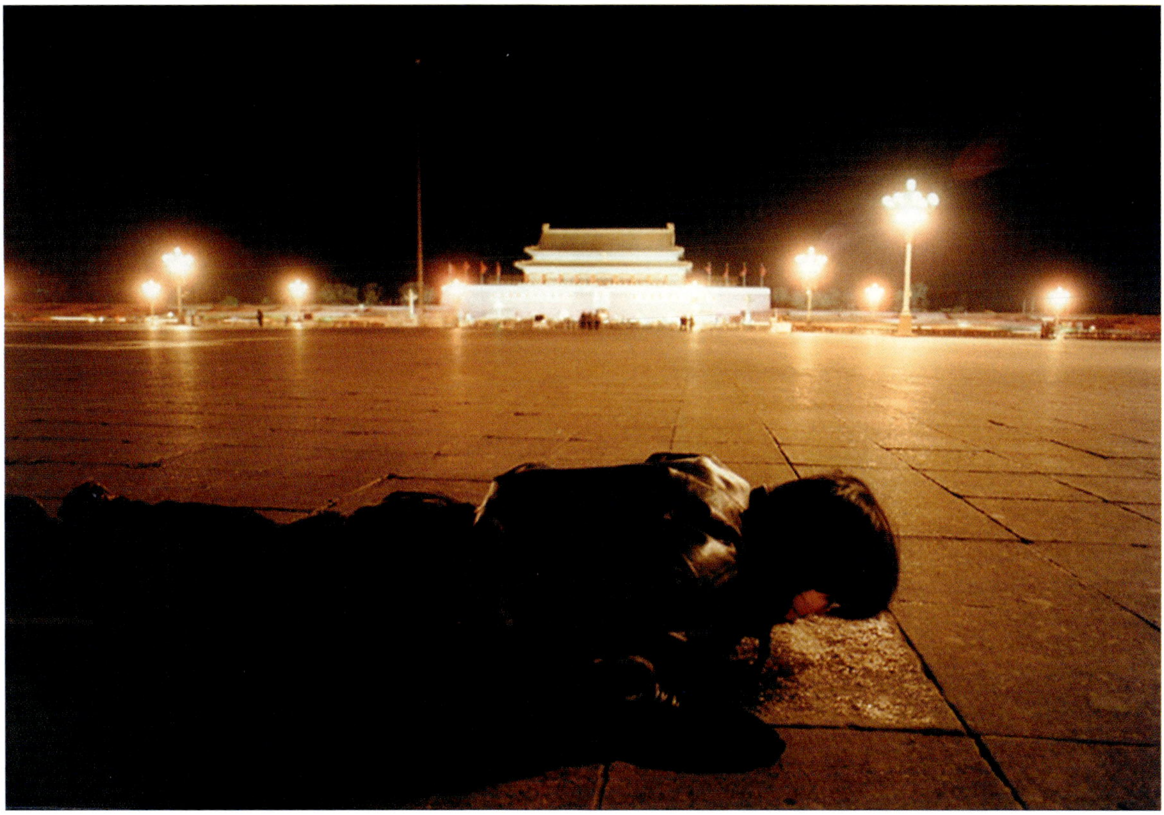

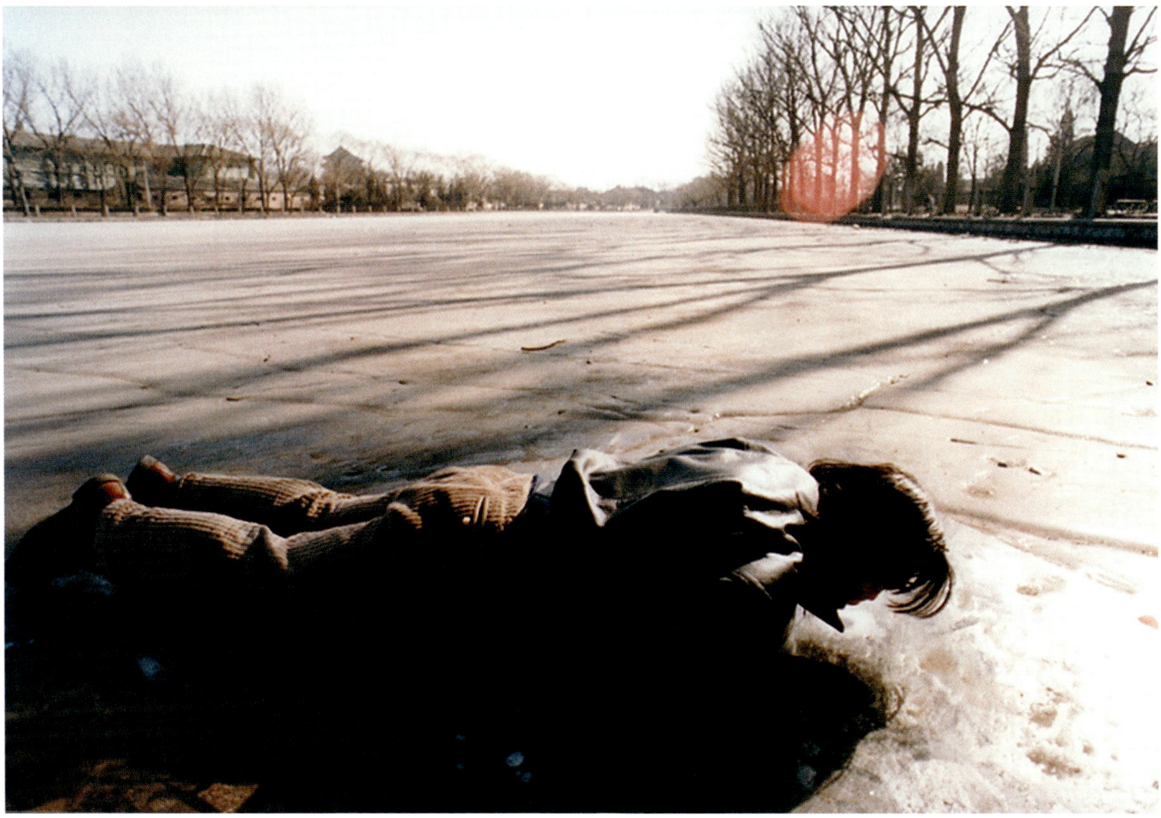

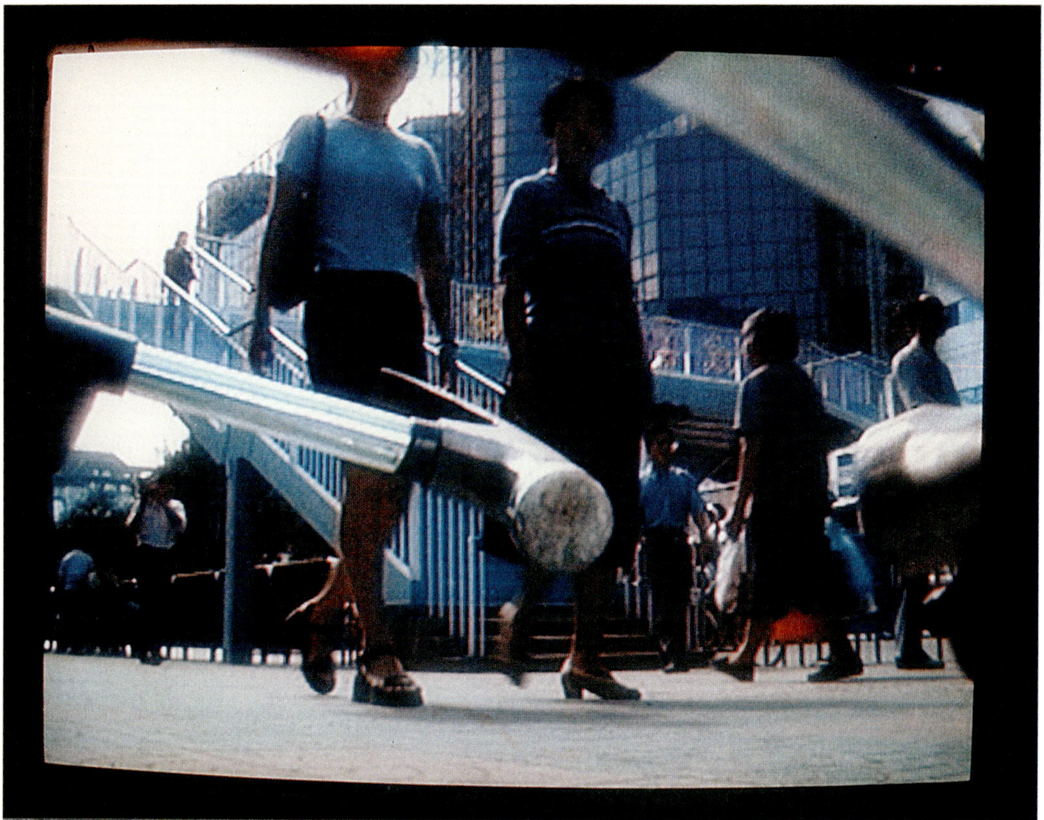

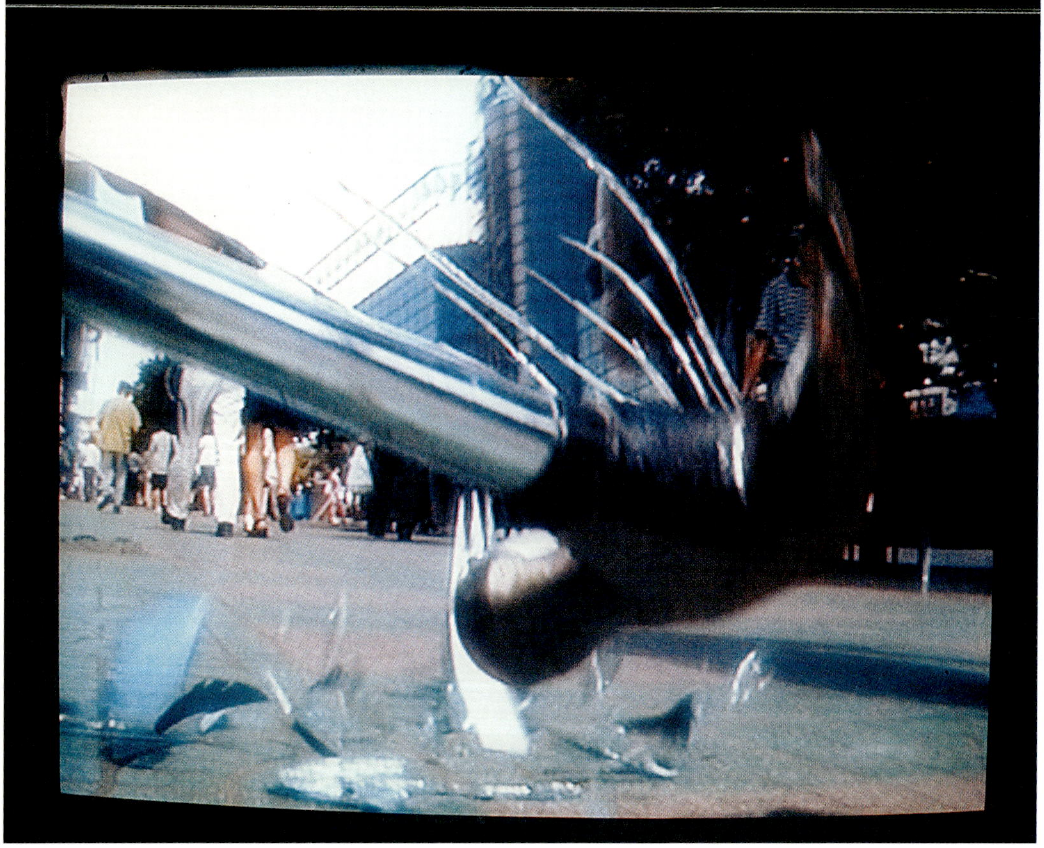

FACING PAGE: *Broken Mirror*, 1999. Stills from video.

THIS PAGE, TOP AND BOTTOM: *Waste Not*, 2005. Installation view, BTAP Gallery, Beijing.

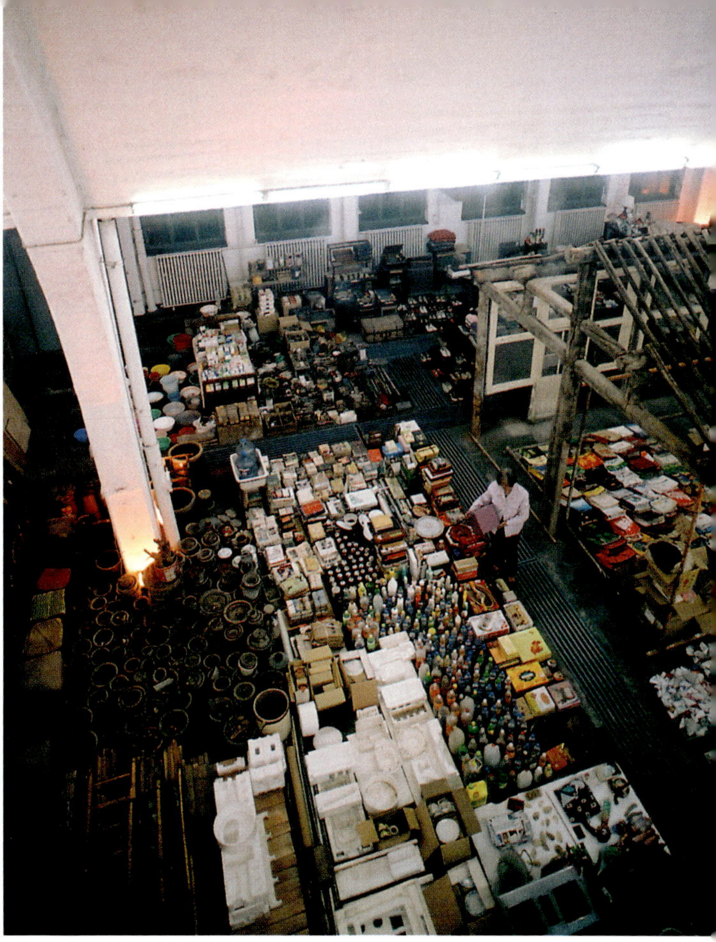

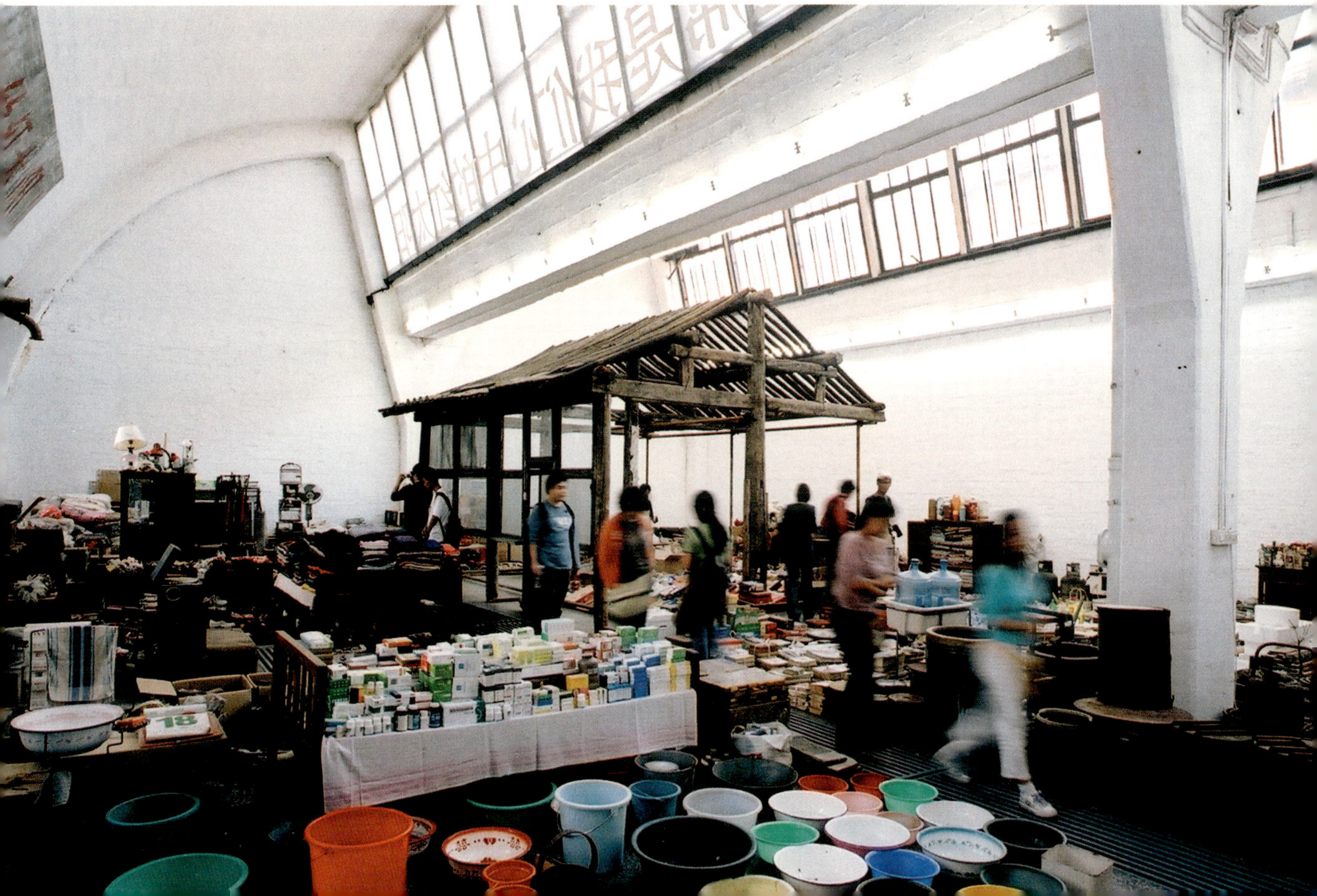

Wang Guangyi

Born 1957, Harbin, Heilongjiang Province

THIS PAGE: *Eternal Halo No. 1*, 2003. Oil on canvas, 78½ x 118 in.

FACING PAGE, TOP: *Great Criticism—Coca Cola*, 1993. Oil on canvas, 78½ x 78½ in.

FACING PAGE, BOTTOM: *Frozen North Pole*, 1985. Oil on canvas, 39 x 59 in.

OVERLEAF: *The Materialist*, 2003–2005. Iron. Each figure 78½ x 47 x 31½ in.

In a country where even the weather is controlled—as shown by the quest of Beijing's Office of Weather Manipulation to improve the city's environmental conditions for the 2008 Olympic Games—control of the population and of the system is predictable. A similar sense of hegemony and control, once the preserve of the Communist regime, is evidently still present in today's consumerist society. Wang Guangyi, founder of the Northern Artists Group in the 1980s—a group of artists openly antagonistic to "official" culture—and considered by many to be the father of the Chinese art movement known as Political Pop, is a keen observer of Chinese society as it enters a "fast-forward" phase of change.

Wang's artistic discourse is centered around the affinities between capitalism and socialism, both of which can be described as ideologies that exert control over the population by using popularized images and catchwords to create a community—of consumers in the first case and of citizens in the latter. In contemporary society, the difference between these two ideologies seems to dissolve, thus their visual regimes can be easily juxtaposed.

Growing up during the Cultural Revolution had an undeniable effect on Wang's art. When he was a schoolboy, every pupil was asked to come up with some propaganda drawings. Forced into an awareness of the art of the Communist regime that surrounded him, Wang was deeply impressed, and this was the beginning of his particular interest in the use of symbols.

Wang's early works, in the mid-1980s, have humanistic traits and quietly optimistic messages in surreal settings. The abstract human figures in the painting *Frozen North Pole* (1985), for example, appear to be harmoniously moving on and heading to a possibly auspicious future. Toward the end of the eighties Wang abruptly changed to the nonhumanistic style that made him famous. Demystifying political icons, he popularizes them, depriving them of their original power with the use of irony and mockery. His juxtaposition of the two clashing ideologies of consumerism and socialism suggests confrontation, and skillfully indicates the thorny points of confluence between China's Maoist past and its current booming growth.

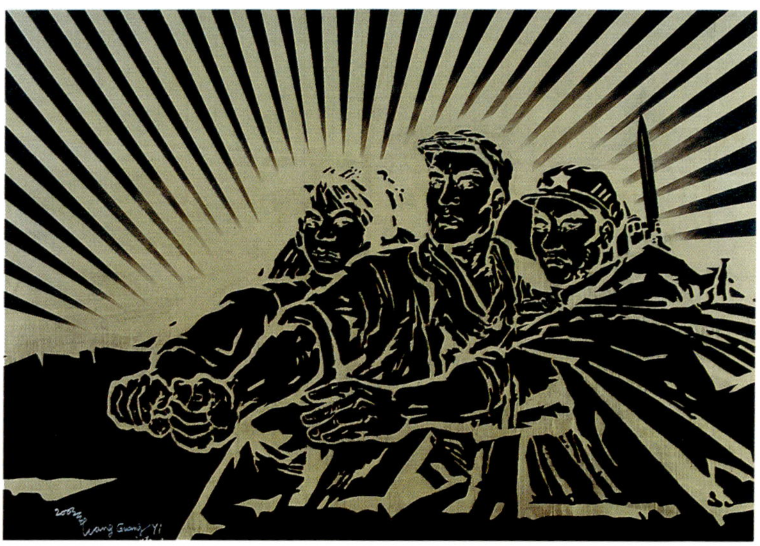

Recently Wang's paintings appear deprived of brand names; *Eternal Halo* (2003) has muted color, and darker images. The artist seems to be moving toward a more personal level in his expression, as though he desires to return to the essence of things.

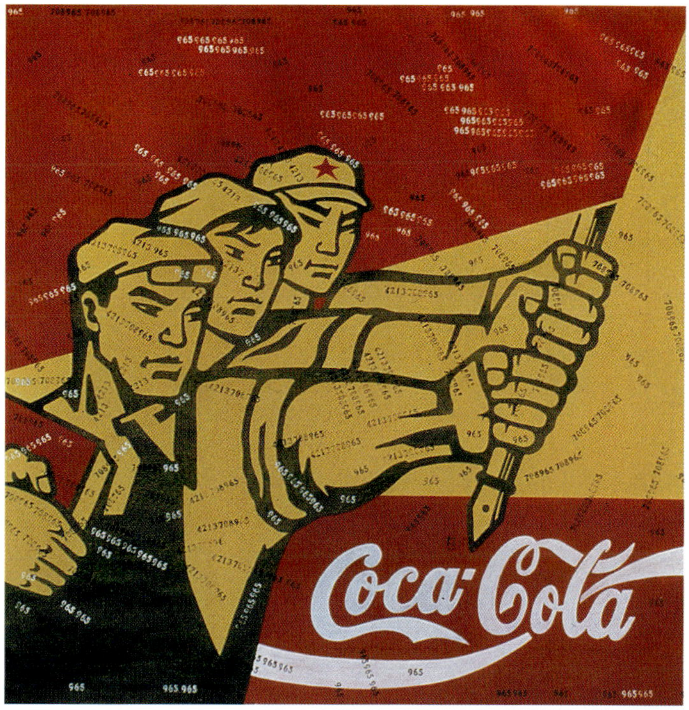
Coca-Cola

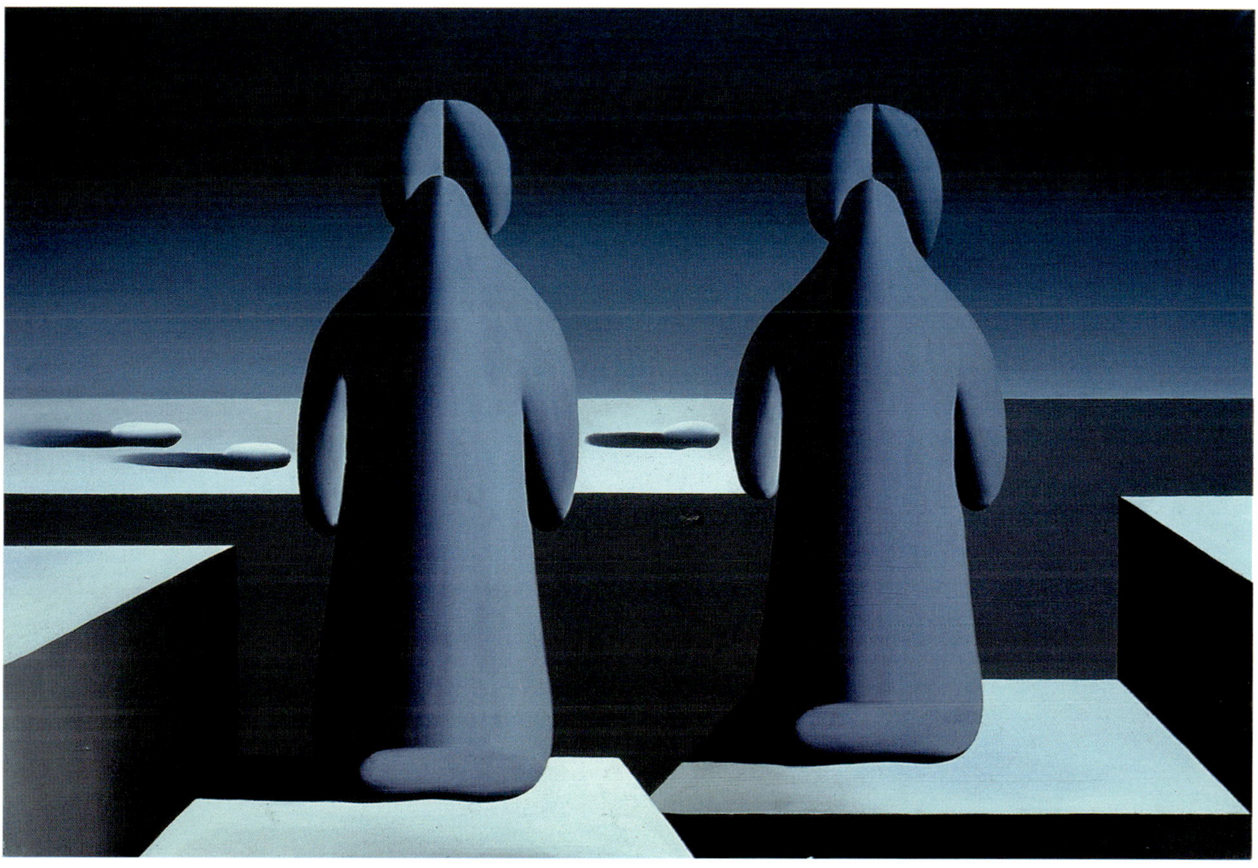

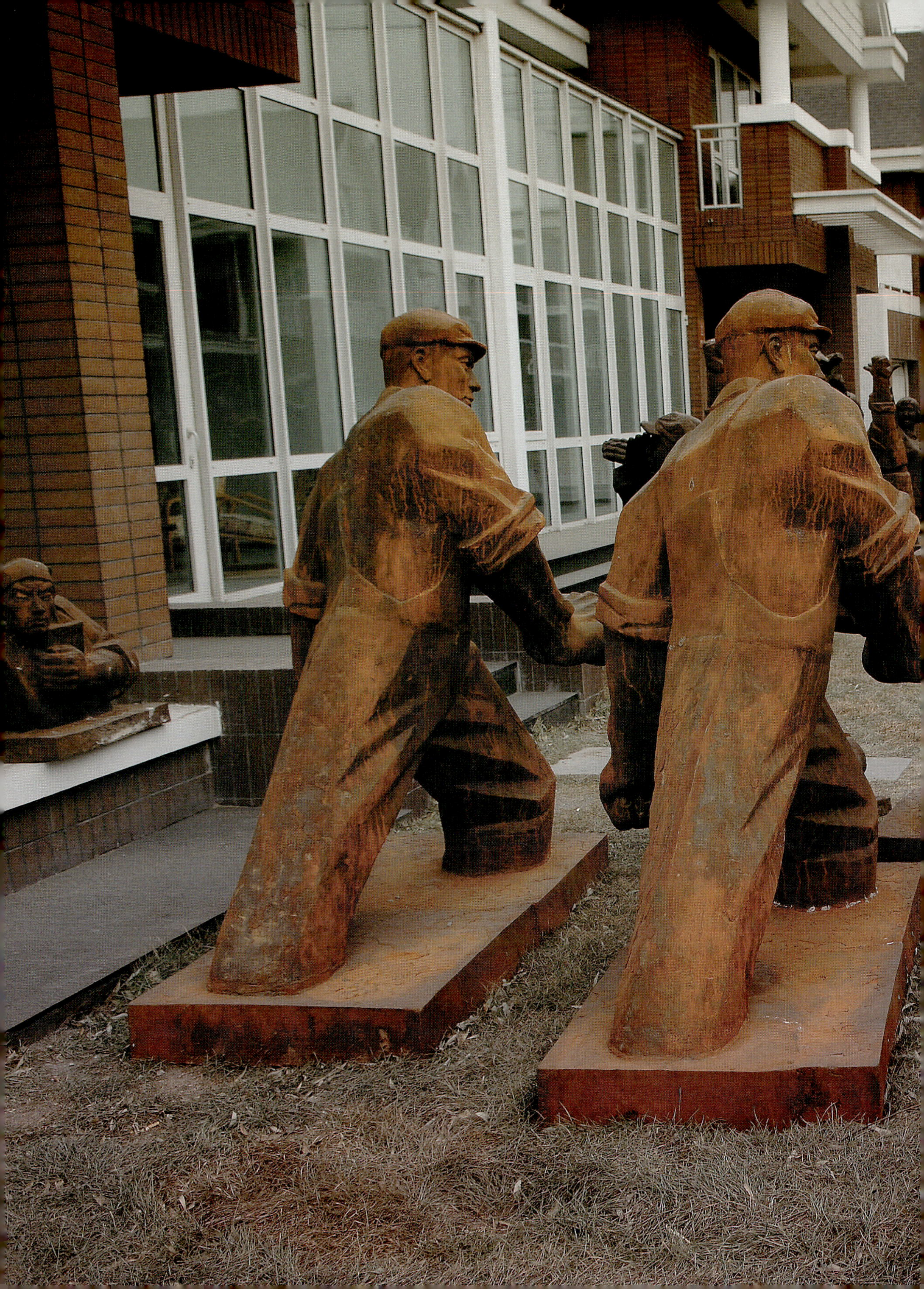

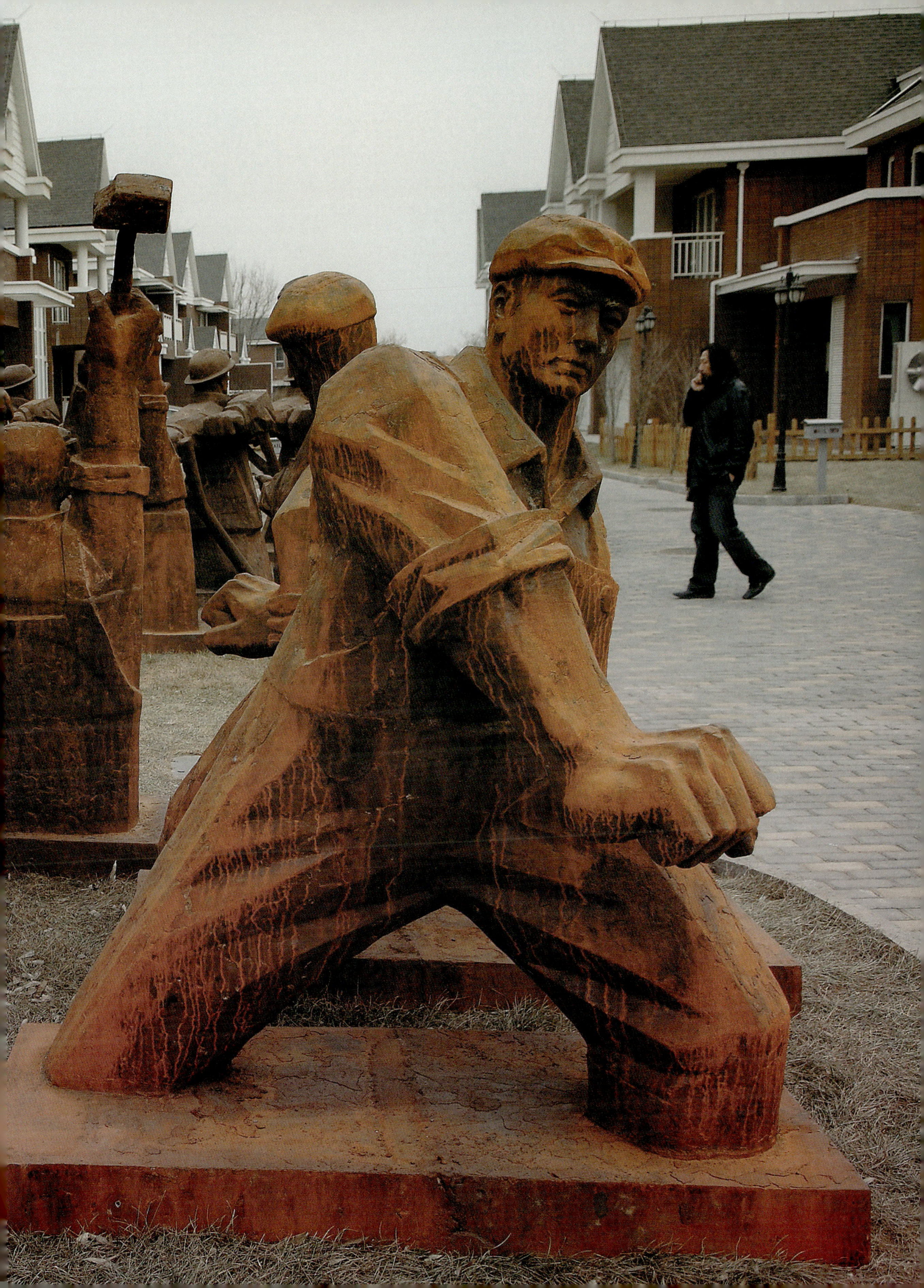

Wang Jianwei

Born 1958, Sichuan Province

Artist and theater director Wang Jianwei grew up during the Cultural Revolution, and managed to train himself in painting while working alongside the peasants as a "young intellectual," an experience that gave him a humanistic approach to life.

Influenced by Sartre, Camus, and Borges, Wang refers to his art as a "form of experimental knowledge." In 1995 he started working in film, and he has documented social issues in pieces such as *Living Elsewhere* (1999), about itinerant laborers, and created theater-related works such as *Screens-Paravent* (2000), a complex multimedia theater piece based on a famous painting from the Tang dynasty.

The video piece *Spider 1* (2004), set in the offices of an Internet company in Beijing, is an exploration of the overlap between an imaginary and a real space, and the relationship between contemporary art and society. Differing from *Spider 2* (2005), where family members interact in common spaces such as living room, kitchen, and bedroom, the four actors in *Spider 1* embody different aspects of history, culture, and society in four different areas of a company—meeting room, general office, manager's office, and corridor—thus creating new relationships in the shifting and overlapping of spaces and behaviors.

Dodge (2006) uses architectural installations, human prototypes, and video to create conventional and imaginary landscapes that offer an uncertain yet thought-provoking view of the world.

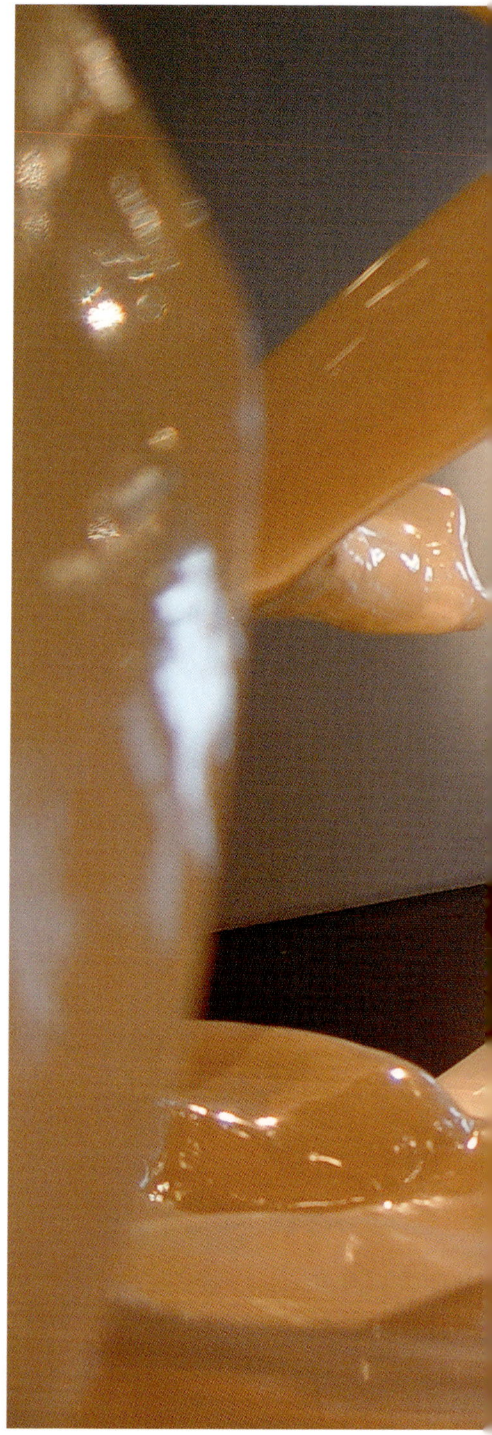

Dodge, 2006. Installation: sculpture, photography, video.

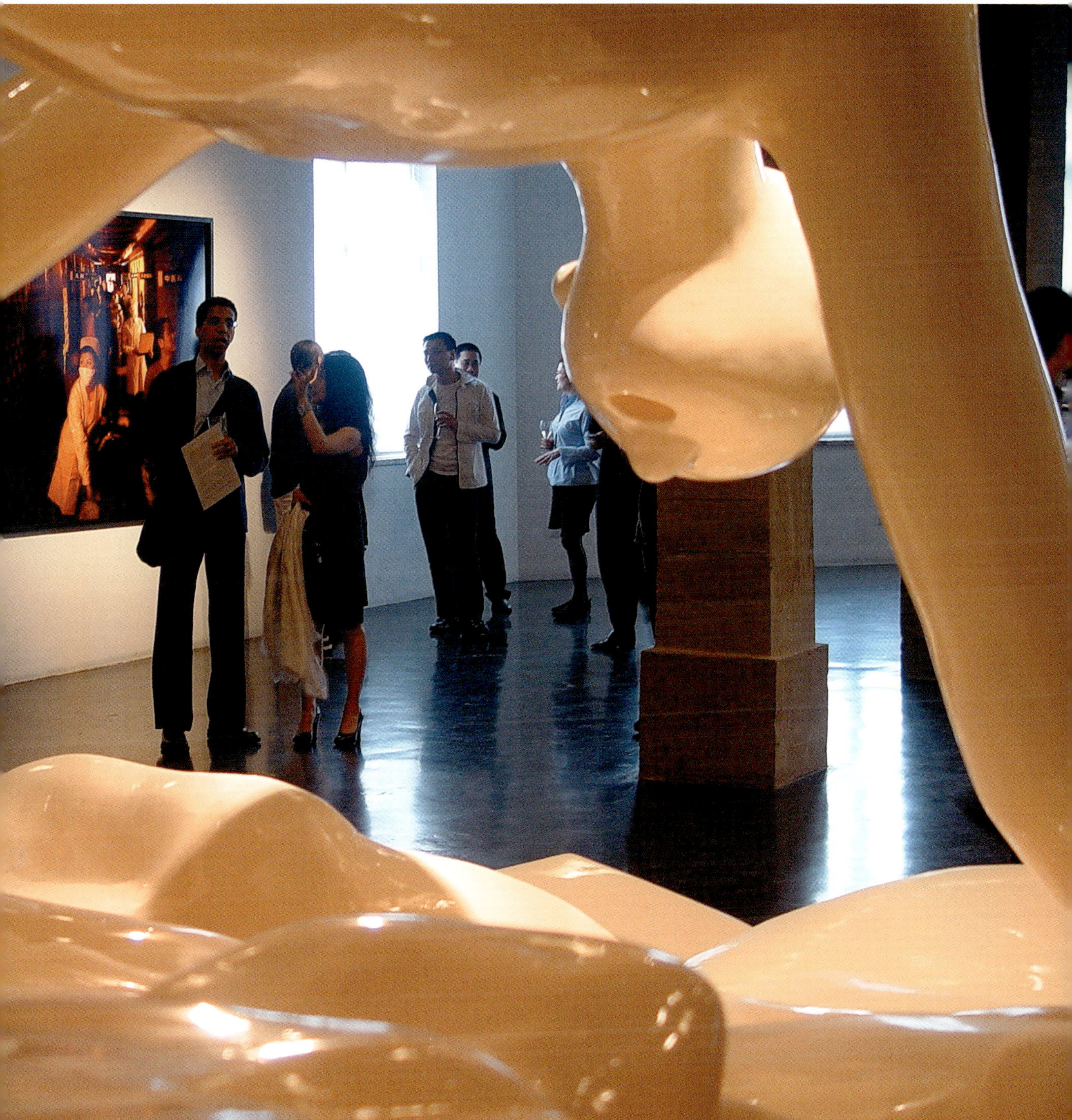

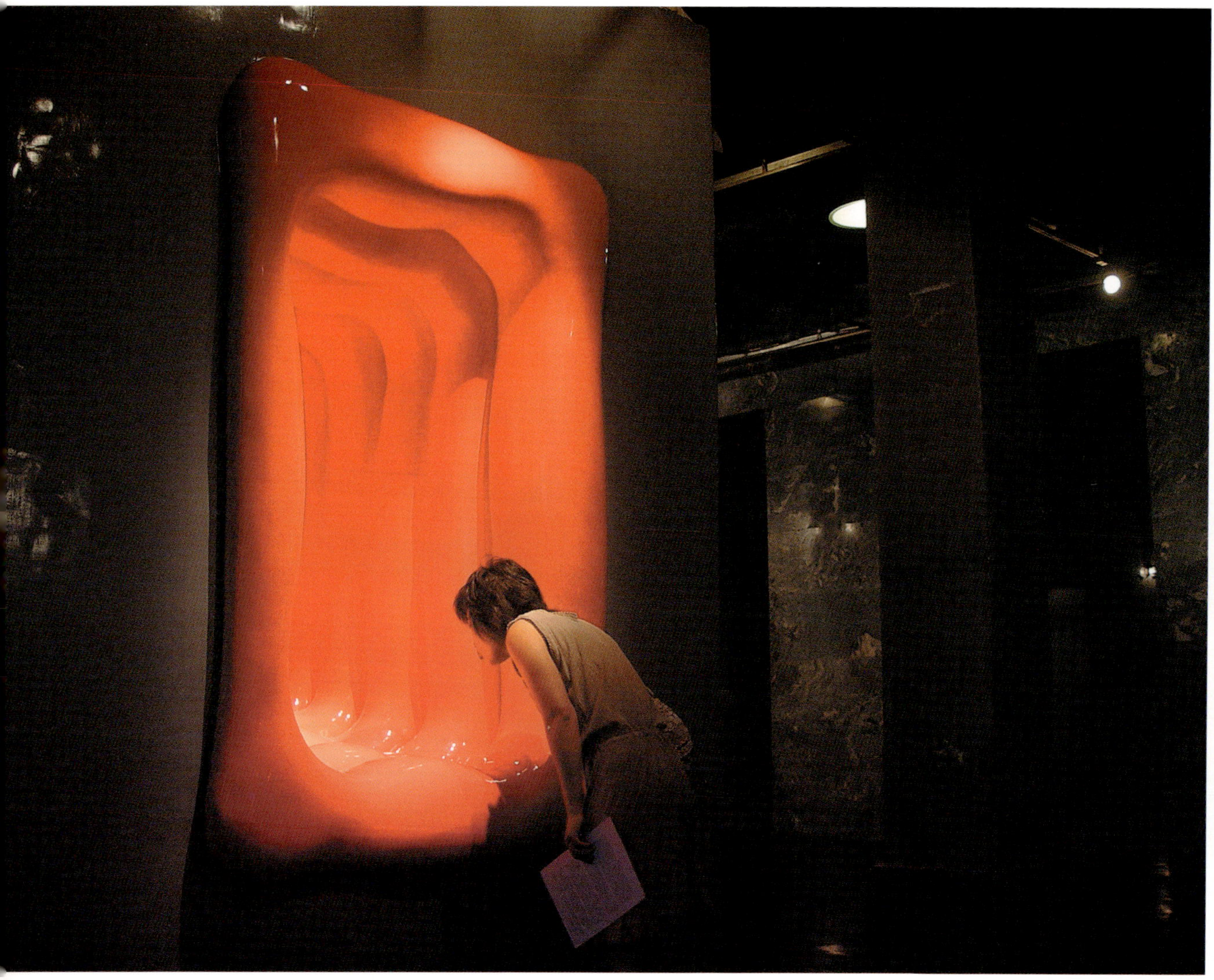

THIS PAGE: *Dodge*, 2006. Installation: sculpture, photography, video.
FACING PAGE: *Spider 2*, 2005. Stills from video.

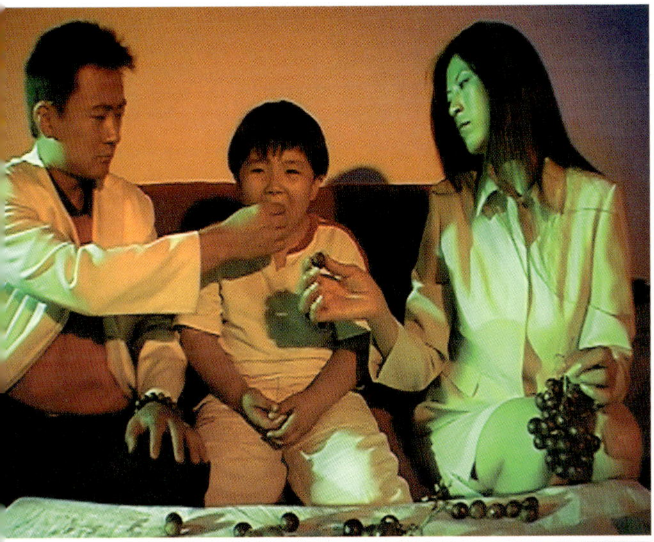
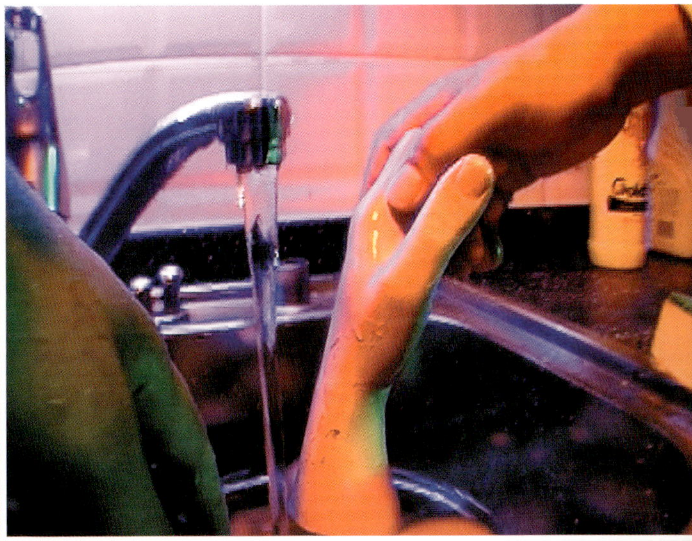
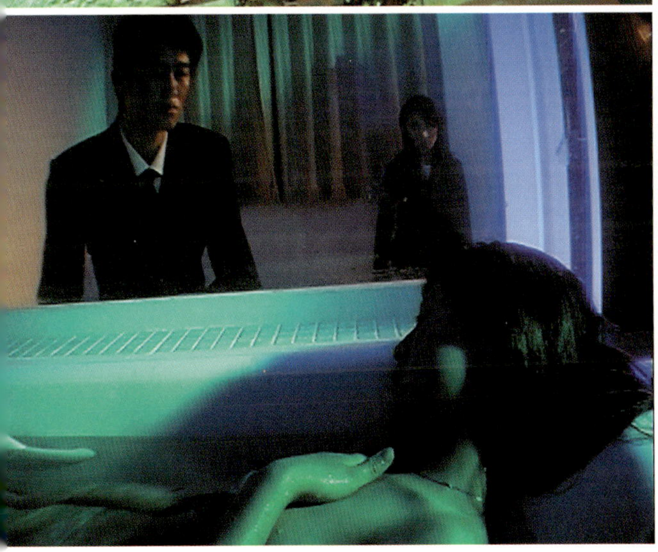
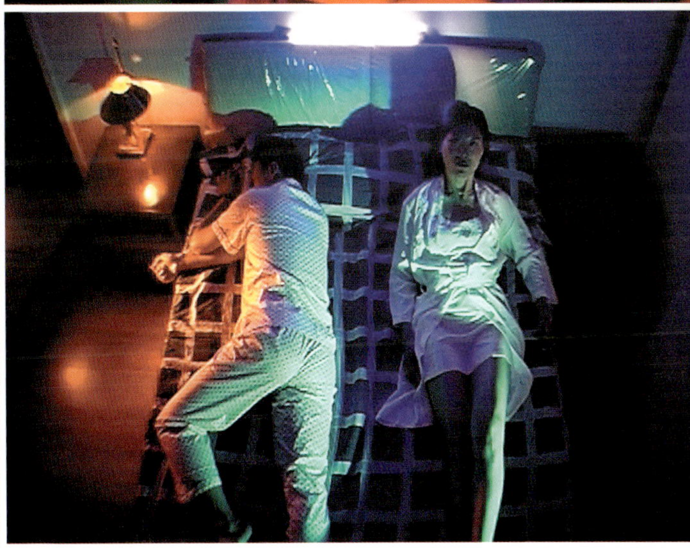

Wang Xingwei

Born 1969, Shenyang, Liaoning Province

THIS PAGE: *Untitled (Penguin and Hole)*, 2004. Oil on corrugated board, 37½ x 83 in.

FACING PAGE: *HELLOHOWMUCH*, 2001. Acrylic on canvas, 109 x 129 in.

Wang Xingwei is a master director, moving his characters around against a backdrop of colorful and surreal settings. Wang's chameleonic production, as many curators like to define it, is gradually gaining recognition at home and abroad. Wang is continuously reinventing himself, his discourse, and his techniques—his use of corrugated board for paintings such as *Untitled (Penguin and Hole)* (2004) an indication of his eagerness to experiment—but his work is distinguished by recurrent characters such as the hostess, the nurse, the penguin, and the sailor. His authenticity lies in the language he uses: references to political and social questions, autobiographical hints, revisions of collective and personal history, and allusions to the history of Western and Chinese art. *Death of Panda* (2004) alludes to Giotto's *The Lamentation*, and *The Legend of the White Snake* (2006) is inspired by the eponymous classical Chinese novel.

In paintings such as *Mein Kampf—Wang Xingwei in 1936* (1996), the yellow-shirted character represents the artist himself. In later works, his characters take on a stronger symbolism. The nurse's face and the hostess's face are strikingly similar, as are the faces of the sailor and the golfer; only their clothes and the roles they play are different. They are like fragments of the artist's inner life, conveying a sense of solitude tinged with humor, and are often portrayed in problematic and absurd circumstances. In *Hellohowmuch* (2001), the hostess stands rigid beside a sofa, in the foreground of a Las Vegas-style nightscape, as though presenting a TV shopping show. Her gaze conveys desolation, and silent acceptance of a state she wouldn't have chosen herself.

In Wang's 2007 solo exhibition Large Rowboat, the figures inhabiting his paintings were cartoonlike sketches. *Untitled (Woman Pulling a Man)* (2006) compares the contemporary couple's relationship to playing golf in the desert.

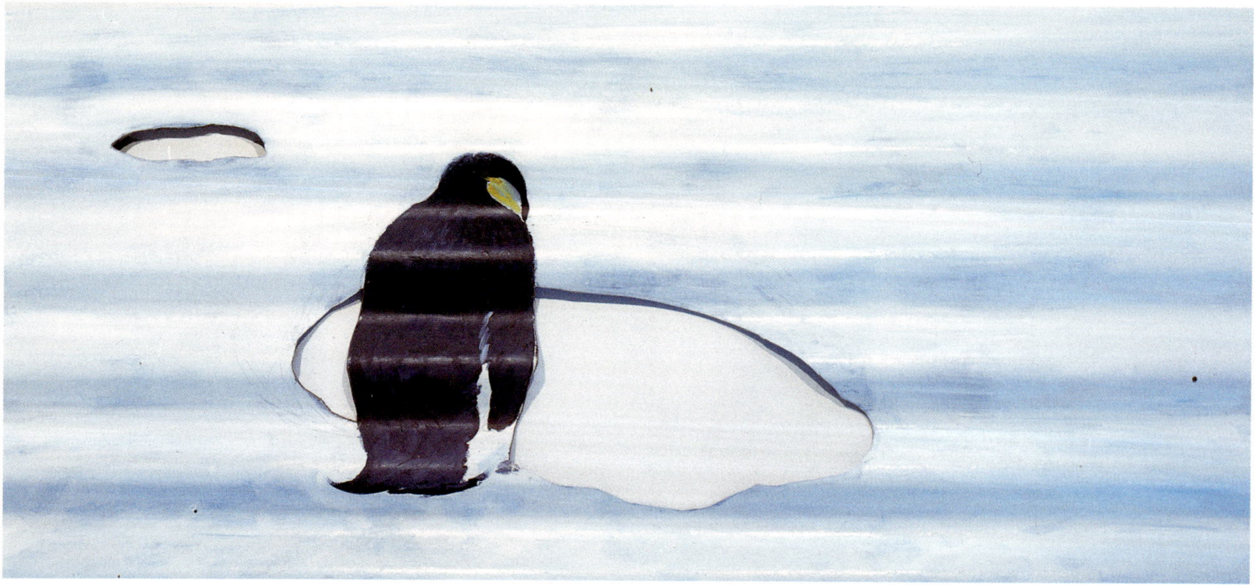

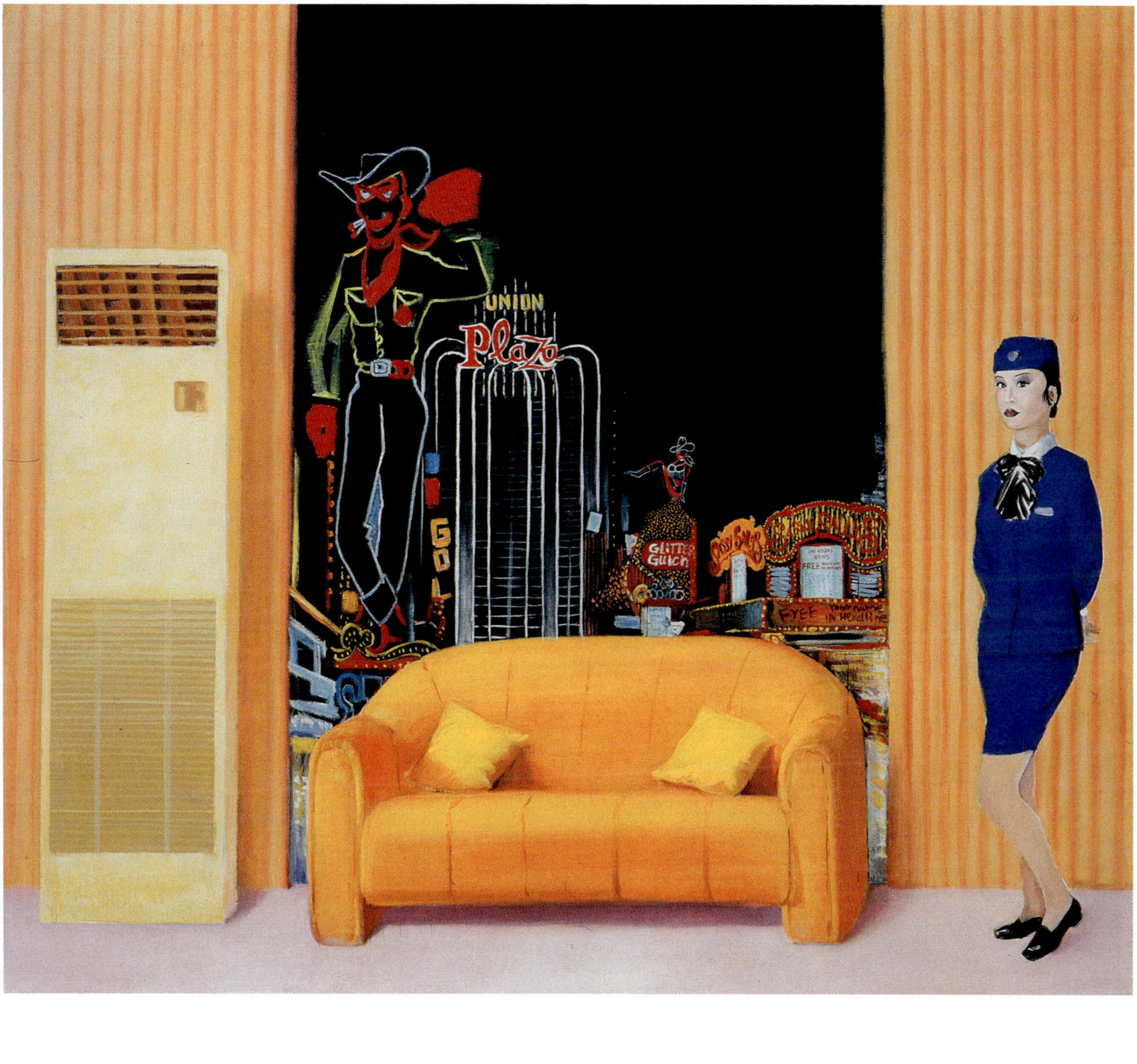
UNION
Plaza
GLITTER GULCH

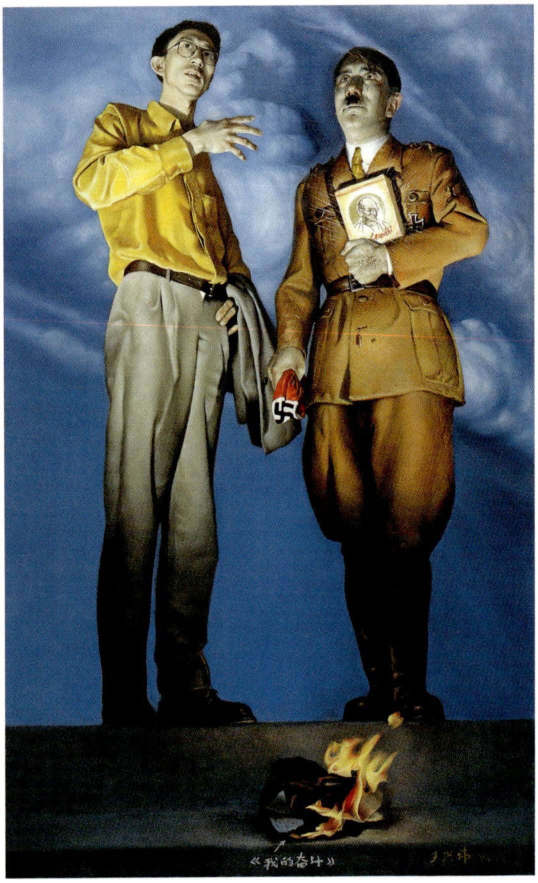

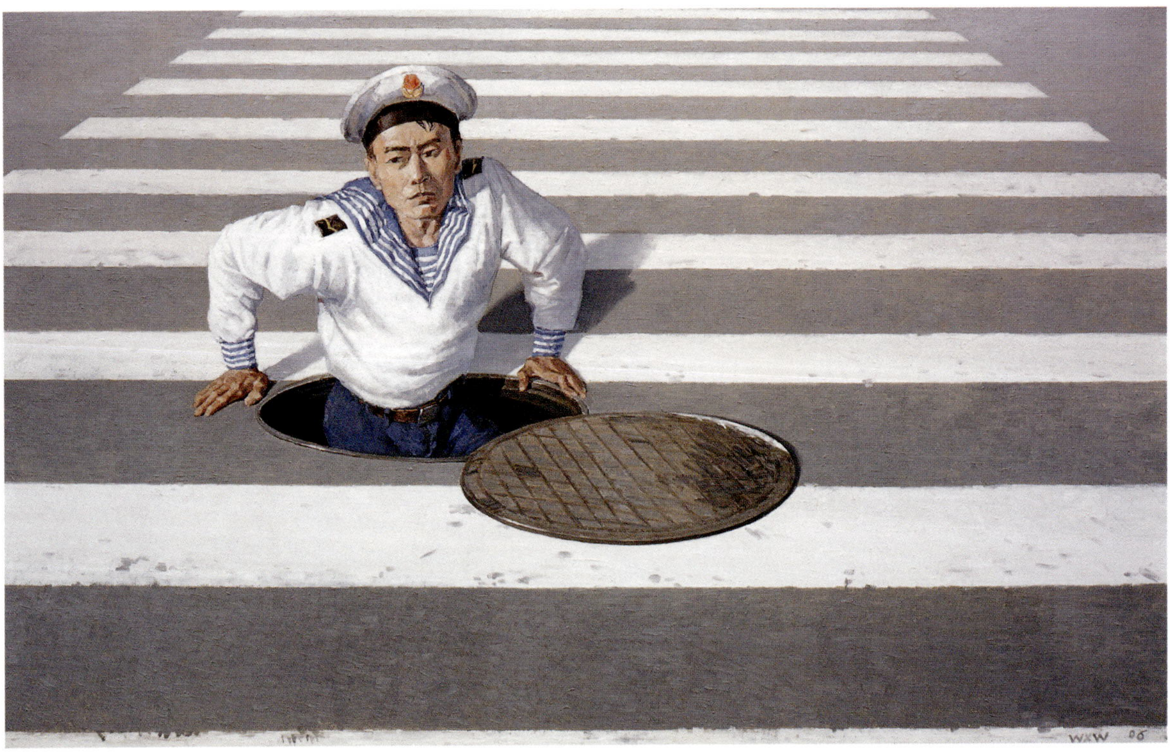

THIS PAGE, TOP: *1936 Mein Kampf—Wang Xingwei in 1936*, 1996. Oil on canvas, 86½ x 53 in.

THIS PAGE, BOTTOM: *Untitled (Sailor and Zebra Crossing)*, 2006. Oil on canvas, 79 x 128 in.

FACING PAGE, TOP: *Death of Panda*, 2004. Oil on canvas, 61 x 79 in.

FACING PAGE, BOTTOM: *Untitled (Woman Pulling a Man)*, 2006. Oil on canvas, 63 x 87 in.

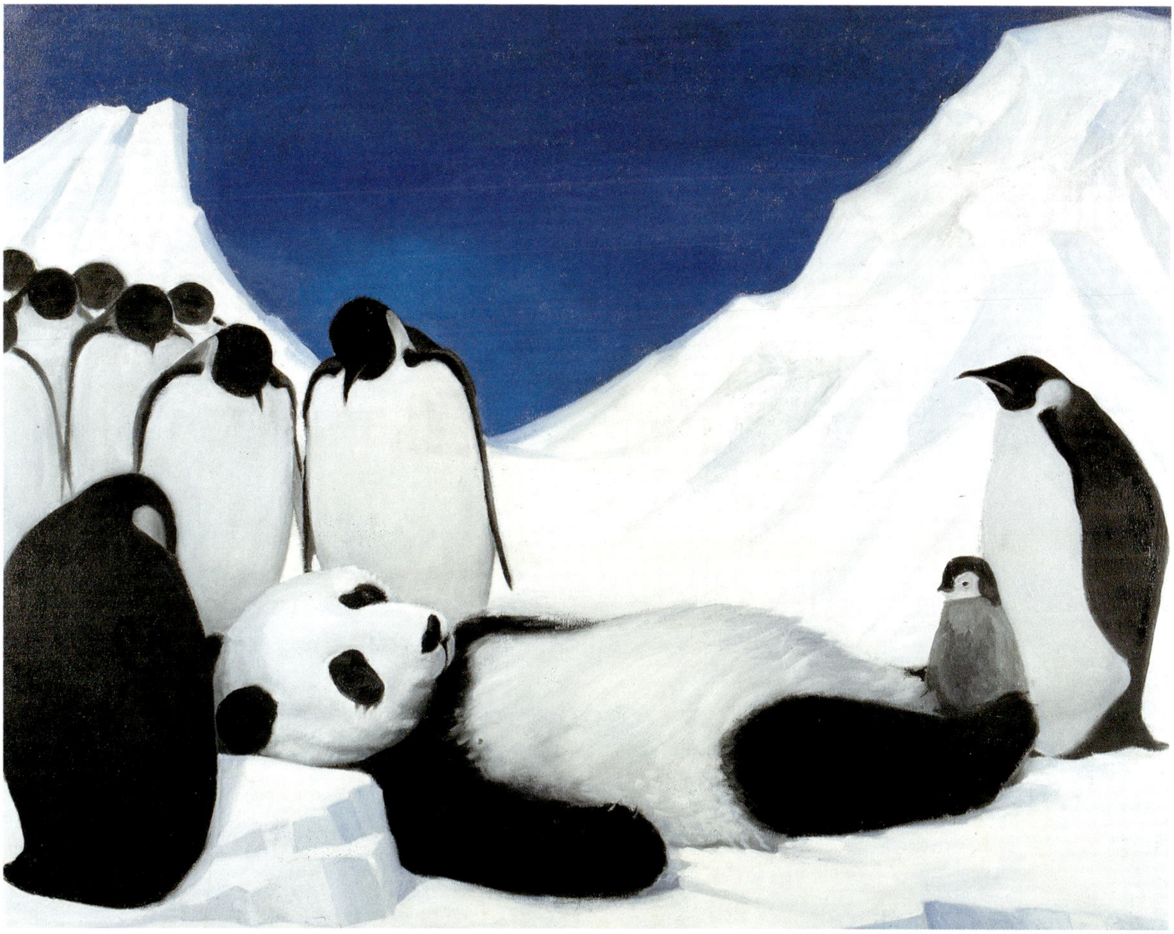

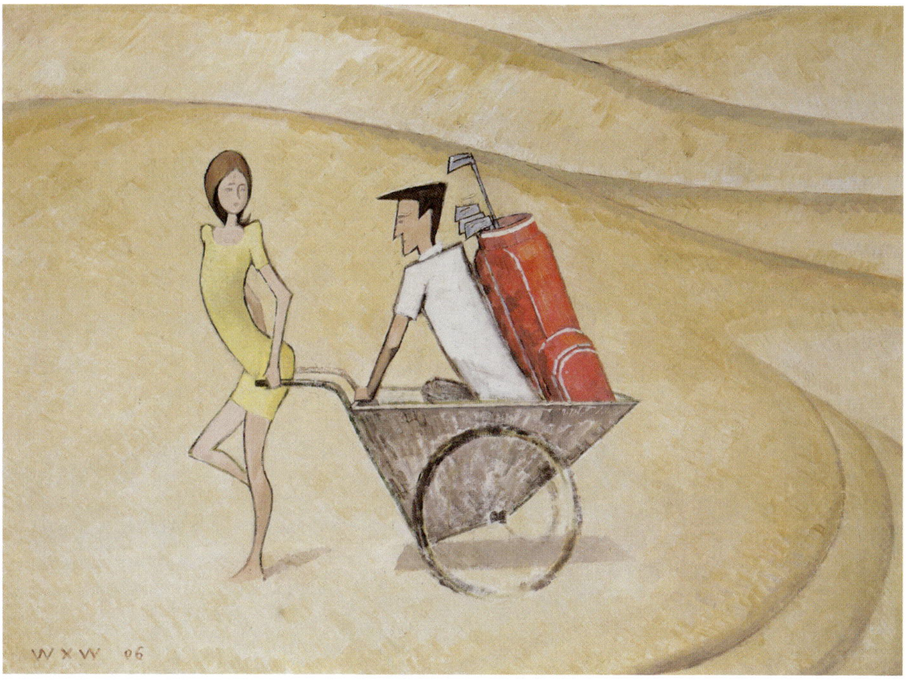
WXW 06

Weng Fen

Born 1961, Haikou, Hainan Island

In Weng Fen's famous photography series *On the Wall* (2001–) it would be natural to assume that the girl sitting on the wall facing the world beyond represents the artist himself, contemplating the new landscape taking shape during China's construction craze. Interested in issues of modernity, and in the consequences of the nation's rapid economic development, Weng Fen (also known as Weng Peijun) is a skillful observer of society's response to these phenomena, and the clashes between people's expectations and the reality that surrounds them. In *On the Wall* and the subsequent ongoing photography series *Bird's Eye View* (2002–), Weng invites us to survey the scene from over the shoulder of his characters, and to share their solitude as they look out across the vista of new urban landscapes.

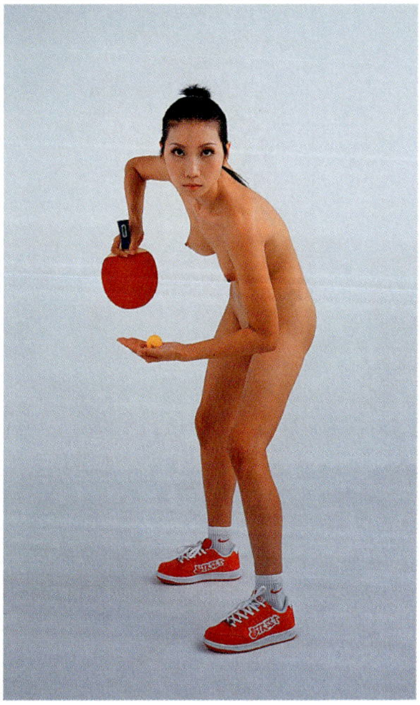

THIS PAGE: *My Olympics—Pingpong*, 2007. C-print, variable dimensions.

FACING PAGE, TOP: *Bird's Eye View—New Beijing (9)*, 2007. C-print, each 49 x 63 in.

FACING PAGE, BOTTOM: *On the Wall—Haikou 2*, 2002. C-print, dimensions variable.

"As precarious as a pile of eggs" is a famous ancient Chinese saying that dates back to the Spring and Autumn Period (770–476 BC) and is used to refer to an extremely dangerous situation. In Weng's two-year project *Accumulating Eggs: Weng Peijun's Terrific New World* (2004–2005), a miniature model city made of eggs demonstrates the precariousness and fragility of the new world being built during the country's desperate process of modernization.

The site-specific installation *View Stand—Bathing Sandy Beach* (2004) displays a crowd of sunbathers relaxing on the beach and, behind a barricade, a multitude of unknown people wearing masks, as though waiting to spring into action. In a world where conflict and antagonism seem to increase day by day, and with particular reference to the September 11 incident, Weng attempts to show the dichotomy between people enjoying their lives and those bearing anger in their hearts. Living in a world of changes, where our roles often overlap from viewing to being viewed, the artist presents two different ways of thinking and feeling. "Antagonism lies constantly and quietly beneath the surface of everything, and it could unexpectedly break out at any moment," says Weng.

The *My Olympics* series (2007) depicts women and men photographed naked in a variety of sporting poses, a comment on China's effervescent state in the run-up to the Beijing 2008 Olympic Games, and the fact that the games themselves seem to have become a mere matter of politics, nationalism, and economic interest. The nakedness of the athletes seems to imply a world without happiness where individuals have no spirit or status.

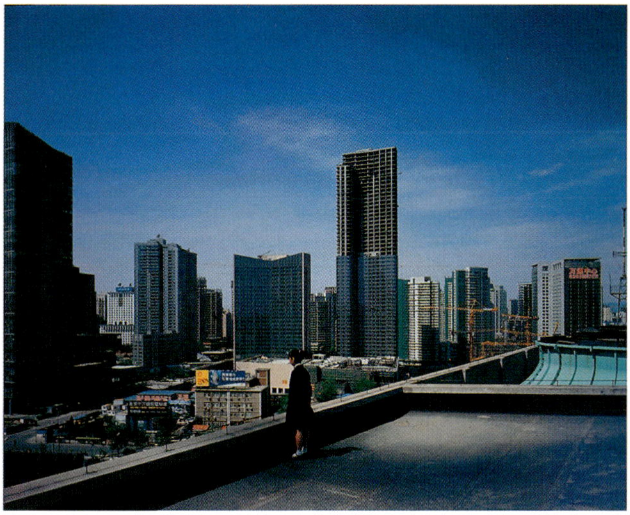
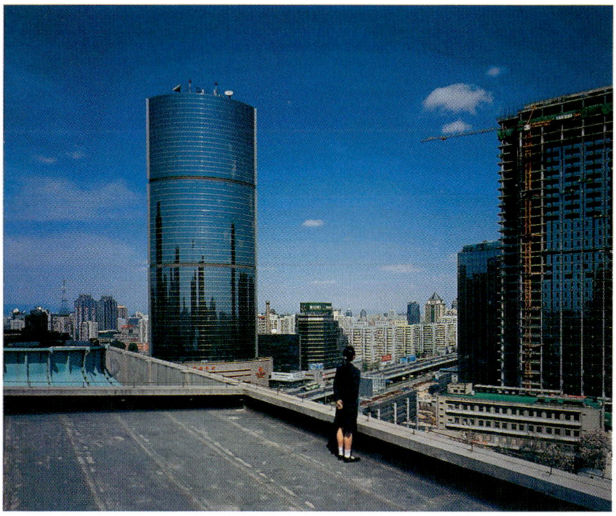
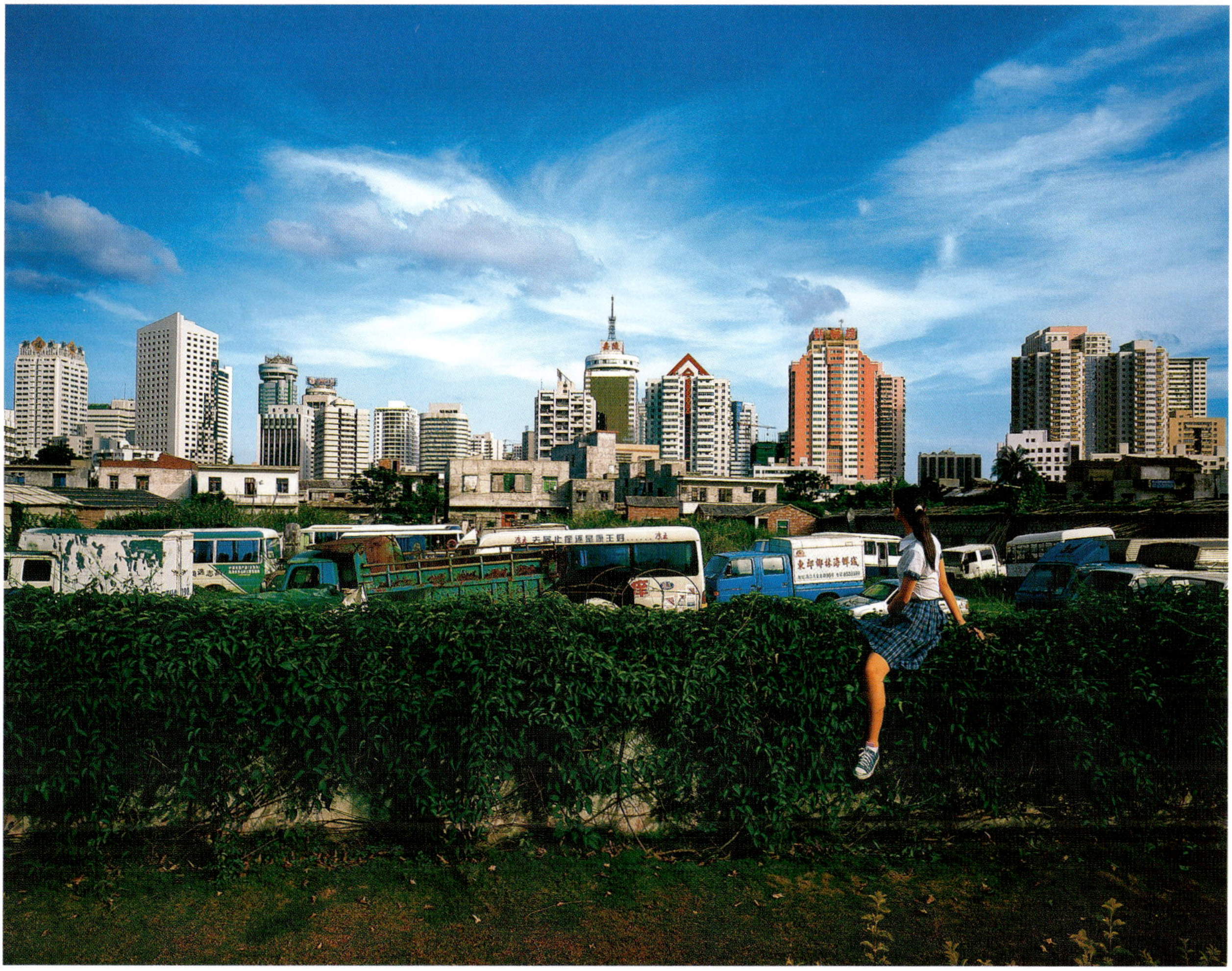

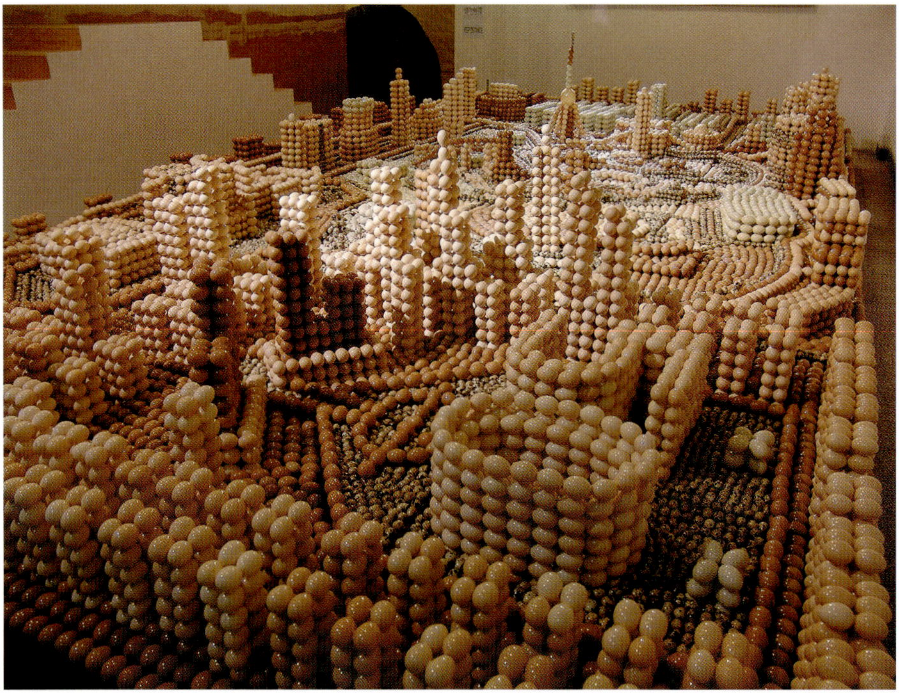

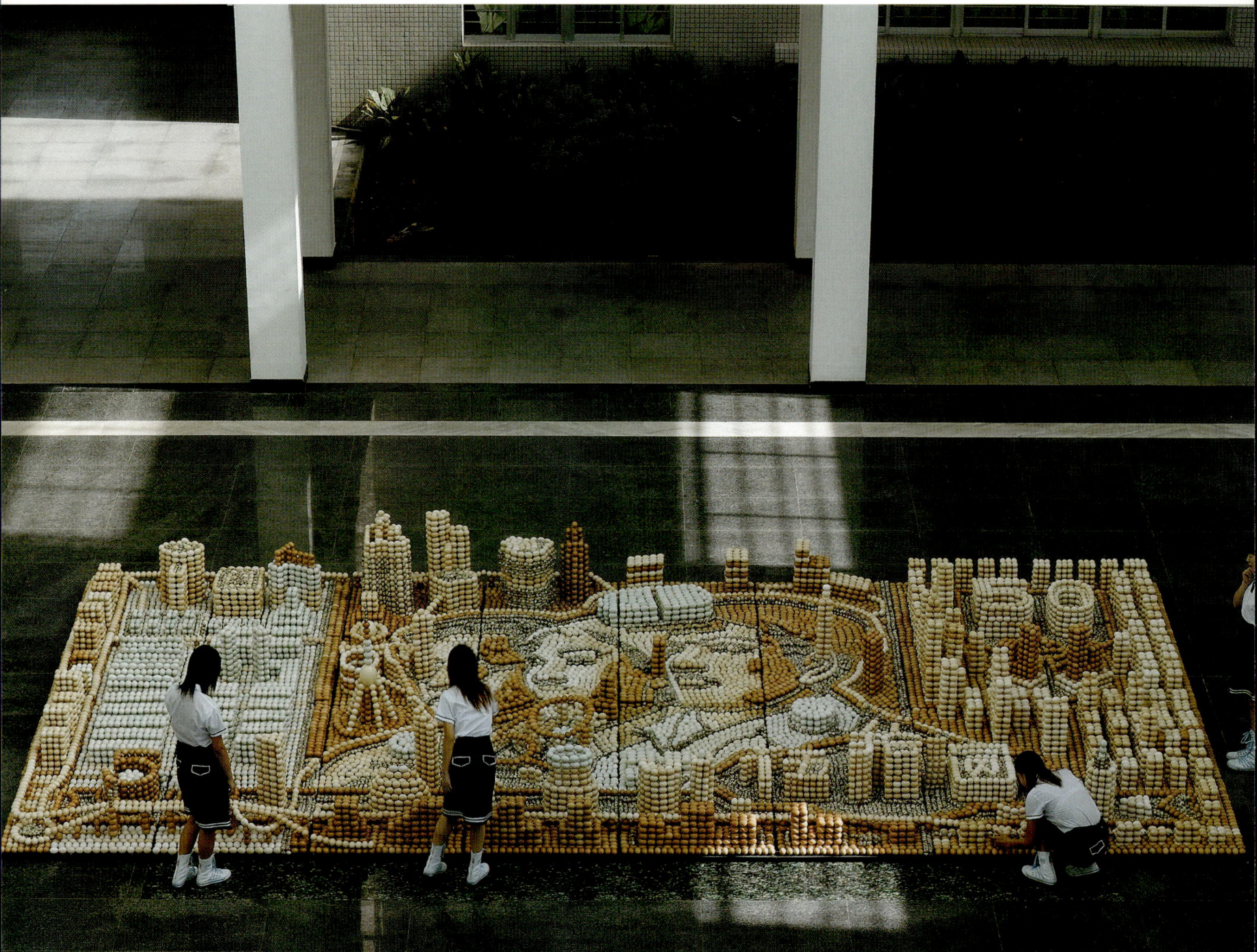

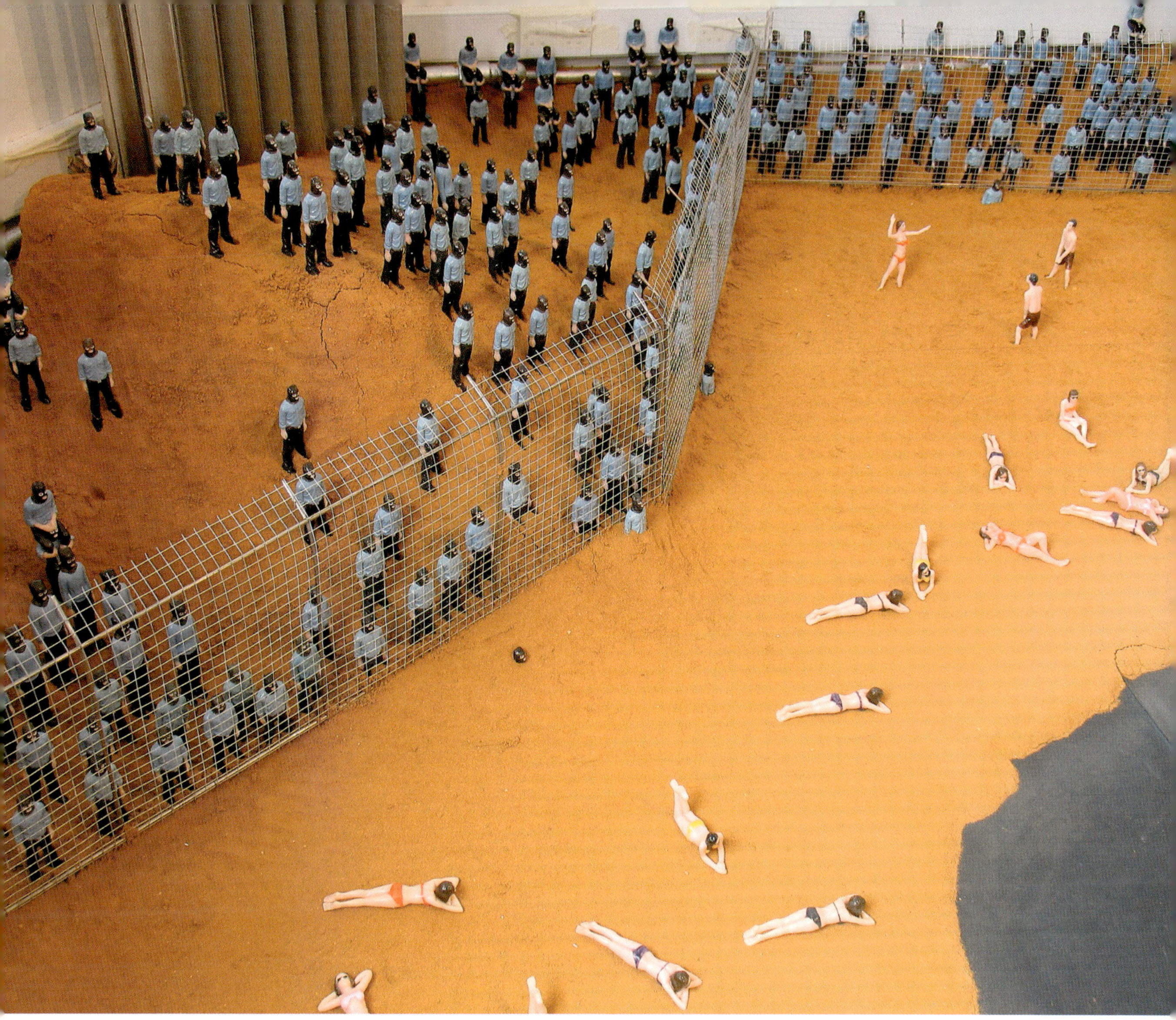

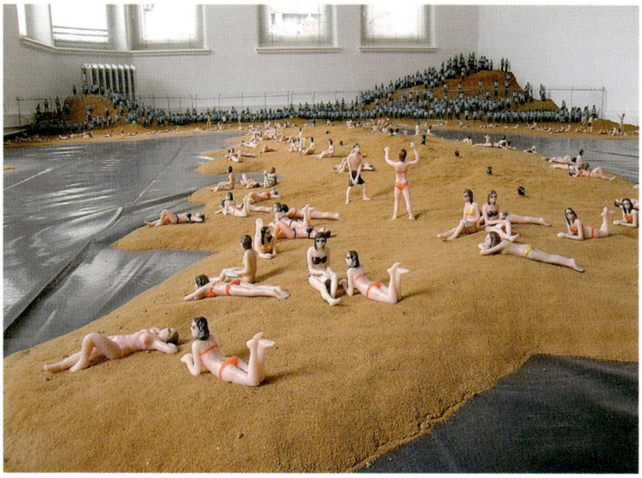

FACING PAGE: *Accumulating Eggs: Weng Peijun's Terrific New World*, 2005. Installation view and detail. Eggs (chicken, duck, ostrich, etc.), wood, glue, varnish, 157½ x 315 x 35½ in.

THIS PAGE: *View Stand—Bathing Sandy Beach*, 2004. Installation view and detail. Sand, wire netting, resin, mixed media, 393½ x 393½ x 19½ in.

Xiao Lu

Born 1962, Hangzhou, Zhejiang Province

BELOW: *Fifteen Shots . . . From 1989–2003,* 2003. Performance, Beijing Shooting Range.

FACING PAGE, TOP: *Sperm*, 2006. Installation/performance, Kangda Hotel, Yanan, Shaanxi Province.

"When I want something, and I really long for it, I make every effort to get it. My art is the means through which I get what I want." Xiao Lu's artworks are limited in number but deeply sincere in essence. *Dialogue* (1989), a performance that took place at the China Avant-Garde Exhibition at the National Art Gallery, Beijing in February 1989, was a comment on Xiao's own life and also a metaphor for the contradictions and miscommunications inherent in our daily exchanges. The piece consisted of two telephone booths, and two figures, one dressed as a man and one as a woman, standing in the booths as if they were talking on the phone. But the phone mouthpieces dangle there, communication curtailed. The performance ended with the artist firing two gunshots—one for herself and one for the man she loved—into a mirror placed between the telephone boxes, as she committed symbolic suicide. The unexpected gunshots shocked the audience, and her lover, the artist Tang Song, who was photographing the performance, was arrested on suspicion of firing the gun himself.

Xiao was then silent for fifteen years, a denunciation of the pain she suffered in her relationship with Tang and of life in a society that lacks real communication. She was silent until 2003, when she opened fire in the performance *Fifteen Shots,* one shot for each year she spent with Tang. In *A Dialogue about Dialogue* (2004), the artist stood in front of the two phone boxes, read out a dialogue about the events of 1989, her silence afterwards, and her feelings. She then offered each member of the audience a copy of the dialogue and a wisp of her hair.

In the installation *Sperm* (2006), the artist used a form of art to try to achieve her long-cherished wish of having a baby. During a forum on art and education, she invited twelve members of the audience to donate sperm so she could undergo artificial insemination. Even though the experiment failed due to a lack of donors, she stated: "I wanted a baby and I felt I had the right to demand it. Men can always get what they want, why can't I?" In conjunction with the installation, Xiao organized a discussion on love, marriage, sex, and ethics. "Again, I used my art to fulfill my needs."

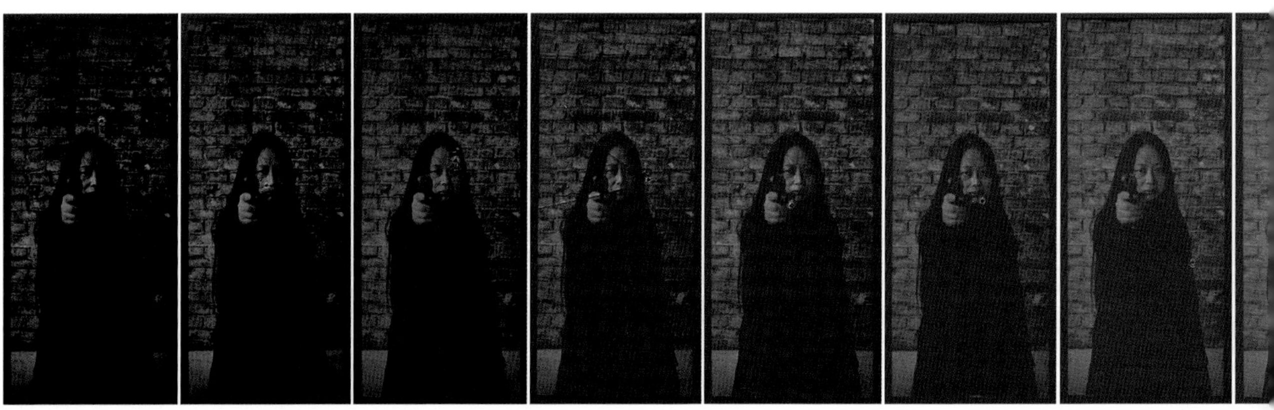

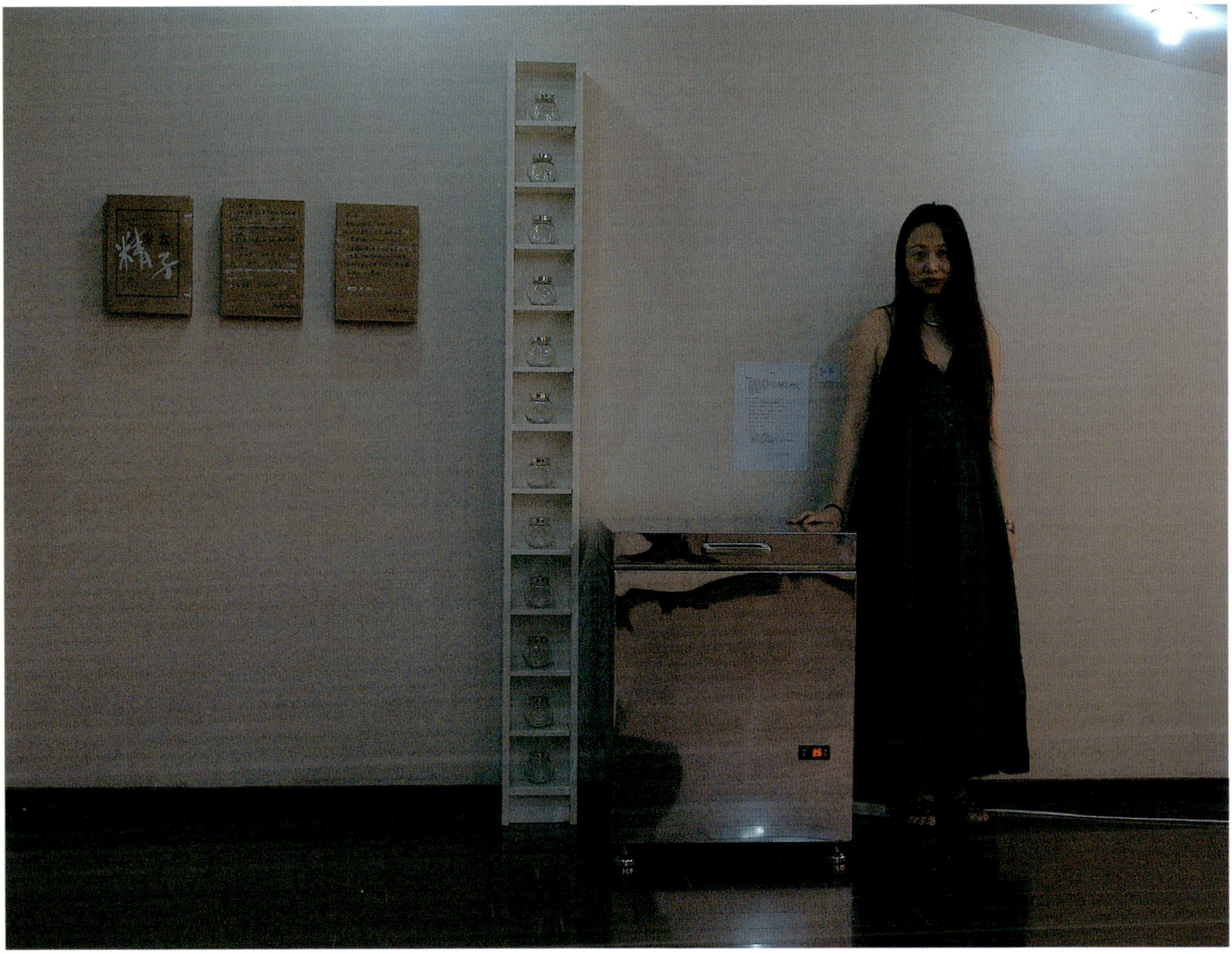
精子

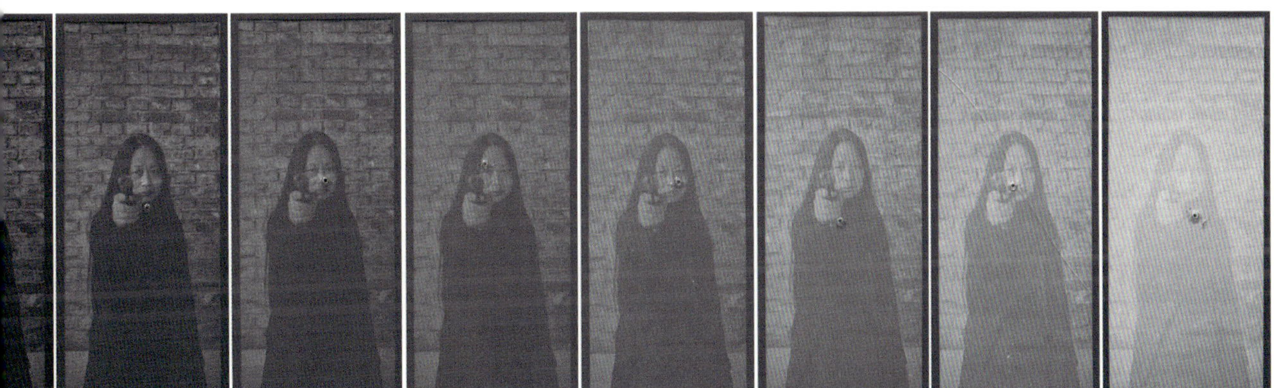

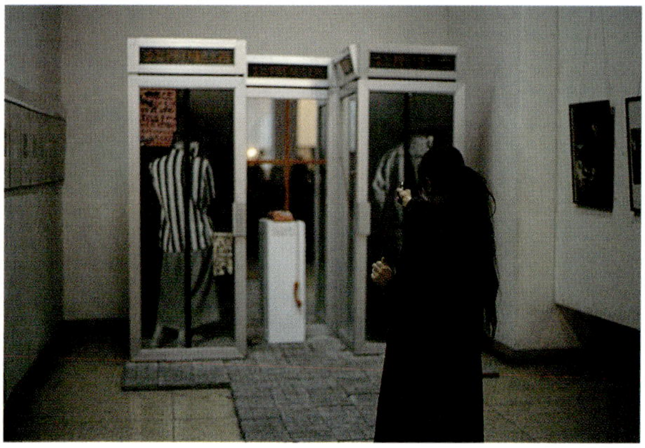

THIS PAGE, TOP: *Dialogue*, 1989. Performance, National Art Gallery, Beijing.

THIS PAGE BOTTOM, FACING PAGE: *A Dialogue about "Dialogue,"* 2004. Installation, 798 Space, Beijing.

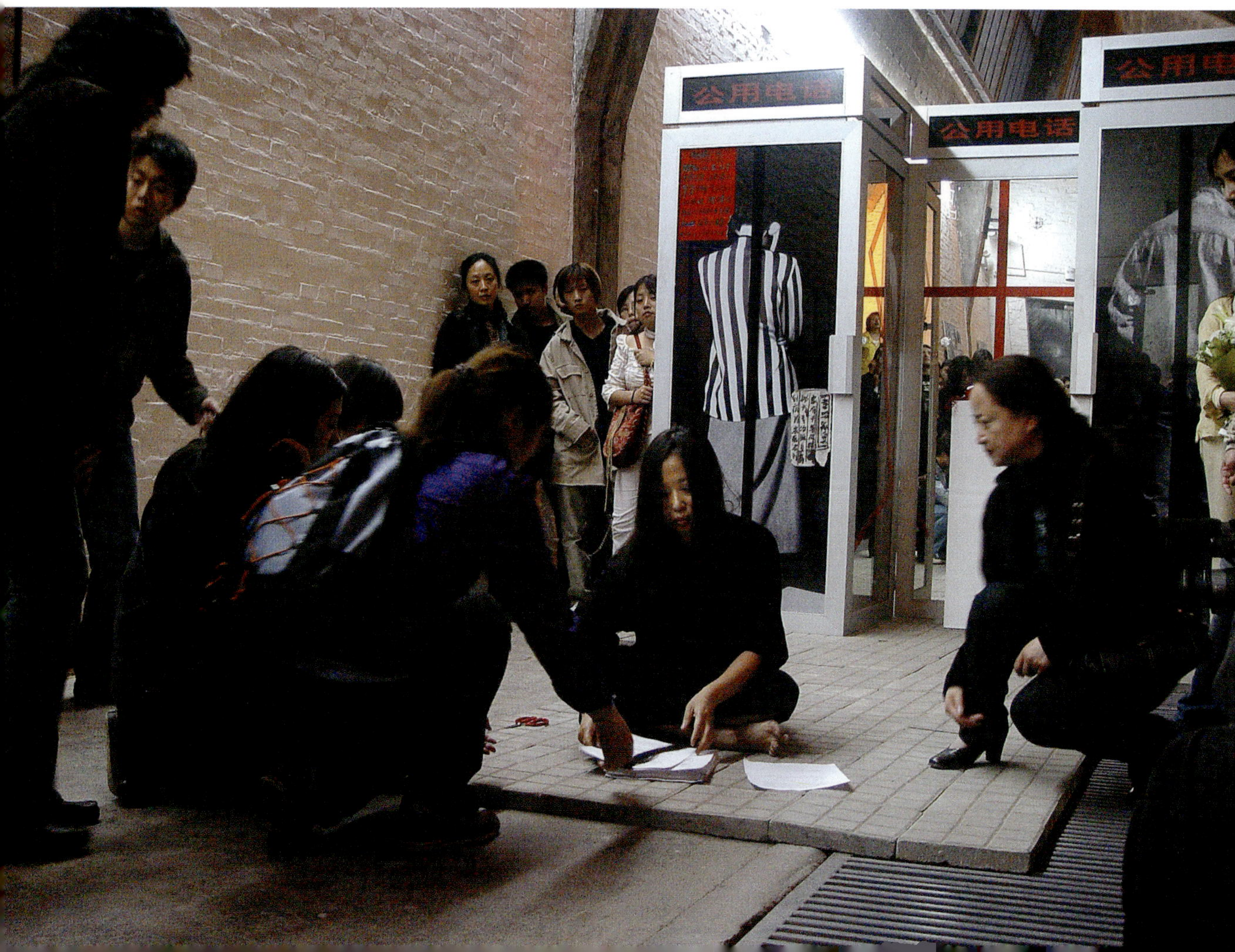

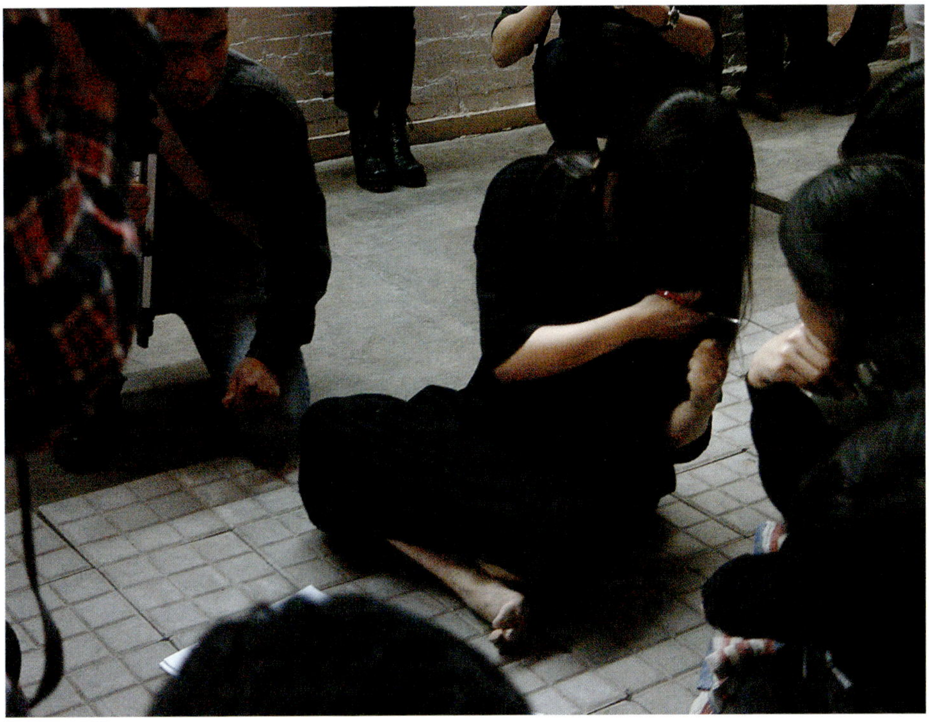

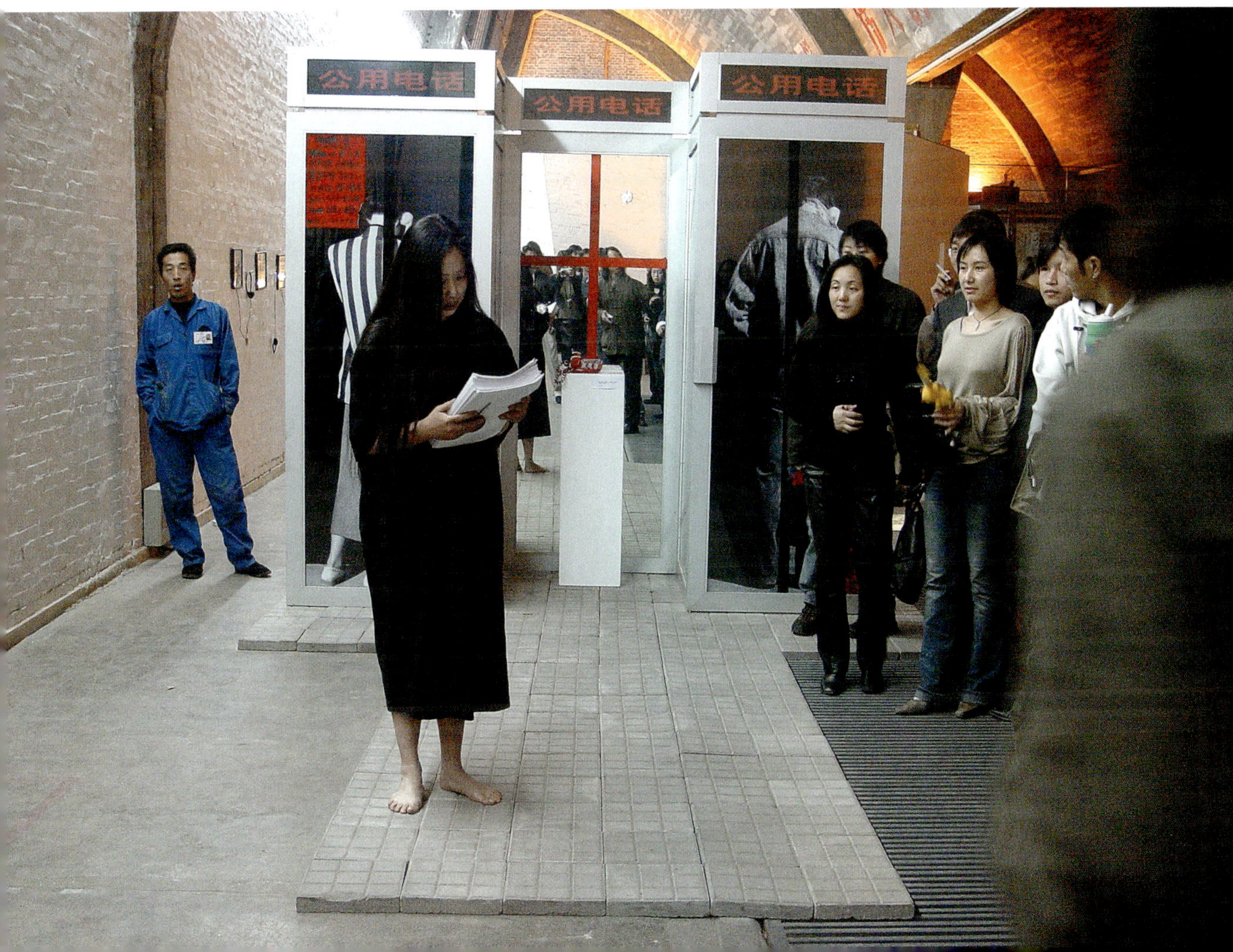
公用电话
公用电话
公用电话

Xie Nanxing

Born 1970, Chongqing, Sichuan Province

Original and enigmatic, conceptual, and with a solid technical base, Xie Nanxing's photorealistic paintings have inhabited the international art scene since the 1990s. Exhibited at biennials, triennials, at German art exhibition Documenta, and in world-renowned art museums, Xie's large canvases, characterized by unique shapes and tricks of light, astonish and captivate.

Xie's "psychological realism"—to borrow the term coined by Chinese curator Feng Boyi—tends to bewilder the viewers: his canvases imbue the ordinary with something gloomy and surprising, yet his approach to art is very logical. His talent lies in his ability to make art out of everyday subjects. These subjects, after undergoing a process of identification, video recording, and being photographed, are eventually transformed into paintings. Availing himself of the most advanced technology in order to reproduce images, Xie dissects reality and continuously reproduces it in different spaces and from different viewpoints, demonstrating that the subject maintains its unique character regardless, and revealing the puzzling nature of things we previously regarded as commonplace. Critic Nataline Colonnello observed that his work is a mapping process, a superimposition of layers, the creative construction of an idea that changes continuously until its ultimate rendering, immortalized by a touch of light. This process can be seen in his *Untitled* series (2001–), whose landscapes induce simultaneous feelings of unease, terror, and eroticism in the viewer.

From his position behind the camera lens, the artist analyzes his reality as if he were examining himself; he provides the viewer with a reality that can be understood at different levels while it gives shape to the artist's unconscious feelings. "I paint the illusions, the images, the visions of my heart," said Xie in an interview with Colonnello. "I display them and let them become everybody else's."

Xie's series *He* (2007), appears to be a radical departure from his usual way of working. In an interview with American curator and writer David Spalding, Xie explained that this new style of painting was inspired by the type of visual puzzle where, after looking at it for a while, the viewer is supposed to be able to make out other shapes. "It's a joke!" he stated. *He No. 1*, for example, symbolizes a sportsman falling into the water where fish are hungrily swimming around.

THIS PAGE AND FACING PAGE: *Untitled (Picture of Voice I)*, 2001. Oil on canvas, triptych, each 86½ x 110 in.

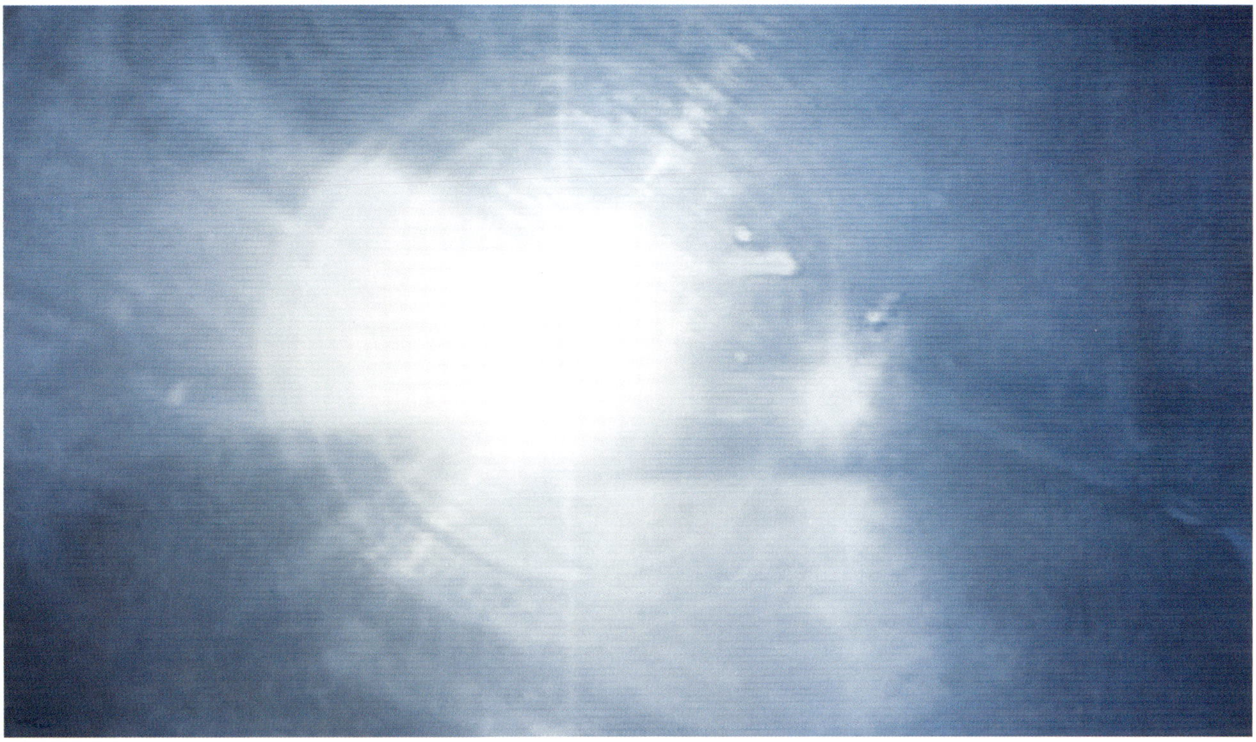

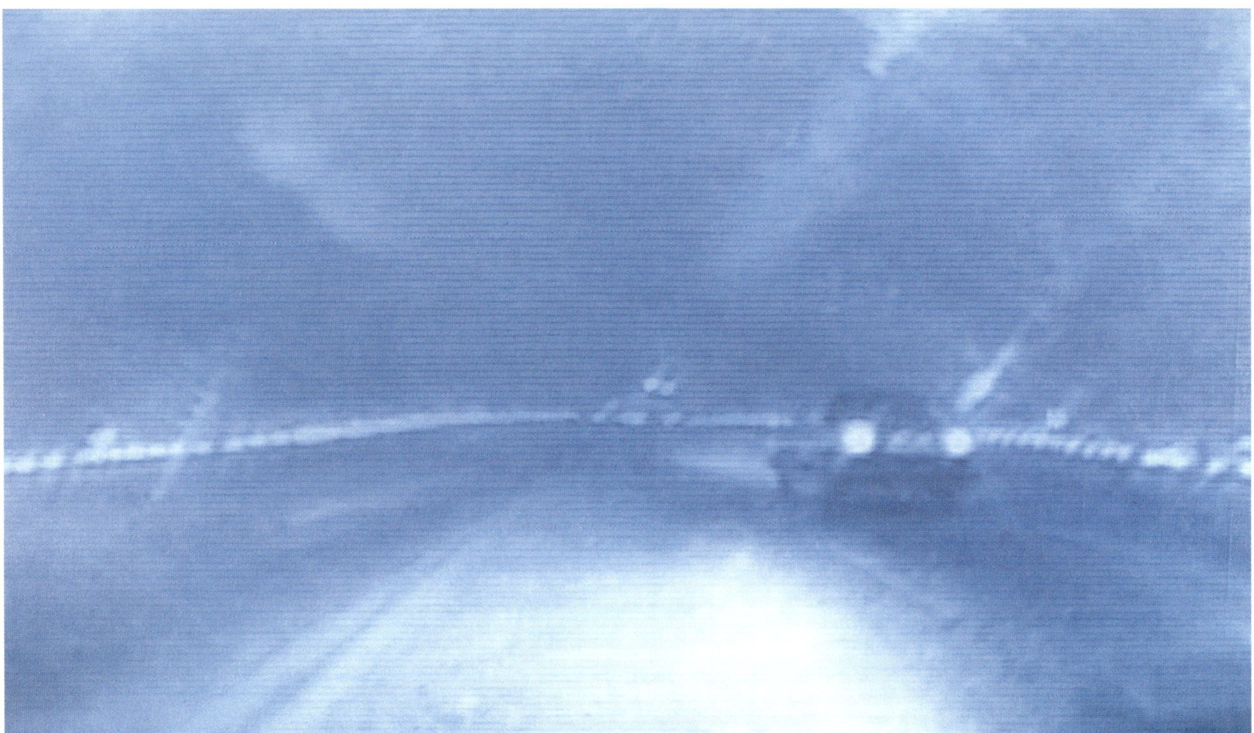

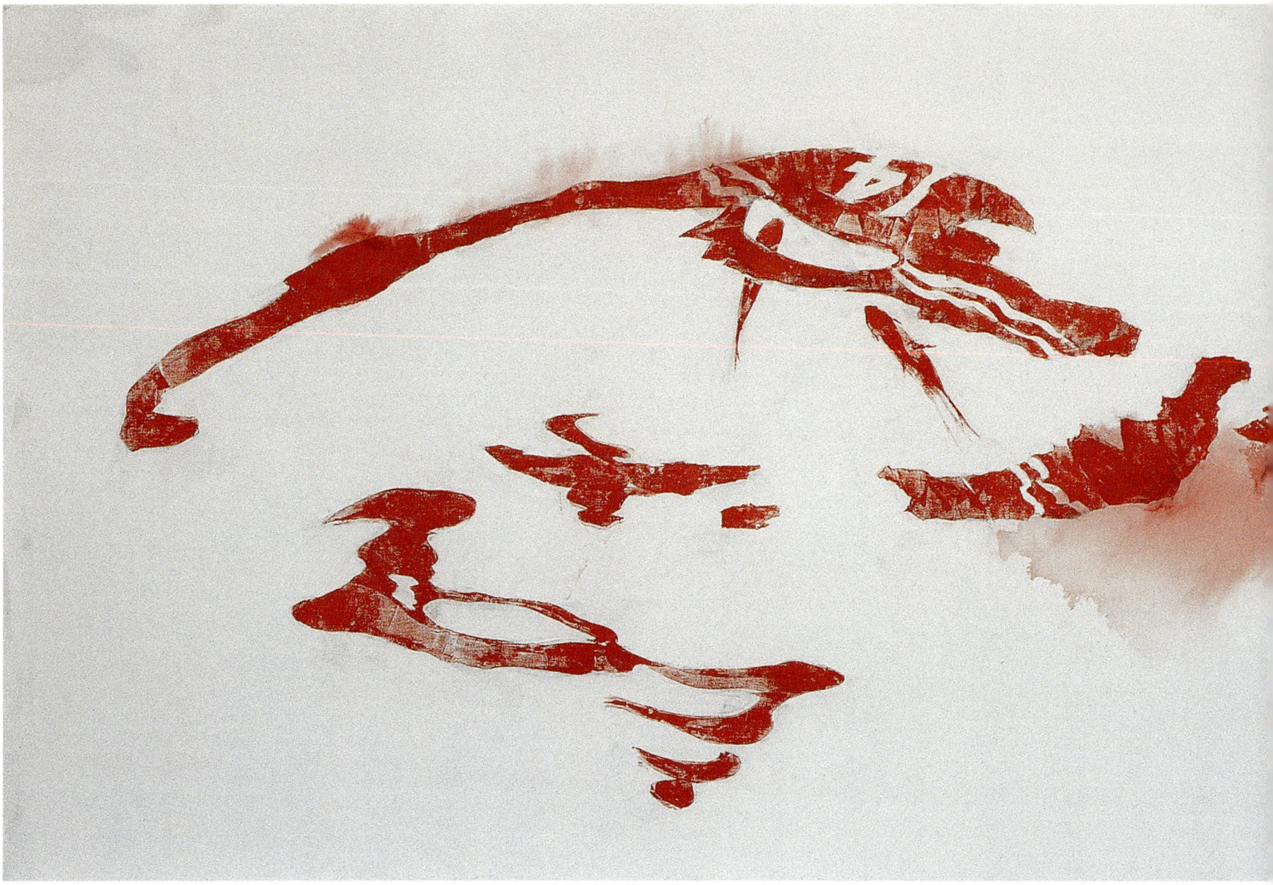

ABOVE: *He No. 1*, 2007. Oil on canvas, 58 x 141½ in.
RIGHT: *Untitled (No. 2)*, 2002. Oil on canvas, 59 x 141½ in.

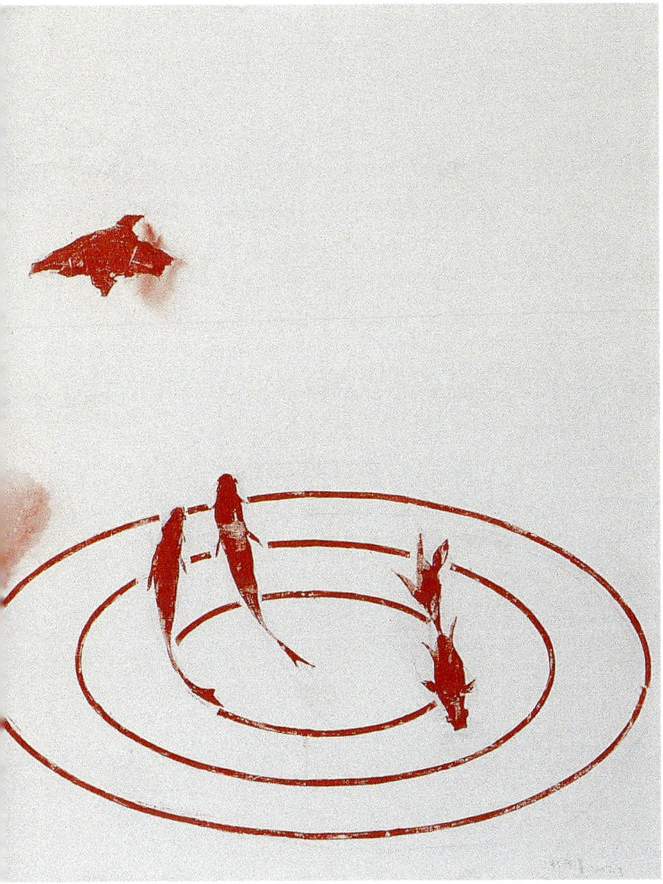

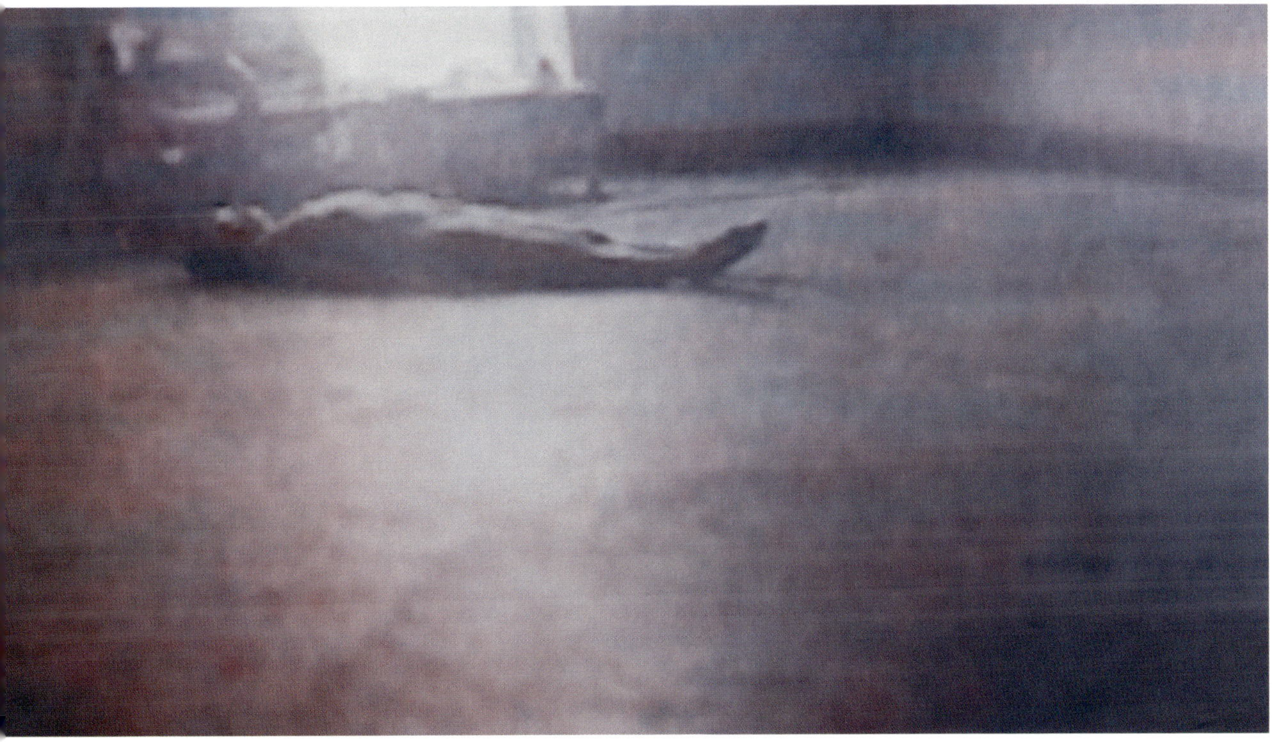

Xing Danwen

Born 1967, Xian, Shaanxi Province

With themes that include dislocation, the fusion of memory and reality, and the lives and preoccupations of urban dwellers, Beijing-based artist and photographer Xing Danwen captures small-scale human dramas and represents them in an ironic way by combining reality, fiction, and illusion.

Her interest in urban landscapes began when she lived in New York from 1998 until 2002, during which period she also traveled extensively to Europe. Her frequent trips to different places made her aware of how modern cities look, and how they function in relation to people's lives. During these years, she created *Sleep Walking* (2000–2001), a multimedia installation including two videos showing images of cities in Europe and the United States. Accompanied by the sound of Chinese instruments and the noise of everyday life in China, this work shows "how our mind can take images from different locations and weave together the cultural differences we experience into one continuous memory."

The series *disCONNEXION* (2002–2003), documenting the huge amounts of electrical trash shipped from industrialized countries and dumped in the suburbs of Guangdong province, draws our attention to the social and environmental problems that are a result of living in an era when people rely on high-tech tools that quickly become obsolete. In *Duplication* (2003), Xing portrays a society that seems to be running to a program, and where people are striving simply to achieve the standard model. "I often have the feeling of being trapped inside a machine that never stops, where there is less and less space for individuality," says Xing.

In *Urban Fiction* (2004–2007), Xing photographs the maquettes created by real estate companies to promote new housing developments in China, then transforms the real into the illusive by adding fictional representations of real life to these plastic models. The architectural structures become the setting where imaginary plots unfold; her figures are real and unreal at the same time, a comment on the state of urban life today and how the commercial world is controlling people's wishes in an imaginary space. "Modern cities in China are plastic and the urban design seems to conglomerate its citizens," Xing explains.

The *Wall-House* series (2007) is the result of a project in which Xing and seven other photographers were invited to stay in the Wall House, the world-famous building designed by architect John Hejduk in Groningen, the Netherlands, and to record their experiences through their photography.

THIS PAGE, LEFT: *Duplication, image 5*, 2003. Chromogenic color print, 58¼ x 47¼ in.

THIS PAGE, RIGHT: *disCONNEXION, image B03*, 2002–2003. C-print, 58¼ x 47¼ in.

FACING PAGE: *Urban Fiction, image 24* and detail, 2006. C-print, 88 x 67 in.

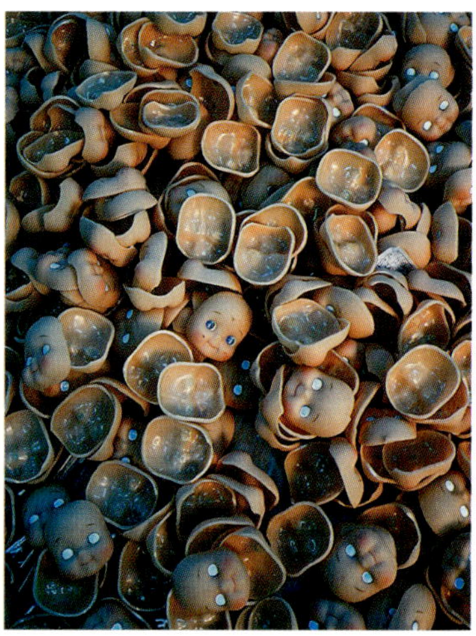

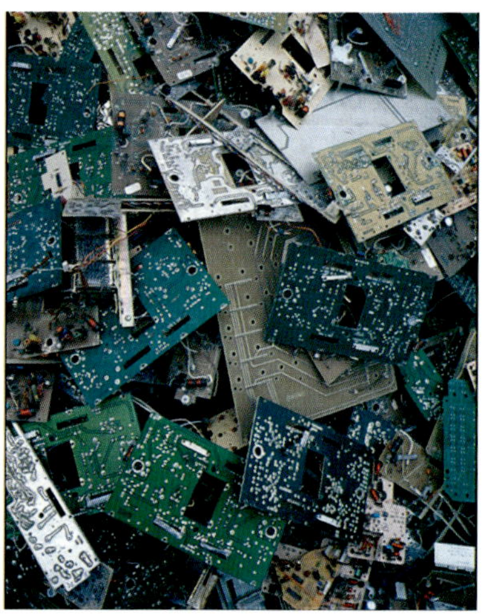

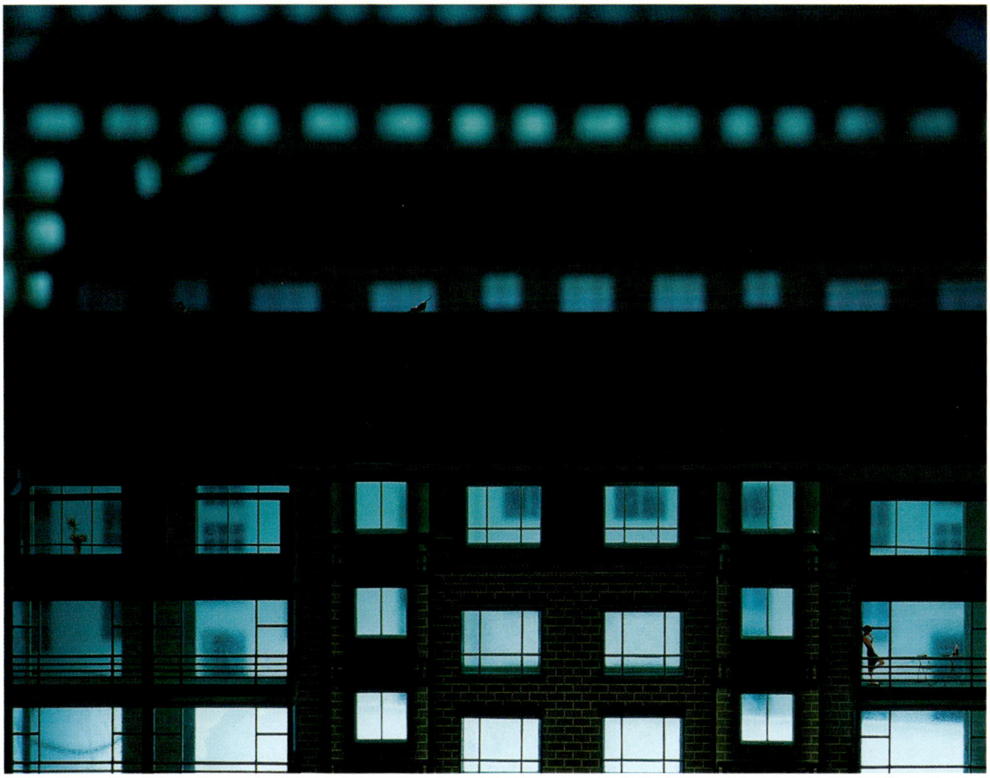

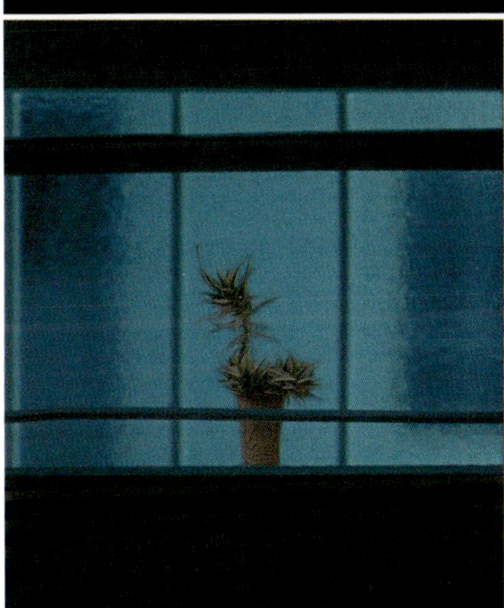

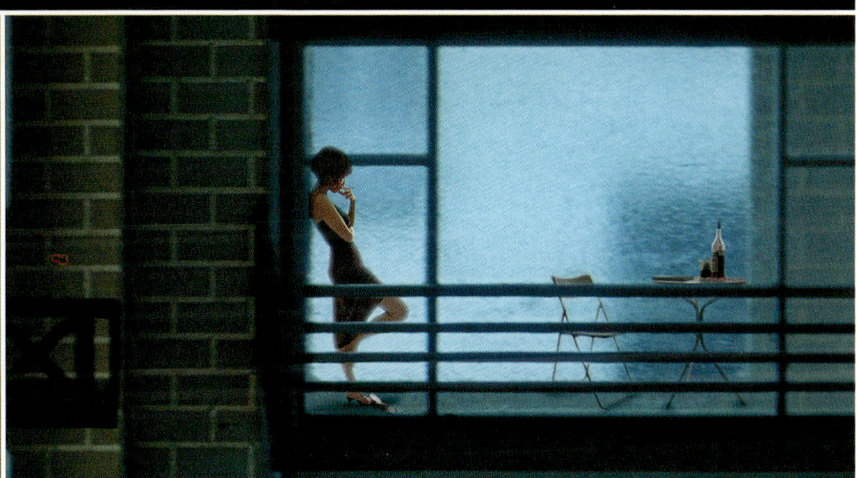

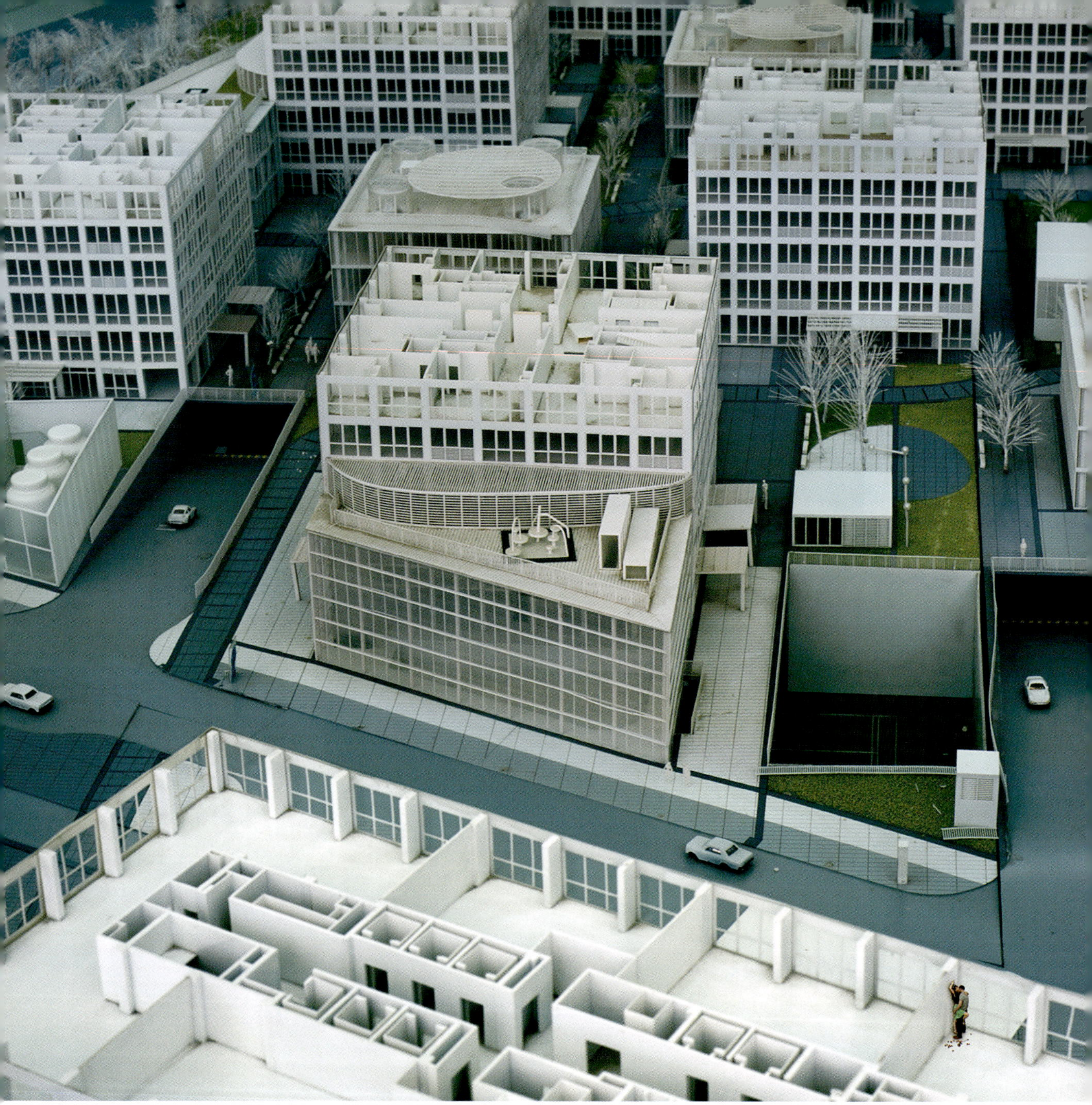

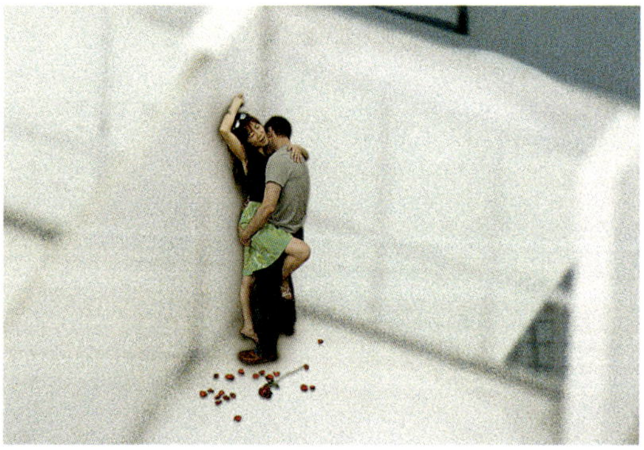

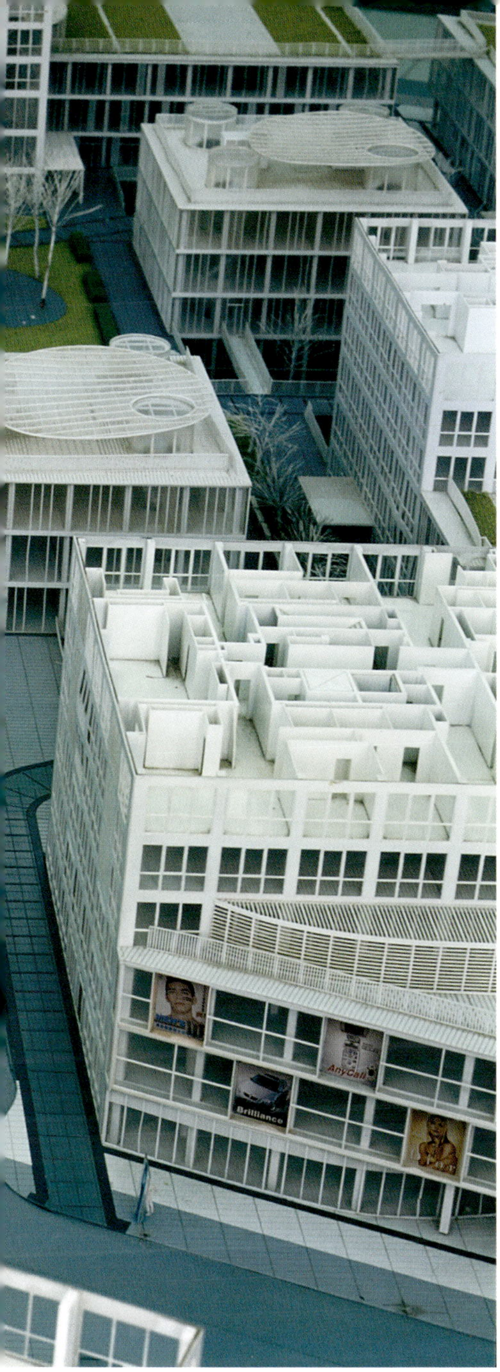

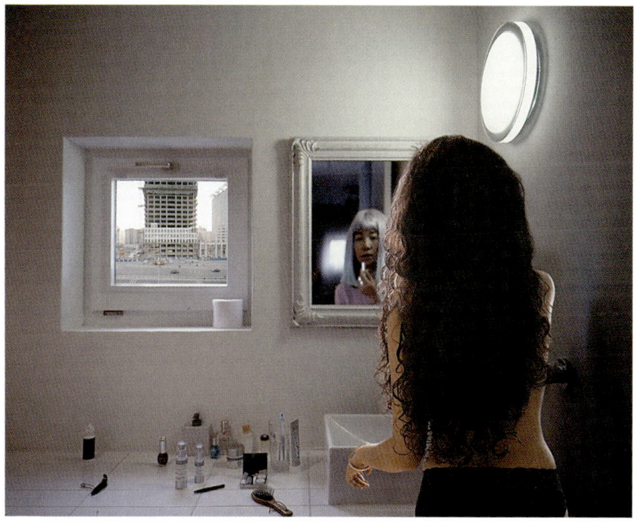

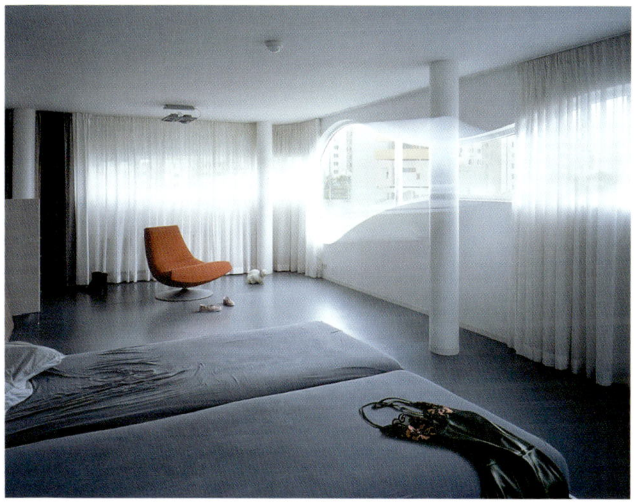

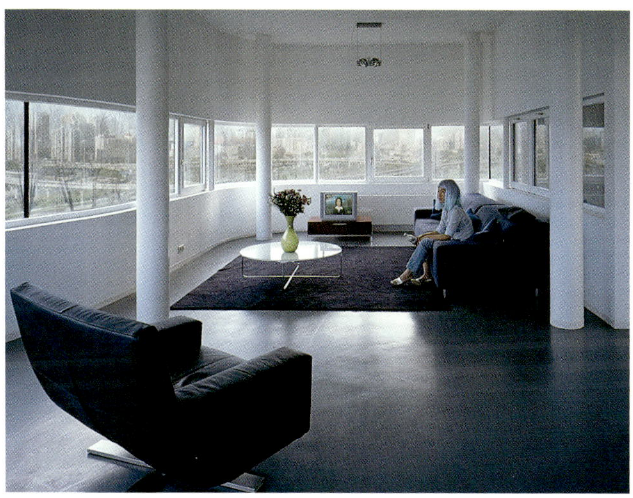

FACING PAGE, TOP AND BOTTOM: *Urban Fiction, image 13* and detail, 2005. C-print, 67 x 86½ in.

THIS PAGE, TOP: *Wall House, image 2*, 2007. C-print, 31½ x 39½ in.

THIS PAGE, CENTER: *Wall House, image 4*, 2007. C-print, 35½ x 47¼ in.

THIS PAGE, BOTTOM: *Wall House, image 1*, 2007. C-print, 47¼ x 63 in.

Xu Zhen

Born 1977, Shanghai

To some, the piece that talented young artist Xu Zhen presented at international art show Art 37 Basel in 2006 might seem like a move on the renowned strategic board game *Risk*. Xu's *18 Days* (2006) is a video installation recording an eighteen-day trip the artist undertook with the purpose of crossing China's borders and invading unsuspecting neighboring countries, equipped with an armory of remote-controlled toys. Xu attempted to cross the border with Russia, Mongolia, and Myanmar in a van stuffed with cameras, speakers, and his toy weapons. The resulting film surpasses political or social critiques to become a display of the artist's theatrical approach as well as an exploration of aspects of the new Chinese social and human reality.

One of Xu's earliest pieces is *Rainbow* (1998), a video that in 2001 was presented at the 49th Venice Biennale. Deeply concerned with the physical body, skin, and nudity, as well as sexuality, Xu records a naked male back, repeatedly beaten by a whip—the agonizing sound of which is the only thing recognizable—until the pink skin becomes fuchsia. Provoking the audience through the senses, Xu invites people to ponder upon the meaning of common categorizations such as male and female, life and death, facts and universal truth. The performance *Throwing a Cat* recorded in the video *I Am Not Asking for Anything* (1999), in which the artist locks himself in a small room and repeatedly beats against the floor the body of what appears to be a dead cat, brought remarkable attention upon Xu and his work. The video and installation piece *Cutting Off the Top of Everest* (2005) depicts Xu climbing Mount Everest to remove six feet (1.86 meters)—the artist's own height—from the top. By making us wonder whether he really did this or not, Xu challenges us to reconsider the importance we give to "facts," such as the continually discussed height of Everest.

In other works, Xu deals with the issues of space, both private and public. In the video installation *From Inside the Body* (1999), the artist deals with the intimate spheres of our lives that often end up the subject of mere public entertainment: a man and a woman are thus portrayed in the act of smelling their own and each other's naked bodies.

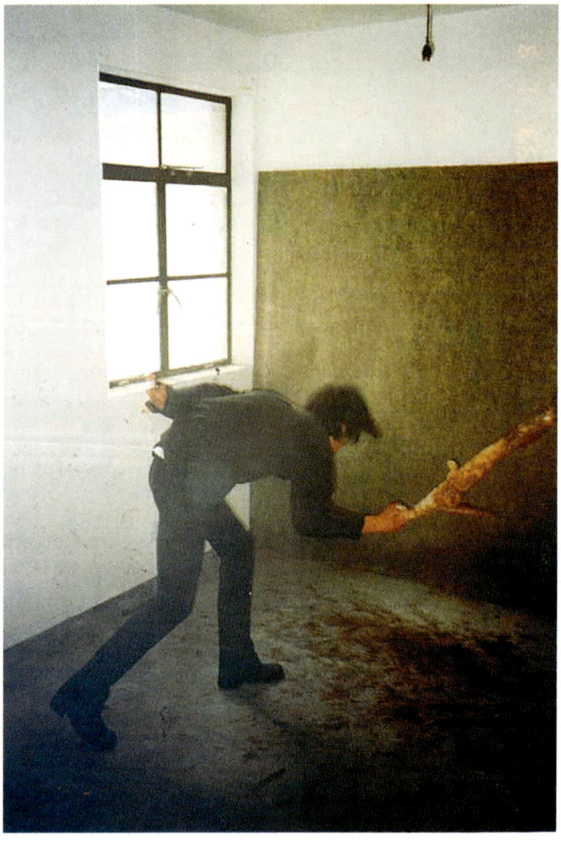

THIS PAGE: *Throwing a Cat*, 1999. Performance from the video *I Am Not Asking for Anything*.

FACING PAGE: *From Inside the Body*, 1999. Video installation.

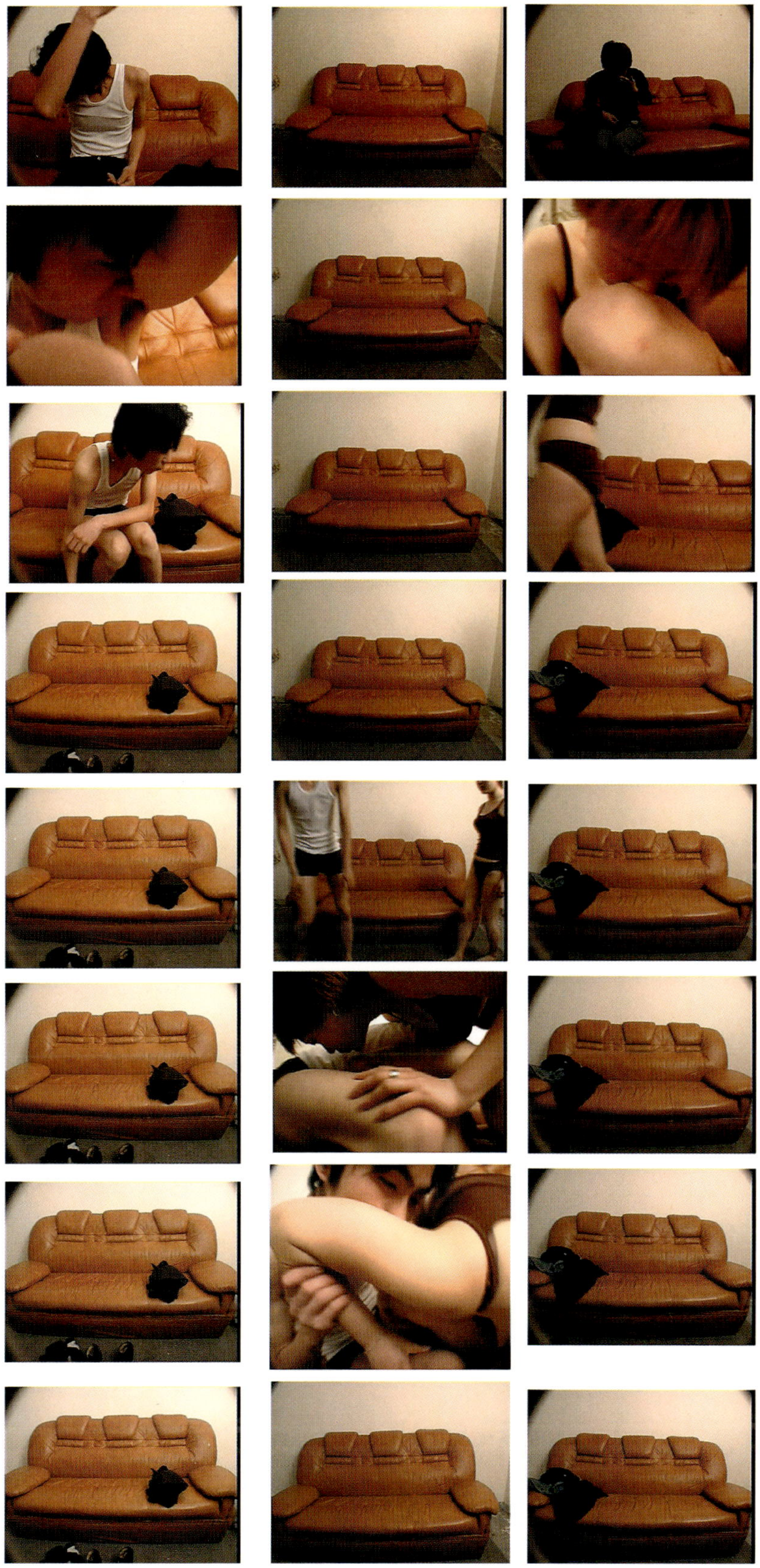

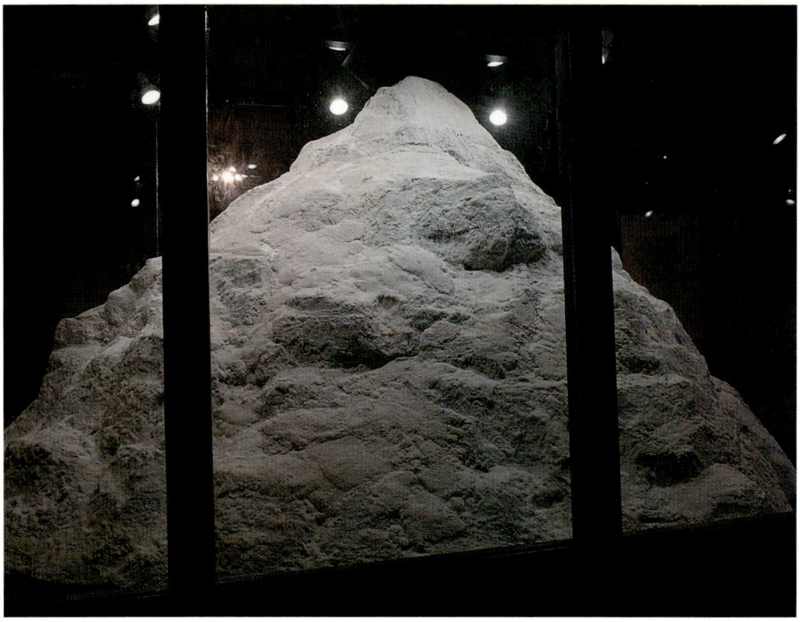

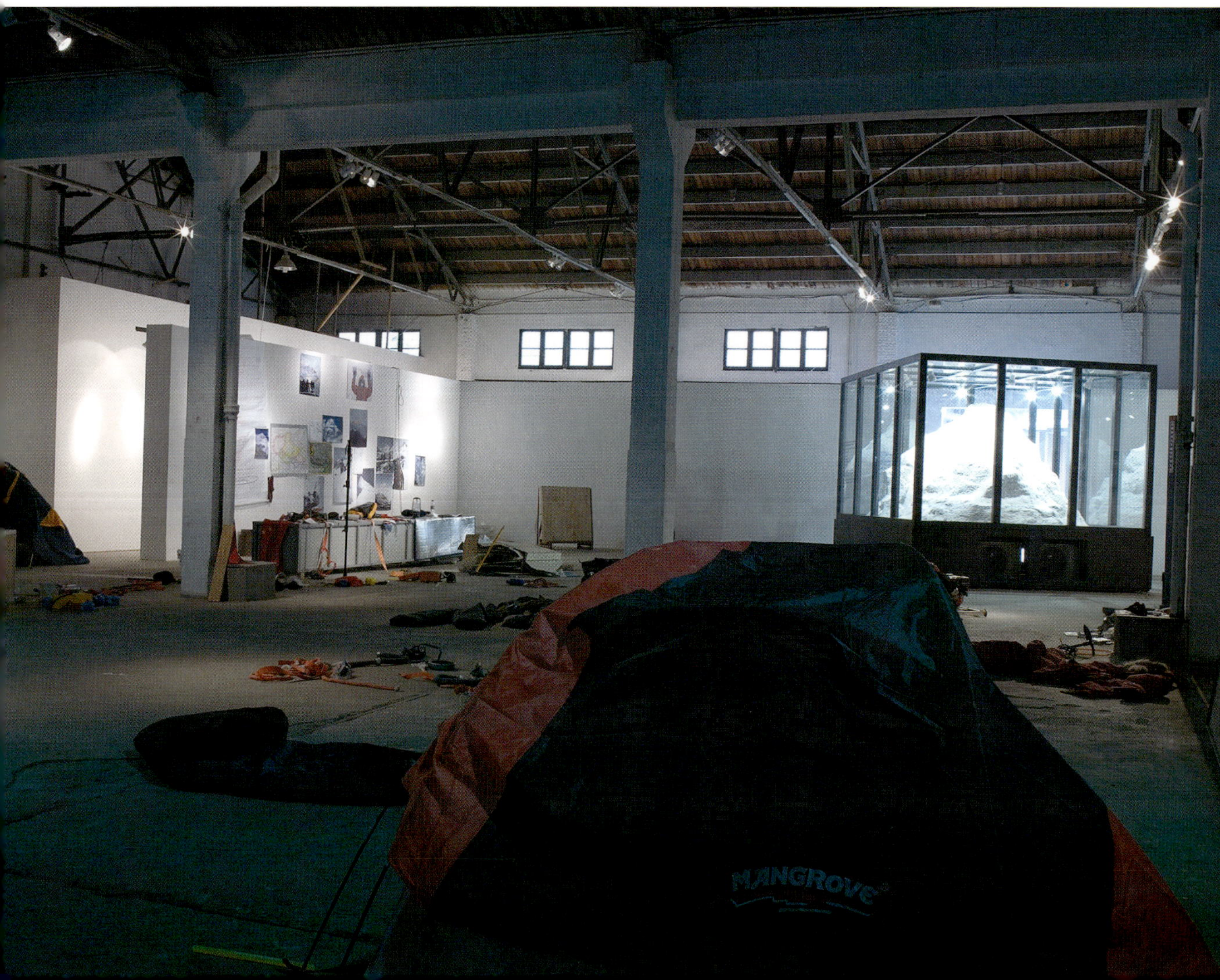
MANGROVE

FACING PAGE: *Cutting Off the Top of Everest 8848–1.86*, 2005. Installation view.

THIS PAGE: *Rainbow*, 1998. Stills from video.

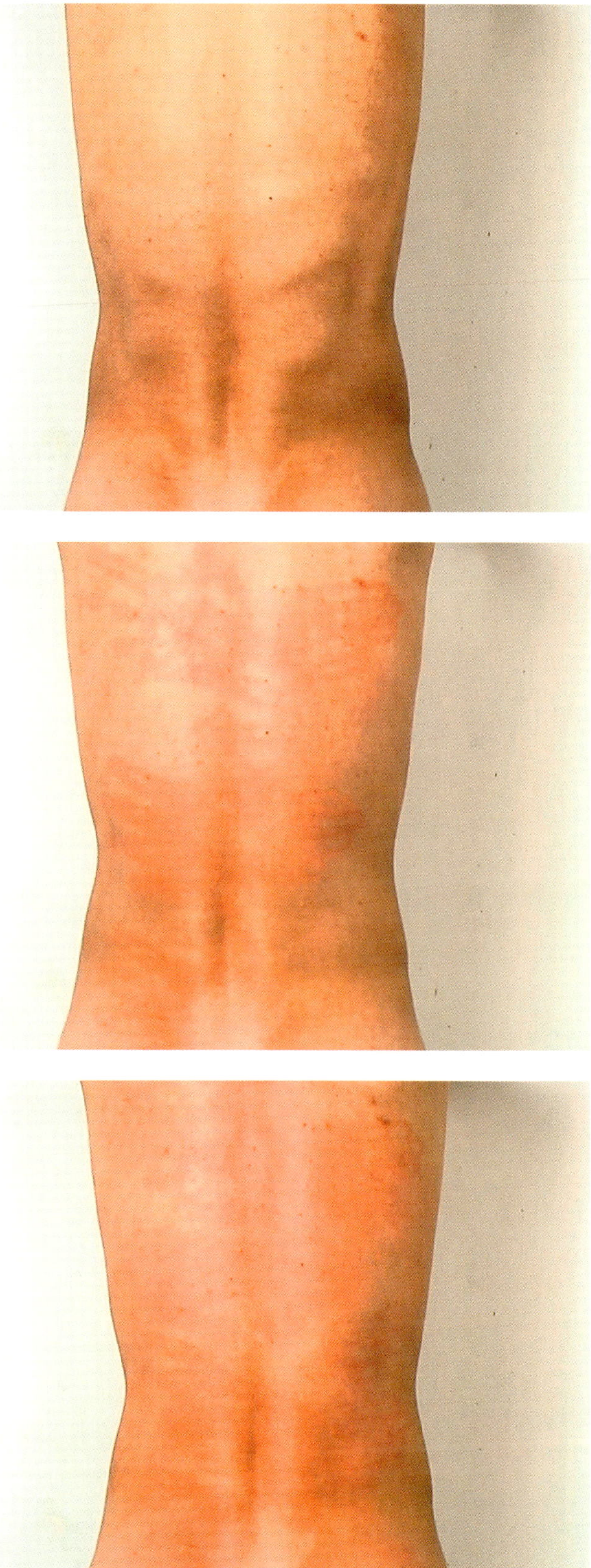

Yan Lei

Born 1965, Langfang, Hebei Province

THIS PAGE: *Invitation*, 1997.

FACING PAGE: *A Gift from Beijing to Istanbul*, 2007. Stills from video of live performance by Brain Failure at the Istanbul Biennal.

Yan Lei became a prominent and influential figure on the Chinese art scene in the 1990s with his interventionist critiques on art institutions and commentary on the structure and function of the globalizing art world. Yan analyzes the relationship between contemporary artists and curators, and between artists and collectors. His artworks are an investigation into the relationship between the action of painting and its expression. He observes and analyzes the artist's own creative method, and from his critical position denounces the inevitable standardization of artistic expression which is currently leading to what many believe is nothing more than a mere system of production and distribution.

Yan's critical and harsh comments on the state of the arts and the role of the institutions that govern the arts can be seen in the astonishing work *Invitation* (1997), a collaboration with fellow Chinese artist Hong Hao. In this work, the artists created a series of fake invitations to the German art exhibition Documenta and sent them out to Chinese artists, who were unaware they were being tricked. The ensuing scandal drew attention to both the failure of overseas curators to understand the needs of Chinese artists, and to the fact that many artists are more concerned with taking part in international exhibitions such as Documenta than producing good work.

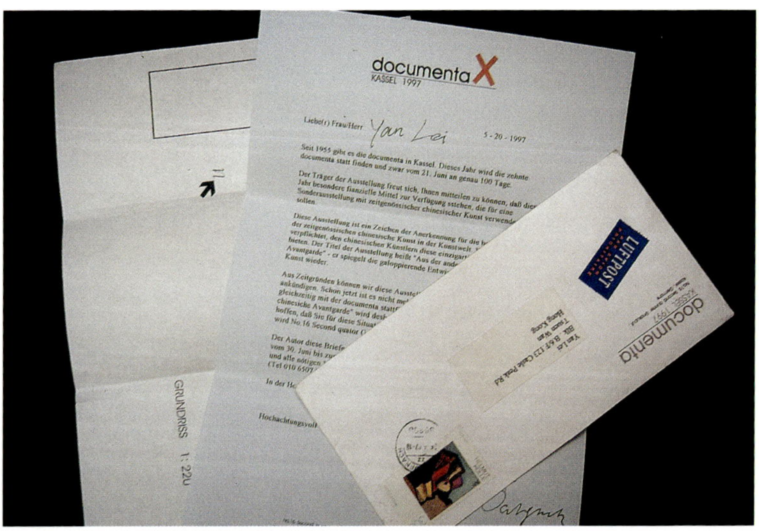

Yan perceives the lack of a real pattern of language in Chinese contemporary art. Choosing a graphic approach, Yan attempts to find a more penetrating language by focusing on the medium and the method. "You see," he says, standing up from the pool table where our interview takes place, and pointing to the bull's eye of the *Color Wheel* canvas that hangs on the wall, "I painted this canvas while I was playing pool. Each line corresponds to the color of the ball I hit. A shade of a color corresponds to a number, so a painting can be composed by applying a color of a certain number to an area of a certain number. It's simple, there is no other meaning in my work." He turns back to the table, strikes, and the ball rolls into the pocket. Thus the bull's eye in the *Color Wheel* series (2005–) becomes simply a dot around which the artist's painting and thinking whirl.

In 2007, as part of Yan's quest for an authentic artistic language, he invited the famous Chinese rock band Brain Failure to the Istanbul Biennial, and videotaped their performance, which he then showed as an installation. For Yan, the reaction of the audience to this performance is art.

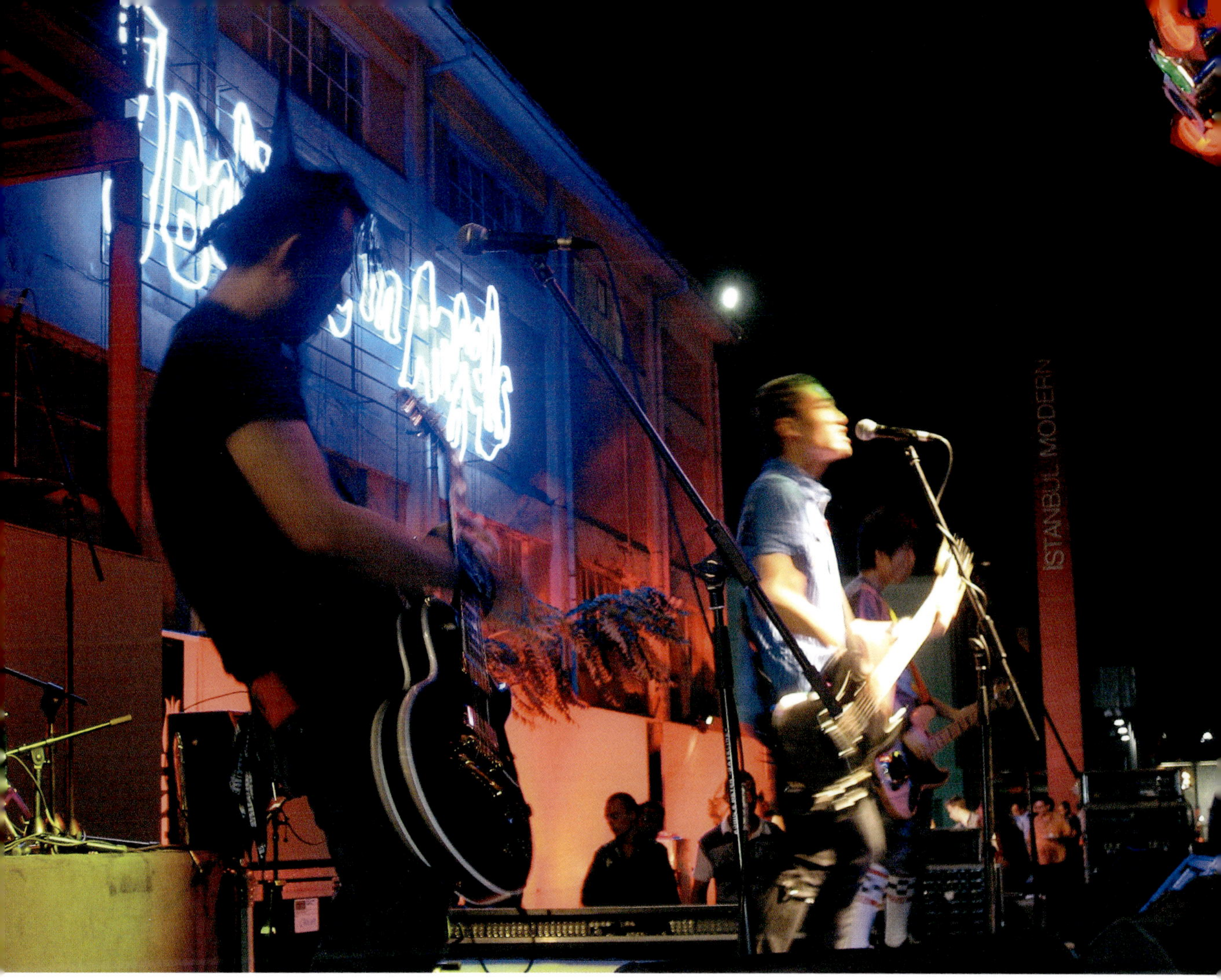
ISTANBUL MODERN

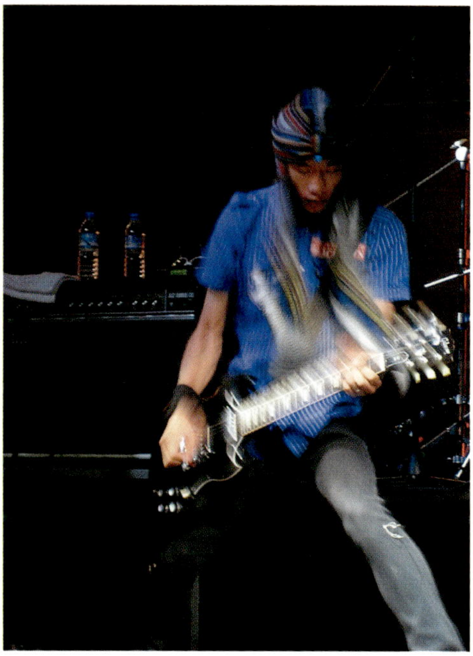

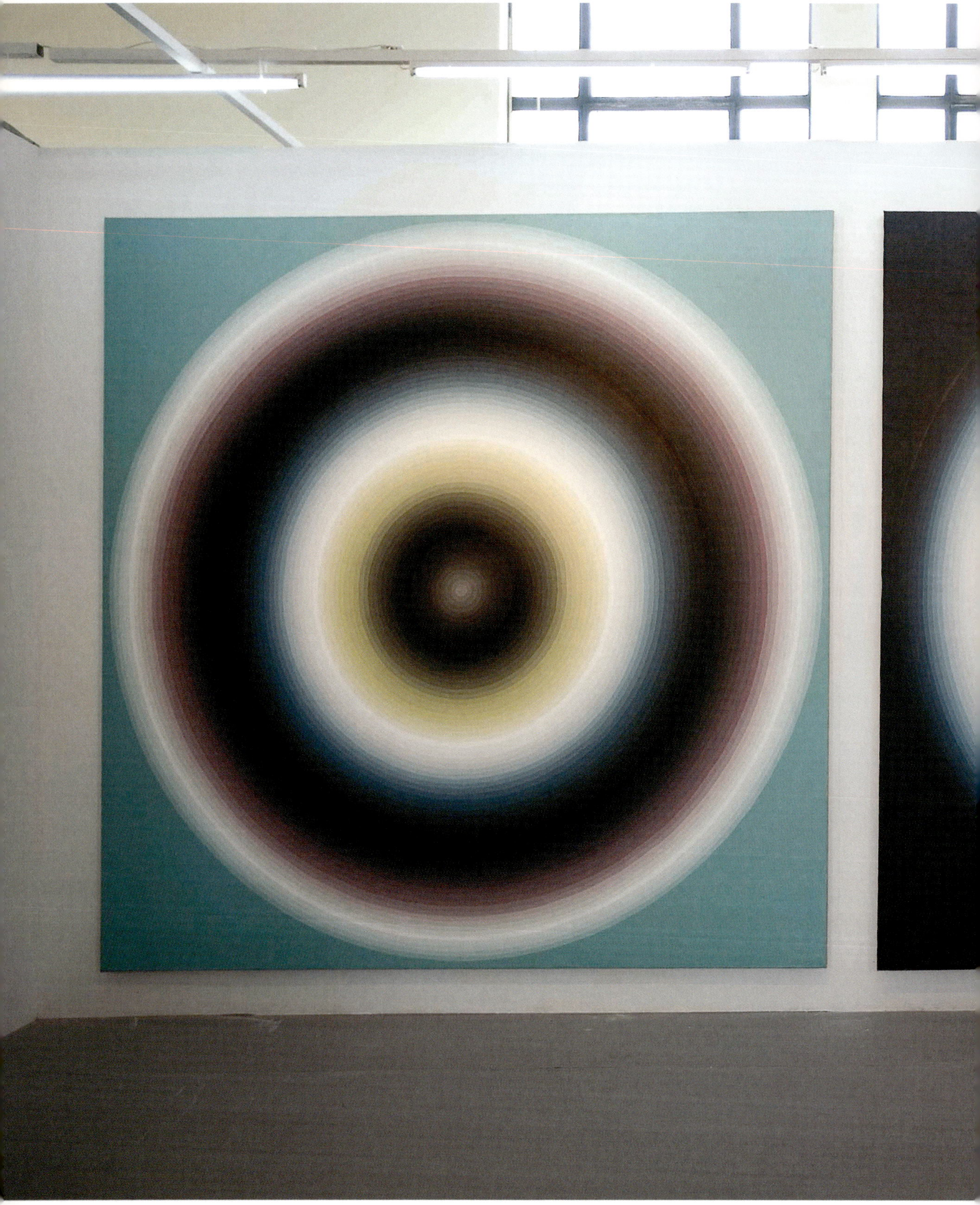

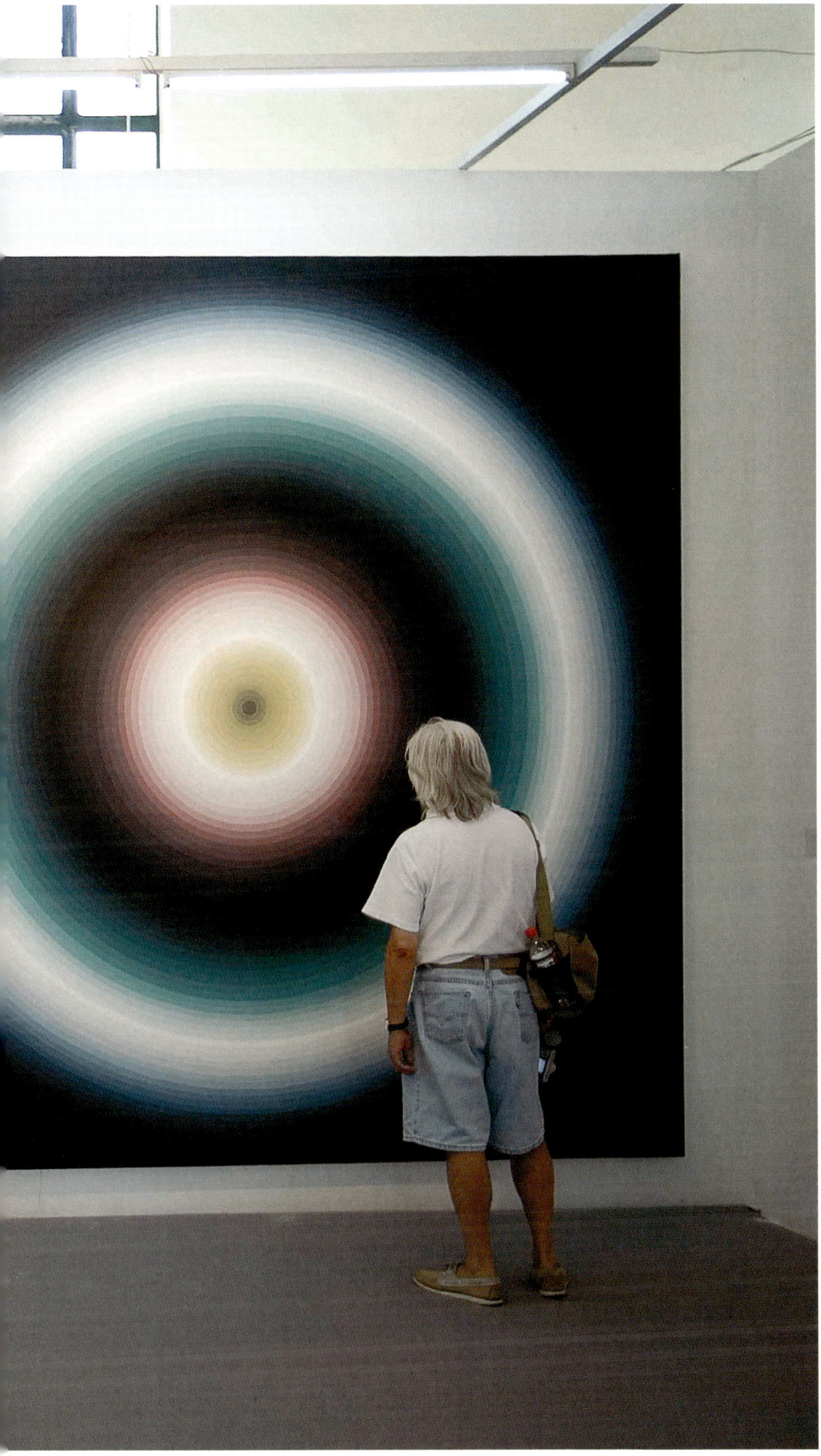

Color Wheels, 2005. Installation view, Galleria Continua, Shanghai Art Fair.

Yang Fudong

Born 1971, Beijing

Graduating in 1994 from the China Academy of Art in Hangzhou, filmmaker, photographer, and video artist Yang Fudong spent three months of his second year at art school in a vow of silence. Misinterpreted by the teaching faculty, Yang's action was in fact part of a project, *Living in Another Space* (1992), for which he decided not to talk, and to communicate only through written messages. Through this ordeal he would experience his emotions more deeply, thoroughly explore his feelings, and allow everything to happen unconditionally. From this early work, we can understand something of the angle from which Yang looks at the reality of contemporary Chinese society and the way he approaches his art.

Yang often reflects upon the sense of alienation at the core of urban life while building a strong narrative discourse that is sometimes difficult to understand. Set in a modern urban context or in natural environments, his narratives tend to focus on the young intellectuals or new middle class of the Chinese metropolis and their ambitions and concerns. His characters are slaves to feelings of uncertainty and vagueness that they don't know how to react to because they don't know whether the problems stem from society or from themselves. This feeling is flawlessly conveyed in *Seven Intellectuals in Bamboo Forest* (2003–), an ongoing black and white video series that takes its title from a Chinese popular tale and whose plot is centered around portrayals of seven men and women in a variety of different scenarios.

Yang's first film work was completed only in 2002 and was presented at the Documenta art exhibition in Germany. *An Estranged Paradise*, shot mostly in black and white using 35mm film, is considered a continuation of Yang's desire to explore the emotional world, and contains psychologically intense meditations on existence while touching on themes such as love and relationships. Both his films and videos are characterized by the use of allusive imagery, carefully chosen sounds, subtitles, and minimal spoken dialogues; the allegories lie in the very slow rhythm and stillness of the scenes where the lives of alienated city dwellers are set.

Even in the description of an ideal, paradisiacal dream world, as in the video *Tonight's Moon* (2000) or in the glimpse of the girl captured in the video *Honey* (2003), there seems to be some hidden aspect, an element that disturbs the overall balance of the contexts, a feeling of estrangement.

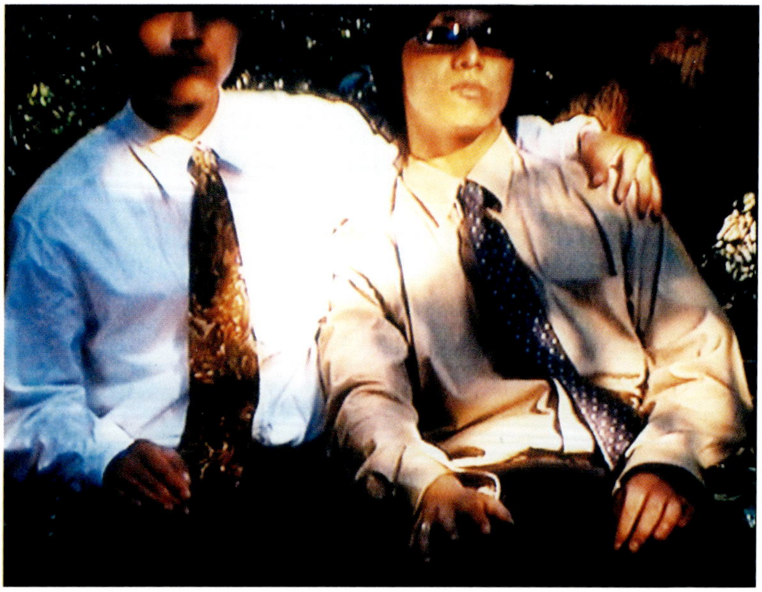

THIS PAGE: *Tonight's Moon*, 2000. Still from multichannel video installation (1 overhead projector, 24 small black and white TV sets, 6 large-screen TV sets).

FACING PAGE: *Honey*, 2003. Still from single-channel video.

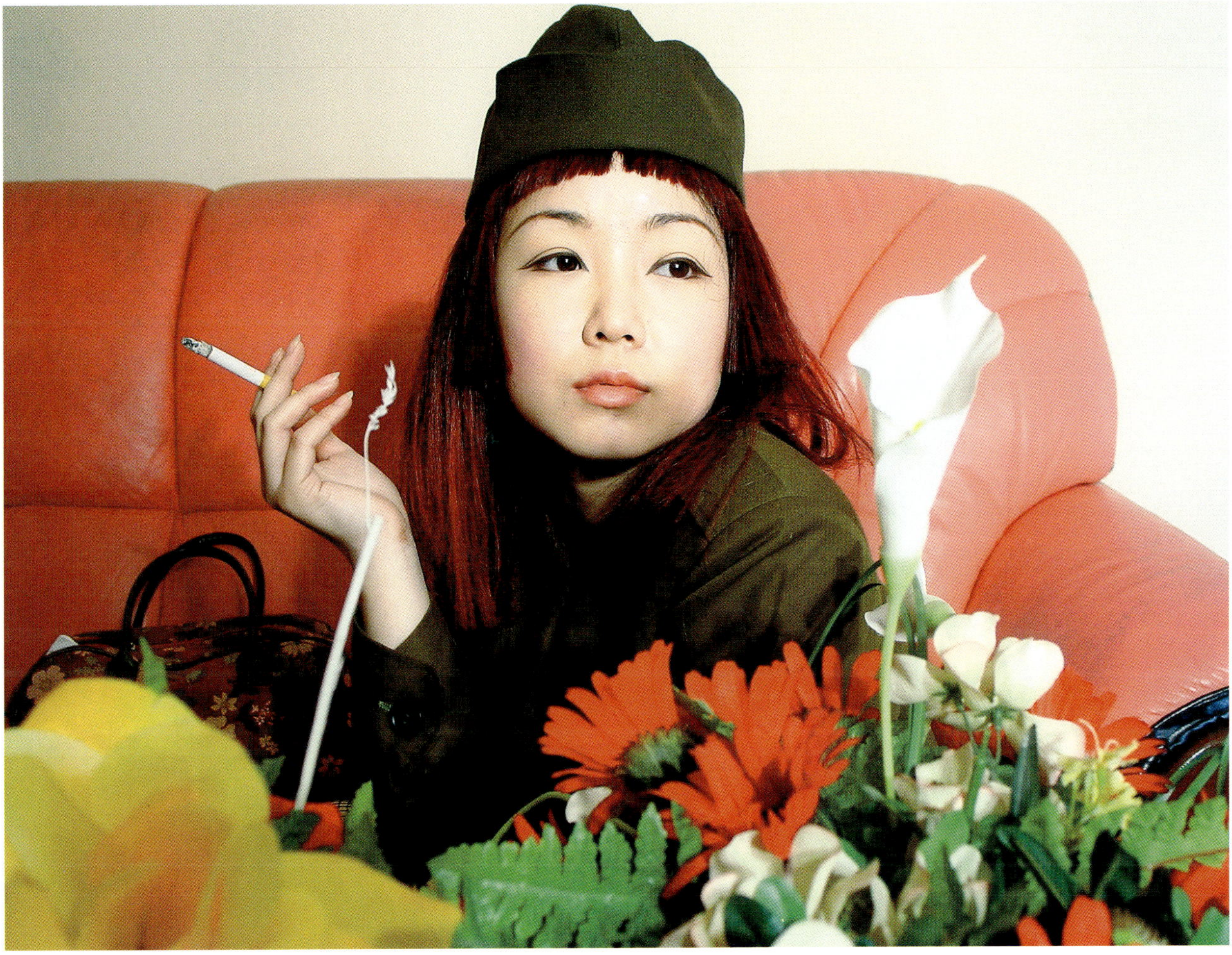

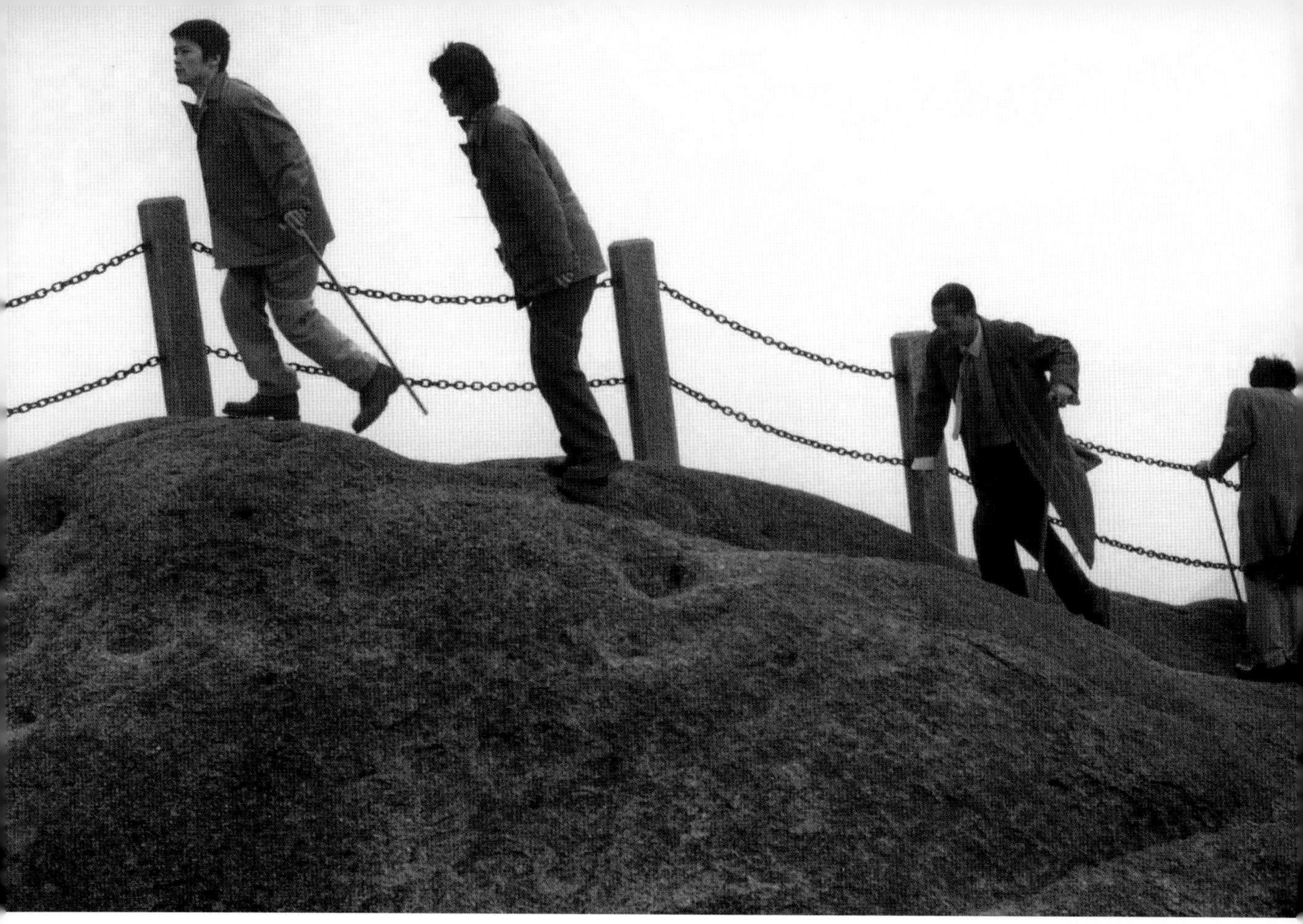

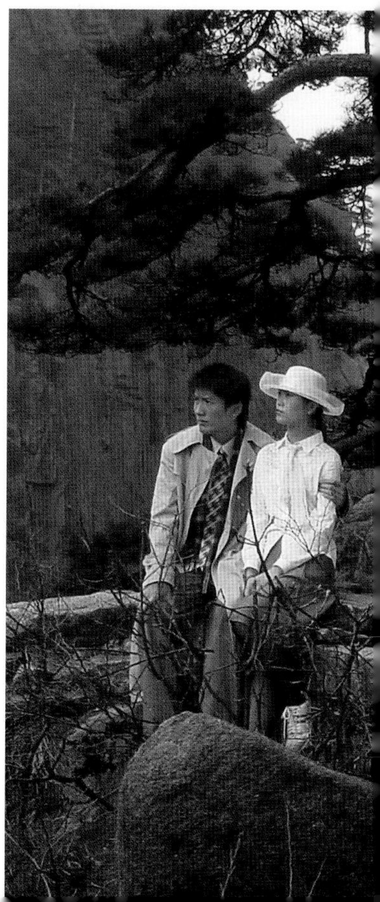

Seven Intellectuals in Bamboo Forest Part 1, 2003. Stills from single-channel video, shot in 35 mm black and white film and transferred to DVD video.

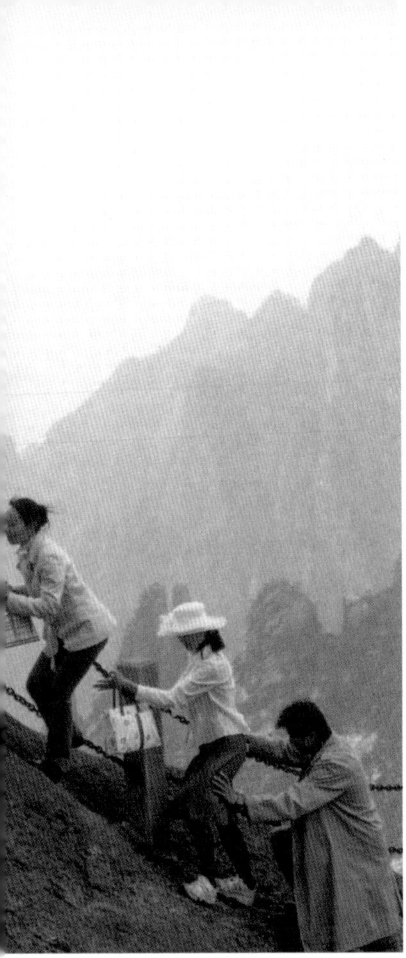

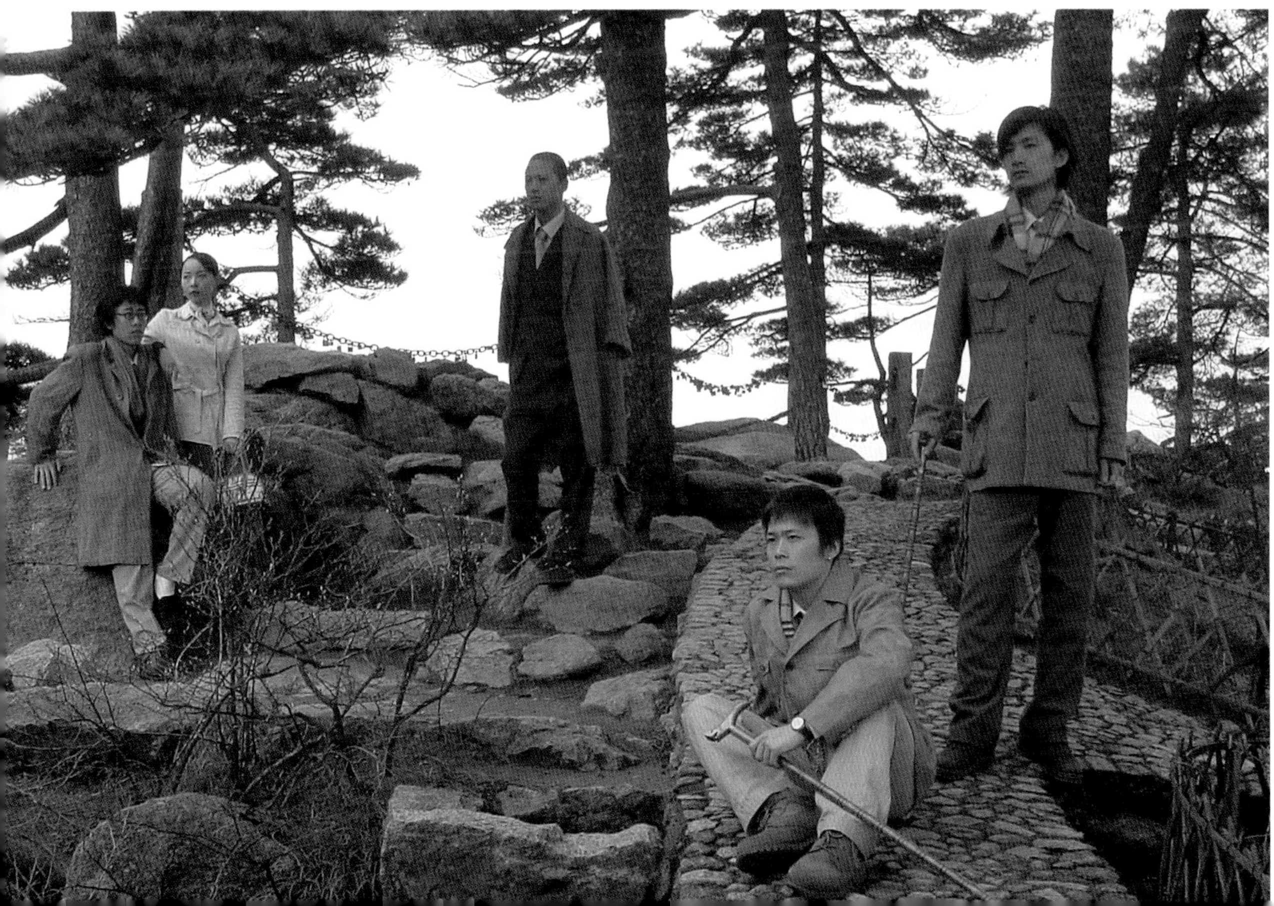

Yang Shaobin

Born 1963, Tangshan, Hebei Province

THIS PAGE: *Untitled 3*, 2007. Oil on canvas, 82½ x 137 in.

FACING PAGE: *Untitled 2000*, 2000. Oil on canvas, 63 x 55 in.

Raised during the Cultural Revolution, a period of lack of information and stimuli, Yang Shaobin is a self-taught artist whose expression is extremely direct and who follows his own natural instincts in a unique and original manner. Yang has not attended any of the Chinese art academies; he was working as policeman in a Public Security Bureau office when, taking inspiration from the everyday events of uniformed life, he began to sketch pictures in his notebook.

Red is the color of the paintings that made him famous: powerful, brutal, heavy brushstrokes in red that transmit unexpectedly real sensations as though the canvases were suddenly surging to life. As he developed his work, Yang moved to the Yuanmingyuan artists' village on the outskirts of Beijing, a gathering place for artists, especially painters, between 1990 and 1995. At Yuanmingyuan, he became involved with the Cynical Realism movement, following in the path of his contemporary Fang Lijun. The professed aim of the movement was to express, through a mix of ennui and black humor, a dissatisfaction with politics and society after the repression and brutality of the Tiananmen incident, and to reflect on the loss of certainties and general societal uneasiness that defined the period.

The spiky satires that are characteristic of his early works, such as *Police Series* (1996) soon changed, however, into a deep analysis of cruelty and an attempt to express the essential violence of human society. Perhaps it was personal experience that brought this to the fore, perhaps his childhood upbringing in the mining areas where violence and brutality were omnipresent. Works such as *Painting No. 19* (2000), *Who Is Screaming* (2003–2004), and *800 Meters Under* (2006) are characterized by images of people fighting, of injuries, and humiliation.

Yang's later works continue to use strong colors, and his paintings are often covered by a thin white layer like a coating of dust, while his sculptures transmit a carnal brutality defined by the superimposition of imperfect layers. Looking at some of his canvases, one can see the influence of Francis Bacon; others show a parity with Hermann Nitsch. The choice of subject and the vigor of the brushstrokes, however, make his style unique.

With works such as *Untitled 3* (2007) seeming to take their inspiration from true episodes of contemporary violence such as terrorism, Yang's canvases continue to speak of anguish and pain. Yet it is precisely in these ugly and unpleasant traits that we can see the beauty of his work.

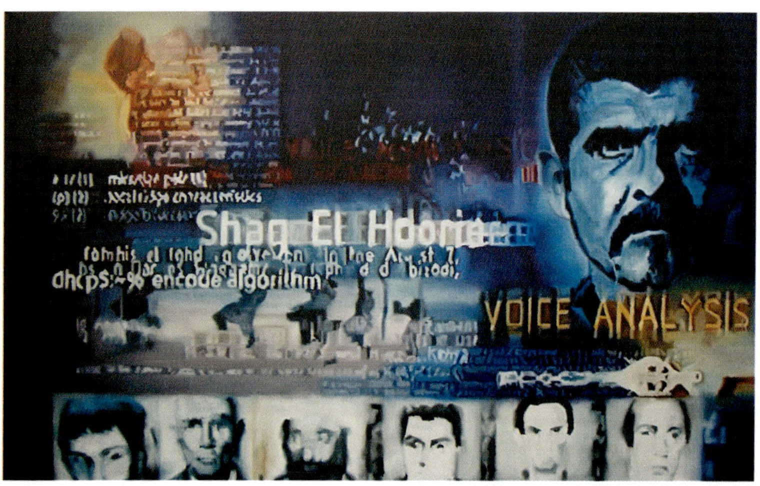

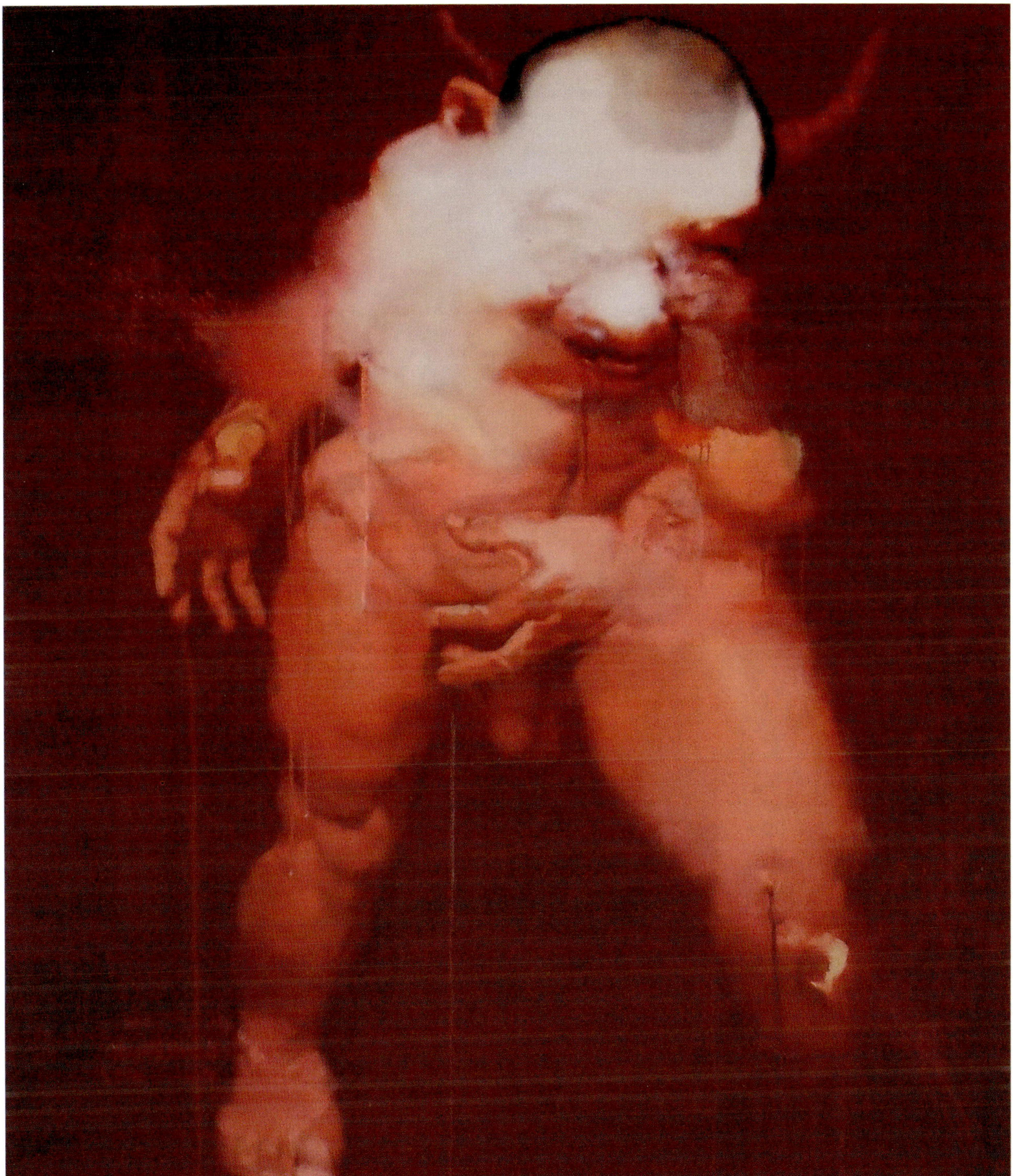

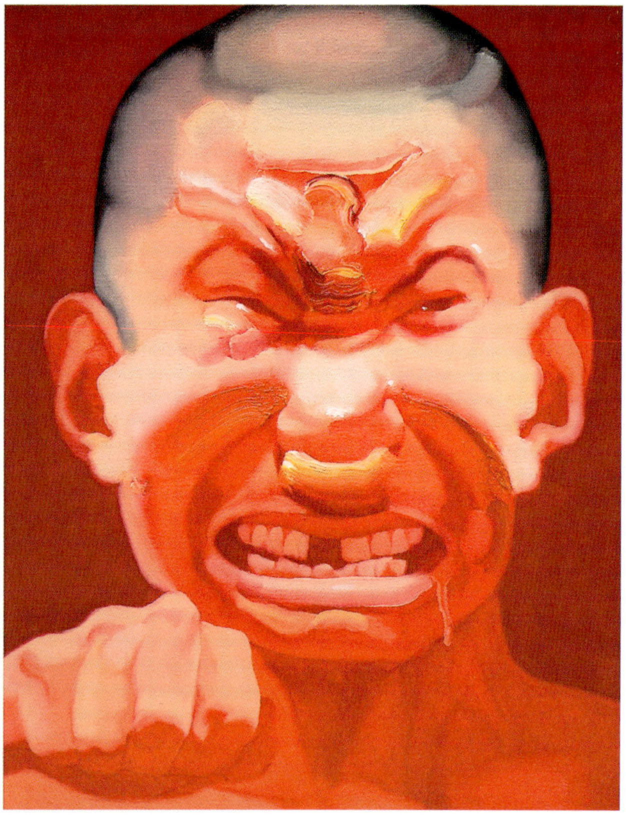

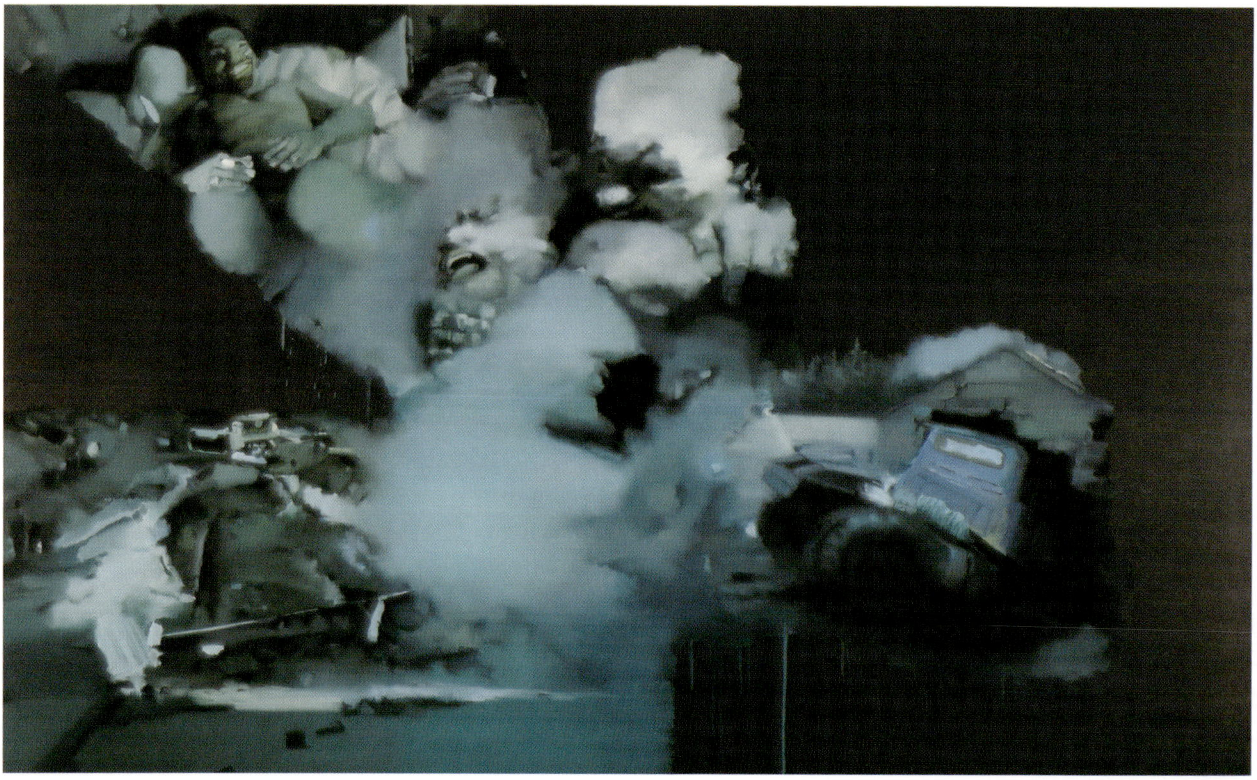

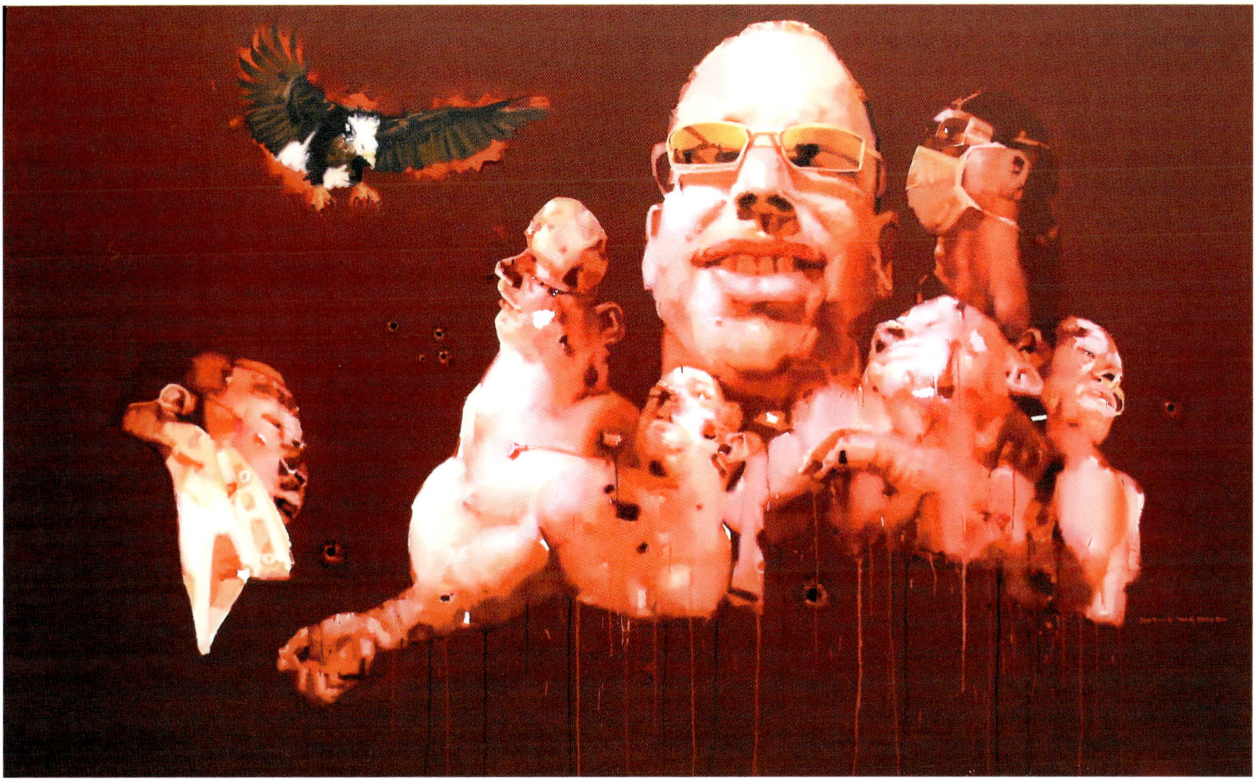

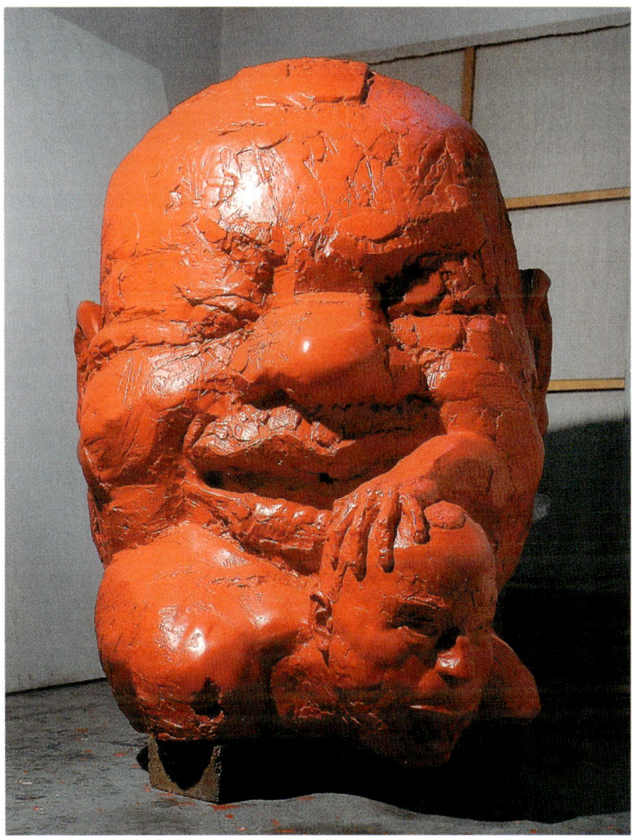

FACING PAGE, TOP: *Police Series No. 46*, 1996. Oil on canvas, 16 x 14 in.

FACING PAGE, BOTTOM: *Who Is Screaming*, 2000–2004. Oil on canvas, 82½ x 138 in.

THIS PAGE, TOP: *Black Hawk Down*, 2007. Oil on canvas, 82½ x 138 in.

THIS PAGE, BOTTOM: *Sculpture 1*, 2001. Fiberglass, 71 x 63 x 55 in.

Yang Zhenzhong

Born 1968, Hangzhou, Zhejiang Province

THIS PAGE: *Light and Easy 2*, 2002. Still from video.

FACING PAGE: *922 Rice Grains*, 2000. Stills from video.

OVERLEAF, LEFT: *I Will Die—Zhongwen (Chinese)*, 2000. Stills from video.

OVERLEAF, RIGHT: *I Will Die—Helan (Dutch)*, 2001. Stills from video.

What if you were asked to pose in front of a video camera and repeat "I will die"? Exploring the different reactions of people to this task, Yang Zhengzhong crosses the border between real life and performance. Starting the project as an experiment in 2000, Yang has made an ongoing work of his video recordings entitled *I Will Die* that questions our relationship with the idea of death. It is interesting to note that as soon as a video camera is placed in front of someone, inevitably this person takes on a new character and starts acting. The audience, on the other hand, experiences contradictory emotions due to the inevitable contrast between the shallowness with which the people caught on camera speak, and the profound meaning of the words recited.

Part of the '85 New Art Movement, whose members investigated new forms of art in reaction to the Socialist Realism style that was prevalent at the time, Yang explores the new urban reality. With no specific plans, he follows his impulses and records the everyday experience. His early single-channel video *Sleepwalking Is a Therapy* (1997), in which a camera is positioned on a moving remote-controlled car, is shot inside a conventional apartment. The innovation is the angle from which we observe the ordinary: the camera is in fact filming from the floor. The ongoing photo series *Cycle Aerobics* (1999–) where a couple sharing a bicycle is portrayed cycling around the city, seems to focus on the triviality of modern life, juxtaposing the practicality of bicycle, a ubiquitous form of transport in China, with its potential use as a fitness machine. The video and digital photographic works entitled *Light and Easy* (2002–) and *Light as Fuck* (2003–) depict the artist holding on the tip of his finger a number of unthinkably heavy objects and huge sculptures, and—even more striking—the city of Shanghai.

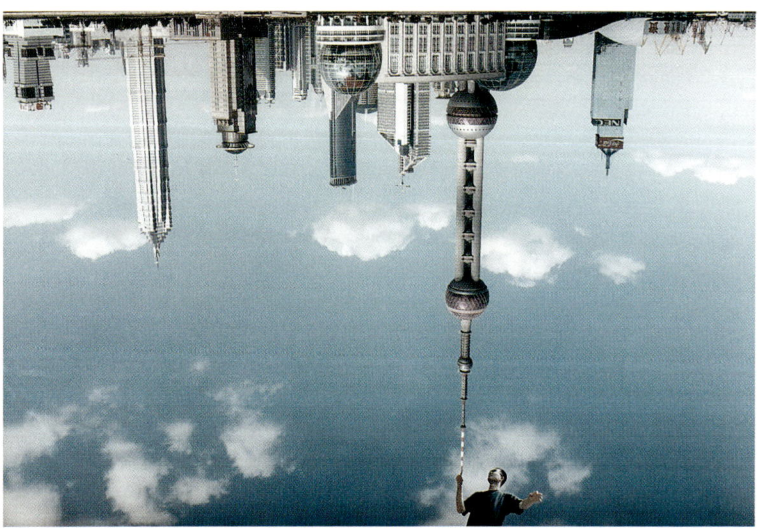

Yang's works focus on his perception of life as a "state of constant recurrence." The videos *We Are Not Fish* (1996) and *922 Rice Grains* (2000) are based on the everyday, and draw our attention to the irritating repetition that is part of the nature of human existence. Later works continue to explore social behaviors. The sound installation *I Have a Dream* (2006), in which members of the audience are invited onto a platform to speak into a microphone, transforms an individual voice into the sound of different people talking at the same time. In the installation *Trashcan* (2006), a trash can which is normally "asleep" opens its "mouth" when a passerby tries to throw something away, a humorous depiction of an inanimate object trying to enter a public space in a human way.

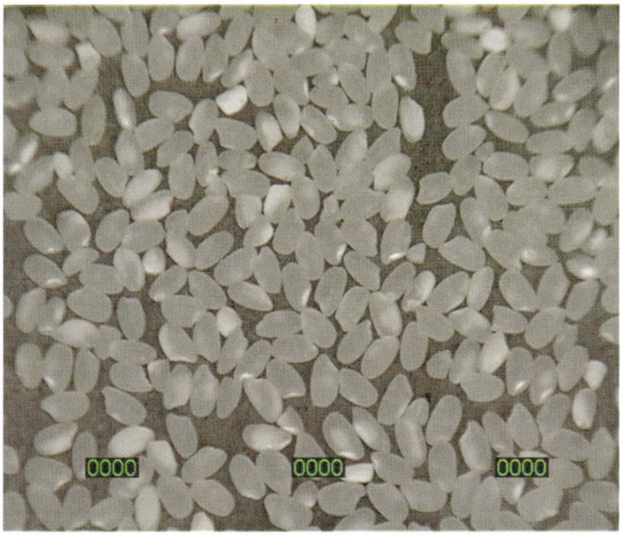
0000
0000
0000

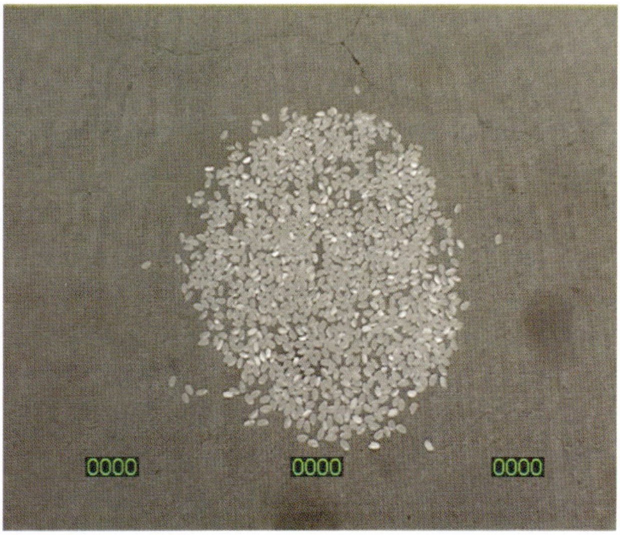
0000
0000
0000

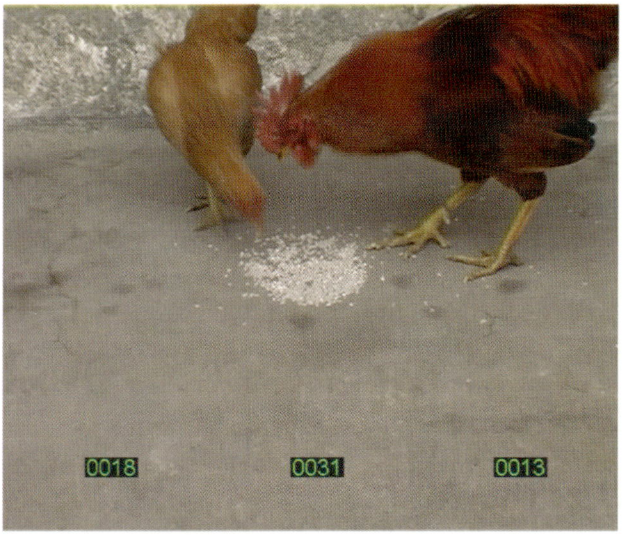
0018
0031
0013

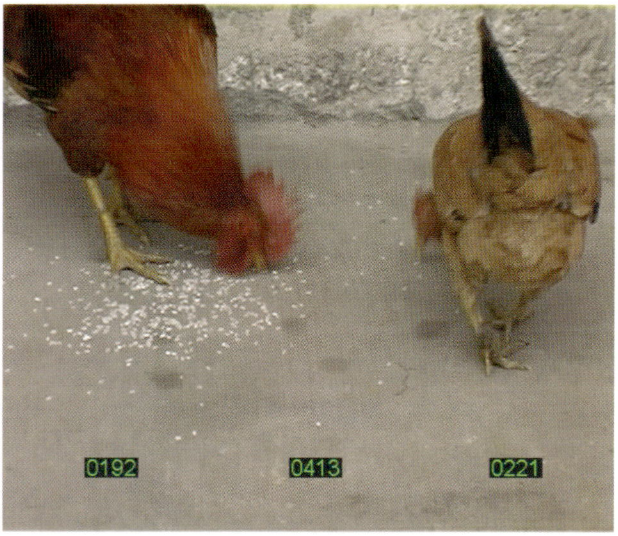
0192
0413
0221

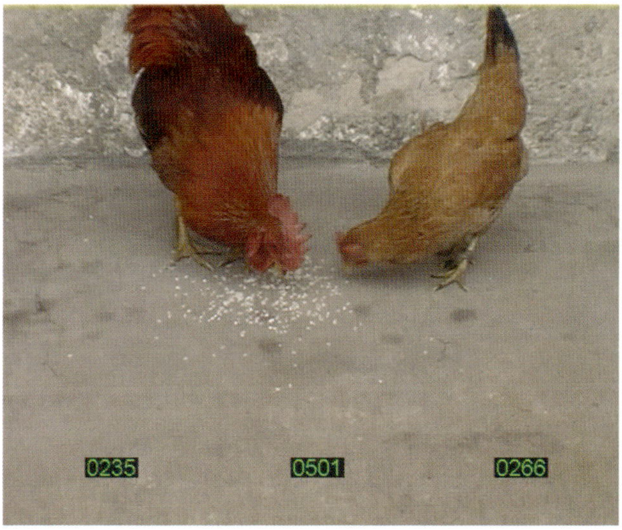
0235
0501
0266

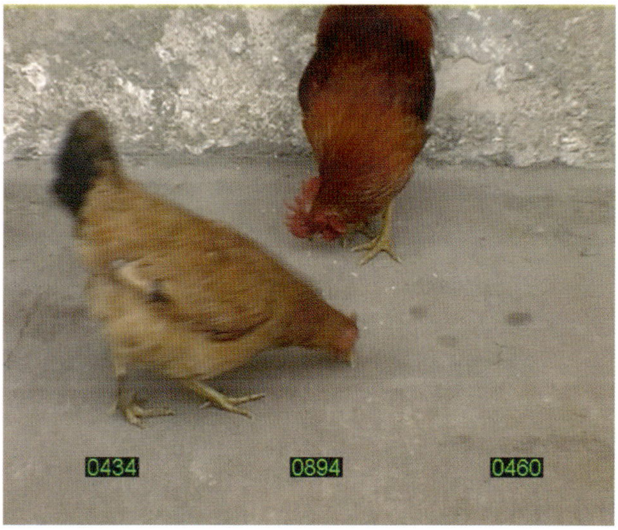
0434
0894
0460

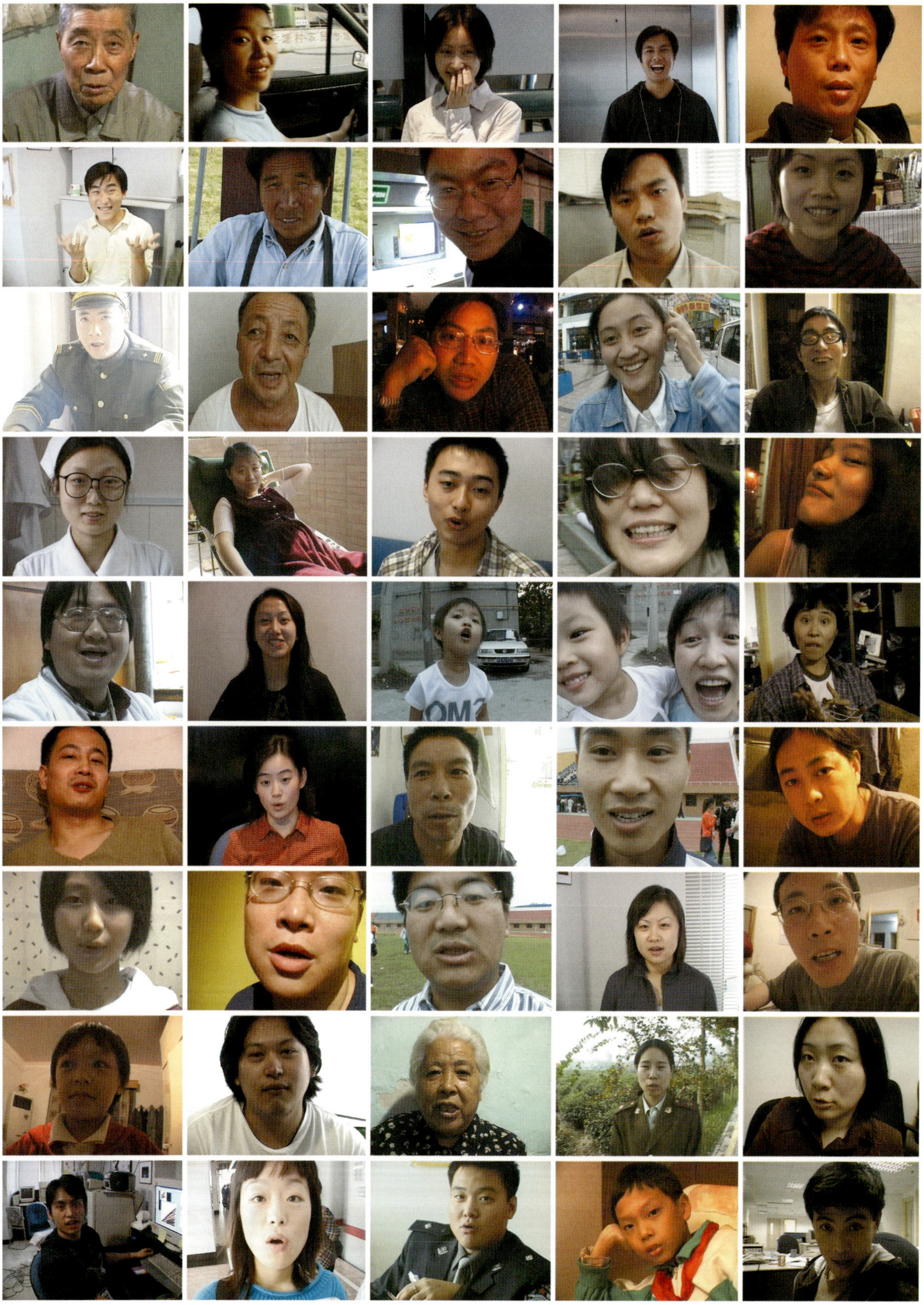

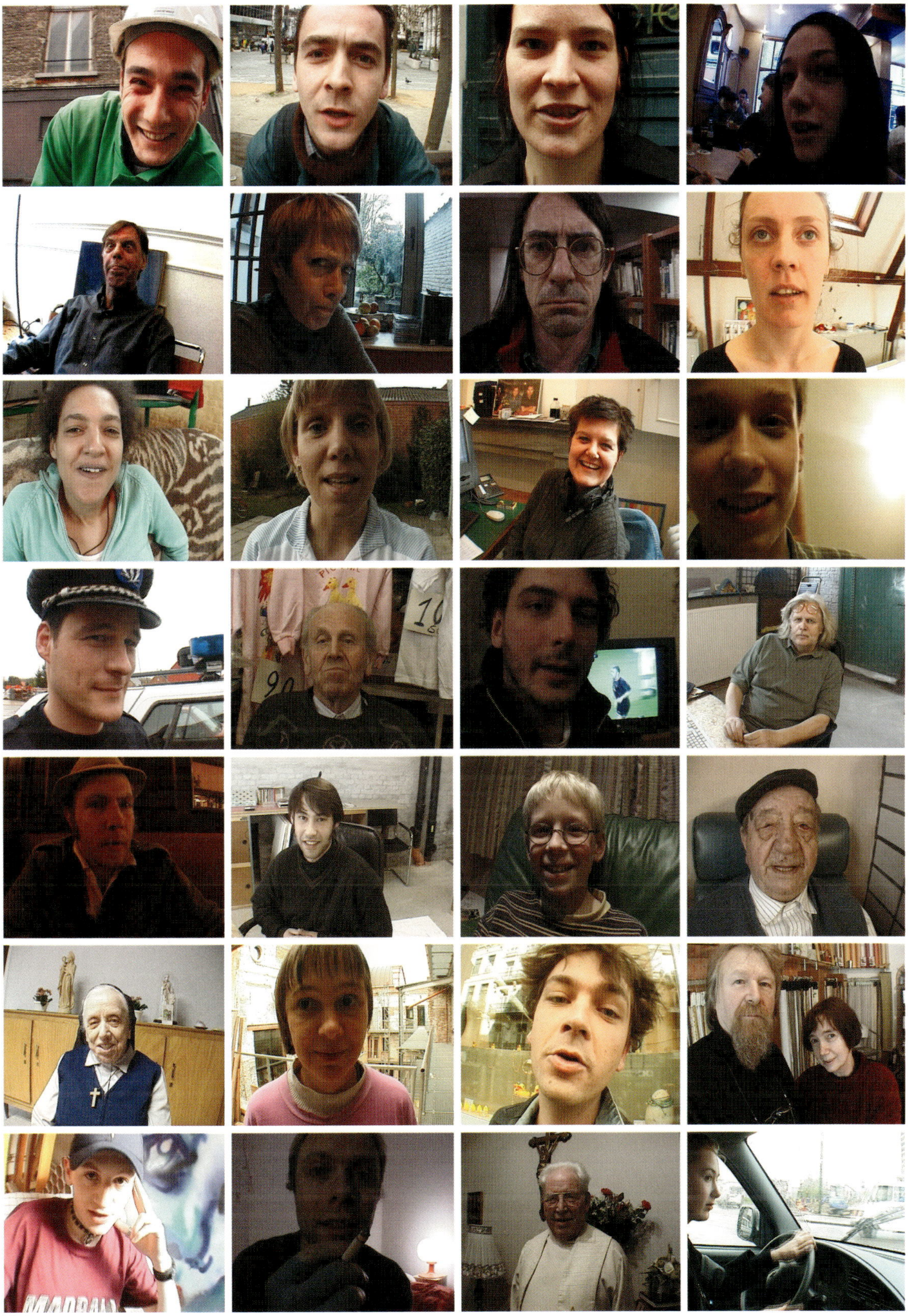

Yin Xiuzhen

Born 1963, Beijing

THIS PAGE: *Weapons*, 2007. Installation view, Venice Biennale. Old clothes from all over the world and everyday objects, 210 pieces.

FACING PAGE: *Portable Cities—Beijing on the Move*, 2002. Mixed media, fabric, suitcase.

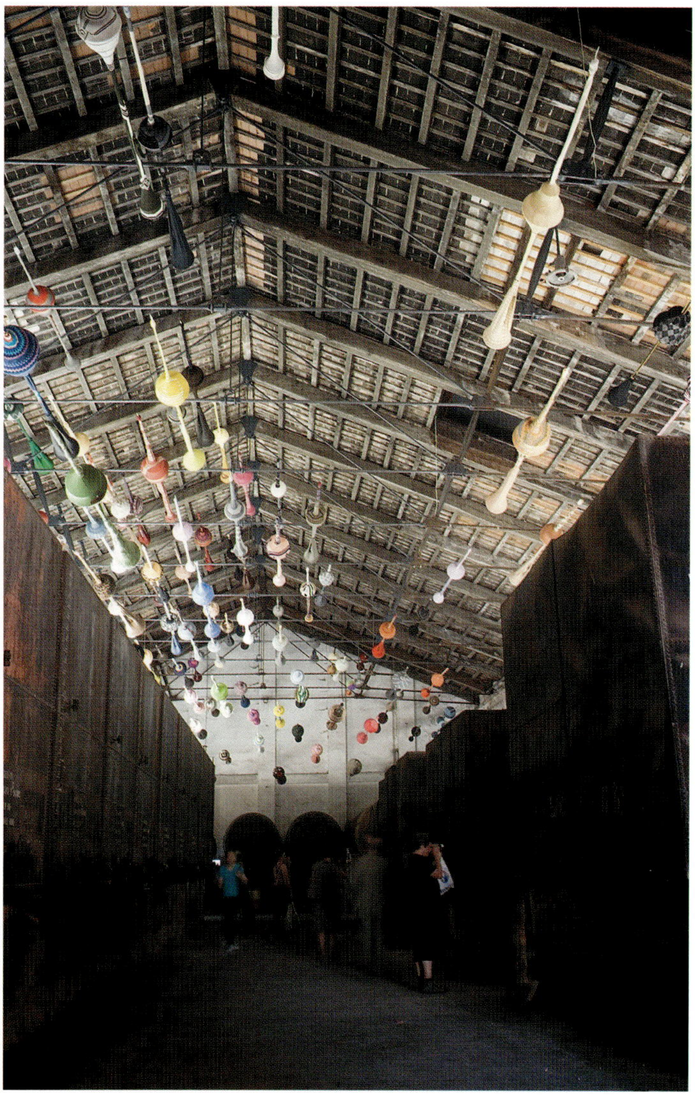

One of four women chosen by curator Hou Hanru to exhibit in the Chinese Pavilion at the 52nd Venice Biennale in 2007, Yin Xiuzhen offers her own unique commentary on the process of modernization in China. Yin uses the notion of memory as a critical tool to analyze the sociopolitical and economic transformations of her homeland, giving a female perspective on issues that tend to be discussed from a male-centric point of view.

The installation *Weapons* (2007), made from 210 items of old clothing and everyday objects collected from around the world, is a testimony to urban mutation and its effects on the individual and the community in the process of China's integration into the global scene. Hundreds of weapons appear hanging from the ceiling to create a menacing scenario, a reflection upon the current reality of excessive economic development, urbanization, and political conflicts.

With an inventive approach to the use of materials and space, Yin's installations are presented in both galleries and natural surroundings. Utilizing her extensive collection of used items, Yin recycles and reformulates to present her perspective. In the series *Portable Cities* (2002) she recreates the landscapes of various cities inside suitcases, using a patchwork of different materials and old clothes to represent the human feelings and events coursing through the urban realm.

Clothes and textiles have a feminine quality, which gives a thought-provoking contrast to the forms they are assembled to represent. Their soft, tactile texture is imbued with an awareness of history and experience: these are objects that contain individual lives. Through her work, Yin explores the ability to store, retain, and subsequently retrieve information, and moves her discussion to a metaphorical level to highlight the political, social, environmental, and human constructs that contribute to the problems brought about by China's sudden process of modernization.

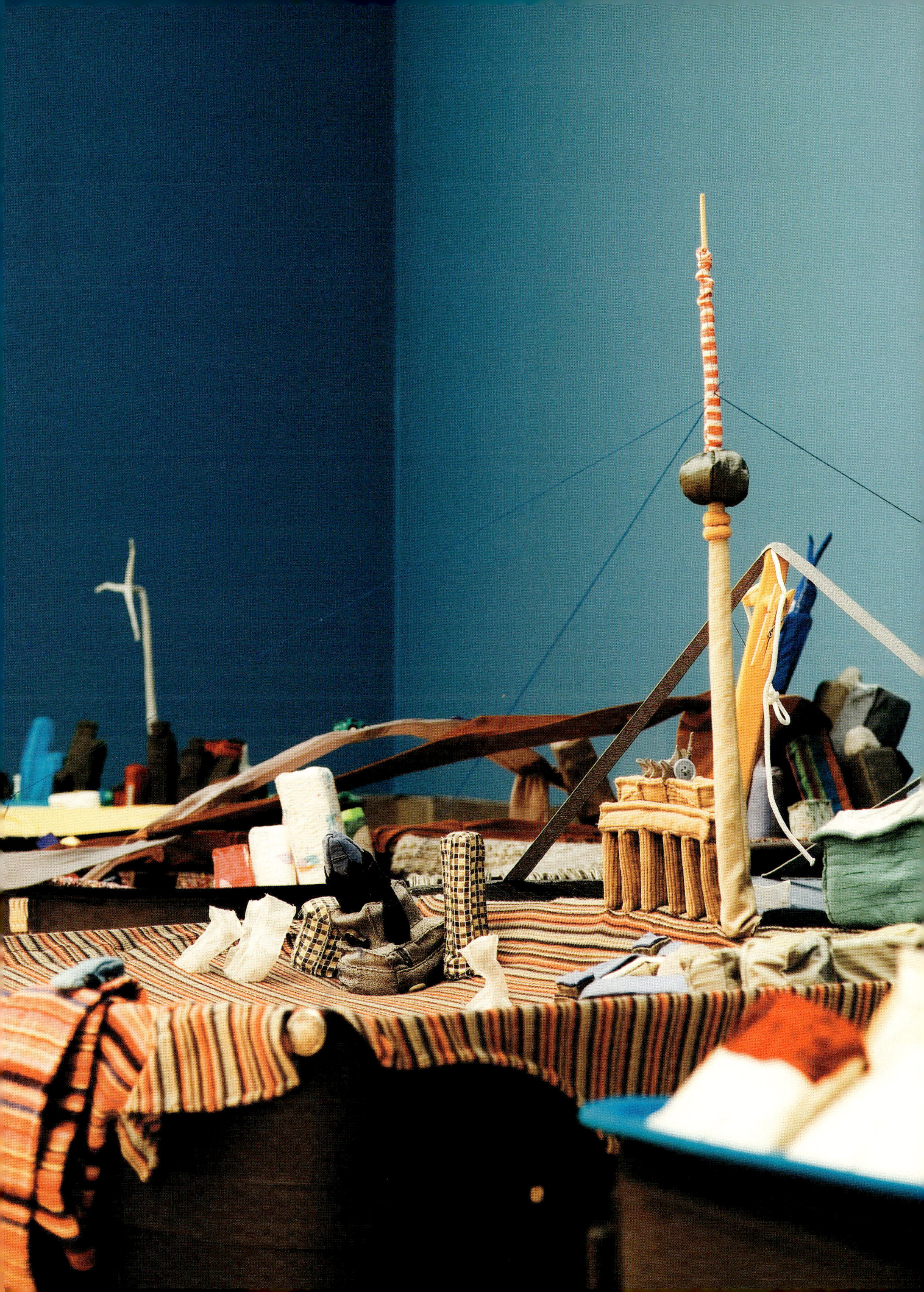

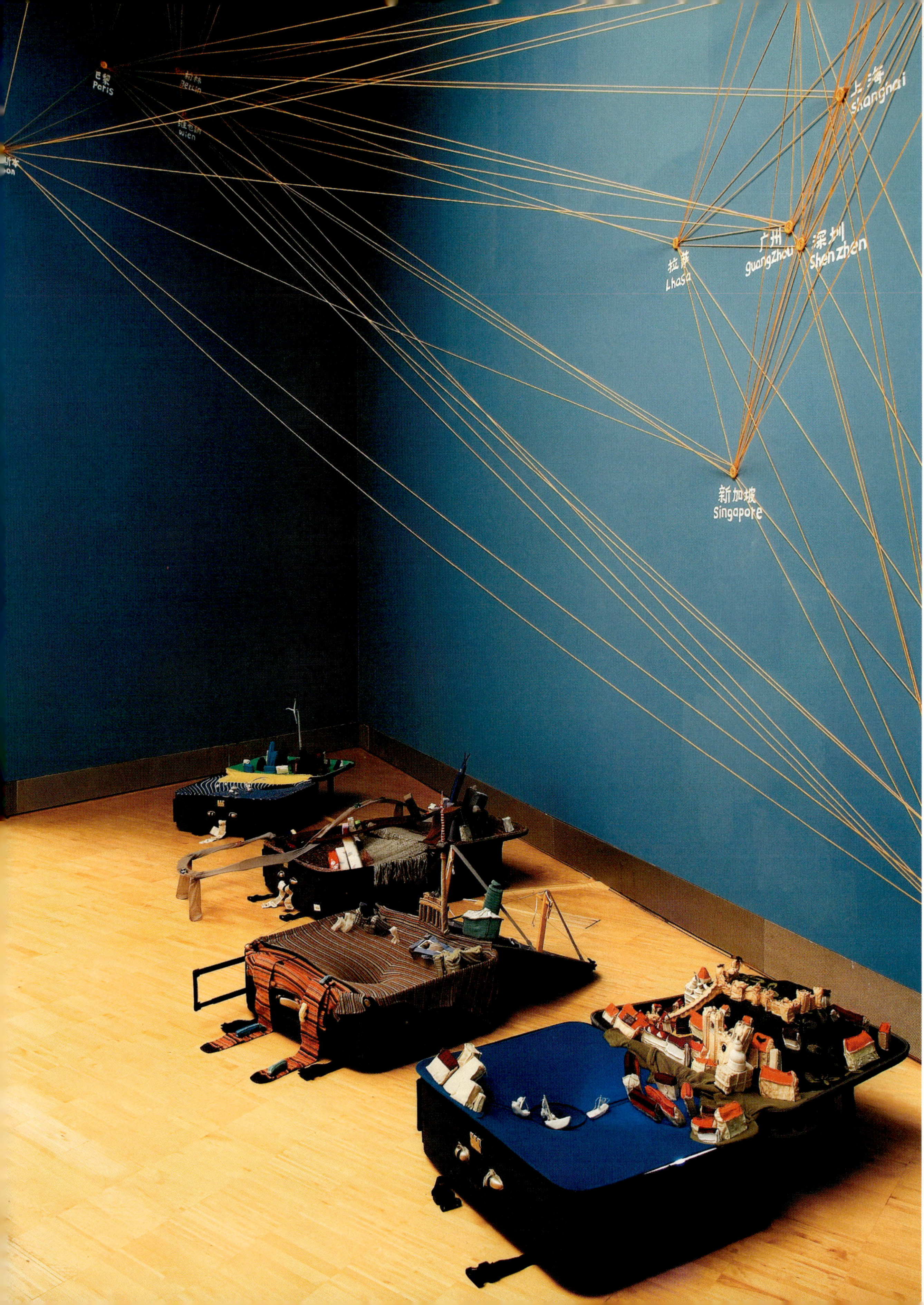

巴黎
Paris
柏林
Berlin
维也纳
wien
上海
Shanghai
广州
Guangzhou
深圳
Shenzhen
拉萨
Lhasa
新加坡
Singapore

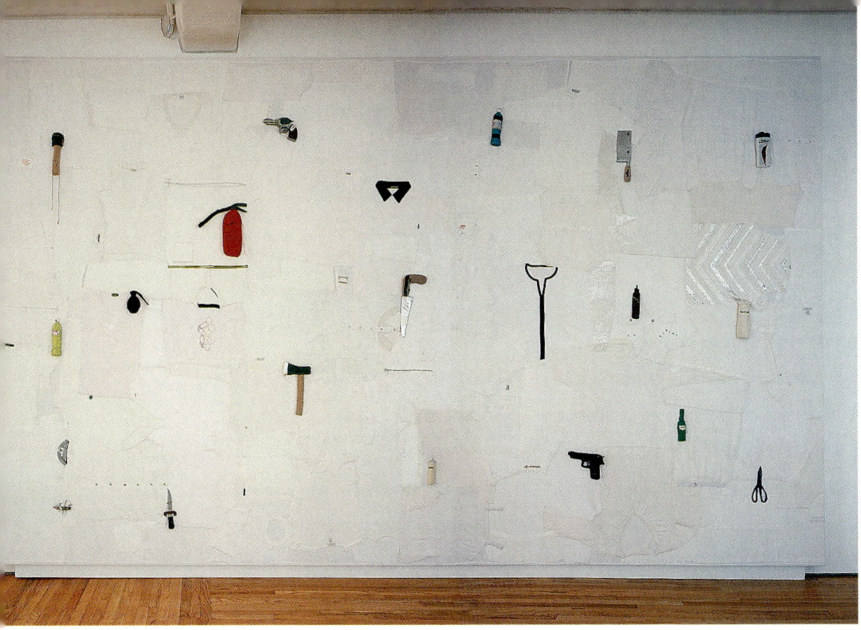

FACING PAGE: *Portable Cities*, 2006. Installation view, Essl Museum, Klosterneuburg, Austria.

THIS PAGE, TOP: *Dangerous Things in Baggage*, 2006. Fabric, buttons, wood, 118 x 197 x 8 in.

THIS PAGE, CENTER: *Fashion Terrorism*, 2004. Mixed media, fabric, suitcase. Dimensions variable.

THIS PAGE, BOTTOM: *International Airport Terminal 1*, 2006. Installation view, Alexander Ochs Galleries, Berlin.

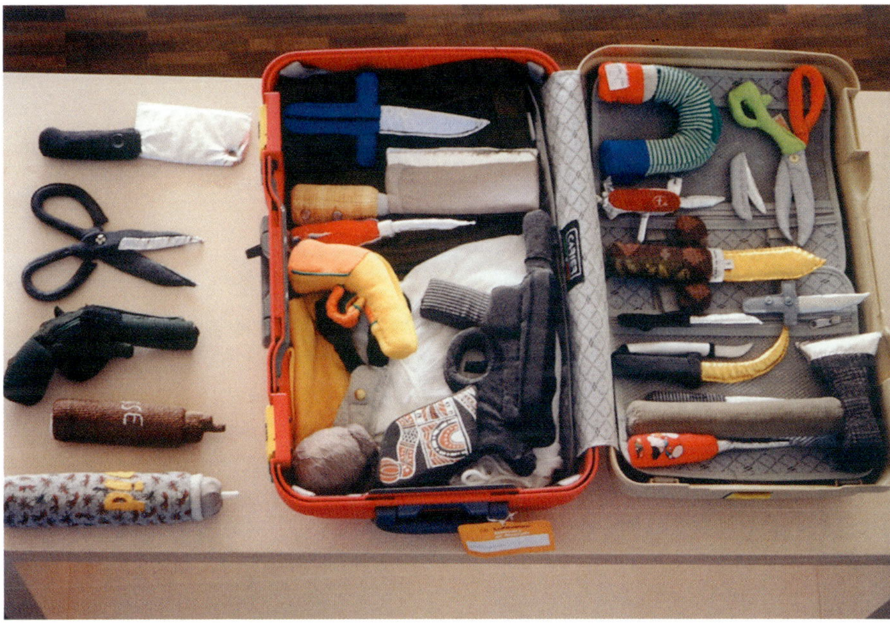

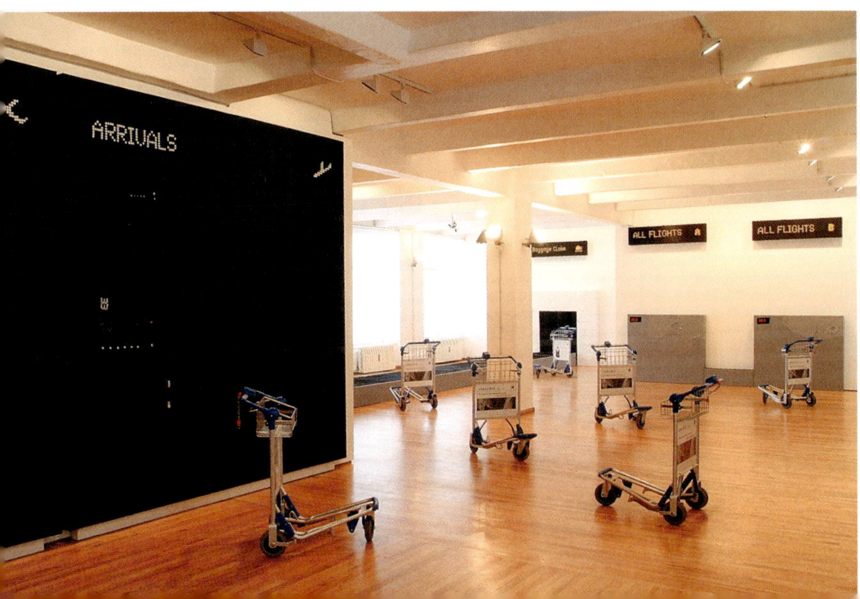

Yue Minjun

Born 1962, Daqing, Heilongjiang Province

THIS PAGE: *Maze Series—Looking for Whom Being Defined as Terrorist*, 2006. Acrylic on canvas, 86½ x 118 in.

FACING PAGE: *Contemporary Terracotta Warriors 6*, 2005. Bronze sculpture, 73 x 31½ x 23½ in.

The laughing clones that Yue Minjun creates have become his trademark feature. Yue expresses his dissatisfaction with society through this obsessively repeated self-image, the "superficial idol," as art critic Li Xianting has termed it. Using himself as model, Yue draws faces that are strong yet self-mocking, and which deride people and their precarious relationships, portraying emptiness, boredom, and indifference toward everyone and everything. Growing up during the Cultural Revolution—as a child educated to emulate models for exemplary communist behavior, and as an adult consigned to the regimented "work unit" with no access whatsoever to the world beyond the work unit—he became cynical and disillusioned as a result of the hypocrisies that surrounded him.

Since the early 1990s, Yue has devoted himself to this huge mocking grin, which began on canvas and has since extended to sculptures and silkscreen prints. Using a minimal palette of radiating colors, his works have a strong visual impact. Yue's approach could be described as simplistic, but the artist has said that his work emits a sense of laxity that describes his own personality exactly. Reminiscent of Pop Art, his style belongs nonetheless to the school of Cynical Realism, of which he is one of the most influential exponents. A term coined by Li Xianting, Cynical Realism was developed during the early 1990s among the artists living in the Yuanmingyuan artists' colony in Beijing. These painters used irony and mockery to criticize society.

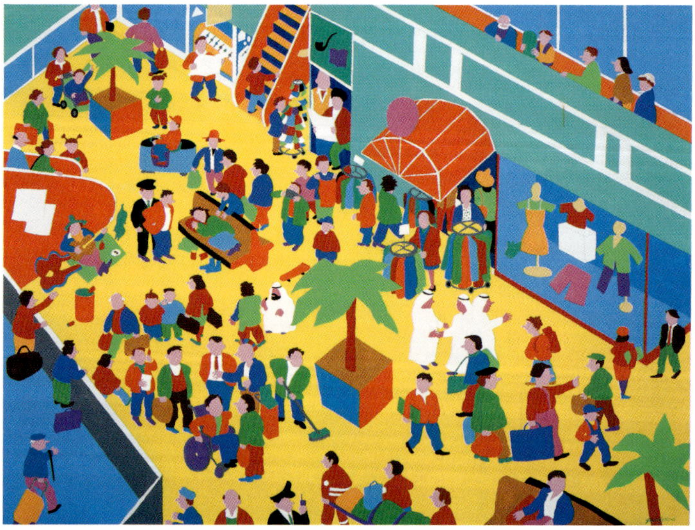

Yue's grinning protagonists bring to mind the fool, an image that can be traced back to classical Taoist philosophy, whose ancient scholars often chose to give up when faced with hopeless problems. Yue reminds us that the act of giving up is utterly human, and that laughter—which allows us to become detached—is a way of dealing with difficult situations.

Perhaps most unsettling are Yue's paintings of men engaged in killing. He has stated: "My compositions are full of mock shooting and killing, carried out in laughter. This is a way to ridicule those who try to solve conflicts through violent means." The use of colors typical of Chinese rural paintings, radiating richness and happiness, adds to the mocking element.

In the *Maze Series* (2006), Yue wonders what we are looking for in the search for terrorists if not for something that we have created ourselves. Through the use of bright colors and a childlike aesthetic, he softens this formidable issue, creating a new approach to the problem.

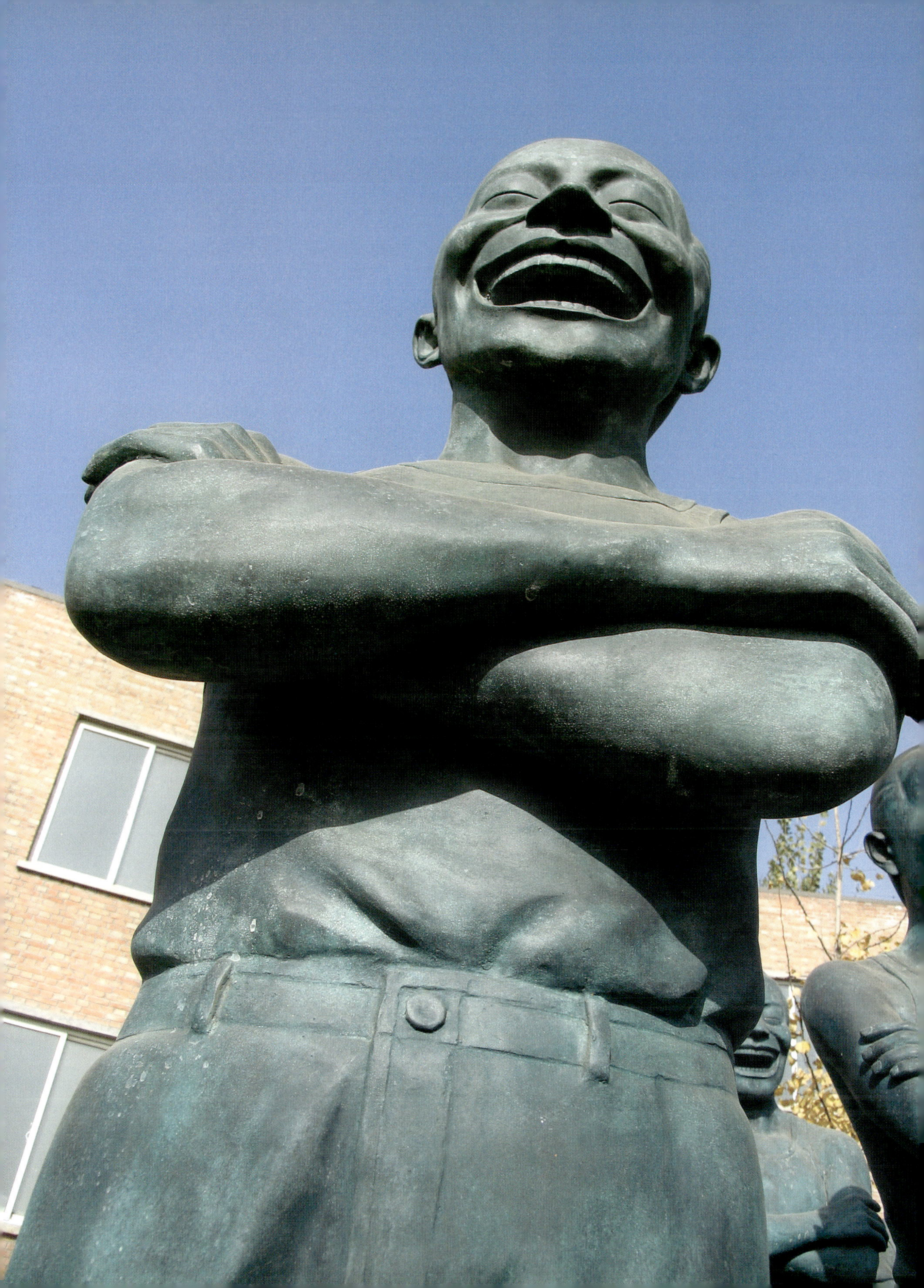

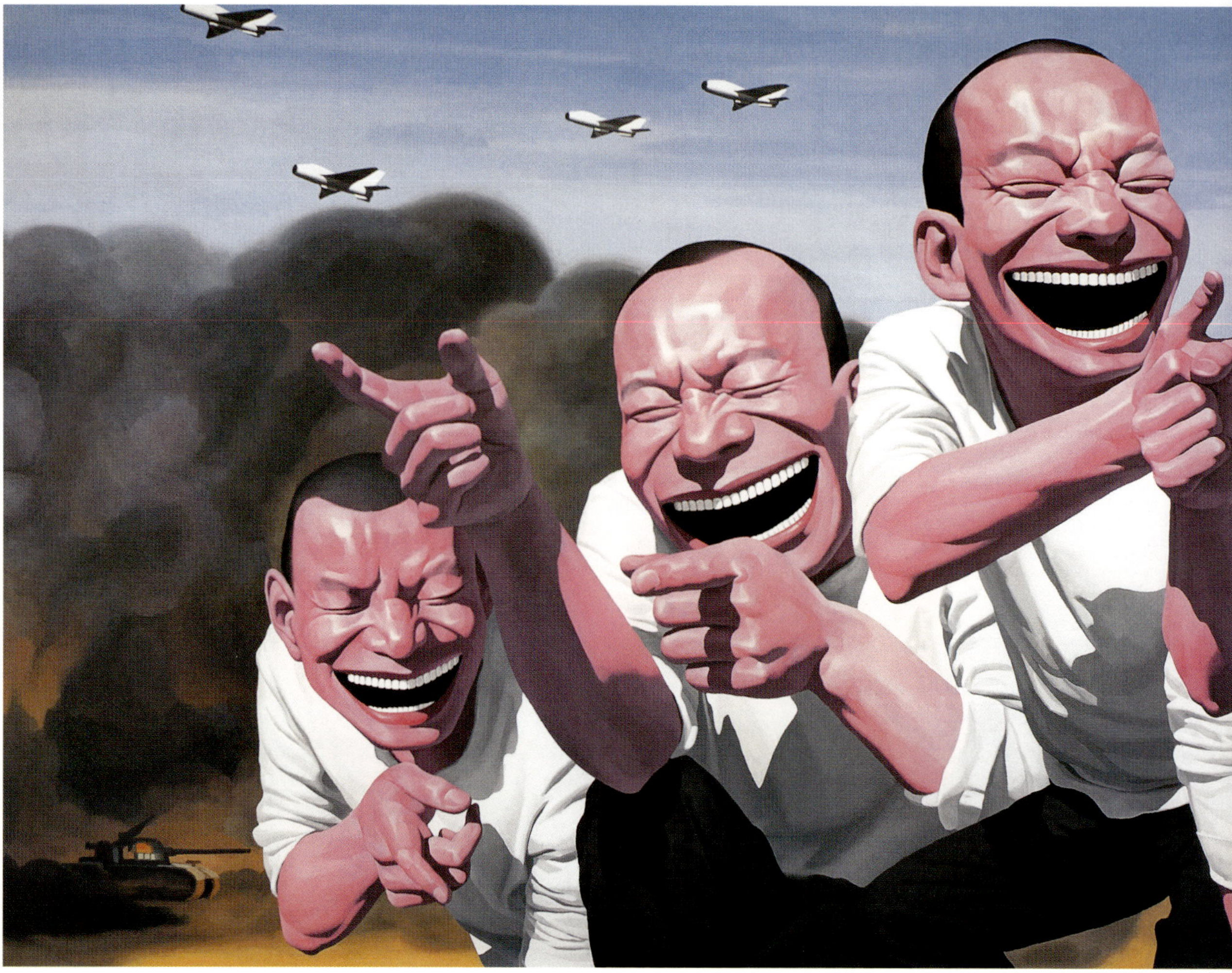

TOP: *Fighting*, 2002. Acrylic on canvas, 71½ x 197 in.

BOTTOM: *Freedom Leading the People*, 1995–1996. Oil on canvas, 98½ x 142 in.

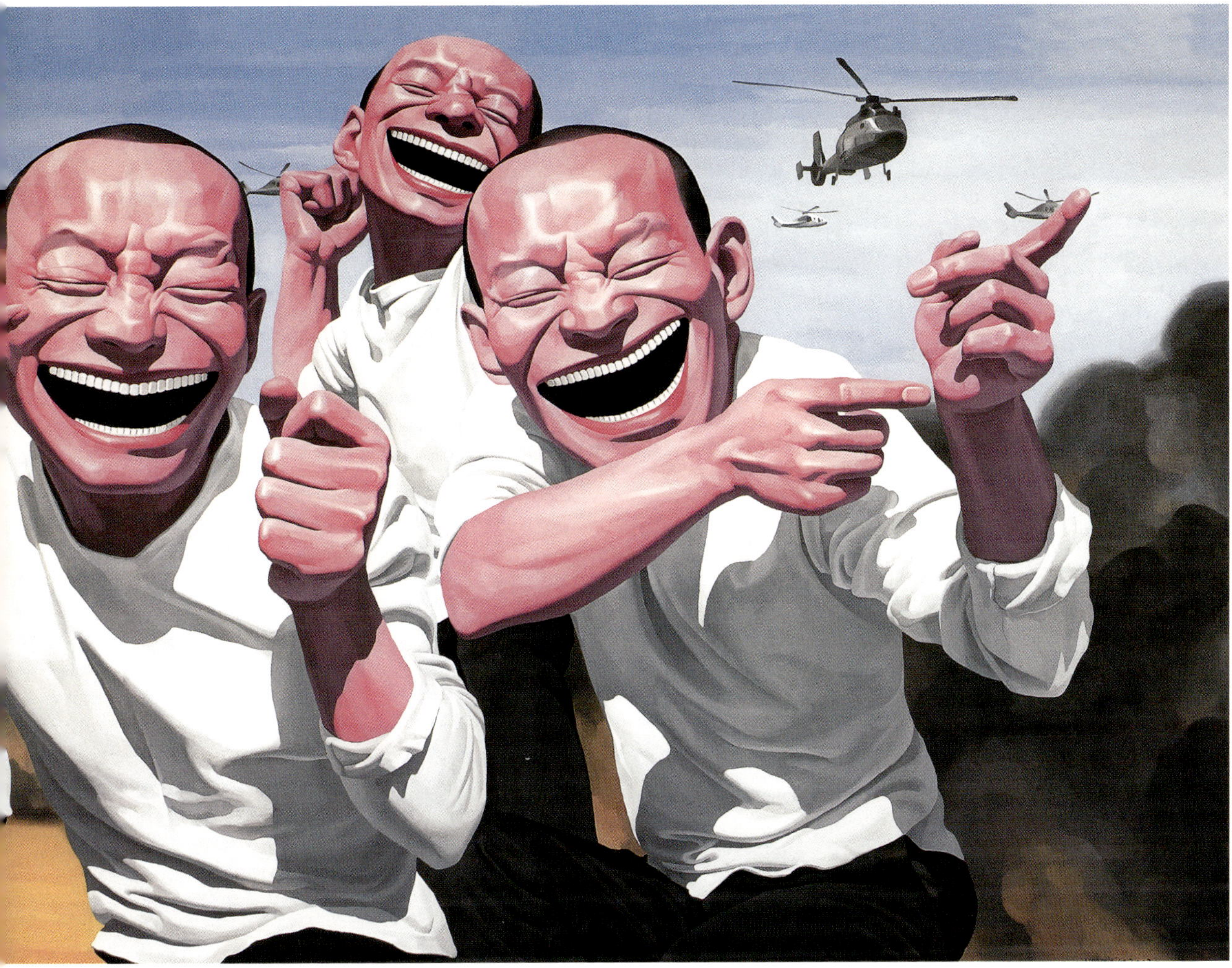

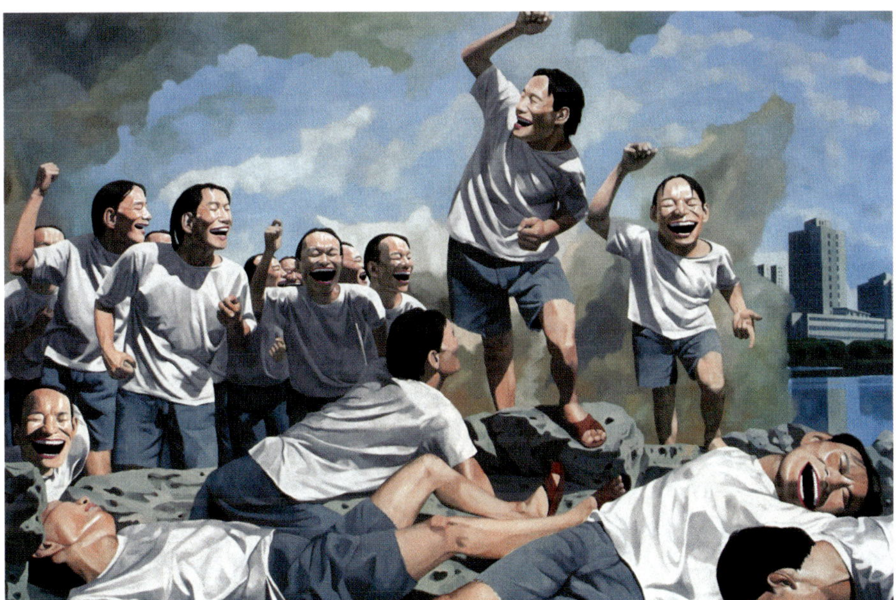

Zhang Huan

Born 1965, Anyang, Henan Province

THIS PAGE: *To Raise the Water Level in a Fishpond*, 1997. Performance, Beijing.

FACING PAGE: *12 Square Meters*, 1994. Performance, Beijing.

Zhang Huan first became notorious in the early 1990s when he was a member of Beijing East Village—an experimental artists' community in the suburbs of Beijing—for his repertoire of ostensibly ritualistic work in which his body becomes a living metaphor for his art.

His theatrical performances bring art practice startlingly close to life, as if through psychophysiological experiences he can achieve a totally involved body enactment: his performances convey the experience of immediacy, thus reality. Zhang is distinguished for his masochistic actions in his first public performances, for example *12 Square Meters* (1994), where he covered himself in honey, allowing his body to attract insects. After he moved to the United States in 1998, he shifted his focus to more socially conscious works related to issues of identity and to his responses to his new surroundings, for example, the installation *My America* (1999).

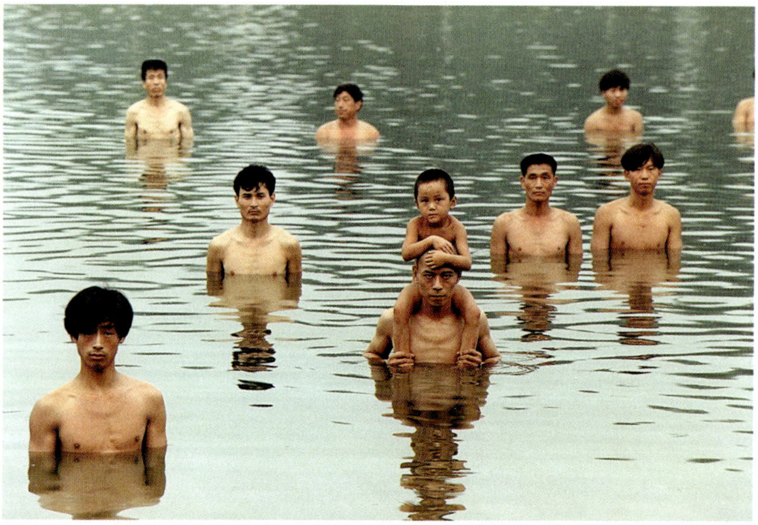

Using an eclectic combination of cultural references, Zhang's body becomes a work instrument, a sheath from which he can temporarily free himself through extreme practices. Measuring himself against insurmountable obstacles—like Yukong, the old man in an ancient Chinese story who decided to move a mountain that was in his path, piece by piece—Zhang engages his inner strength in order to explore the limits of his body. Aware of the fact that he will never have the energy to achieve the impossible, as revealed in *To Raise the Water Level in a Fishpond* (1997) where he proved that attempts to raise the water level by one meter were of no avail, Zhang nonetheless tries to do what is unachievable so as to understand his body's impotence.

Zhang's use of Chinese elements, such as people, architecture, animals, and materials, is fundamental to his work and gives his actions a strong identity. Site-specific and linked to his personal experiences, Zhang sometimes seems to be striving for a kind of purification in his performances. In conceptual works such as *Family Tree* (2000), he focuses on his need for personal definition by writing Chinese characters on his face, and in *Window* (2004) he deals with political concerns by examining the relationship between master (his body) and servant (a donkey), an allegory that refers to the condition of both animals and the masses in rural China. In *Donkey* (2005), a donkey with an oversized penis penetrates the Jin Mao Tower in Shanghai, symbol of urban development and landmark of the city. Beset by the hectic and domineering presence of skyscrapers in the city, Zhang provokes the audience with an absurd and ironic scene.

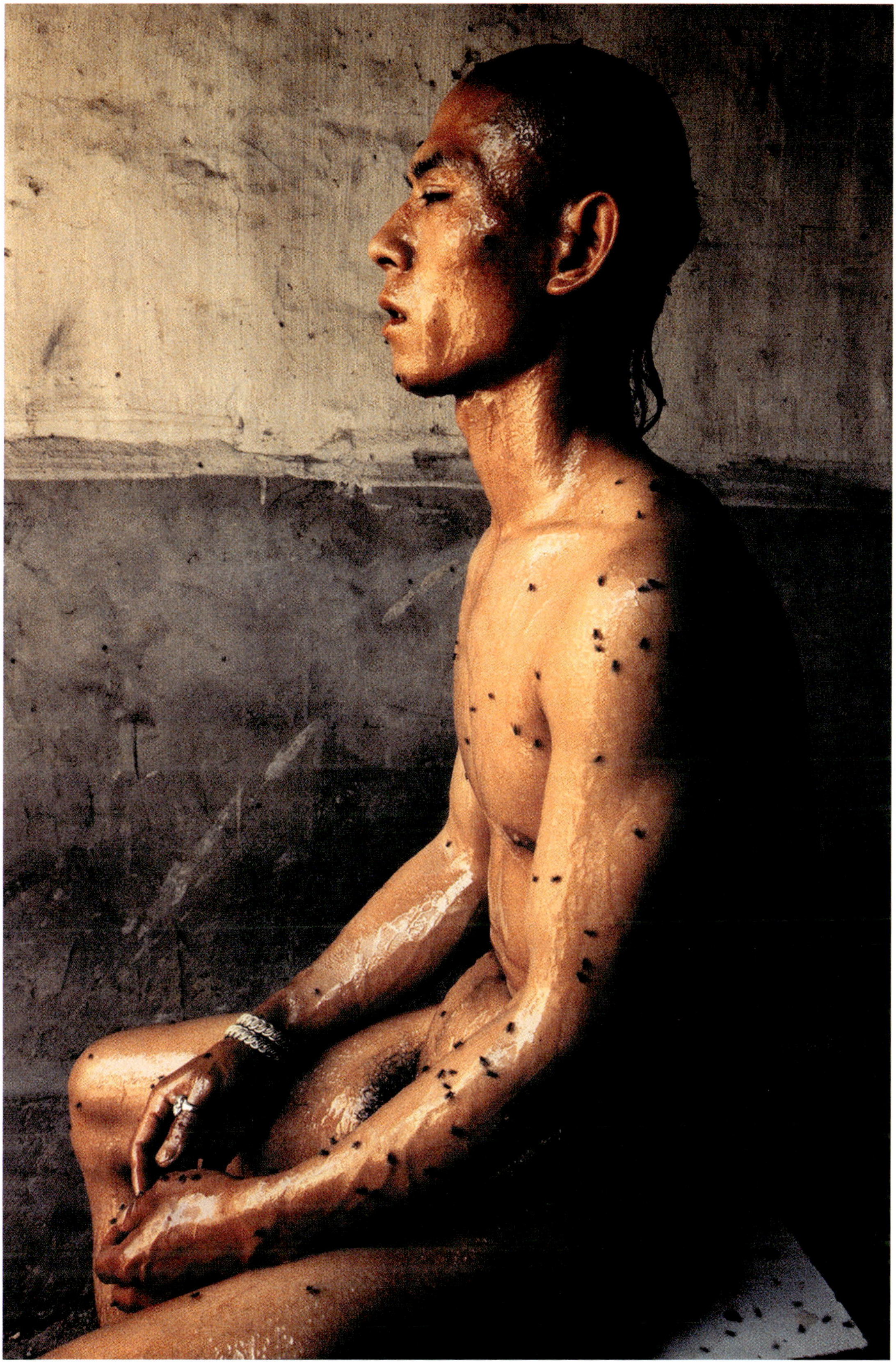

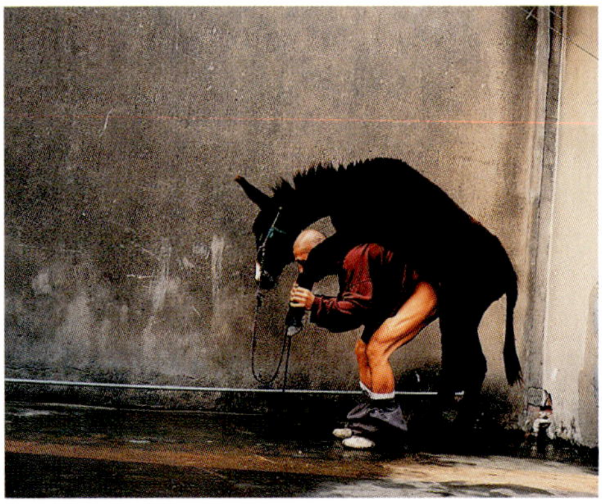

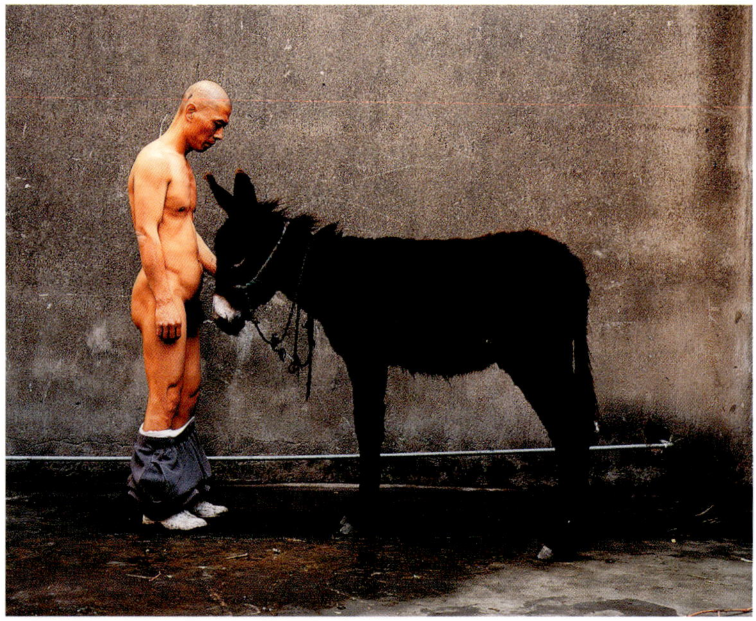

THIS PAGE: *Window*, 2004. Performance, Shanghai.

FACING PAGE: *Donkey*, 2005. Steel, taxidermied donkey, 127 x 78½ x 31½ in.

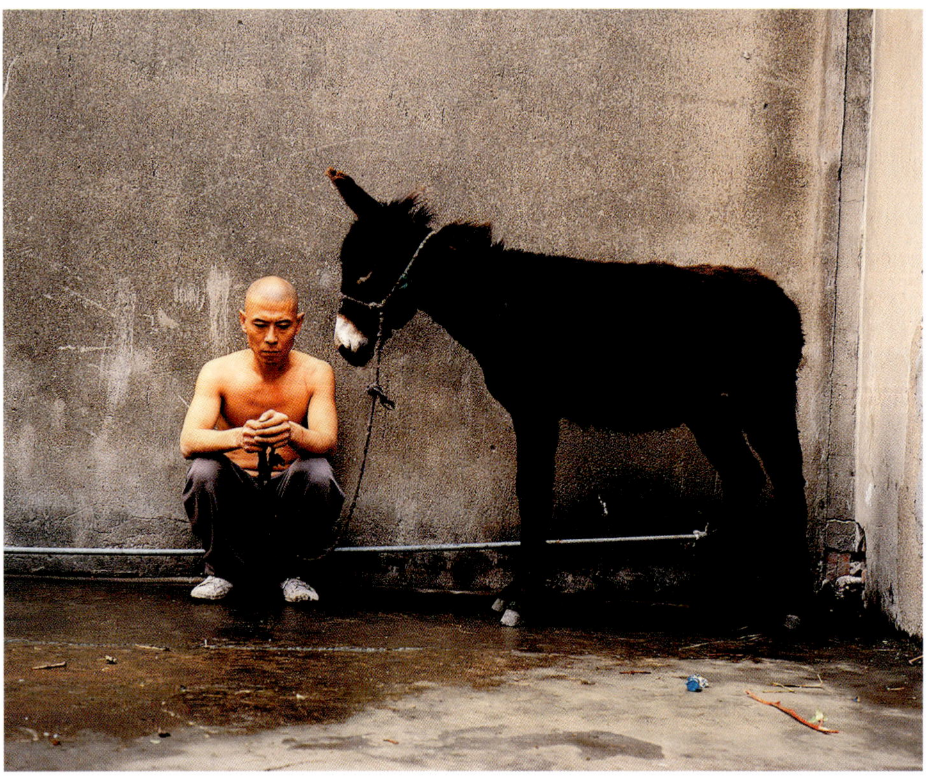

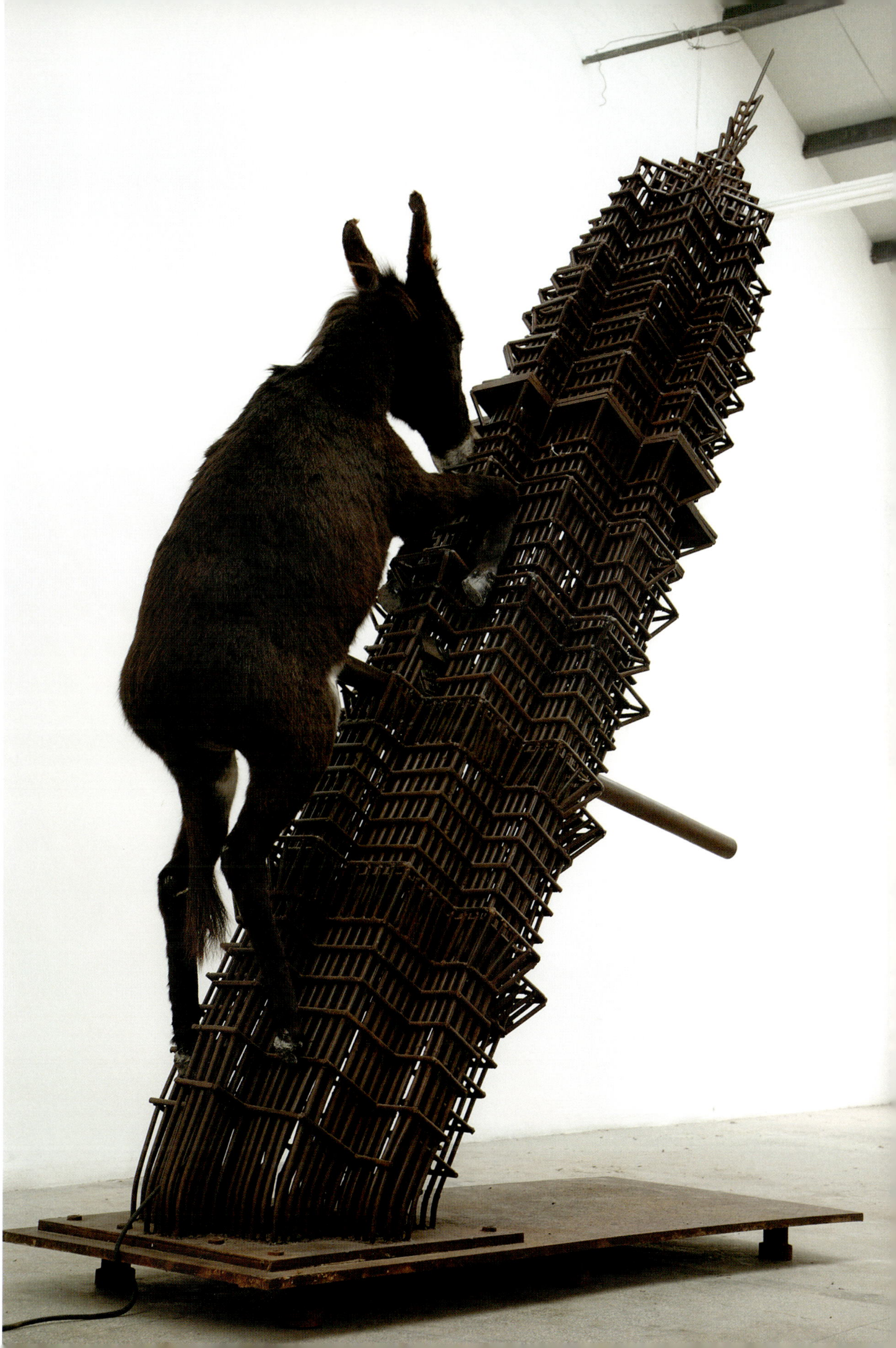

Zhang Peili

Born 1957, Luoyang, Henan Province

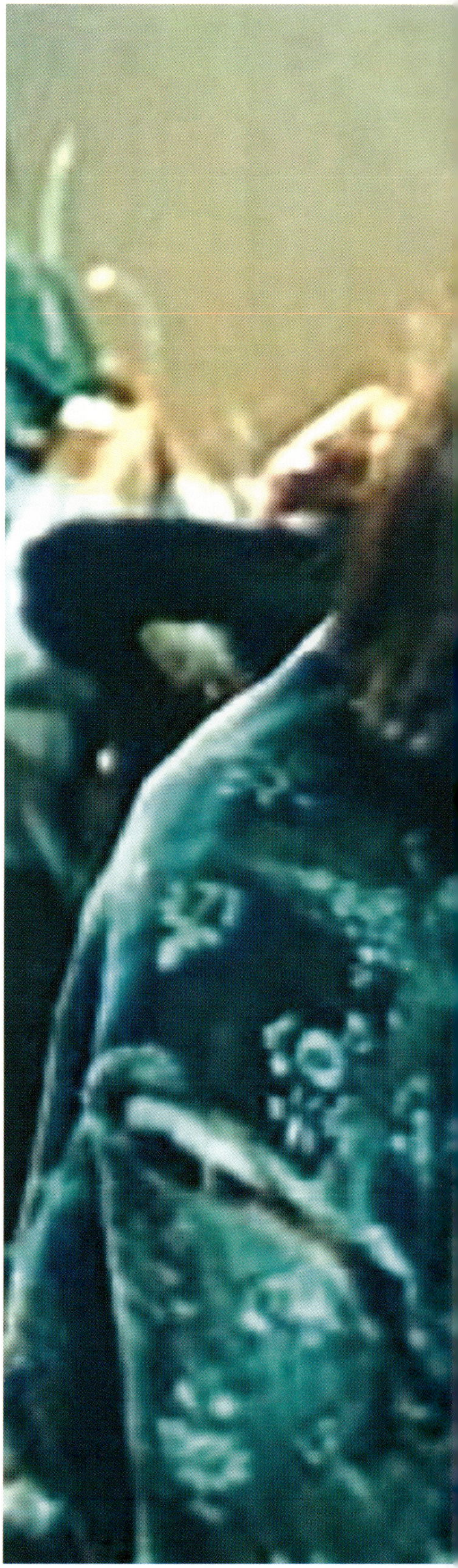

THIS PAGE: *Last Words*, 2003. Single-channel video.

Progenitor of video art in China, artist, professor, and head of the Department of New Media Art at the China Academy of Art in Hangzhou, Zhang Peili's specialty is video installation. His focus is on ordinary people and their simple and common actions. The notion of repetition is an important component in Zhang's works. *30 x 30* (1988), his first video work, records the artist breaking a mirror and gluing the pieces back together over and over again. *Last Words* (2003) is a remaking of Chinese patriotic movies of the 1950s and 1960s. Zhang extracts the scenes where communist heroes gasp their last words before dying and builds a new narrative that he screens using a dual format projection: one screen shows the normal sequence of the assemblage, the other shows it in reversed play.

In *Uncertain Pleasure* (1996), twelve video monitors show a hand repeatedly scratching a shoulder, arm, belly, and hips, transforming the action to something between self-torture and pleasure. Having grown up during the Cultural Revolution, Zhang's videos hint at the psychological pressures people suffered, pressures that caused them to confine their actions to the mere habitual and methodical in order to affirm the self.

Short Phrase (2006) and *Happiness* (2006) are comprised of remakes of excerpts from Chinese revolutionary films of the 1960s. Working on a rhetorical narrative structure, Zhang attempts to free these works from the symbolism they are filled with.

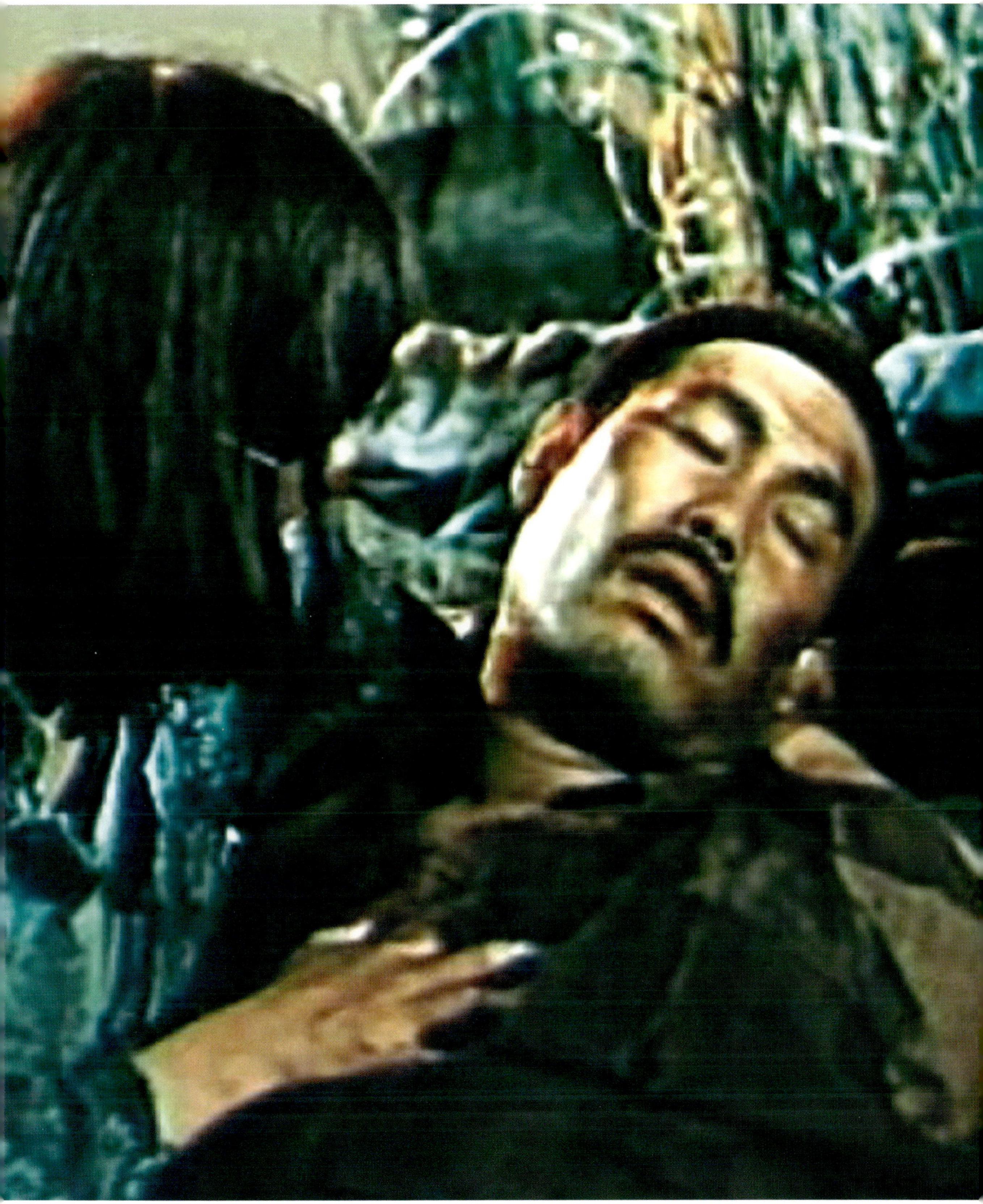

THIS PAGE: *Happiness*, 2006. Stills from video.

FACING PAGE: *Uncertain Pleasure*, 1996. Video Stills from video.

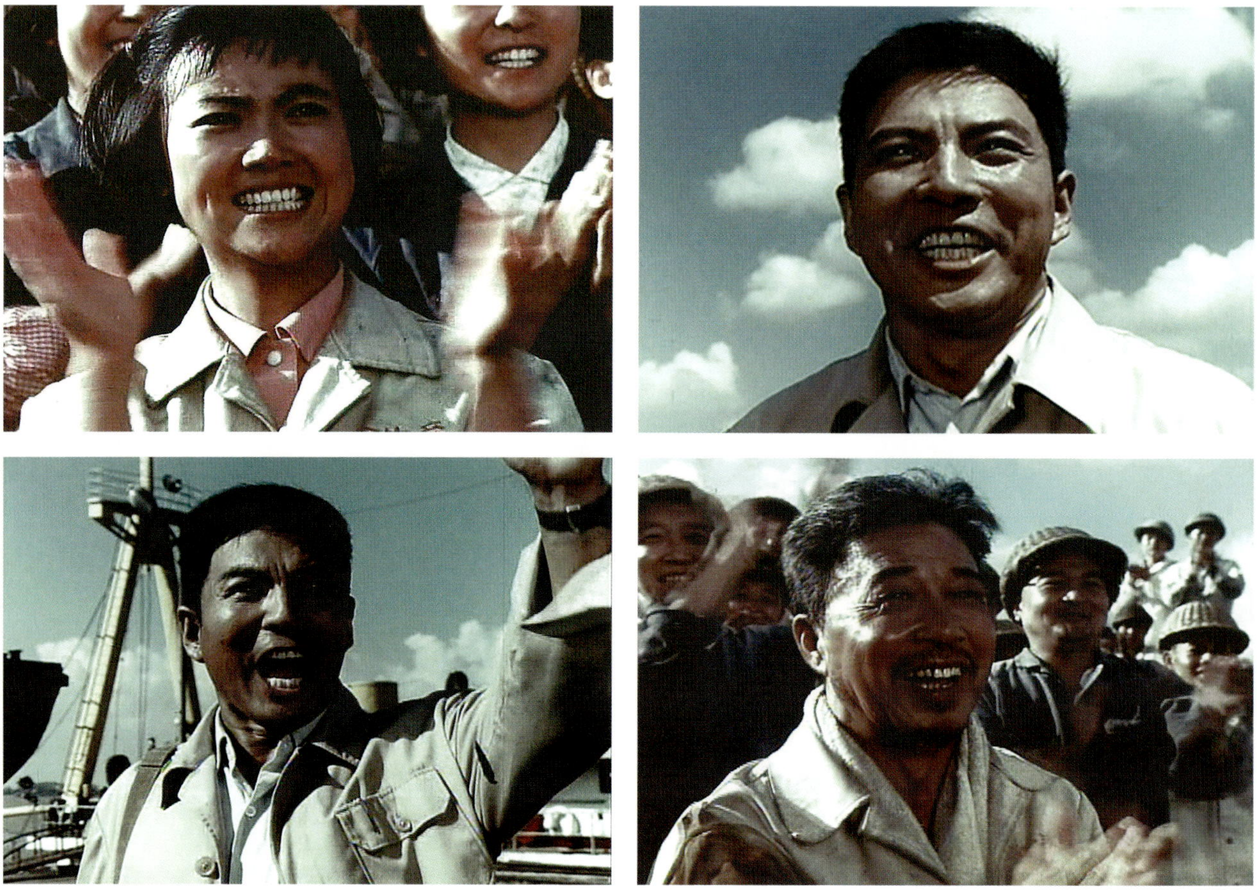

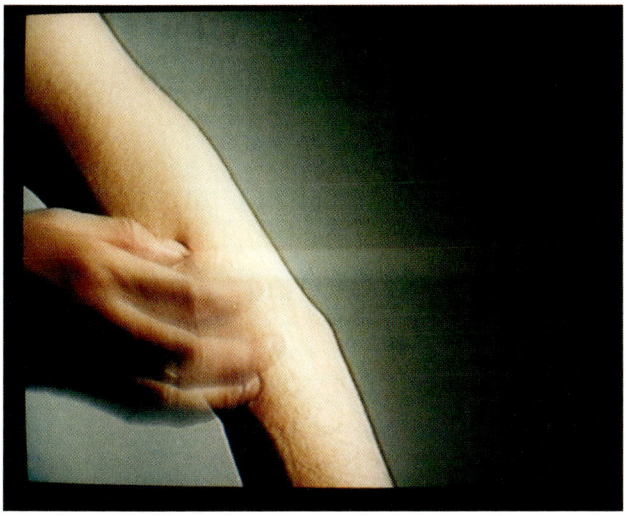
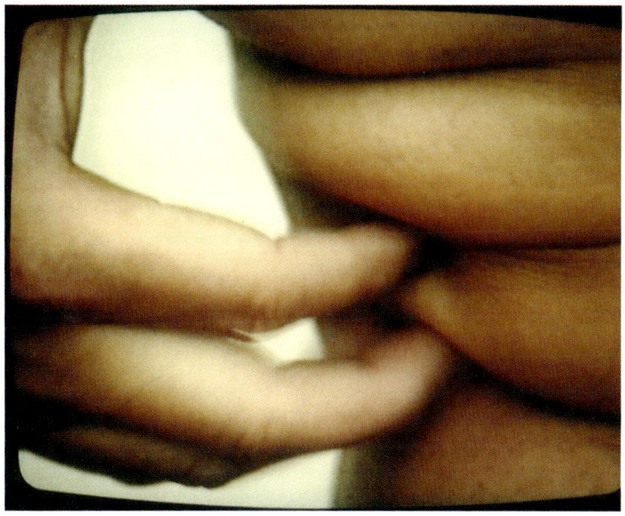
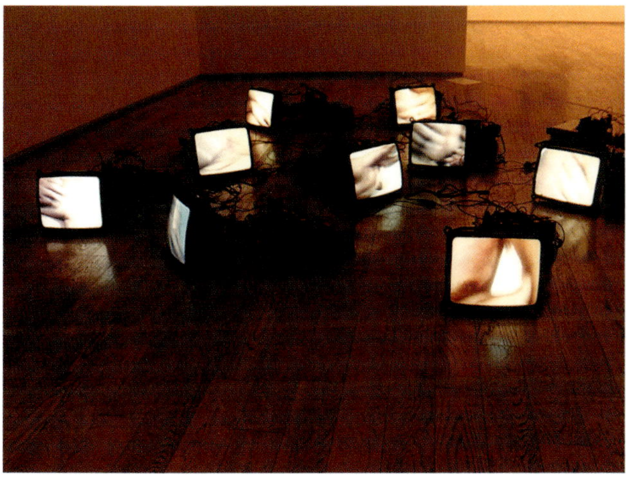
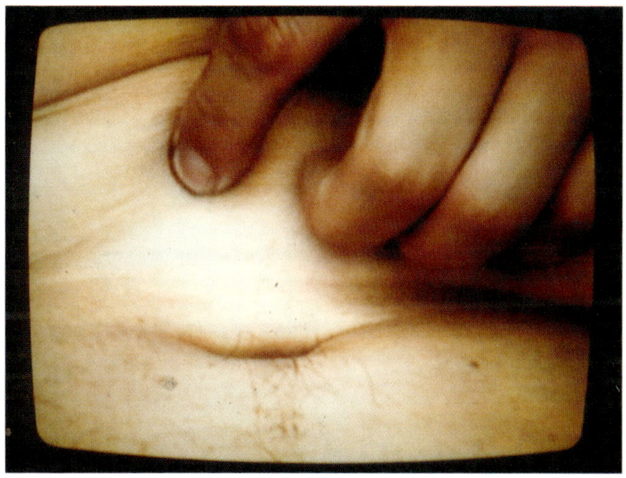
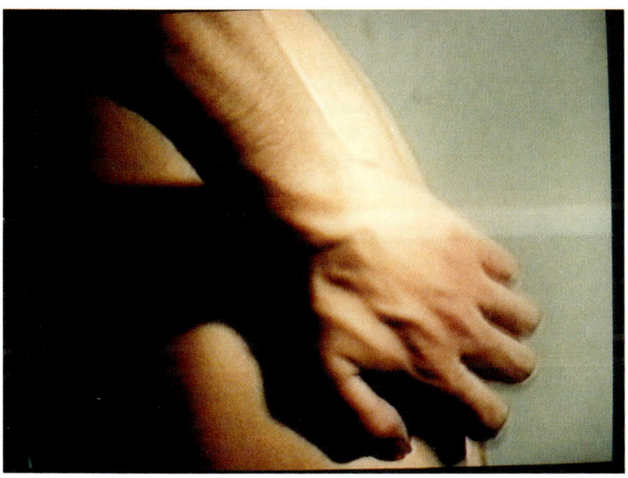
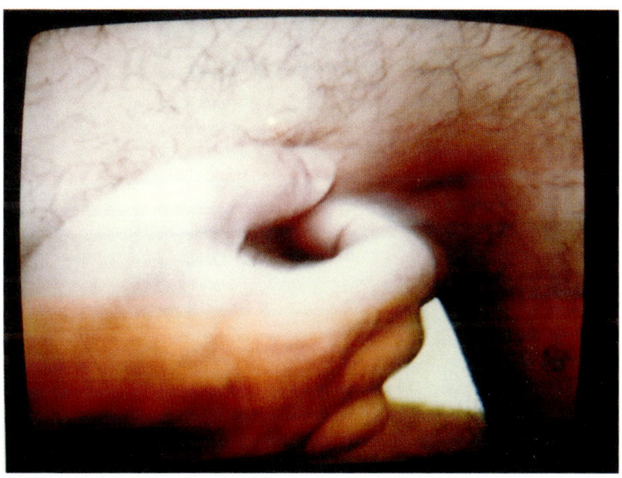

Zhang Xiaogang

Born 1958, Kunming, Yunnan Province

Breaking records at international auction houses, Zhang Xiaogang's sought-after works are characterized by an iconography and style that has established his position in the international art world and made significant contributions to the artistic language of contemporary Chinese art.

Zhang trained in oil painting at the Sichuan Fine Arts Institute, and after graduation started to work for a dance troupe, designing costumes and scenery. In that period he learned about Western painting, especially Surrealist painting, which seems to have had a strong influence on his work, thanks to its resonance with the fantasy, imagination, and sense of wonder also prevalent in Chinese literature. After the Tiananmen incident, Zhang spent one year overseas and when he came back, he started to put into paintings all the secrets and memories from his childhood. Delving into the mysteries of his family, he found himself deeply touched by the figure of his mother, whose mental illness probably drove Zhang to focus on the relationship between the individual and society. His early canvases seem to convey a sense of strain, emphasized by the thick layers of brightly colored paint, but *Bloodline* (1993–) and *Amnesia and Memory* (2003–), the two series that made him famous, use thinner layers of paler colors, like the ones in old photographs, to show an almost depressing calm; an anomalously unperturbed stillness. Based on his personal experiences, Zhang deals with the connections between people, often portraying a sense of constraint and a lack of real feelings. Inspired by old family photographs, he creates false portraits that hint at turbulence and suppressed emotions below the surface. Zhang stated in an interview with Michel Nurisdany that he believes bonds between people are complex; that we learn how to protect ourselves in our secret place while pretending to be in perfect agreement with other members of our family or society. The red line in the paintings, the "bloodline," as critics define it, represents historical and cultural bonds. Physical flaws on his subjects are said to represent moral flaws. These superficial infirmities hint at hopes and desires that have been suppressed and turned inwards.

Zhang's 2006 series *In and Out* unexpectedly shows a radical change of subject and style that makes it hard to recognize the artist's hand, but is actually a further journey into memory and still haunted with the same melancholy atmosphere.

THIS PAGE: *Tiananmen*, 1993. Oil on canvas, 39 x 51 in.

FACING PAGE, TOP: *In and Out—02*, 2006. Oil on canvas, 59 x 78½ in.

FACING PAGE, BOTTOM: *In and Out—05*, 2006. Oil on canvas, 59 x 78½ in.

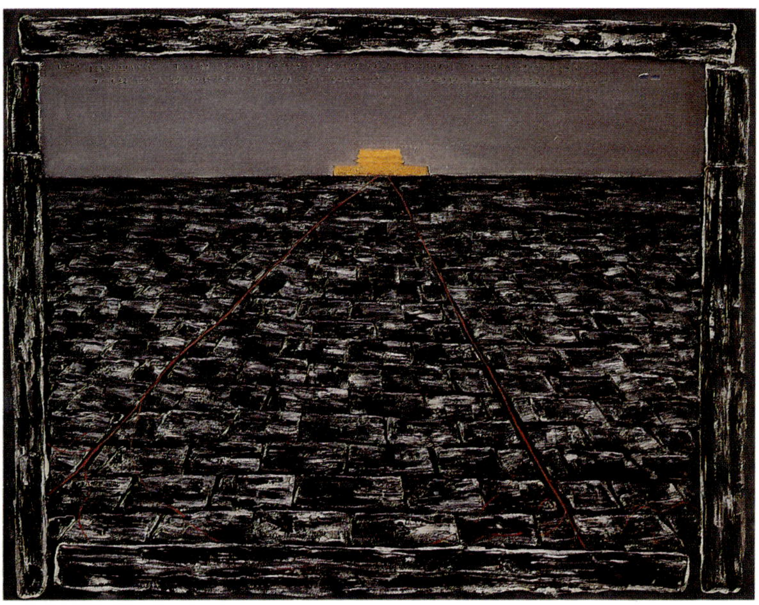

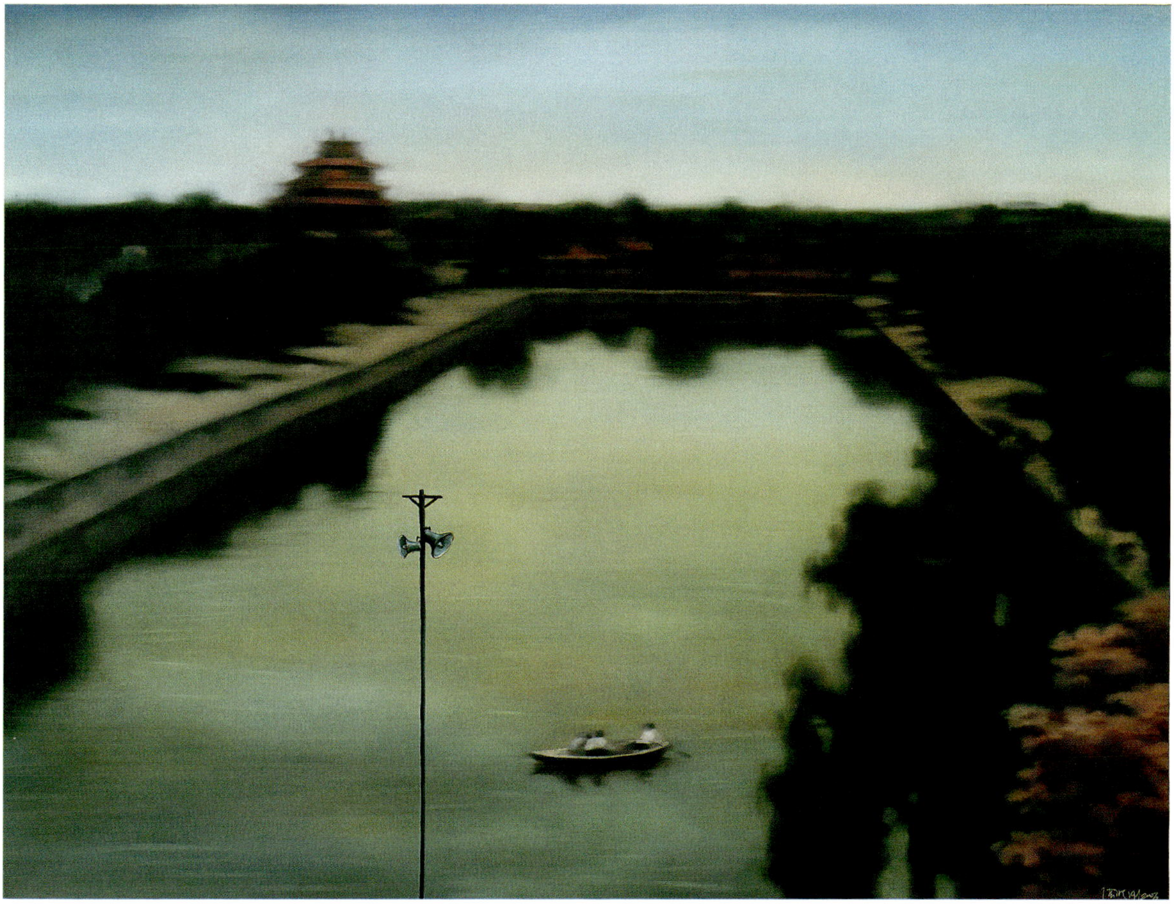

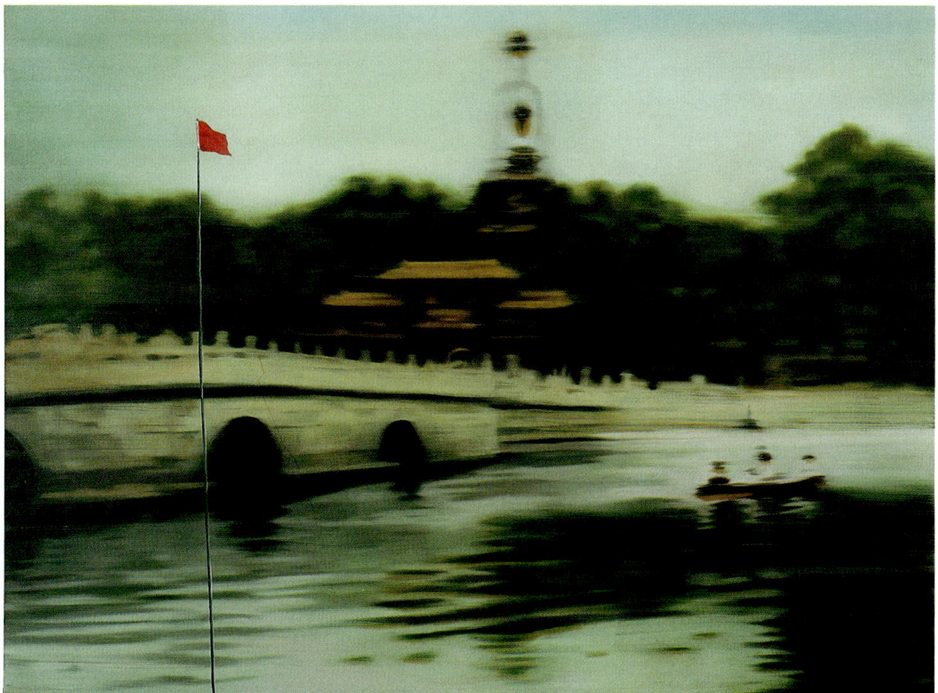

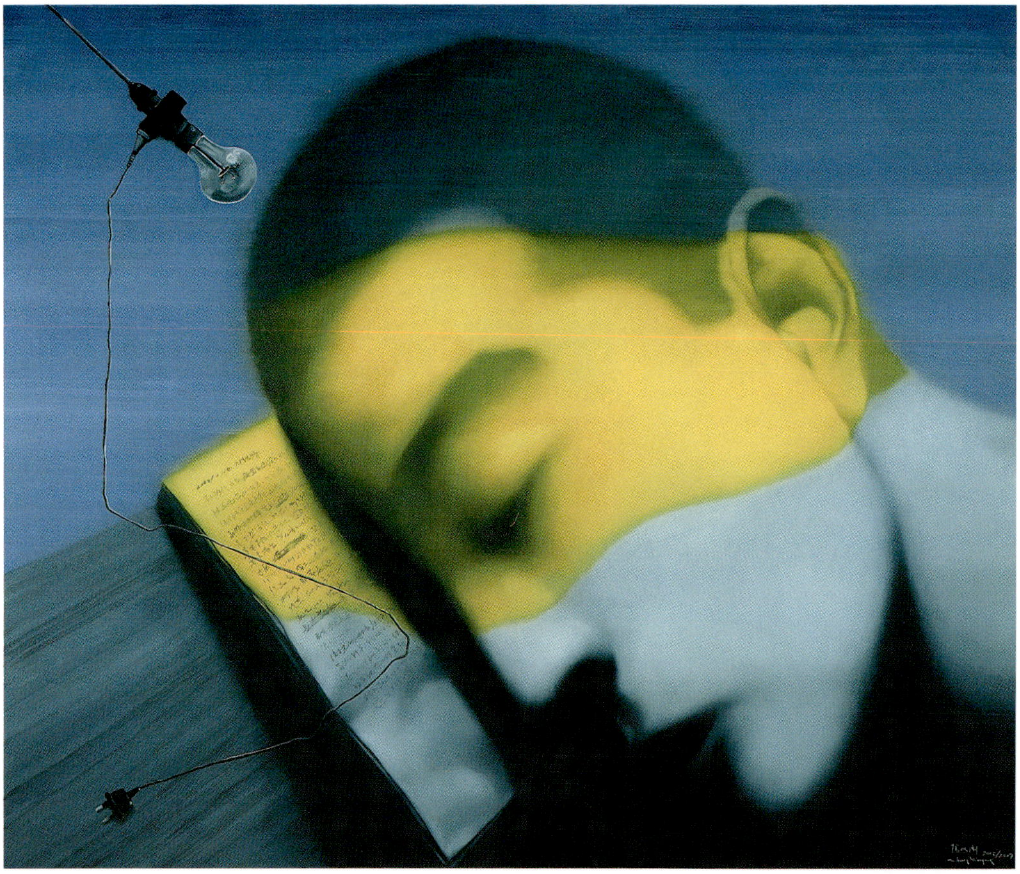

THIS PAGE, TOP: *Amnesia and Memory*, 2003. Oil on canvas, 47 x 59 in.

THIS PAGE, BOTTOM: *Amnesia and Memory—01*, 2007. Oil on canvas, 98½ x 118 in.

FACING PAGE: *Bloodline: The Big Family*, 2007. Oil on canvas, 39 x 51 in.

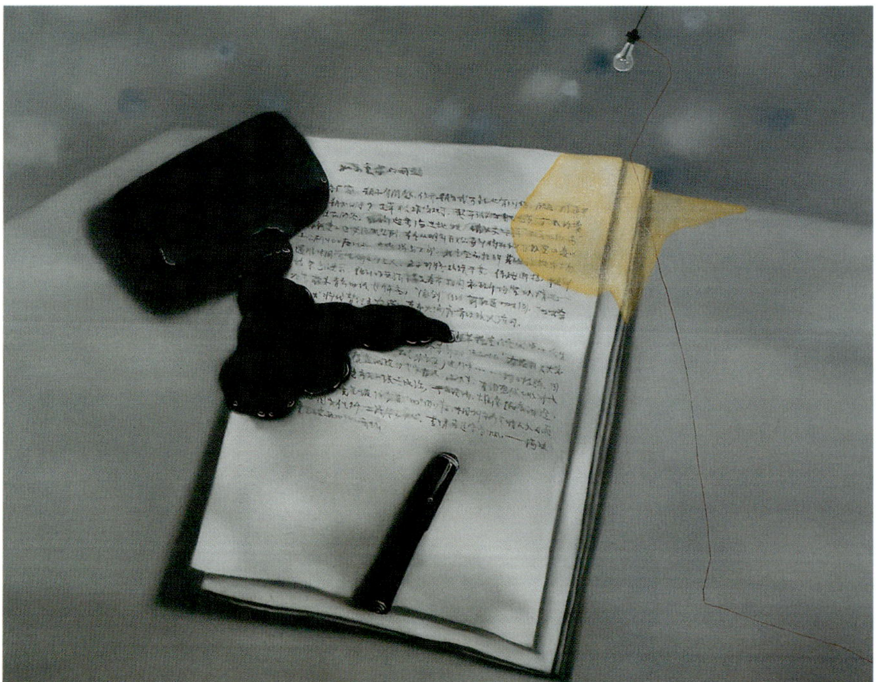

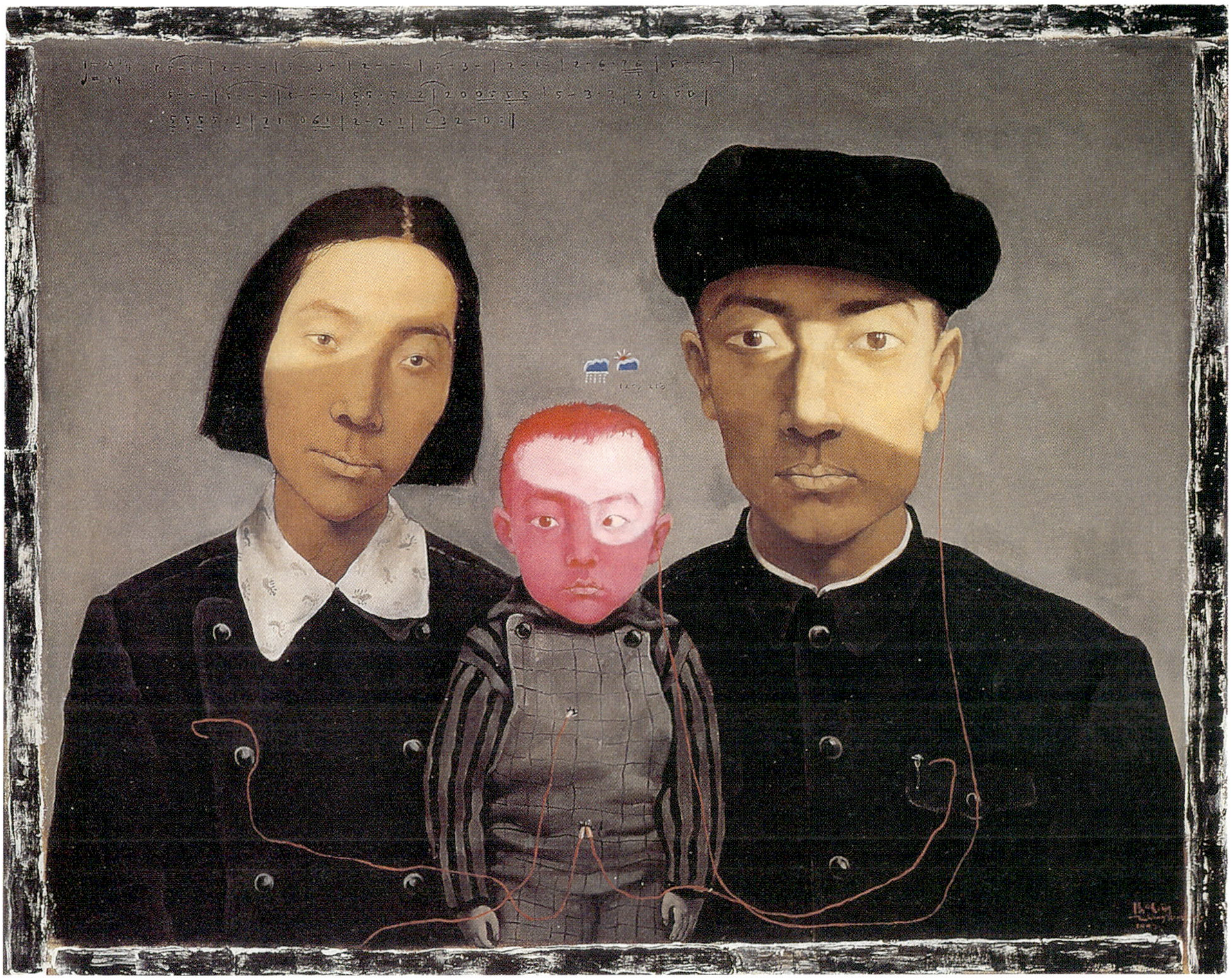

Zhang Yue

Born 1987, Xishuangbanna, Yunnan Province

Zhang Yue's thought-provoking work challenges the precarious equilibrium of the Chinese contemporary art system and brings forth new ideas and new approaches. Aiming to "make work that resonates meaningfully with the particular context of its creation," Zhang creates temporary and site-specific projects. For *177 Wuding Lu* (2007) she embroidered tablecloths with common Chinese phrases and the outlines of plates and bowls. The tablecloths were used on the tables of a restaurant due to be knocked down the following day. With the intention of prompting the conversation of people eating there, she recorded portraits of the customers sitting at the tables and, at the end of the day, she collected the stained tablecloths showing the traces of a situation that no longer existed. This project addresses the common phenomenon of destruction in China today and how it affects us as individuals.

Bravely attempting a critique of the art world and its system, Zhang questions the value of art institutions and the future of Chinese artists who appear as branded products to export, and whose quality has to be checked by the specialized foreign eye, just like mass-produced manufactured goods. The 5,000 Zhang Yue Industries brand-name toothpaste boxes she arranged in the shape of China in the installation *Your Friend Your Enemy* (2007), ironically underline this concern.

Kaiten Camera (2005) is a video recorded by a camera positioned on a conveyor belt in a Japanese restaurant. Offering a humorous and lively portrayal of individual restaurant customers while exploring their gestures and attitudes, Zhang wonders, "What if art could be made on a conveyor belt?"

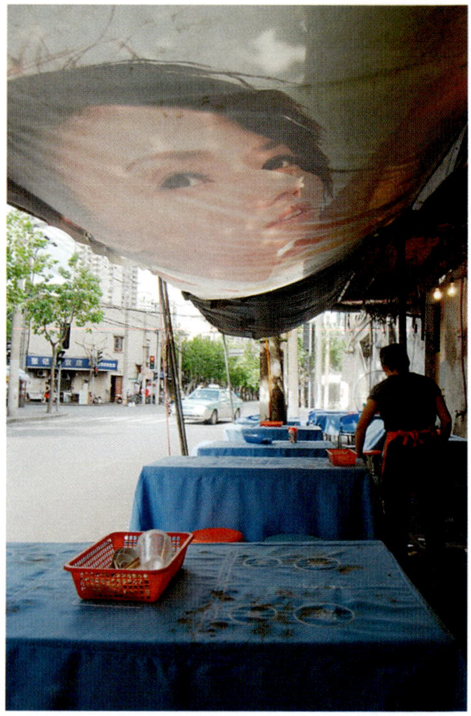

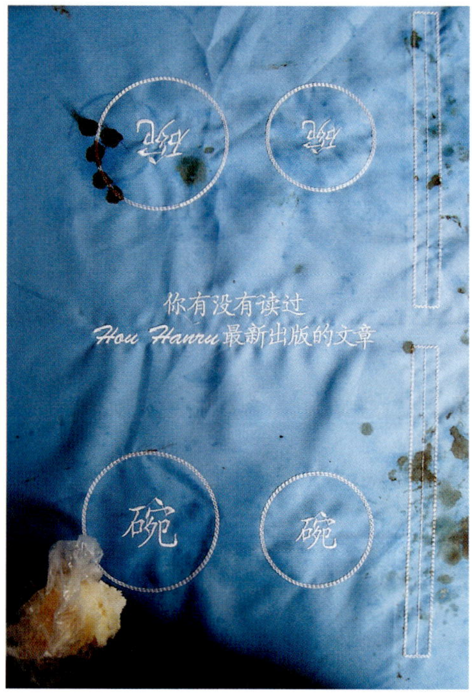

THIS PAGE AND FACING PAGE: *177 Wuding Lu*, 2007. Site-specific installation.

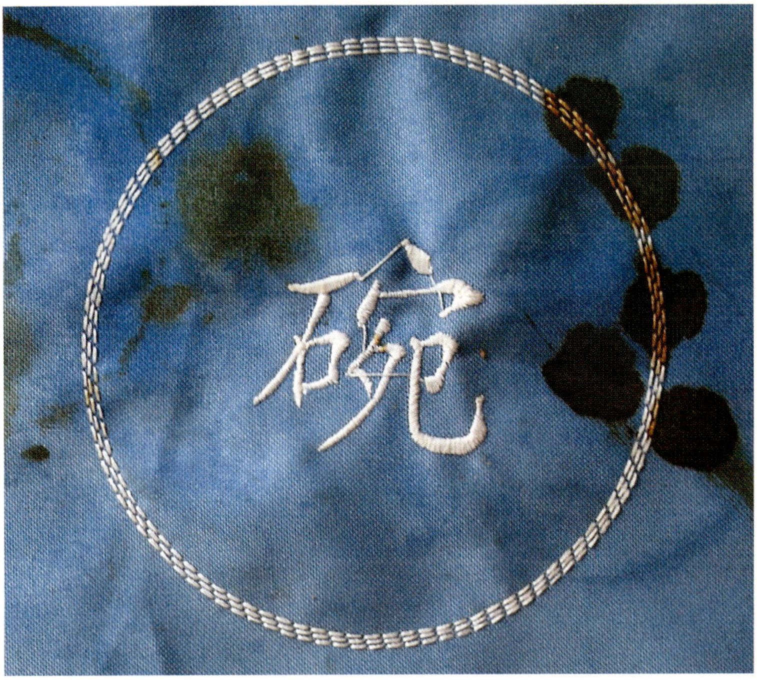
碗

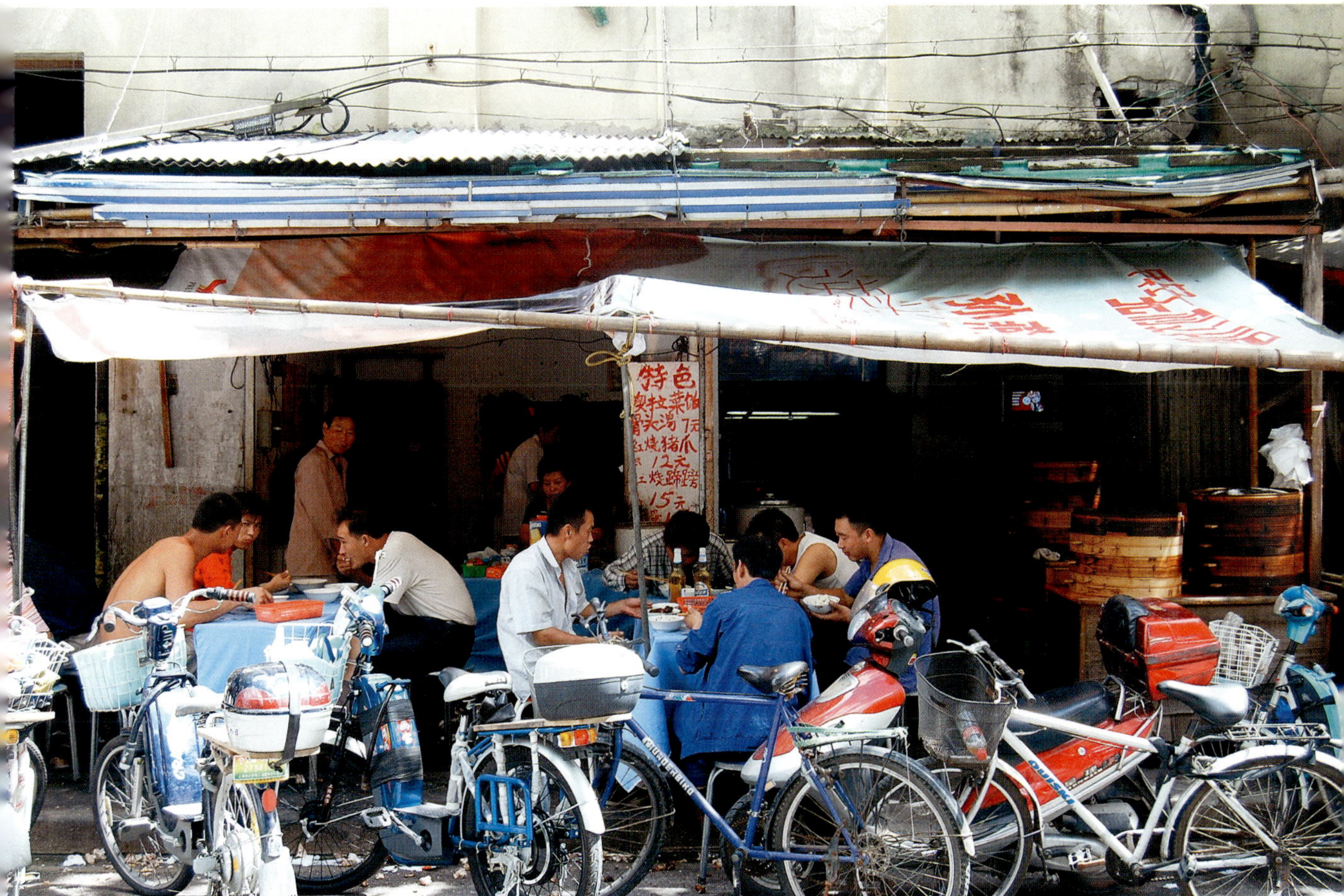
特色
7元
红烧猪爪
12元
15元

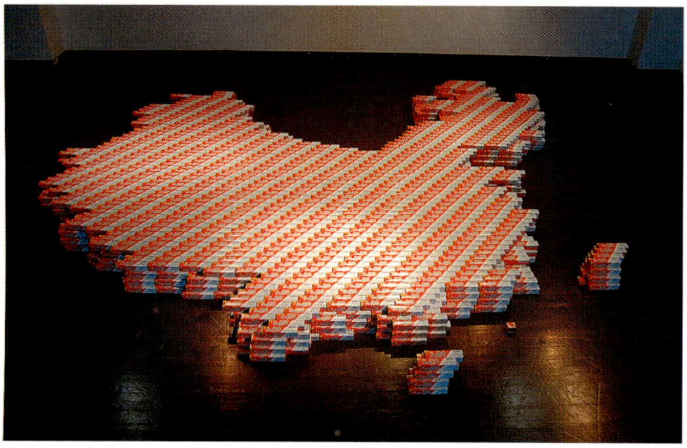

THIS PAGE: *Your Friend Your Enemy*, 2007. Installation. 5,000 toothpaste boxes.

FACING PAGE: *Kaiten Camera*, 2005. Stills from video.

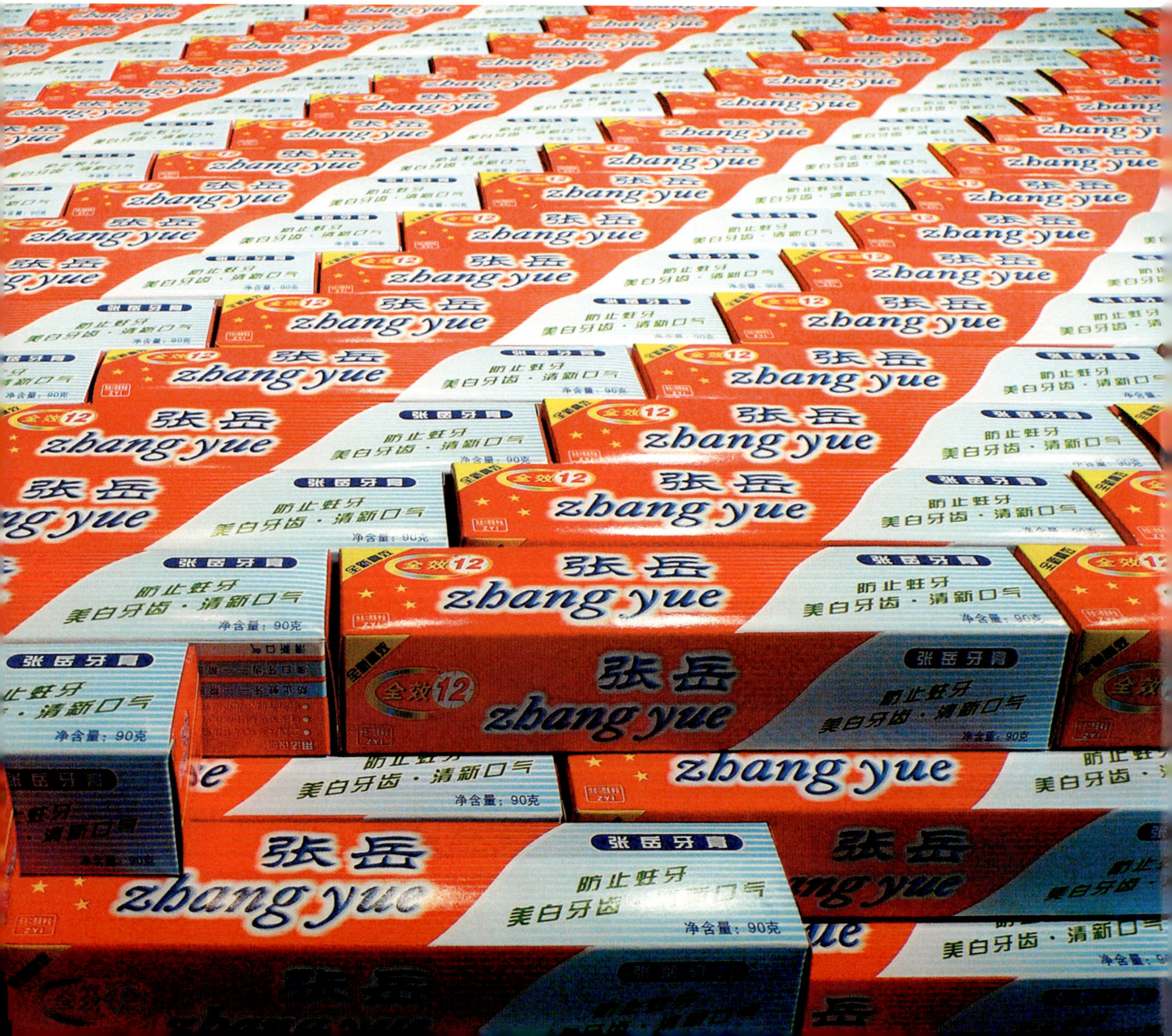

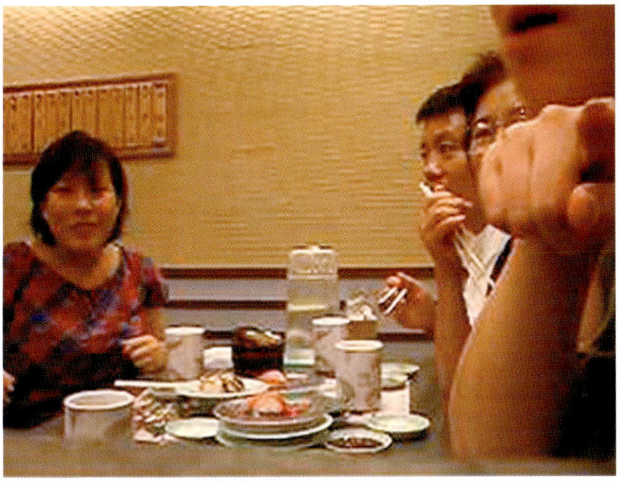
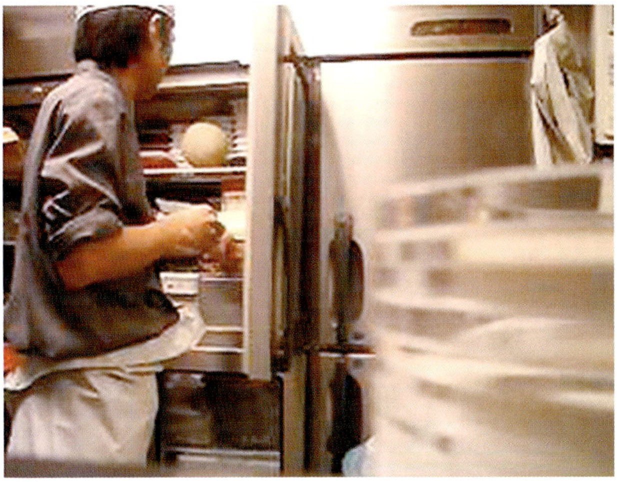
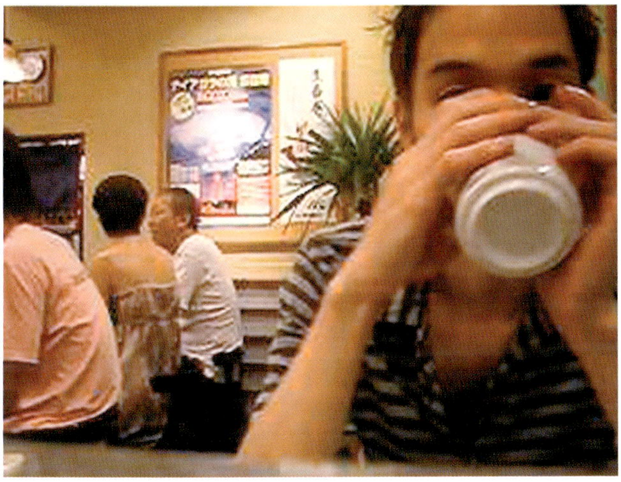
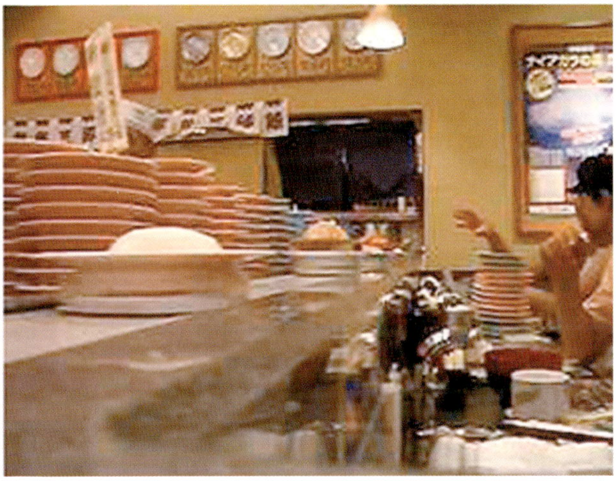
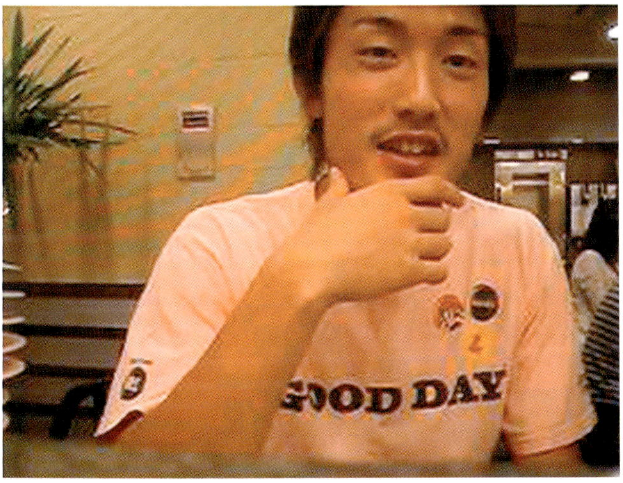
GOOD DAY
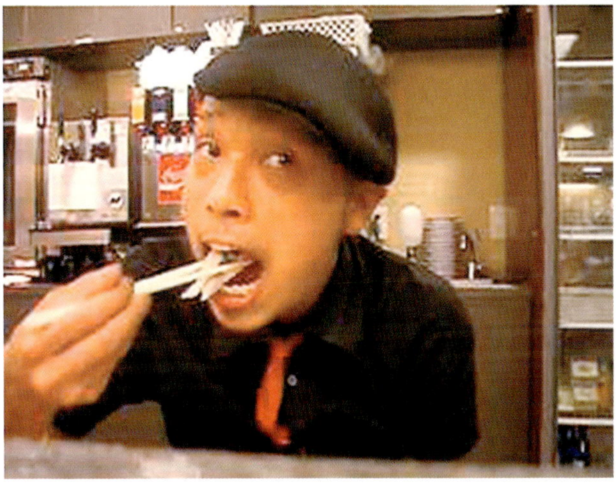

Photo Credits

Copyright for all images belongs to the respective artists except where otherwise stated.

Page 6, courtesy Yue Minjun.

Page 8 top, all the information and images of works in the annex © Cao Fei, courtesy Vitamin Creative Space, Guangzhou.

Page 8 bottom, courtesy Galerie Urs Meile, Beijing-Lucerne.

Page 9 top, courtesy Wolfgang Joop and Alexander Ochs Galleries Berlin/Beijing.

Page 10 top, courtesy Galerie Urs Meile, Beijing-Lucerne.

Page 10 bottom, courtesy Xing Danwen.

Page 11 top, courtesy Lin Tianmiao.

Page 12 top and bottom, pages 14–15, courtesy Galerie Urs Meile, Beijing-Lucerne. Page 13, courtesy Galerie Urs Meile, Beijing-Lucerne, Erlenmeyer Stiftung Switzerland, Leister Foundation Switzerland.

Page 16, photo: Hiro Ihara, courtesy Cai Studio. Page 17 top, photo: Tatsumi Masatoshi, courtesy Cai Studio. Page 17 bottom, photo: Hiro Ihara, courtesy Cai Studio, reproduced by kind permission of Deutsche Guggenheim, Berlin, Germany. Pages 18–19, photo: Hiro Ihara, courtesy Cai Studio, reproduced by kind permission of Seattle Art Museum and Massachusetts Museum of Contemporary Art.

Pages 20–23: All the information and images of works in the annex © Cao Fei, courtesy Vitamin Creative Space, Guangzhou.

Pages 24–27, courtesy Chen Ke.

Pages 28–31, courtesy Chen Lingyang and the Marella Gallery, Beijing.

Page 32, page 34, courtesy UniversalStudios-beijing. Page 33, page 35, courtesy Chen Shaoxiong.

Pages 36–39, courtesy Cui Xiuwen and the Marella Gallery, Beijing.

Page 40 top, courtesy private collection and Alexander Ochs Galleries Berlin/Beijing. Page 40 bottom, courtesy The Chaney Family Collection and White Space Beijing. Page 41, courtesy Wolfgang Joop and Alexander Ochs Galleries Berlin/Beijing. Page 42–43 top, courtesy Museum of Modern Art, New York. Page 42–43 bottom, courtesy Collection Laurent, Paris, and Alexander Ochs Galleries Berlin/Beijing.

Pages 44–47, courtesy Feng Zhengjie.

Page 48, courtesy Galleria Continua, San Gimignano, Italy. Pages 49–51, courtesy Gu Dexin.

Pages 52–55, courtesy He Sen.

Pages 56–59, courtesy He Yunchang.

Pages 60–61, courtesy Jiang Zhi. Pages 62–63, courtesy Jiang Zhi and the Marella Gallery, Beijing.

Pages 64–67, courtesy Galleria Continua San Gimignano/Beijing.

Pages 68–71, courtesy Liang Yue.

Pages 72–75, courtesy Lin Tianmiao.

Pages 76–79, courtesy Liu Ding.

Pages 80–83, courtesy Liu Wei.

Page 84–87, courtesy Ma Liuming and the Marella Gallery, Beijing.

Pages 88–91, courtesy RongRong and Inri.

Pages 92–95, courtesy Shi Jinsong and the Marella Gallery, Beijing.

Pages 96–99, courtesy Song Dong and TOKYO GALLERY+BTAP.

Pages 100–103, courtesy Wang Guangyi.

Pages 104–107, courtesy Wang Jianwei.

Pages 108–111, courtesy Galerie Urs Meile, Beijing-Lucerne.

Pages 112–115, courtesy Weng Fen.

Pages 116–119, courtesy Xiao Lu.

Pages 120–123, courtesy Galerie Urs Meile, Beijing-Lucerne.

Pages 124–127, courtesy Xing Danwen.

Pages 128–131, courtesy Xu Zhen.

Pages 132–135, courtesy Yan Lei.

Pages 136–139, courtesy ShanghArt Gallery, Shanghai.

Page 140, courtesy Alexander Ochs Galleries, Berlin/Beijing. Page 141, Ralf Schmerberg, courtesy Alexander Ochs Galleries, Berlin/Beijing. Page 142 top, courtesy Hong Kong Schoeni Art Gallery. Page 142 bottom, collection Zhang Haoming. Page 143 top, courtesy Alexander Ochs Galleries Berlin and White Space Beijing. Page 143 bottom, private collection, USA, courtesy Alexander Ochs Galleries, Berlin/Beijing.

Pages 144–147, courtesy Yang Zhengzhong.

Page 148, courtesy Beijing Commune and Alexander Ochs Galleries, Berlin/Beijing. Page 149, page 151 center, courtesy Yin Xiuzhen. Page 150, courtesy Caspar H. Schübbe, Switzerland and Alexander Ochs Galleries, Berlin/Beijing. Page 151 top, courtesy Alexander Ochs Galleries, Berlin/Beijing. Page 151 bottom, courtesy Alexander Ochs Galleries, Berlin/Beijing.

Pages 152–155, courtesy Yue Minjun.

Pages 156–159, courtesy Zhang Huan.

Pages 160–163, courtesy Zhang Peili.

Pages 164–167, courtesy Zhang Xiaogang.

Pages 168–171, courtesy Zhang Yue.

Acknowledgments

Thank you Cathy! First of all, my most sincere thanks to my editor, Cathy Layne, without whom I would have never been able to work on this book. Thanks for your patience, support, and precious help, and for letting me be a mouthpiece for the amazing world of Chinese contemporary art. I feel really privileged.

I would like to thank Hugo Dobson from the School of East Asian Studies of the University of Sheffield, UK, who made it possible for Cathy to contact me, thus smoothing the way for this project to happen.

Working on this book has been a wonderful experience, mainly because of the avatars as well as superheroes that I have chosen to be in it. I would like to express my warmest thanks to the forty artists, some of whom are also really good friends. I am delighted that this book also gave me the chance to meet those that I didn't know before. All of them welcomed me with kindness and enthusiasm; they entered my life and filled it. I feel honored to have the responsibility of introducing these artists to my readers.

I would like to say my kindest thanks to the galleries, without whose cooperation I would have never been allowed to show the images of the art works included in this book.

My gratitude for the support and help of all my friends in Beijing who have been unstinting with both time and friendship. In particular, I would like to say thanks to Maria Santonastaso, Javier del Puerto, Tom Husband, and Mark Broom who carefully looked over my English, Oak Taylor Smith, Vanessa Trento, Michele Matteini, Stefano Avesani and Marcella Campa and their little baby Leonardo, Fabrizio Zambuto, Jacopo Calza, Beatrice Leanza, and Federica Seravesi. My heartfelt thanks to Neil Sansom who assisted me with his love and confidence, precious gifts from a very important person in my life.

I owe a great deal also to my sister Giulia, an amazing companion and friend who was always there for me and incessantly sustained and strengthened my energy and devotion. Her unwavering temperament has been of treasured significance.

Warmest thanks to my friend and colleague Eleonora Battiston and to Marella Gallery, who gave me the opportunity to work on this project and without whom I would have never become so deeply involved in the world of the arts. Eleonora's illuminating comments on the work of many of the artists featured in this book have been a valuable resource. Great thanks to all those in the art field who inspired me and taught me so much more than what can be contained within the pages of this book.

Last but not least, I would like to thank my family, who never stopped comforting and supporting me all throughout the period of this project. Their true love and faith will never abandon me and it is to them I would like to dedicate this book.

And I could not leave without a phrase from Francis Bacon which I bring to mind that goes, "Some books are to be tasted, others to be swallowed, and some few to be chewed and digested."

(英文版)コンテンポラリー・チャイニーズ・アーティスト
Avatars and Antiheroes

2008年2月29日　第1刷発行

著　者　クラウディア・アルベルティーニ
発行者　富田 充
発行所　講談社インターナショナル株式会社
〒112-8652 東京都文京区音羽 1-17-14
電話　03-3944-6493(編集部)
03-3944-6492(営業部・業務部)
ホームページ　www.kodansha-intl.com
印刷・製本所　大日本印刷株式会社

Printed in Japan
ISBN 978-4-7700-3071-9

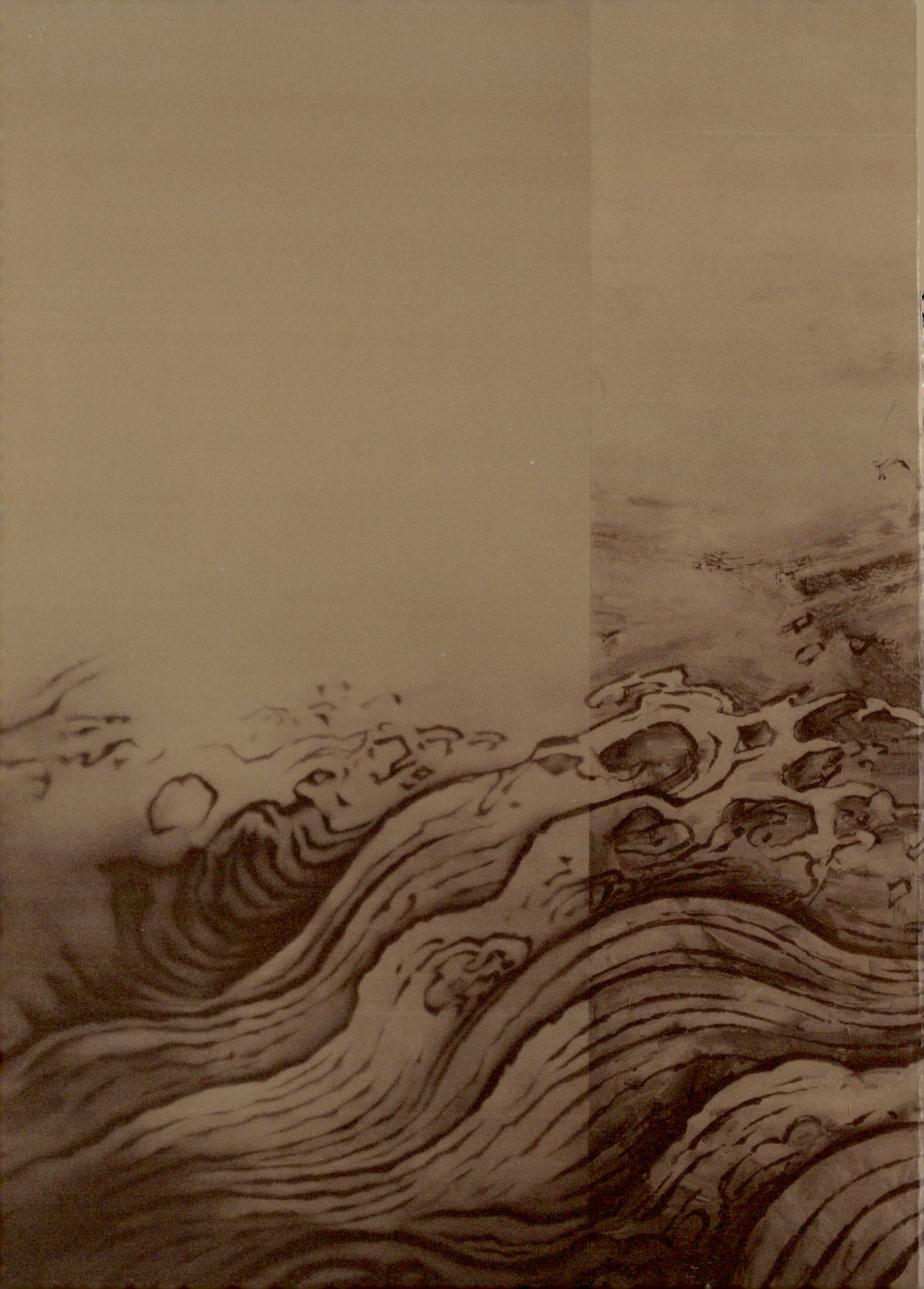